what was then research and analysis department FCO kindly tracked down press coverage of the events of 1967 in Beijing, while David Coates, then a colleague in Beijing, read much of the Beijing manuscript and provided helpful comments, as did Alan Waters, a former management officer in Beijing. Fred Sharf did the same.

When the FCO allowed me a year off at the International Institute for Strategic Studies, Gerry Segal gamely hid his disappointment at my historical approach which failed to produce the promised *Adelphi Paper* but encouraged me to write about the Beijing embassy. Paul Norbury and his colleagues at the Curzon Press have been tolerant and understanding publishers, unfailingly encouraging while perhaps inwardly despairing of ever seeing a manuscript. Lord Hurd, himself once a member of the Beijing embassy, kindly agreed to contribute a foreword. Above all, Susan has encouraged and helped in the project from the first days in Seoul to its completion so long afterwards. To others who have helped, but who are not mentioned here, I extend my thanks nevertheless. Of course, the views expressed are my own, and do not necessarily represent those of Her Majesty's Government.

Crown copyright material appears by courtesy of the comptroller of the Stationery Office.

J. E. Hoare
London, Spring 1999

Notes

1 J. E. Hoare, *The British Embassy Compound Seoul 1884–1984* (Seoul: Korean-British Society, 1984).

2 J. E. Hoare, 'Building Politics: The British Embassy Peking, 1949–1992', *The Pacific Review* vol. 7, no. 1 (1994), 67–78.

3 J. E. Hoare, 'The Tokyo embassy 1871–1945', *Japan Society Proceedings* no. 129, (Summer 1997), 24–41.

4 Lionel Munby, *How much is that worth?* (Salisbury, Wilts.: Philmore for the British Association for Local History, 1996).

the order in which they were originally drafted. China now comes first, followed by Japan, and then Korea.

Names for Chinese, Japanese and Korean follow the traditional convention of surname first, followed by given name(s). For transliteration of Chinese, I have followed the now almost universal *pinyin* system, even though this jars with the historical account. As the late Walter Graham, former consul-general in Beijing and later minister to Seoul, pointed out to me many years ago, the Americans in China had always referred to 'Beijing' and to the seaside resort used by its foreign community each summer as 'Beidaihe'. The British, by contrast, stuck to the well-established 'Peking', and following a literal reading of the Wade-Giles' system, talked always of 'Pater-ho', but they all meant the same places. For Japanese, I have used a modified Hepburn, avoiding the diacritics, and for Korean, a modified McCune-Reischauer, also without the diacritics. The exceptions to all these rules is that I have stuck with personal names as people have chosen to write them, and where place names or other words appear in titles or in quotations, I have left them as they were. From time to time, I have indicated how prices in the past compare with those today – in this case mid-1998. The reader is warned that this is in no sense a scientific attempt to equate prices in the late nineteenth century, for example, with those today. The pitfalls of such an exercise have been ably spelt out by others.[4] Those that are included here are merely designed to give the casual reader some idea of the real bargains which were concluded in the past.

As will already have become obvious, this is a work which has been dependent on the help, support and encouragement of many people. A number of ambassadors have relatively cheerfully tolerated the destruction of their favourite stories, or in other ways encouraged this project. From Seoul, they include John Morgan – also full of useful information about Beijing – the late Nick Spreckley, and Tom Harris. From Beijing, Percy Cradock, Alan Donald and Robin MacLaren told me about their early years in China, as well as about their time as ambassadors. Helpful comment and information about Tokyo came from Michael Wilford – who also contributed a few anecdotes about China – Hugh Cortazzi and John Boyd. Sally and David Wright, first from Seoul and then from Tokyo, were helpful and encouraging. The late Sir Arthur de la Mare, who served in both Seoul and Tokyo, wrote me a most entertaining account of the former, so candid in its comments that it could only be used with the greatest discretion. I was amused but not surprised to see that he had exercised a similar discretion in his memoirs.

The staff at the Public Record Office, including Nicholas Cox, and Oliver Hoare, my second son, have been more than helpful. So, too, have colleagues in the FCO library; in particular the late Margaret Cousins was even more assiduous than me in searching out obscure works while I was in China. I am sorry that she is not here to see the final result. Her successors in the hunt included Michael Veasey and Carole Edwards. From the records branch of the FCO, Joan Macpherson, has been a regular source of help and assistance, and several of her colleagues have been equally assiduous in tracking down obscure – and sometimes wrong – references. Rod Wye in another unexpected bonus. I knew, because there was a foundation stone to prove it, that the ambassador's residence in Seoul had been built while one Walter Caine Hillier was consul-general. Of Hillier, I knew that he was an important member of the British consular service in China, but little more. One night, discussing this with the friends with whom we were staying, our host, Andrew Hillier, said that he thought that his cousin had some photographs belonging to Walter Hillier, who happened to be a great-great-uncle. This serendipity produced some excellent pictures of the original Korean-style house on the present embassy site, as well as a series of photographs which Walter Hillier, an accomplished amateur photographer, had take of the present buildings under construction and just after completion. All fell into place, and the result was the little book on *The British Embassy Compound Seoul, 1884–1984*, which appeared in 1984.[1]

There it all might have rested, except that in 1988 we were, very unexpectedly, asked to go to Beijing. After several months of cliff-hanging suspense, as the post decided whether or not it wanted a research officer rather than a generalist officer, we arrived in Beijing in the summer of 1988. I was far more aware of the history of British representation in China than I had been of its counterpart in Korea, but it was not really until 1990, and the lull in bilateral relations following the events of June 1989, that I began to explore the history of the old legation and the new embassy, both of which had had some stirring moments. The fact that 1991 marked 130 years since there was first a British diplomatic presence in Beijing was an added spur, and in June 1991, I gave a paper to the Beijing International Society describing the history of Britain's diplomatic presence in China from 1861 to 1991. Later, after our return to London in 1991, I gave a revised version of this paper to the Great Britain-China Centre. Thanks to Gerry Segal of the International Institute for Strategic Studies, and the founder-editor of the *Pacific Review*, an account which focused in particular on the years after 1949, appeared in that journal in 1994.[2]

Tokyo is the only one of the three posts where I have not served. Yet in some ways, I was aware of Tokyo long before I had any but the haziest idea of Seoul or Beijing. Although it was not until 1976 that I visited the Tokyo embassy, I had known about it since I had began studying for a Ph D in 1964. A request from the then minister, Adrian Thorpe, in 1995 for a history led me to begin collecting material on the embassy, and it was not until 1997 that I succeeded in completing a history of the embassy. This, in modified form, has become the Japanese section of this history. Again, this time thanks to the Japan Society, a partial account of this has already appeared, but the version here is much expanded.[3]

Writing of the three sections, has, therefore, spread over some sixteen years. In putting them together, it has become essential to work out an order. In one way or another, all three posts can claim a 'first' for their embassy. Seoul now has the oldest and the longest continually inhabited set of buildings. Tokyo has the oldest site, while Beijing was the first permanently established, and was certainly seen as the most important of the three in its origins and up to the Pacific War. In the end, I have reversed

Acknowledgements and Thanks

The origins of this book go back to 1976, when I was temporarily covering Korean affairs in the then research department of the Foreign and Commonwealth Office (FCO). One of the counsellors at the embassy of the Republic of Korea, Mr Lee Jong Chan, later a well-known politician and currently (Spring 1999) the head of the National Intelligence Service, asked me if I could let him have details of the first Korean mission in London and of the British diplomatic presence in Seoul. I spent some enjoyable hours tracking down the relevant material at the Public Record Office, then in Chancery Lane, and in the FCO library, photocopied the results and sent them off.

There were three immediate results. Mr Lee was most grateful, both then and later when I was posted to Seoul, and he and his family remain friends to this day. My own department was less than happy, and I was severely reprimanded for having ordered photocopies without permission. Finally, the then British ambassador in Seoul dismissed my attempt at historical reconstruction as 'very laboured'. It was therefore a less than totally auspicious beginning.

When, unexpectedly, I found myself posted to Seoul in June 1981, it was not long before I found that there were various tales told about the British embassy and its nineteenth century core buildings which did not ring true. The story was that the buildings dated from the period of the Boxer rebellion in China (1900), and had been erected, using bricks carried by Mongolian ponies by the Royal Engineers on their way home from helping to raise the siege of the Beijing legations. But I was new and unwilling to challenge the views of my ambassador, who told the story with great flair and authority. We were celebrating, as embassies do, a hundred years of diplomatic relations, and the stories were regularly repeated. It was even 'suggested' that I should include it in a short piece I wrote about British graves and monuments in Korea. Such suggestions could not be ignored without evidence, and so I did – but only in a footnote.

Home on leave in 1983–84, mindful of the fact that Britain had first had a consulate-general in Seoul in 1884, I decided to pursue the matter further, and with much aid from Dr Nicholas Cox, then at the Public Record Office, I found what I needed. This was the files of the Office of Works relating to Seoul. These proved a treasure trove, even if they were among the most badly organised files I have ever come across. But I had

Foreword

by the Rt Hon. Lord Hurd of Westwell CH CBE

Just over a year ago I broke away from the commercial mission which I was leading in Beijing and walked alone through a grey polluted afternoon from our hotel to the old legation quarter. I wanted to revisit the old compound where forty years earlier I had spent as a young diplomat two of the most cheerful years of my life. The old compound is shut now to the public, and an ugly block of flats has been built over the gardens of my bungalow. The chapel has gone, but the gate which the Boxers besieged still stands, as do the scarlet pillars of the No 1 House behind it.

Something of the former magic of the place flowed back with memories to my mind. Diplomatic compounds arouse strong emotions for and against among those who inhabit them. It is excellent that Dr Hoare has laboured valiantly over years to tell the story of three of them. These buildings are a vivid part of the story of British diplomacy.

The Beijing compound is no longer ours but Tokyo and Seoul remain. Seoul now has the oldest buildings. The Tokyo houses are not architectural masterpieces but their combination of grey stone and quiet trees contrasts pleasantly with the tumult of the modern city. These buildings, resisting the occasional efforts of the Treasury to diminish or over-exploit them, leave their stamp not just on those who live in them but on all those who, by passing through their gates, absorb a particular impression of Britain past and present. Their tale is well worth telling.

Spring 1999

List of Illustrations

CHINA

1. 'Legation Court at Leong-Koong-Fu' 1861.
2. Beijing legation under snow, 1899.
3. Beijing c. 1902. Lady Susan Townley leans on a lion.
4. Harry Lester does the same some 50 years later.
5. Beijing c. 1895. Looking towards the main gate.
6. Beijing c. 1902. A busier scene near the main gate.
7. The Beijing embassy side gate c. 1937, with the 'Lest We Forget' Wall.
8. Beijing main gate, outside view from across the Imperial Canal, 1900.
9. Today, the gate is recognizable, but the Royal Arms have gone.
10. Siege 1900: sandbagged verandas.
11. Siege 1900: manning a gun.
12. Siege 1900: reinforcing the outer wall.
13. Siege 1900: the temporary graveyard.
14. Siege 1900: badly damaged student quarters.
15. Registry stool and desk, 1920s.
16. Office armchair, 1920s.
17. Beijing 1991: the lectern in the offices, a link with 1900.
18. Beijing 1937: a small member of the British community sits between the Boxer cannons.
19. Beijing 1950s: third secretary Douglas Hurd and colleagues at the Great Wall.
20. and 21. The residence from the gardens and the offices.

JAPAN

1. Entrance to Tozenji temple, site of Britain's first legation in Japan c. 1860.
2. Tozenji today.
3. Sir Rutherford Alcock (1809-97).
4. British legation Yokohama c. 1867.
5. Sir Harry Smith Parkes (1828-85).
6. Tokyo: British embassy, c. 1905.
7. Tokyo minister (Sir Harry Parkes) and staff early 1870s.
8. Architect's drawing of the house of secretary of legation (the second in command), as modified in the late 1870s.

Contents

Dedicated to the Memory
of

Nick Spreckley
(Sir J.N.T. Spreckley)
1934–1994

H. M. Ambassador Seoul
1983–1986

British High Commissioner
Malaysia
1986–1992

who would have enjoyed
the tales told here

EMBASSIES IN THE EAST: THE STORY OF THE BRITISH EMBASSIES
IN JAPAN, CHINA AND KOREA FROM 1859 TO THE PRESENT

First Published in 1999
by Curzon Press
15 The Quadrant, Richmond
Surrey, TW9 1BP

© 1999 J.E. Hoare

Typeset in Garamond Light 11 on 11½pt by LaserScript Ltd, Mitcham, Surrey
Printed and bound in Great Britain by Bookcraft, Avon

British Library Cataloguing in Publication Data
A catalogue record of this book is available from the British Library

Library of Congress Cataloguing in Publication Data
A catalogue record for this book has been requested

ISBN 0–7007–0512–0

Embassies in the East

The Story of the British Embassies
in Japan, China and Korea
from 1859 to the Present

J.E. HOARE

CURZON

Embassies in the East

Introduction

The British in East Asia, 1600–2000[1]

———⟡———

With the transfer of Hong Kong to Chinese sovereignty in 1997, to be followed by the return of Macau in 1999, the long wave of Western imperialism in East Asia will have finally spent its force. Of course, the European withdrawal from Asia long predates these two events. The sweeping Japanese victories of 1941–42 marked one phase of the end of empire. The US domination internationally after 1945 was another. The end of the British Empire in India in 1947, followed within twenty years by the virtual end of all British military links East of Suez, the Dutch withdrawal from the East Indies in 1949, and the French defeat in Indo-China in 1953, were all major landmarks on the road to the 'end of imperialism'.

Yet the Europeans were at the centre of Asia for a long time, and have left their mark from Afghanistan to the Pacific. The Portuguese and the Spanish led, with the British nearly a century behind. It is not even clear when the first Britons arrived in the waters of East Asia. Sailors often served under many flags, and it may be that well before 1600, storms or the fortunes of war had brought Britons to the shores of China or Japan. But the evidence is lacking, and it was not until the arrival of William Adams in Japan in 1600 that the first known Briton stepped ashore in East Asia. A pilot from Gillingham in Kent, working at the time for a company based in Rotterdam, he would never return to England, dying in Japan in 1620.

It was typical of the period that Adams was serving on a Dutch rather than an English ship when he reached Japan. By 1600, however, his fellow countrymen were preparing to exploit the 'wealth of the Indies', now widely known throughout Europe as details of the Portuguese and Spanish voyages spread far and wide. In 1600, Queen Elizabeth I gave a charter establishing the East India Company. Further charters were granted by her successor, King James I (and VI of Scotland). It was a Europe-wide trend.

1

The Netherlands East India Company was founded in 1602, the Danish in 1616, while a French equivalent waited until 1664.

It was not long, therefore, before Adams was joined in Japan by representatives of the new East India Company, led by Captain John Saris. They established their 'factory' or trading settlement at Hirado in western Japan, and for a time enjoyed reasonable trade. However, the small factory was beset with difficulties. There were disputes among its members, the Japanese imposed restrictions on its trade, and the Dutch conspired against it. There were also allegations of mismanagement and possibly fraud. By 1622, the court of directors at Batavia (present-day Jakarta) in the East Indies had had enough and the factory was closed down in 1623.

During the remainder of the seventeenth century, the East India Company would make occasional attempts to re-establish a presence in Japan, but they all failed. After 1623, the Japanese became steadily more suspicious of foreigners and Christianity, especially the Roman Catholic Church under the direction (principally) of the Jesuits. When Charles II married a Portuguese princess, Catherine of Braganza, in 1662 it was easy for the Dutch to portray England as a country leaning towards Catholicism. Japanese listened to such claims, and acted accordingly, rejecting all further British attempts at trade. Not surprisingly, the East India Company, remembering the difficulties of the first factory and faced with continuing Japanese hostility, lost interest.

Meanwhile, however, the British, again somewhat late, had 'discovered' China. An attempt in 1596 to deliver a letter from Queen Elizabeth I to the Emperor of China, as a prelude to establishing trading relations, failed, and only one member of the expedition survived to tell the tale. The first East India Company ships to reach Chinese waters arrived in the south in 1637. They received an unfriendly reception, but forced their way through Chinese blockades. The British persisted and by the end of the seventeenth century, the East India Company had established itself in the China trade. In 1689, following an imperial edict that opened all ports to foreign trade, the Company set up a factory at Guangzhou (Canton). This became a permanent post from 1715, but on a restricted basis. Its members could only live at Guangzhou for half the year. After the sailing of the East Indian ships (the Indiamen), they had to retire to the Portuguese enclave of Macau, where they spent the rest of the year. But the British had gained a foothold, and now the China trade could develop.

Develop it did. The British may have been late arrivals, and for the East India Company, India would always be more important than China, but soon the British were the principal merchants in China, outdoing all other countries in the volume and value of their trade. Tea, in particular, became a major component of the trade, with exports from Guangzhou more than quadrupling between 1775 and 1785, as the British became a nation of tea drinkers. In general, it was a trade carried on with little formality and virtually no legal underpinning. Contracts were rarely signed; oral agreements sufficed. Inevitably, however, the large numbers of sailors and merchants in port during the season could and did lead to difficulties. The merchants, with rich houses and good salaries, were generally well behaved, but the ordinary sailors were different, and there were clashes with the local Chinese authorities.

When the Chinese prevailed and succeeded in punishing Western malefactors, their methods sent a shudder through the not very squeamish British. It was only a few years since the British had ceased to use torture against prisoners as a matter of routine, and the practice was still common elsewhere in Europe. While there were remarkably few cases of conflict between 1637 and 1834, when the East India Company's formal monopoly over the China trade ended, the merchants, looking at the Chinese system of justice recognized approaches and methods that were already regarded as out-dated and under criticism in Europe. They did not relish the thought of being permanently under Chinese jurisdiction.

Concern at Chinese legal methods was not the only issue. The China trade was heavily unbalanced. The British and others bought a great deal from China, for silks and other products also attracted much custom. By contrast, the Chinese were used to their own products and showed little interest in those of the West. The result was a massive trade deficit in China's favour. The way to redress the balance turned out to be opium, widely produced in India and smoked by all classes in China. To balance the expenditure on tea and silks, the drug was imported in large quantities. Once it was more readily available, its use spread even more widely among the population and penetrated far from Guangzhou. From the late eighteenth century, the East India Company assumed a monopoly of the sale of opium in India. The Company did not itself trade in opium outside India, selling it instead, to other traders, known as the 'country merchants' who were happy to take it to China. When there were protests, the merchants argued that it was just another commodity. To the Chinese authorities, it was a trade out of control, causing immense damage to ordinary people. The path was set for a major clash between two mighty powers.

The clash would not come yet. The end of the eighteenth century saw a number of attempts by the British to put their relations with China on a more normal footing. If Britain had diplomatic relations with the Sultan of Turkey, why not with the Emperor of China? The answer was that of course it should, especially since this would aid trade. In 1787, Colonel Cathcart, who had distinguished himself in the Company's service in Bengal, set out at the request of the government in London to establish formal relations with China. The expedition failed. The ships suffered badly in rounding Cape Horn, Cathcart fell ill, and died within sight of China. The remainder of the embassy crept back to Britain at the end of 1788.

This failure did not dampen hopes in London. In 1791, it was proposed and accepted that another embassy should be sent to China, and that it should be headed by a veteran diplomat, the Irish peer, George, Baron Macartney. Created an earl and a viscount in the Irish peerage as a reward for accepting the role of ambassador to China, Macartney set off with three ships in September 1792. From the start, things did not go smoothly. One of the ships, the *Jackal,* became separated from the other two in heavy seas soon after leaving Plymouth, and never rejoined the group. The *Lion* and the *Hindostan* left on their own.

The Chinese had been given due warning of Macartney's expedition, but it made little difference to the reception that Macartney received. When the embassy arrived in China in 1793, Macartney did succeed in reaching the capital, Beijing, and later found the emperor at the summer resort of Chengde, north of the capital. But the approach of the two sides to the question of relations was too far apart for the visit to succeed. To the Chinese, this was but another tribute mission, albeit from a somewhat unusual source. They had their ways of fitting all sorts of outsiders into their scheme of diplomacy, and if Macartney had been prepared to fit in with this, perhaps relations might have developed in a more productive fashion. To Macartney, however, there could be no question of behaving in front of a foreign potentate in any way different from how he would behave in front of his own sovereign. Even the benefits of increased trade could not be gained at any price. For the emperor and his court, the benefits of trade were seen as of little value, while the presents brought by Macartney seemed no more than highly sophisticated toys. Although Macartney's refusal to perform the ceremonial bowing that became anglicized as the 'kow-tow', may not have been as important as it once seemed, it made little difference in the end. There were some gains at the margin, and Europe was flooded with books and pictures about the embassy, but in so far as its purpose was to establish diplomatic relations and to increase trade, the embassy was a failure. Yet, since Macartney had gained an audience with the emperor, his mission must be accounted more of a success than those that followed. In 1816, Lord Amherst reached the capital but was thwarted in his wish for an audience with the emperor. In 1834, Lord Napier failed to get past Guangzhou.

Meanwhile, the growing British presence in China, and the general expansion of Britain's overseas empire, brought more and more ships to East Asian waters. Between 1791 and 1819, at least four British merchant ships tried to trade with Japan, all without success. Royal Navy surveying ships were also active. The first Royal Navy vessel, and the first foreign ship of war, to reach China was HMS *Centurion*, in November 1741. Others followed, and all refused to be put under Chinese control while in Chinese waters. The frequency of such visits increased during the wars with the French from 1793 to 1815.

The ships did not confine their attention to China. Between 1795 and 1798, William Broughton in HMS *Providence* explored parts of northern Honshu, Hokkaido and the Kurile islands, as well as regularly visiting the Ryukyu islands. Broughton's other main claim to fame is that in the autumn of 1797, he landed near modern Pusan on the southern Korean coast, and thus became the first known Briton to visit Korea. Later, during Lord Amherst's visit to China in 1816, HMS *Alceste* and HMS *Lyra* visited Korean waters, while waiting for the main expedition to return from Beijing. Under Stamford Raffles, the energetic temporary governor of Java, which had been captured from the Dutch, the East India Company made a determined effort to pierce Japanese seclusion in the latter years of the war against Napoleon. A combination of Dutch and Japanese determination prevented it from being successful, and the policy, very much Raffles' own brainchild, ceased with his departure from Java in 1815. The Company remained officially interested in opening trade with Japan, but in practice it was felt to be too difficult and nothing happened.

For the time being, it was China that most preoccupied British traders and policy-makers. By the early nineteenth century, there was growing dissatisfaction among the non-Company merchants with the restrictions that the Company tried to place on their trade in China. It was widely believed that the Company was not pushing hard enough to sell British goods in China, and that its policies towards the possibility of developing trade with Japan were also denying British manufacturers a readily available market. Such complaints figured prominently in the evidence submitted to committees appointed by both Houses of Parliament in 1830 to enquire into the Company's affairs and its China trade. The result was the abolition in 1834, despite all arguments, of the Company's monopoly of the China trade – and by extension, of the potential trade with Japan; Korea does not seem to have been considered.

After January 1834, the affairs of British merchants in China were no longer subject to the East India Company's control. Instead, a chief superintendent of trade was appointed by the British government, to reside at Guangzhou, who would be responsible for the supervision of the British merchants and for normal diplomatic relations with the Chinese government. The man appointed as the first chief superintendant was a sailor, William John Napier, Baron Napier. Napier's tasks included the development of trade in China and further afield, though this was to be done as far as possible without causing local offence. At the same time, he was to avoid confrontation with the Chinese. In effect, he was to mollify the Chinese wherever possible, but at the same time insist that he represented the Court of St James. It was a recipe for inevitable conflict.

Lord Napier's mission was a failure. The years up to 1839 saw a steady deterioration in relations between the Chinese and the British. British merchants, without the Company's restraining hand, became more assertive in their demands for free access to the China market, rejecting in particular that all trade should be conducted through a Chinese guild, the *cohong*. Increasingly, one commodity, opium, began to dominate the trade. Its importation remained officially illegal, but the merchants ignored this theoretical prohibition, and pressed more and more opium on a willing Chinese population. The Chinese authorities in turn became concerned at the spread of opium addiction, although many officials also benefited from the trade. Imperial edicts attempting to stop opium-smoking were generally ignored.

In 1839, the matter came to a head. The Chinese government sent an imperial commissioner to Guangzhou with orders to stop the trade and to punish those responsible. This provoked the first Anglo-Chinese War or, as it is generally known among Chinese, the First Opium War. When it ended in 1842, the British had secured, they thought, official Chinese recognition of Britain's equal status with China for the purpose of diplomatic exchanges; taken Hong Kong island as a colony; opened five Chinese ports to foreign trade and residence (Guangzhou, Ningbo, Xiamen (Amoy),

Shanghai and Fuzhou); introduced the idea that Britons would live under British, not Chinese jurisdiction (though the full principle of extraterritoriality was not spelled out until the United States' treaty of 1843); established the right of diplomatic and consular representation in China; and had also established the principle that British merchants might trade with anybody who was willing to do so, on payment of very low tariffs.

There were two obvious gaps in the treaty, which would cause problems in the following years. Despite pressure, the Chinese would not concede that British diplomats should reside in Beijing; the superintendent of trade lived in Hong Kong. The treaty also failed to address the question of opium. The British foreign secretary, Lord Palmerston, laid down that Britain would make no demand on this matter, and would certainly not push for British rights to engage in what the Chinese authorities might regard as an illegal trade. If British subjects chose to engage in such a trade, they must take the consequences. So, in British eyes, the First Opium War was not about opium at all, but about free trade. British merchants continued to engage in the opium trade, safe in the assurance that their government and its local representatives would uphold the principle of the freedom to trade.

The British treaty was followed by others, which, through the use of 'most-favoured-nation' clauses, quickly created an interlocking net of arrangements, whereby the benefits gained by one country became available to others. Thus as each new set of negotiators arrived, the range of foreign 'rights' and privileges was steadily extended. The Chinese, beaten in war in 1842, and faced with multiple rebellions throughout the 1840s and 50s, could do little formally to resist a process that equally steadily undermined their sovereignty.

The opening of the five ports brought larger numbers of foreigners than ever before to China. Trade grew, but before long some of the old problems reasserted themselves. Foreigners found that they could not trade as freely as they expected. Internal taxes restricted both imports and exports. Monopolies continued, and Chinese officials were seen as arbitrary, officious and greedy. To the consuls now appointed to administer extraterritoriality, their nationals were not above reproach. The continued illegality of the opium trade brought many problems, as did large the numbers of sailors who were now regular visitors to the open ports.

Unsettled conditions in China allowed the foreign communities established at the newly opened ports to ignore Chinese authority. This was especially the case at Shanghai, where the breakdown of imperial control in the 1850s allowed the foreign community to create a quasi-independent foreign city, which would survive until 1941. When the Chinese attempted to reassert control over the foreign communities, the resulting tensions eventually led again to war. The ostensible reason for the renewed fighting in 1856 was the question of the registration of a boat called the *Arrow*; hence this is sometimes called the '*Arrow* War', but the real problem was the continued clash between two very different ways of life and approaches to trade. To the Chinese, it has always been the 'Second Opium War'. The *Arrow* incident has another minor claim to fame, for it was his role in this incident that first brought the young British consul at Guangzhou, Harry Parkes, to wider attention.

France, whose main interest in China at the time was the protection of Roman Catholic missionaries, joined with Britain in the second phase of the war, in 1857, and a joint Franco-British force defeated the Chinese. The *Arrow* War ended in 1858, with the treaty of Tianjin. This provided for diplomatic representation in Beijing; the opening of ten more 'treaty ports'; travel by foreigners, including missionaries, in the interior; the standardization of the internal transit tax on foreign goods at a maximum of 2.5 per cent; the payment of an indemnity; and the legalization of the opium trade. The British government appointed Frederick Bruce, brother of Lord Elgin, the negotiator of the 1858 treaty, as minister to Beijing. However, when he and his French counterpart tried to reach the capital in 1859, they met stout resistance, and the war recommenced.

The fighting finally ended in 1860, and China once more lost heavily. In addition to the terms of the 1858 treaty, the 1860 Convention of Beijing added further indemnities payable to Britain and France; opened Tianjin, the capital's port, to foreign residence; and Kowloon, opposite Hong Kong island, was ceded to the British, to become part of the Crown colony. The 'defects' as foreigners saw them, of the earlier treaties were now remedied. The legal protection offered by extraterritoriality was further consolidated and extended. The treaty port system, with its consuls and consular courts, its foreign-language newspapers, its clubs, bars and associations was firmly established as the norm in East Asia. There would be marginal changes, further ports would open, and some would close, but essentially, by 1860–61, a system was in place that would outlive the Chinese empire, lasting until 1943. This did not go unchallenged by the Chinese. There were occasional attacks on foreigners, such as the 'Tianjin massacre' of French missionaries in 1870, and the more serious outbreak of anti-foreign violence that became known as the Boxer Rebellion between 1898 and 1900. Although such events shook the self-confidence of the foreign communities in China, they tended to lead to further concessions to the foreigners, rather than ending their special status.

The British dominated the China treaty ports. Although virtually all European countries and the United States had concluded treaties with China before the end of the nineteenth century, the British were the largest and most conspicuous of the foreign communities. British trade flourished, British shipping companies commanded the China coastal and, increasingly, the river trade. British banks were financial powerhouses, loaning to governments as well as to merchants. Only Britain made the effort to provide full consular coverage wherever there was an open port, training a special China consular service to do so. Britons ran the press, the clubs, the racecourses, and the chambers of commerce. They were employed by the Chinese government, running the Imperial Maritime Customs and other services. Not until the arrival of the Japanese in large numbers in China after the 1894–95 Sino-Japanese War was there a real challenge to this dominance. The one area where the British did not predominate was missionary activity. Although there were many British missionaries in China after 1860, China came second to India in British missionary eyes. The British missions were never as numerous as those from the United States.

The significance of the Western advance into China between 1839 and 1860 did not escape the Japanese and Koreans. Both countries realized that it could only be a matter of time before the pressures from the West would be turned on them. The Japanese, kept informed of developments in China by the Dutch at Nagasaki, hoped to cope by building up strong defences and maintaining their policy of avoiding foreign contact. The Koreans, nearer to China, with which they shared a long border, watched anxiously as their traditional mentor and protector buckled before the Western onslaught.

The most obvious warning sign was the steady increase in Western shipping in Japanese and Korean waters after 1839, as well as in the Ryukyu islands. Previously, the occasional ship had called, with many years between visits; now it was not unusual for several ships to be sighted in the course of a single year. Some crews landed and had to be persuaded to leave. From 1825, in a departure from the eighteenth-century practice, Japanese forts began to fire upon any ship that came too close or looked as though it might attempt to land. The success of the British in China in 1839–42 led to a further change, however. The Japanese took note of the British firepower and from 1842 onwards, ships in distress calling at Japanese ports began to receive assistance, rather than being driven off at the first approach.

Expansion in China revived British interest in Japan, as did the need of the growing whaling trade for ports where the whalers might re-supply their ships. The British were also concerned at Russia's increased role in East Asia, eventually marked by treaties with China from 1858, and an increased naval presence around Japan's northern coasts. While officials on the ground in China were eager to take positive steps towards establishing relations with Japan, the British government was in no hurry to pursue the question, and was content for the United States to take the lead. Commodore Perry's visits to Japan were, of course, watched with interest, but Britain's concerns were mainly with China, and from the spring of 1854, with the conduct of the Crimean War. Ironically, it was the latter that led Britain's Admiral Stirling to Japan in 1854, where, without instructions or authority, he negotiated a treaty similar to that of Perry.

Admiral Stirling's treaty was generally a disappointment, and was replaced in 1858 by a new one, negotiated by Lord Elgin. (Perry's treaty was also unsatisfactory, and replaced.) When this was ratified in 1859, Japan too entered the treaty port era. As instructed by London, Lord Elgin essentially introduced into Japan the same approach to the issue of foreign residence and trade as had developed in China. Foreigners would live in separate 'foreign settlements' at the 'open cities' and 'open ports', protected by extraterritoriality, and enjoying the benefits of a relatively low tariff. Restrictions on trade would be reduced to a minimum. There would be minor changes over the next ten years or so, but essentially, the China model that was introduced in 1858 would last until Japan reversed the 'unequal' treaties between 1894 and 1899. Symbolic of the importance of the 'China pattern' in British thinking was the appointment of Rutherford Alcock, from the China consular service, as the first British representative in Japan. Alcock was followed by Sir Harry Parkes, an appointment that served to reinforce the impression that it was the China pattern that counted.

As in China, the British rapidly came to dominate the Japan treaty ports, running the clubs, the parks and the press, as well as being the most active in trade. British companies played the main role in commerce until well into the twentieth century. Only in missionary activity, again, did the British fall behind the United States. In sheer numbers, the British would be outnumbered by Chinese from about 1870 until the Sino-Japanese War in 1894, but in power and influence, it was the British who counted.

Until surprisingly late, this power was largely exercised by the men on the spot. Although the telegraph reached China in the 1860s and Japan in 1871, London did not use this new means of communication to control the activities of its diplomatic and consular agents on the ground. A newly-appointed minister might receive some form of broad guidance as to what policies he should follow on appointment, but this was by no means certain. Even as late as 1900, and in the aftermath of the Boxer Rebellion, Lord Salisbury was reluctant to give any guidance to Sir Ernest Satow on his appointment to Beijing. Once in China, Satow would be better able to judge what could be done than those sitting in London.

There was, however, one area of tight control, which had little to do with policy issues, but which caused many a dispute. For the men who ran the British diplomatic and consular missions in China, and later in Japan and Korea, it was self-evident that they should live in comfortable houses, work in adequate offices, and be able to have them repaired as required. From the earliest days of British diplomatic representation in East Asia there were problems with this apparently simple proposition. The man on the spot might suggest a scheme for his house, whether it was a purpose-built bungalow or a grand palace, albeit one fallen on hard times. This would then be put to the Foreign Office in London.

The Foreign Office, however, had no control over the matter. For financial approval, the Foreign Office had to go to the Treasury. The Treasury might or might not authorize the required works, depending on how well its staff were convinced of the value of what was proposed. Their assessment of the latter was not based on any idea of local conditions, but on what seemed reasonable to them, sitting in Great George Street in London. If they approved of the work, this was conveyed to the Office of Works (later the Ministry of Public Building and Works), one of the oldest of the government departments in Britain, though perhaps not one of the most dynamic. Works, as the department was generally known, would instruct a local representative to authorize the work to be done. Following the opening of China to foreign residence, the representative was based in Shanghai, and could not always go in person to Beijing, Tokyo or Seoul to supervise work. The result was a regular, and triangular, stream of complaints about lack of work done, lack of authorization, or, most frequently, what seemed sheer bloody-mindedness on the part of one or other member of the triangle. Only in the latter part of the twentieth century, did the Foreign and Commonwealth Office, as the Foreign Office had now become, take over the role of the Ministry of Public Building and Works, and begin to manage its own estate. It was a move that did not solve all problems, though it eased some. Further devolution of financial control in the 1990s may lead to an even better system, although ultimately, the Treasury still exercises a considerable degree of control.

To return to the main story. Japanese resistance to the presence of foreigners was fierce. The opening of the ports was followed by a string of attacks and assassinations, which only ceased in the early 1870s. More important in the long run were the attempts by the Japanese government to revise the treaties, and end what was seen as Japan's humiliation. Successive Japanese governments would suffer what they saw as humiliation on this issue, and came to see the British as their main opponents. For Britain, for a long time it seemed important to have a series of protective arrangements in place, such as foreign judges, before Britons could be entrusted to Japanese protection. In the end, however, the revised British treaty of 1894, which became the model for all other revised treaties, contained no such provision. From 1899, Britons and all other foreigners moved under Japanese jurisdiction with none of the awful consequences that had been predicted.

Korea did not follow the pattern established in China and Japan, as far as the British were concerned. Here the British took a back seat. Although rumours about the Korean peninsula's fabled wealth were widespread in Asia, the small number of visitors before the treaties reported on a poor country, with little obvious sign of riches. The Japanese took the lead in forcing Korea to abandon its long-established policy of isolation, signing a Western-style treaty in 1876. (The British and others were not slow to note that while protesting against 'unequal treaties' directed at Japan, the Japanese were happy to compel the Koreans to sign just such a treaty.) Western goods reached Korea long before the first Western treaties were signed in 1882, but they came in the packs of Chinese or Japanese peddlers, and the Korean market would remain small.

The early United States and British treaties, concluded like the first treaties with Japan by naval officers, were felt in both countries to be unsatisfactory. They were soon replaced by ones modelled, again, on those with China. In the British case, Sir Harry Parkes again enters the scene, first as British minister in Japan from 1865 to 1883, where he was a determined advocate of a policy of 'opening' Korea, and then as British minister in Beijing. In the latter role, he formally concluded negotiations with the Koreans in 1883 on a new treaty, and became the first, non-resident, British minister to Korea. Day-to-day business in Korea was in the hands of a consul-general, and this remained the pattern of British representation in Korea until the end of the nineteenth century. Then, John Jordan, of the China consular service, became first (1898) chargé d'affaires, then from 1900, minister plenipotentiary, to the court in Seoul. When the Japanese protectorate ended Korea's independence in 1905. Jordan left to become minister in Beijing. Extraterritoriality and other foreign privileges ended in 1910, with the Japanese annexation of Korea as a colony. Thereafter, a small group of Britons remained in Korea until the outbreak of the Pacific War in 1941, but its numbers never matched those of the United States' community.

At the beginning of the twentieth century, Britain's position in East Asia appeared unassailable. While British treaty rights had been given up in Japan, Anglo-Japanese relations seemed to be at their peak, especially after the signing of the Anglo-Japanese alliance in 1902. Although formally abolished, the former treaty ports were still at the centre of foreign life, and the British remained the largest group among foreigners. In China, the collapse of the ruling Manchu dynasty and the resulting confusion tended to increase foreign influence. British predominance continued in the treaty ports, and British banks and British merchants were closely involved with the new forces that emerged in China.

Yet there were signs that the predominant British role was nearly over. The French, German and Russian intervention in 1895 at the end of the Sino-Japanese War was one warning. Another was Russia's role after the suppression of the Boxers. The First World War took its toll on Britain's investment in East Asia. Japan's influence in China steadily increased after the Sino-Japanese War of 1894–95, and the Japanese made further advances during the First World War, as Western preoccupations turned elsewhere. After 1918, it was the Japanese who were predominant in much of China, with the Americans second. The British were still there, and clung to some of their former positions of power, but the trend was clear. Britain's willingness to discuss issues such as tariff reform and the end of extraterritoriality were increasingly seen as signs of weakness.

In Japan, the 1923 Tokyo earthquake marked a watershed; after that, the British would never again predominate, being steadily replaced by the Americans. British political influence in Japan also declined, especially with the end of the Anglo-Japanese Alliance in 1921. By the later 1930s, much of the goodwill that had marked Anglo-Japanese relations in the earlier years of the century had dissipated.

Then came the Pacific War, with the capture of Malaya, Singapore, Burma and Hong Kong, and Japanese armies reaching to the edge of the Indian empire. These were shattering blows for Britain's prestige in East Asia, showing that Britain could no longer defend its empire. There was further humiliation for those captured by the Japanese. Although the British government had been encouraging the departure of civilians from East Asia from the middle of 1940, many had stayed, and now fell into Japanese captivity. At best they were treated with indifference; at worst their Japanese captors determined to humiliate them and through them, the British empire. British troops captured by the Japanese generally fared worse; consciously or unconsciously, many Japanese now sought revenge for what they felt were past British humiliations of Japan.

During the War, Britain and the United States finally conceded to Chinese demands for the end of the old 'unequal' treaties. In 1943, both countries gave up extraterritoriality and all the other privileges associated with the treaty-port system. In some ways it was perceived as an empty gesture, since a number of the remaining treaty ports, including Shanghai, were in Japanese hands. Yet for the Chinese, the concession was important and welcomed both by government and press. Another break with the past also occurred in 1943, though it was less noted in East Asia. In that year, the 'Eden reforms', named after the then secretary of state for foreign affairs, Anthony Eden, ended the separate China and Japan consular services. This marked a further symbolic end to the system created after 1842. By that stage, of course, the exigencies of war had scattered the members of these two services far and wide throughout the British government, but the reforms would have an important effect on how British diplomatic and consular posts would be staffed after the end of the war.

At the end of the Pacific War in 1945, Britain returned to East Asia but the balance of power had shifted even more dramatically than had been apparent in 1918. Superficially, much continued as before, especially in China where Britain still had large investments. At the same time, it was impossible to hide the fact that the United States had now well and truly replaced Britain as the leading Western power in Asia. The Americans controlled access to Japan and Korea. In China, it was different, but although British firms resumed their trade with China, the preponderance of American power, and the role that the United States was playing in the Chinese Civil War between the Communists and the Nationalists, effectively marginalized the British.

Britain's decision to recognize the People's Republic of China in 1950 might have made a difference, given the United States' refusal to do so. The ambiguity of Britain's position over Taiwan, and by June 1950, its involvement in the Korean War, severely reduced any influence that Britain might have hoped to have with the new China. After 1954, relations improved but they were fragile. How fragile were shown in 1967, when the spread of the Chinese 'Cultural Revolution' to Hong Kong led to the house arrest under appalling conditions of the then Reuters' correspondent, Anthony Grey, and to the sacking of the British mission by Red Guards.

At the end of the twentieth century, Britain is not without significance in East Asia, though its role is much reduced from that which it had up to the 1920s. Britain maintains a strong diplomatic presence in China, Japan and South Korea (the Republic of Korea). Although Britain does not have diplomatic relations with North Korea (the Democratic People's Republic of Korea), diplomats from the two countries maintain a low-key dialogue. As well as embassies, in China, there are consular posts in Shanghai, Guangzhou, Hong Kong (restored to Chinese sovereignty in 1997) and, to be opened soon, in Chongqing. In Japan, the consulate-general at Osaka is the only surviving representative of the net of consular posts that once covered all Japan, but which modern means of communication render unnecessary. Britain remains a trading nation, and trade plays a major role with all the countries of East Asia, apart perhaps, from North Korea. Britain's role on the United Nations' Security Council still commands respect in East Asia, as does its support for new initiatives such as the Europe-Asia meetings, the second of which was held in London in April 1998.

If much of Britain's former powerful position in East Asia has disappeared, there have been new developments. The British Council, the cultural arm of the British government, is an important contributor to the understanding of British culture and knowledge of English. Britain is still a major investor in East Asia, playing an important role in, for example, the development of the South Korean automobile and shipbuilding industries. Not that this is all a one-way movement; since the 1980s, there has been a steady growth in Asian investment in Britain. British fashion and design finds a ready market in Beijing's Wangfujing or Tokyo's Ginza. British charities and non-governmental organizations helped South Korean reconstruction in the 1950s, and are helping hungry North Koreans in the 1990s. Students from China, Japan and South Korea study in large numbers in Britain, and an increasing number of British students attend educational institutions all over East Asia. British universities teach Chinese, Japanese and Korean. The 'good old days of Sir Harry Parkes' may have gone, but the British involvement with East Asia lives on.

Notes

1 This introduction makes no pretence at originality, and therefore there are no footnotes. The following works, while by no means an exhaustive list, have proved useful:

W. G. Beasley, *Great Britain and the Opening of Japan*, (London: Luzac and Company, 1951; reprinted Folkestone: Japan Library, 1995);

J. E. Hoare, 'The centenary of Korean-British diplomatic relations: aspects of British interest and involvement in Korea, 1600–1983' *Transactions of the Royal Asiatic Society, Korea Branch*, vol. 58, (1983), 1–34.

Peter Lowe, *Britain in the Far East: A Survey from 1819 to the Present* (London and New York: Longman, 1981).

Evan Luard, *Britain and China* (London: Chatto and Windus, 1962);

Colin Mackerras, *Modern China: A Chronology from 1842 to the Present* (London: Thames and Hudson, 1982).

D. Massarella, *A World Elsewhere: Europe's encounter with Japan in the Sixteenth and Seventeenth Centuries* (New Haven, Conn., and London: Yale University Press, 1990).

H. B. Morse, *The international relations of the Chinese Empire* 3 vols., (London: Longman, Green, 1910–18; reprinted Taipei, Taiwan: Ch'eng Wen Publishing Co., 1978).

Alain Peyrefitte, *The Collision of Two Civilisatons: The British Expedition to China 1792–94* (London: Harvill, 1993).

Sir John Pratt, *Britain and China* (London: Collins, n.d.).

Part One

<u>China</u>

China

$$\boxed{1}$$

The Beginning: The Duke of Liang's Mansion and the Establishment of the Legation 1860–1900

———————❦———————

It was the Treaty of Nanjing (Nanking) of 1842 which 'opened' China to the West and which established diplomatic relations between Britain and China. This was the culmination of years of pressure to force China to follow Western ways of commerce and diplomacy, a pressure determinedly resisted by the Chinese. Even when the principle of diplomatic relations on a supposedly equal footing was conceded by the Chinese, they continued to resist successfully for some years more the establishment of diplomatic missions in the capital itself.[1]

Only after two years of fighting and the signing of the treaties of Tianjin (Tientsin) with Britain, France, the United States and Russia in June 1858, was the right to establish diplomatic missions in the capital conceded by the Manchu court. It was a right which the Chinese promptly sought to take away. The Chinese, whatever they had signed, had no intention of allowing the foreigners into the capital.[2] When Elgin's brother, Sir Frederick Bruce,* fresh back from London with the British ratification of the treaty, and now appointed British minister to the court at Beijing, and his French counterpart, M. de Bourboulon, together with the US minister, J. E. Ward, arrived at the port of Dagu in June 1859 in preparation for their entry to Beijing to exchange ratifications of the treaty, they were forcibly prevented from travelling.[3] They left for Shanghai the following month, where they spent the winter.

In March 1860, determined to return to the task, they demanded an apology and an indemnity for the events of the summer of 1859, and the right to enter Beijing, as stipulated in the treaty. These demands were

———————

*Bruce, later Sir Frederick, and minister to Washington during the early part of the Civil War, was the third son of the seventh Lord Elgin, of Greek marbles' fame, and thus the youngest brother of the Lord Elgin who had negotiated the 1858 Treaty. He acted as secretary to his brother on that occasion, but was no stranger to East Asia, having first come out to Hong Kong as colonial secretary in 1844.

refused, and by June 1860, there was further conflict. By late August, Tianjin was occupied by British and French forces, and the two plenipotentiaries of 1858, Baron Gros for France and Lord Elgin for Britain, had arrived in the city to begin a further round of negotiations. During this period, the British interpreter, Harry S. Parkes and a number of his colleagues were captured, imprisoned and tortured. Most died and the incident became one of the justifications for the decision to burn the Summer Palace. Parkes, however, survived and will feature regularly in these pages.[4] The outcome of all this was that the 1858 treaties were reinforced by the Convention of Beijing of October 1860. The right of diplomatic residence in the capital on Western terms was now firmly established. In Chinese eyes, it was perhaps less a right than a concession seized from them at the point of a gun. China's modern diplomatic relations could hardly be said to have got off to a good start.

The two embassies, the British under Lord Elgin, the French under Baron Gros, took up residence in Beijing on 27 October 1860 with a strong military escort. Writing some thirty years later, Parkes's biographers could not resist a degree of triumphalism in describing the occasion:

> The representative of the Queen was at last within the walls of Peking. The long struggle of twenty years had ended in victory. Half measures were tried and failed, and tried again. At length the only step that could decide the issue for ever was taken, and what ought to have been done in 1842, what was obtained and abandoned in 1858, had finally, after a treacherous tragedy, been accomplished.[5]

For temporary lodgings, the British were placed in the mansion of one of the officials who had been responsible for Parkes's mistreatment; not surprisingly, Parkes found a certain satisfaction in this.

While in Beijing for the exchange of ratifications, both the British and the French ambassadors demanded accommodation for the permanent missions which both planned to establish. This the Chinese were obliged to provide under the terms of the treaties. That autumn of 1860, the French and the British were each assigned a palace to the south-east of the Forbidden City near the long established Russian Orthodox Church. This was an area long associated with the presence of foreign envoys in Beijing, for it was near the site of the hostel where the Korean, Annamese, Burmese and Mongolian envoys who arrived on their regular tribute missions were lodged. There they were also coached in the elaborate etiquette necessary for their presentation at court. Now it was to see the beginning of the official French and British presence in Beijing, and the birth of the Beijing legation quarter.[6] Neither property was in good condition, and so it was decided that the ministers would withdraw from the capital for the winter of 1860–61, to allow time for redecoration and alterations to be put in hand. Junior officers were left in charge, entrusted with this task, while the ministers retired to the protection of Tianjin for the winter.[7] They planned to return the following spring to formally open their respective legations in the capital, resisting continued Chinese attempts to keep them away from the city proper. Despite all Chinese efforts at procrastination, the French minister entered the city on 25 March 1861, and his British counterpart the following day.

The *Liangongfu*, where the British legation was situated, was the larger of the two palaces, and the British legation would always remain the largest of the legations. It lay to the west of a canal that ran north from the water gate in the wall of the Tartar or Manchu city to the Forbidden City itself. On the opposite side of the canal was another palace, the *Suwangfu*. To the south were Chinese-occupied buildings, below which was the Russian legation. Immediately north was the Hanlin academy, once the highest academic institution of Imperial China, with a famous library. By the 1860s, however, it was little used. On the west side, from south to north were to be found first, an open piece of ground known as the Mongol market, for sometimes traders from Mongolia actually came there, and then the Imperial Carriage Park. This, like the Hanlin academy, was much faded from its former glories. The Dukes of Liang, who owned the property, were descended from the Kangxi emperor, who died in 1722. By the 1860s, when its head was holding a command 'in the neighbourhood of the Great Wall', the family had fallen on hard times, and were happy to let their mansion to a foreign envoy.

At first, the new legation compound consisted only of the original Duke of Liang's house and subordinate buildings. Dr Rennie, a British army doctor who spent twelve months with the new legation, described it in some detail:

> The Leang-koong-foo may be described as consisting of two sets of quadrangular courts, running parallel to each other, north and south, with a covered passage between them. These courts contain blocks of buildings, built in the ordinary Chinese style of architecture. The set of squares on the eastern side form the palatial portion, and contain the state apartments. The roofs on this side are covered with green glazed tiles, and supported by heavy columns of wood . . . The interior, though out of repair, is still very handsome; the ceilings of the state apartments being beautifully decorated with gold dragons within circles on a blue ground, which again are in the centre of small squares of green, separated by intersecting bars in relief of green and gold.

The western side of the compound had less showy buildings, but they still had 'elegance and great taste'. What they perhaps lacked in beauty was compensated for by curiosities such as the names given to some of the rooms. Those used by Rennie were in the 'hall for the nourishment of virtue', while the housekeeper, at that point still on her way from Shanghai, was to live in the 'hall for the study and development of politeness'. It was this western section of the compound that was first occupied, while elaborate repairs began on the eastern section.[8] Outside, the mansion faced what in theory was the Imperial Canal, but which was in such a sorry state that most of the stone embankments that had once lined it had collapsed. According to a slightly later account, their collapse had contributed to the blocking of the canal, which became a series of stagnant pools in the dry season, and a sluggish sewer in the wet.[9]

The rent for all this was fixed at taels 1500 a year in perpetuity, abated for two years because of the repair work required. The tael then in use was the 'customs tael', valued at six shillings and eightpence (33 pence in Britain's 1999 currency) per tael, or three taels to one pound. The rent therefore was £500 a year, and, after the abatement period was up,

> . . . for forty years [sic – in fact, no rent was paid after 1900] the rent was regularly paid, in silver ingots taken in a mule cart by the Chinese Secretary of Legation to the Yamen [the Zhongli Yamen, or Foreign Ministry, established in January 1861] every Chinese New Year.

Another version has it that the senior of the legation's language students went each year with the rent, wearing a top hat kept specially for the purpose.[10]

Both the French and the British properties were in poor condition, and there was a need for extensive repairs. At the British legation, these were set in hand under the care of Colonel Neale, later to be chargé d'affaires in Japan, together with a Chinese clerk of the works. Within a month of Bruce's arrival, Dr Rennie noted, there had been speedy progress, and the question of redecoration was under discussion. Rennie provided a detailed account of one estimate which proposed the use of various forms of oil and grease to prepare the surfaces for painting. For this the government contractor wanted Mexican $1050. (The Mexican dollar was then one of the many standard coins accepted in China and Japan, and elsewhere in East Asia, and prices were often quoted in it. Its value steadily declined from the 1860s to the 1890s, when it was replaced by other coins.[11]) Another painter, who offered to do the same amount of work, quoted $750. Dr Rennie does not record which contractor was chosen, but, as we shall see, whoever did the work did not do a good job. Subsequently, other contractors were used to complete other pieces of decoration.[12]

In September 1861, an additional plot of land with some buildings was bought from one of the Duke of Liang's brothers. The asking price was taels 8000, but after some negotiating, the legation got it for taels 3500. This property had been briefly used by a Prussian delegation in May 1861, and would later provide a site for a hospital and accommodation for second secretaries. This piece of land and its buildings were made available for use as a medical missionary centre to the Anglican church, and later as a hospital. Thus began the close links between the legation and the Anglican mission. The premises were used again by the Prussian (by then North German Confederation) legation in 1866, but were thereafter firmly incorporated into the British plot.[13]

On 24 May 1861, Queen Victoria's birthday was celebrated for the first time in Beijing. To mark the occasion, Bruce invited the staff of the French legation to dinner, and toasts to Queen Victoria and Emperor Napoleon III were cordially exchanged. Another great event for the inhabitants of the new legation was the arrival of a 'large oil painting of Her Majesty the Queen in a massive gilt frame, sent out by the Foreign Office . . . .' on 20 June 1861. The picture was by Sir George Hayter, and was life size. The Chinese workmen much admired it and all filed past to pay their respects. Markbreiter in *Arts of Asia* (May–June 1983) has a fine picture which is probably of the Liangongfu state apartments as restored with the Queen's picture in prominent position. The portrait was to have a remarkable history.[14]

The new legation clearly impressed its occupants. Rennie's enthusiasm is evident throughout his two volumes. Ernest Satow, later to be minister in Beijing, spent some months on the compound in 1861–62 , studying Chinese before beginning the study of Japanese. He wrote of living in '. . . the splendour of the newly restored buildings of the Liang Kung Fu . . . .' (Satow, later renowned as a pillar of rectitude and author of the standard *Guide to Diplomatic Practice*, and a friend amused themselves while in the legation by shooting pieces off the roof of the Hanlin academy next door. In the 1870s, other students smashed a hole in the wall of the Imperial Carriage Park in order to get in, an action that led to official Chinese protests.[15])

Satow's friend, Algernon Mitford, who arrived in Beijing in 1862 as an attaché at the British legation, described the site and the general effect of the newly occupied building in equally enthusiastic terms:

> Our Legation is situated in the southern part of the Tartar city. We occupy a most picturesque palace called the Liang Kung Fu . . . which like all Chinese buildings of importance, covers an immense space of ground. There are courtyards upon courtyards, huge empty buildings with old pillars, used as covered courts, state approaches guarded by two great marble lions, and a number of houses with only a ground floor, each of us inhabiting one to himself.[16]

Thus it was in the spring and summer. In the autumn, however, Mitford seems to have found it all rather less congenial. In October 1865, he wrote a graphic passage indicating the drawbacks of the wide courtyards and ancient buildings:

> Outside the rain is falling fitfully and the wind blowing a hurricane, it moans and howls dismally through the courts and cranky buildings of the Legation, piercing its way into all sorts of odd nooks, and routing out old bells that jangle in a harsh and discordant way from the quaint eaves, as if they were angry at being disturbed in their dusty dens. Doors are creaking in every direction, and the windows threaten to burst in, but the stout Corean paper holds good, though it gets stretched and flaps unpleasantly like loose sails in a calm, and on the whole I confess I prefer glass.[17]

The truth was that much of the repair work carried out in the early days had not been of high quality. Perhaps in the rush to make the old palace habitable, too many corners had been cut, while subsequent maintenance appears to have been poor. Mitford wrote:

When the Legation first came to live here the whole place was put in repair, and redecorated in the Chinese fashion with fluted roofs of many colours, carved woodwork, kylins of stone and pottery . . . Unfortunately, the repairs were badly executed, and nothing further was done to keep matters straight, so the Legation, which ought to be as pretty as possible, is really a disgrace to us. The gardens are a wilderness, the paving of the courts is broken, the walls are tumbling down, and the beautiful place is going to rack and ruin . . . Fancy a residence in the heart of a great and populous city where foxes, scorpions, polecats, weasels, magpies, and other creatures that one expects to find in the wild country, abound. That will give you an idea of how space is wasted in Peking.

Mitford was a man of strong views. Much of his complaint was not about the premises themselves but about the very fact that they were in the middle of a large and to him clearly uncongenial city. Like many others, he disliked the smell and dirt of Beijing and the fact that the countryside lay several miles outside the city. Indeed, again like many others, he believed that a great opportunity had been missed in 1860 to force the Chinese to move the capital from Beijing to a more attractive position. Writing in 1900, with the siege of the legations fresh in his mind, he argued again that unless the capital was moved from Beijing, there would be a repetition of that 'death-trap' in 'ten, twenty or thirty years', opinions he had first expressed in 1862 or thereabouts. He also felt that the Russian Orthodox mission, by the 1860s established in the far north-eastern corner of the Tartar city, was in a much healthier and safer place. But these were unfashionable views, and were to remain so at least until the 1950s.[18]

As far as the quality of repairs was concerned, a more sober official report in 1867 noted that considerable sums had been spent in 1862 and 1863 on repairs – £5750 in 1862, and £257 in 1863. The reporter, Major Crossman of the Royal Engineers, who had been appointed by the Treasury to examine the condition of the diplomatic estate in China and Japan, was less than impressed by the quality of repairs carried out in Beijing. Of course, the problem was, as the Treasury itself had minuted, in commissioning Major Crossman in December 1865, that 'Her Majesty's Government are in the power, to a great extent, of native builders, whose workmanship is defective, and whose charges are extravagant'. It was to be a theme often repeated in the years to come.[19]

Whatever doubts the young Algernon Mitford had about the British legation, it was clearly in Beijing to stay. In 1865, Sir Frederick Bruce was replaced by Sir Rutherford Alcock, lately minister in Japan, but a man with a long experience of China. Mitford watched with a jaundiced eye as the Alcocks' luggage arrived, noting carts and packing cases containing furniture, pianos and harmoniums. There were also 'games of croquet', though Mitford felt that these were likely to fall victim to another defect of the legation grounds '. . . for there is not a blade of grass nearer than the park around the Temple of Heaven . . . .'[20]

Alcock was to be minister at Beijing from 1865 until his retirement from the diplomatic service in 1871. His biographer, the long-time China resident Alexander Michie, wrote in 1900:

During the time of Sir Rutherford and Lady Alcock their hospitalities rendered the British Legation the chief centre of social interest, while the unaffected kindness which inspired these courtesies endeared its inmates to all their fellow residents. That, indeed, was the golden age of the British Legation, and it may be added, of the general social life of the Chinese capital.[21]

In a further burst of lyricism, Michie described the British legation and other such compounds as 'These seductive oases in a wilderness of garbage in a city of great distances . . .', which tended to make the foreigners turn in upon themselves. Mitford, writing of the same period, noted that the total foreign community was only about seventy or eighty. He, too, detected a tendency for this group to turn in upon itself. In January 1866 he wrote: '. . . we have been leading the lives of vegetables in our own gardens; with a skating rink inside the Legation there is no excuse for facing the wind and dust outside'. The only problem was to keep up the rink, for hot sun and dust played havoc with the quality of the ice. Ten years later, Mrs Fraser, wife of the then head of chancery, or chief political officer, found the attractions of the legation's 'little world in itself' so beguiling that she scarcely ventured outside the compound for the first two or three months after her arrival.[22] Later, she too was to find that the sense of being cut off from the outside world was even stronger in winter. Between December and April, when the port of Tianjin was effectively closed, the foreign community was entirely on its own. The diplomatic and consular communities set about the serious business of dining, with all ranks entertaining each other, until, towards the end of the winter period, supplies began to run out.[23]

Skating, and possibly croquet, were not the only recreational facilities on offer. An undated plan in the Foreign Office records, which seems to be from the early 1860s, shows a library, probably for official use, a chapel and a bowling, or skittles, alley. Until about 1867, there was also some sort of gymnasium, though this was later converted into residential accommodation for the accountant. Another building was used as a theatre. There was also a social library for the student interpreters, set up in 'a dark old Chinese apartment' above their quarters. This was perhaps not as well stocked as it should have been. According to Mrs Fraser, the London bookseller who had been given £500 to stock it had taken this as a golden opportunity to rid himself of ancient volumes no one else wanted; the students seem to have found it a dreary collection, with little relevance to their entertainment or work needs. By Sir John Walsham's time as minister in the 1880s, tennis was also being played on the compound.[24]

Another reason for staying in the compound was that so much of the outside world came to its inhabitants. Not only were there official callers, but from the earliest days, curio dealers would bring their goods to sell on the compound. At times of financial or other crisis, real bargains were to be had in this way, but even in ordinary times, there was a constant flow of such tradesmen. Whatever profits they made from the deals also helped to keep the legation's head gateman in a suitable style. It was perhaps no wonder that few felt the need to venture forth into the smelly and dangerous city beyond.[25]

For those who did decide to go out, however, there in fact were plenty of things to do. W. P. Ker's diary for the last three months of 1892 records expeditions to temples in the hills, with occasional overnight stays until late October, less targeted riding expeditions in the Beijing countryside, shopping for silks and curios outside the Qian gate, trips to the Great Wall – usually a journey of two or three days – as well as dinner parties, picnics, and skating as the winter came on. A visit to the Lama temple in Beijing with George Curzon and Cecil Spring-Rice, visiting from London, and his consular colleague John Jordan, cost some $3.60; as today, there were separate charges to enter the main halls.[26]

During Alcock's time as minister, there were several changes to the original compound. The following account follows Major Crossman's report to the Treasury in 1868, already cited. Two new pieces of land were added to the original site in the 1860s, while various alterations were carried out to the existing buildings and new ones added. The new land was acquired to provide two sets of stables, one for general use, the other for the minister's private use. Crossman clearly had grave doubts about the wisdom of the second purchase, indicating that he thought room could have been found on the existing site. He added, however, that since the stables were convenient, perhaps it was just as well the land had been purchased, especially as additional horses were already on their way from India. Besides the stables, a cottage for the constable in charge, rooms for the Chinese grooms, forage rooms and harness rooms were all situated on the new ground acquired.

Numbers of staff grew. As more consular posts opened, more student interpreters had to be trained. After some two years of study, punctuated by the need to help out with copying and the other mundane tasks that fell to members of the chancery, these young men would provide the British staff of the consular service, as well as the Chinese secretariat in the legation; by 1867, eight students were in residence and five more on the way. All lived on the compound as did their Chinese teachers; eventually, the latter were moved away from their original position 'where they were a great nuisance', to one which intruded less on the other occupants.

The new buildings tended to be in European rather than Chinese style and so the distinctive mixed appearance of the compound, so apparent in old photographs, began to emerge. The alterations to the older buildings were generally designed to make them more comfortable; Chinese open pavilions might be attractive to look at, but on a Beijing winter's night they could be very cold and draughty. For similar reasons, Major Crossman accepted that the corridor around the minister's house should have a wooden floor. Although the corridor was long and wood was expensive, he considered it was 'quite necessary for the health and comfort of the inmates in winter'. In total, Major Crossman's proposals for expenditure for Beijing came to £17,390 10s. 7d. The Treasury agreed.[27]

In Major Crossman's opinion, the various new buildings required by 1867 left the compound unduly crowded and with little space for recreation.

After Alcock's departure, another two new pieces of land were acquired in 1876. One had already briefly been leased in the early 1860s, and was now substantively incorporated into the British legation. The other was a small plot of land bought for Mexican $250. The former was to provide the site for the 'First Secretary's House' – i.e. the number two to the minister. It is not clear what purpose the second piece was put to, but no doubt it relieved the general pressure on space.[28]

There were to be no more additions to the British compound before 1901. A description given in 1883 by one of the daughters of the newly arrived minister, that same Sir Harry Parkes who had enjoyed the triumph of the entry to Beijing in 1860, probably represents as good a picture as any of the residence and to some extent of the compound as it was before the great changes of 1901. Miss Parkes was fresh from the much larger legation compound in Tokyo, and her account echoes Mitford's first impressions some twenty years before:

> How can I describe the house to you? It is so unlike anything we have seen or lived in before. It really was originally a series of Chinese temples [sic] and has been adapted for the use of Europeans by having odd little rooms built on, at odd and inconvenient corners. The entrance is very fine; first come two courts, with handsome red pillars; the carving and painting of the roofs is very picturesque and the colouring really beautiful. From the court you mount a flight of steps, and enter the hall, or Queen's room as it is called – her picture being there. It is used for the reception of mandarins when they call, and is a fine square hall with a stained wooden floor, and windows on either side of the door, – nice, bright and sunny. On either side of the hall are two rooms; they are not very large, but face the south and get all the sun, and are therefore the most cheerful for sitting rooms. The remainder of the house is divided and built round a stone court with shrubs in the centre. It looks bare and dreary at present, but I think if we can get a few flowers to grow, it will brighten it up and make it more cheerful . . .
>
> There are long corridors which run all round the house – great, bare desolate places. which really look quite like a barn. On one side of the courtyard are the drawing room and the dining room, both handsome rooms, the latter panelled half way up the wall, and with open carved wood over a red ground; it is rather sombre and dark looking. The drawing room is also panelled . . . The grounds here are small but very nice; each person has his own little home, and it reminds me much of a cathedral close; it is very peaceful and quiet.[29]

Writing much later, the China coast journalist J. O. P. Bland remembered the world of the legations in Beijing in the 1880s as being content to '. . . pass its lotus-eating slumbers in the slumberous shade of the spacious Legation compounds, emerging thence to tea and tennis and tittle-tattle at the funny old ramshackle club under the Tartar wall . . .', with the easy tenor of life disturbed only by '. . . the little storms, born of feminine enmities or Chancery jealousies, which from time to time disturb the diplomatic tea-cup . . .'[30]

One must not exaggerate, but perhaps Bland reflected something of the truth. The excitements of the 1860s and 1870s faded into memory. Routine took over. As far as the British legation was concerned, there were only minor changes to the site after the 1870s. Buildings were added to or modified. Various improvements were made to the chapel under the direction of the then chaplain, Bishop Scott of North China, in 1886–87. A new baptismal font and altar were dedicated in 1887, a reredos painting of the meal at Emmaus in 1898. That year, a large bell was hung in a bell tower outside the chapel to mark Queen Victoria's Diamond Jubilee in 1897. It still hangs in the present embassy compound and is the origin of the name of the embassy social club, 'The Bell'. The chapel was used by the wider foreign community as well as by legation staff.[31]

The basic layout of the compound remained the same up to 1900. Battles were fought with London over relatively minor matters; the number of gardeners, the duties of the 'engineer'. The gardeners' tasks were obvious. They filled the courtyards with potted plants, and even in the depths of winter, could find roses on Christmas morning.[32] The engineer seems to have kept the boilers going, and by 1898 to have helped man the legation's two fire engines. The amounts involved were small – Mexican $472 (about £100) in 1898 paid for the maintenance of the electric bells, a gardener, a carpenter, an engineer and two groundsmen – but principles were everything, and each proposal for change was fought hard from London. They were not one-sided battles. Beijing won those relating to the maintenance staff. Others, perhaps more dear to the minister's own heart, such as a plea for a grand piano for the ballroom as provided to most other legations at government expense, or so it was claimed, fell on deaf ears. The then minister, Sir Claude MacDonald, was told firmly in 1897 that since it had '. . . not hitherto been the practice to supply pianofortes to missions . . .' it could not be done for Beijing. He gave up.

The following year, he had another battle. By 1898, the number of student interpreters training and living on the compound was about to rise to eighteen, and the minister made a plea to London for a common-room for them. Otherwise they had nowhere to go except their quarters or the club 'where there is a liquor bar'. This time he won without a struggle. Whatever doubts MacDonald had about the students using the club do not seem to have extended to the more senior staff of the legation, and a number of its members served as officers of the club.[33]

In 1898, just before the events which were to change the whole legation quarter, a report by Mr Boyce of the Office of Works – of whom more later – listed the buildings on the site as follows:

(i) The Residence. The old palace of the Dukes of Liang, much added to;
(ii) Minister's stables for ten horses;
(iii) The First Secretary's house, a modern purpose-built building;
(iv) The Chinese secretary's house, old one-storied Chinese building;
(v) Second secretaries' house, modern six-roomed, two storey;
(vi) Quarters and mess for three assistants, eight rooms and offices;
(vii) Doctor's residence, as Chinese secretary's;

   (viii) Assistant Chinese secretary's house, a six-roomed detached bunga-
           low;
     (ix) Accountant's house, the same;
      (x) Students' quarters, mess and reading room;
     (xi) Old escort quarters, now occupied by three students;
    (xii) The Chancery, an eight-room detached bungalow;
   (xiii) Sergeant of Escort's quarters;
   (xiv) Church, an adapted Chinese building;
    (xv) Stables for twenty-one horses, with harness and *mafoo* (grooms)
           rooms, forge, storage and smithy;
   (xvi) Dispensary;
  (xvii) Constables' quarters, a two storied house with stable yard.
           Accommodation for two, but only one occupant, with a store room;
 (xviii) A fives' court;
   (xix) A bowling alley (presumably the new bowling alley opened in
           1892;[34]
    (xx) A theatre.

Mr Boyce noted that the compound was surrounded by high walls and
totalled seven acres. He estimated the value of the buildings at £80,000. Most
of the properties were in good order and satisfactory, except the second
secretaries' and student accommodation, but these could be made suitable
by adding a second storey to the secretaries' accommodation and converting
the old escort building for the students. Otherwise, the only carping note
was that the road in front of the legation was disgraceful and £300 should be
spent on it immediately. Looking forward, Boyce suggested that it would be
useful to acquire more property if it became available and indicated that the
old Imperial Carriage Park should be taken over if possible.[35]
  A similar picture of the compound in 1898, though with more emphasis
on the human occupants, was given by Sir Meyrick Hewlett, writing some
forty years later. Hewlett had just arrived as a student interpreter and wrote
with affection of the family atmosphere created by the minister's wife, Lady
MacDonald, who was 'a veritable mother to the Students' Mess'. He was
impressed by the green-tiled main buildings and the 'imposing archway'
over the entrance gate. In the compound lived the minister, three
diplomatic secretaries, the Chinese secretary, the assistant Chinese secretary
and the accountant. These three were all members of the consular service
(and were often looked down upon by their diplomatic colleagues). There
was a chancery mess made up of those who had passed their Chinese
examinations and who were destined to be sent to consular posts but who
had not yet been commissioned, and a students' mess, still of fifteen
members when Hewlett arrived. The captain of the marine guards was a
member of the students' mess. The marine guard in normal times was small;
in October 1898, it seems to have been no more than one officer and six
men. There were also of course spouses and dependants and large numbers
of Chinese teachers, servants and grooms.[36]
  By the time Boyce's report was being considered in London and Hewlett
was well into his studies, there was more to worry about in Beijing than the

state of the roads outside the legation or falling off a pony in the Mongolian market. Those events would change the face of the British legation quite substantively, but first the comic-tragic saga of the summer legation, deserves to be told . . .

Notes

1 For the background to these developments, see D. Hurd, *The Arrow War: An Anglo-Chinese Confusion, 1856–1860* (London: Collins, 1967); H. B. Morse, *The International Relations of the Chinese Empire* (London: Longman, Green, 1910–18, reprinted Taipei: Ch'eng Wen Publishing Co., 1978), Vol. II; and on the specific subject of diplomatic relations, M. Trouche, *Le Quartier Diplomatique de Pékin: Etude Historique et Juridique* (Paris: Librairе Technique et Économique, n.d., [late 1930s]), especially Chap.2. For a modern account of the military campaign leading to the Convention of Beijing, which was waged with brutality on both sides, see Raymond Bourgerie and Pierre Lesouef, *Paliko (1860): Le sac du Palais d'Été et la prise de Pékin* (Paris: Economica, 1995).

2 For Lord Elgin's views on this matter, and his defence of his negotiations, together with translations of his correspondence with the Chinese negotiators, see Laurence Oliphant, *Narrative of the Earl of Elgin's mission to China and Japan, in the years 1857,' 58, '59* (New York: Harper and Brothers, 1860), Appendix II, pp. 622–629.

3 F. V. Dickins and S. Lane-Poole, *Life of Sir Harry Parkes*, (London: Methuen, 1894), I, 310–313.

4 Dickins and Lane-Poole, *Parkes*, passim.

5 Dickins and Lane-Poole, *Parkes*, I, 401.

6 D. F. Rennie, *Peking and the Pekingese during the first year of the British Embassy in Peking* (London: John Murray, 1865), I, 24–29; Morse, *International Relations*, II, 49–50; J. Bredon, *Peking* (Shanghai: Kelly and Walsh, 1931, reprinted Hong Kong: Oxford University Press, 1982), pp. 40–41; L. C. Arlington and W Lewisohn, *In search of Old Peking* (Beijing: Henri Vetch, 1935, reprinted Hong Kong: Oxford University Press, 1987), pp. 5–6.

7 Dickins and Lane Poole, *Parkes*, I, 404–5, Parkes to his wife 17 November 1860.

8 Rennie, *Peking and the Pekingese*, I, 55–56.

9 'A student interpreter', '*Where Chineses [sic] drive': English student-life at Peking* (London: W. H. Allen and Co., 1885), pp. 23–24.

10 Bredon, *Peking*, p. 41; Morse, *International Relations*, II, 49, note 2. The top hat version is in Arlington and Lewisohn, *In search of Old Peking*, p. 15; however, even in 1885, it was noted that the top-hat was not often worn: 'A student interpreter', '*Where Chineses drive*', p. 27.

11 J. E. Hoare, *Japan's Treaty Ports and Foreign Settlements: The Uninvited Guests 1858–1899* (Folkestone, Kent: Japan Library, 1994), p. 32.

12 Rennie, *Peking and the Pekingese*, I, 95–97, 337. Much of Rennie's account is reproduced in Stephen Markbreiter, 'In search of an identity: The British Legation at Peking, 1861', *Arts of Asia* (Hong Kong), 13, no. 3, May-June 1983, 120–130.

13 Public Record Office, Records of the Ministry of Works: Public Buildings Overseas (hereafter Works 10)/10, A. Miller, Office of Works, to S. K. Millar, Foreign Office, DC16/124644, 19 Nov. 1942, listing the pre-1901 holdings of the British legation/embassy, not always accurately; Rennie, *Peking and the Pekingese*, II, 79–80; Arlington and Lewisohn, *In search of Old Peking*, p. 15; F. L. Norris, *Handbooks of English Church Expansion: China* (London and Oxford: A R Mowbray and Co., 1908), p. 57.

14 Rennie, *Peking and the Pekingese*, I, 172, 230; Markbreiter, 'In search of an identity', 120–121.

15 E. M. Satow, *A Diplomat in Japan* (London: Seeley, Service and Co., 1921; Rutland Vermont and Tokyo: Charles Tuttle and Co., 1983 – a reprint of the 1921 edition), p. 20; A. B. Freeman-Mitford, *The Attaché at Peking* (London and New York: Macmillan and Co., 1900), p. 66. For Satow and the Hanlin academy, see P. D. Coates, *The China Consuls: British*

Consular Officers 1843–1943 (Hong Kong: Oxford University Press, 1988), p. 86. The story comes from Satow's diary. For the hole in the wall, see Mrs H. Fraser, *A Diplomatist's Wife in Many Lands* (London: Hutchinson and Co, 4th. edition, London, 1911), II, 422.

16 Mitford, *The Attaché at Peking*, p. 163.

17 Mitford, *The Attaché at Peking*, p. 66–67.

18 Mitford, *The Attaché at Peking*, pp. lvii, 67, and 210–211.

19 Parliamentary Papers, House of Commons, (PPHC), 1867–68, vol. XLVIII, C.315. Reports from Major Crossman and Correspondence respecting the Legation and Consular Buildings in China and Japan, pp. 2, 3–4.

20 Mitford, *The Attaché at* Peking, pp. 182–83.

21 Alexander Michie, *The Englishman in China* (Edinburgh and London: Blackwood and Sons, 1900), II, 139–140.

22 Michie, *The Englishman in China*, II, 145; Mitford, *The Attaché in Peking*, pp. vii, 200; Fraser, *A Diplomatist's Wife*, II, 411–412.

23 Fraser, *A Diplomatist's Wife*, II, 431–433.

24 Public Record Office, records of the Foreign Office, General Correspondence China (cited as FO17)/1460, undated manuscript map, bound in at the beginning of the volume. See also PPHC, 1867–68, Major Crossman's Report; Fraser, *A Diplomatist's Wife*, II, 451–452. For the students' view, see: 'A student interpreter', '*Where Chinese drive*', p. 35–36. For tennis, see Coates, *China Consuls*, illustration facing p. 324.

25 Rennie, *Peking and the Pekingese*, I, 337; Fraser, *A Diplomatist's wife*, II, 412.

26 W. P. Ker, diary entries for September – December 1892. I am grateful to Fred Sharf and the Peabody Museum in salem, Mass., for permission to quote from this diary.

27 PPHC, 1867–68, Major Crossman's Report. For the effect of similar housing in Seoul, see below.

28 Works 10/10/110, T. Terrance to G. Howard-Jones, 14 Dec. 1942. This gives details of the various pieces of land making up the British compound in Beijing. Terrance had been the Board of Works' representative in China, and in 1942 had just been repatriated from China.

29 S. Lane-Poole, *Sir Harry Parkes in China* (London: Methuen and Co., 1901), pp. 335–336.

30 J. O. P. Bland, *Something Light* (London: W. Heinemann Ltd., 1924), pp. 105–106.

31 *Guide to 'Peking'* (Peiping: The Leader, 1931), pp. 47–48.

32 Fraser, *A Diplomatist's Wife*, II, 413.

33 See various exchanges of correspondence in FO17/1460, 'Legation House, Peking', 1861–1900. For legation involvement with the club, see W. P. Ker, diary entry, 15 November 1892.

34 W. P. Ker, diary entry, 14 November 1892

35 FO17/1460, *Report on Her Majesty's Legation and Consular Buildings in China, Corea, Japan and Siam*, by Mr R. H. Boyce CB, London 1899.

36 M. Hewlett, *Forty Years in China* (London: Macmillan and Co., second printing, 1944), pp. 4–5.

China

$$\boxed{2}$$

Interlude: The Summer Legation Question

From the first days of the foreign community in Beijing, its members sought to escape the heat, smells and noise of the summer. The easiest way of doing this – indeed, the only way before the coming of the railways in the 1890s – was to move up into the hills some ten or twelve miles to the west of the city. This was a major expedition involving several hours' ride and the movement of much equipment. The majority of the staff and dependants from the various legations would make this move each summer, leaving a skeleton staff in the city. The latter would bring out urgent work – not so common in the days before the telegraph introduced a need for urgency in reporting local developments and responding to instructions – and would be relieved from time to time. In the hills, the easiest form of accommodation was in one or other of the many Buddhist temples that had long been established there. No doubt there were those who worried about such arrangements at first, either from religious or other scruples. Sarah Conger, writing at the turn of the century, noted her own uncertainty about the practice, but went on to say that the places were foreigners stayed were not usually the same as the monks' dwellings: 'They are in reality walled compounds which include many buildings besides the shrine buildings . . . The buildings where the priests live and hold their worship are apart from those rented to foreigners . . . .'[1]

As early as April 1861, Dr Rennie described an expedition to the area around Badachu (The Eight Great Places) '. . . in search of some temple that would be adapted for a residence during the extreme heat that is believed to prevail at Beijing during a portion of the summer'.[2] By 1865, the practice was well established. That year, Mitford noted that the British legation temple was the Biyunsi (Temple of the Azure Clouds), near the imperial hunting ground in the Fragrant Hills Park. It was a quiet spot, and the Russians had taken another temple one-and-a-half hours' ride away, so the British were not completely isolated:

Our habitation consists of several little houses on one side of the temple; we dine in an open pavilion, surrounded by a pond and artificial rockery, with ferns and mosses in profusion; high trees shade it from the sun, and close by a cold fountain pours out of the rock into a pond, in which we can ice our wine to perfection . . . .[3]

The following year, most of the legations hired temples at Badachu. The British legation went to Dajuesi (Temple of Great Perception or Awakening), which Mitford described as 'certainly the prettiest temple and the most charming summer residence that I have seen near Beijing . . .'. Fourteen cartloads of goods went with the vacationers, as well as '. . . our whole poultry yard . . . and a cow with her calf . . .'. It was to remain a favourite visiting place for foreigners until the 1930s.[4]

For the next twenty years from the mid-1860s, the British legation continued to rent temples in the Western Hills each summer without incident. There were excitements. Mary Fraser, who clearly liked her expeditions into the countryside, where the air was clear and the people friendly, nevertheless found the presence of snakes, scorpions and on one occasion, wolves, rather trying. She was also somewhat disturbed by the Chinese habit of leaving unburied coffins in temples until an auspicious occasion for burial should arrive. Sometimes the auspicious occasion had apparently not arrived before all those who might have had an interest in arranging a burial were themselves dead or scattered, and there were temples with mouldering ancient coffins next to the rooms which foreigners rented. Indeed, a stray visitor arriving late might find in the morning that he had been put in with the coffins. One British student interpreter so treated woke to find a coffin opening and a hideous figure emerging. He fled. (Mrs Fraser thought the figure was probably a thief, one of the many who hung around the temples preying on the living and the dead, but the student's reluctance to find out is perhaps understandable!) Others, who slept too soundly, were apt to wake to find that nocturnal visitors had removed all their clothes in the night. There would then follow hasty appeals to other temple dwellers to provide at least a modicum of cover.[5]

The pattern of these summer expeditions was soon established. The minister took a large temple which he shared with the student interpreters and others less well off among the staff, and where he would also establish the temporary office, while some of the senior staff took their own temples. Even Sir Harry Parkes, who became minister in 1883, and who was notorious for not taking holidays, was prevailed upon to move to the hills in the summer, though he was not above riding back into the city to make sure that those who remained there worked as expected. In summer 1884, he took the temple of Xiangjiesi (Temple of the Fragrant World), and filled it with '. . . the inhabitants of the various houses which were included in the Legation compound, and intimate friends like Bishop Scott', the Anglican Bishop of North China.[6]

Early in the spring of the following year, Parkes again signed a lease for the temple and paid taels 100, some £26 5s (£26–25p in decimal currency – the contemporary equivalent is some £1200), towards the rent. Before the summer arrived and before the balance of the rent money had changed hands, Parkes was dead. The chargé d'affaires, Mr N. O'Conor, paid another taels 100 so that the benefits of using the temple would not be lost to the staff. He then sought to claim back from the Treasury both his own money, since he claimed he could not afford this expense, and that which Parkes had paid, arguing that the latter sum was owed to Parkes' estate.[7]

The Treasury's response hinted at a sense of outrage – 'When My Lords are asked to pay the rent of this building, They are virtually asked to make an addition to salaries for purposes which those salaries are intended to cover . . .' – and rejected the request. O'Conor stuck to his guns, however, arguing that while a minister's salary might be calculated to include such a rent, that of a chargé was not. He had found an agreement already made and had felt compelled to abide by it. There followed a series of somewhat bad-tempered exchanges, with the Treasury suggesting at one point that, while the bill could be met from the Diplomatic Vote, if there were funds available, the Foreign Office should approach the trustees of Parkes' estate to see if they would pay the bill. This proved too much for the Foreign Office. Having sought reconfirmation that the bill could be met from public funds, the Foreign Office informed O'Conor in March 1886 that he would be reimbursed.[8]

O'Conor left Beijing in 1886, to return some six years later as minister. In the meantime, it is clear that temples were still rented in the summer, though on exactly what basis is not obvious. After O'Conor's return, the legation doctor recommended that staff should not have to stay in the city in the summer and that there should be some form of official summer residence – a number of other diplomatic posts already had such a facility. The official papers relating to this proposal do not appear to be on the files, but in a private letter to the permanent under secretary, the chief civil servant at the Foreign Office, in February 1893, O'Conor made clear that he thought that this was a good idea. He wrote that he had not had time to consider the question of a summer residence but if the doctor's report did not move the Treasury, 'I give it up and you must be prepared to see me go to Chefoo [now Yantai in Shandong province, by then already a great holiday centre much favoured by missionaries] or some temple a couple of days' journey from Peking . . . .'[9]

It is not clear what, if anything, happened next. O'Conor must have argued that there should be a permanent British establishment in the hills, but nothing seems to have come of this by the time he was transferred to Moscow in 1895. The next hint of a continuing problem over the summer residence was a private telegram from the Foreign Office to the chargé d'affaires, W. Beauclerk, in February 1896 which simply said: 'Do your best to get a good temple for Minister and staff in the summer.' Whatever Mr Beauclerk obtained, another problem over summer temples had arisen by the time the new minister, Sir Claude MacDonald, arrived early in 1896.

MacDonald, writing privately in April 1896 to Francis Bertie, assistant undersecretary for Asia in the Foreign Office, noted that the 'elegant row' over the temple had been patched up. Not all the details are recorded, but it is clear from this letter that the Russian minister had hired the Dabeisi

(Temple of Great Sorrow) for the summer of 1896, despite the fact that the British secretary of legation had taken it for the last twenty years. MacDonald believed that the Russian minister had been put up to this by his French colleague. The latter, according to MacDonald, had encouraged the Russians to make a fuss because at the Fuzhou [foreign] club, the Chinese porter's hat had a badge in English and Chinese only, not French. The solution to all the problems which had arisen over the years, according to MacDonald, was that favoured by O'Conor: '. . . the establishment of a sanitarium on the Western hills for the members of this Legation to which they may repair during the four unhealthy summer months . . .'. O'Conor had said that this would cost £8,000 (about £40,000 today), but MacDonald wrote that a good set of buildings could be obtained for half that price.[10]

There followed many months of heated exchanges involving Beijing, the Foreign Office, the Office of Works and the Treasury. The Office of Works disputed the figures, argued that the hills were too far away, and expressed the hope that the problems over hiring temples would go away. If that did not happen, perhaps the minister – no mention of his staff – could spend the summer in Chefoo (Yantai) or in Korea. (This indicated a lack of knowledge of Korea, where few facilities were available for foreigners in the 1890s, and certainly nothing that resembled a summer resort, while the climate of the capital, Seoul, was virtually the same as that in Beijing.) MacDonald resisted all such suggestions. Reluctantly, therefore, Works agreed that their representative at Shanghai, Mr Marshall, who looked after all the Far Eastern posts, could examine sites and make recommendations about buildings. The Treasury adopted an Olympian attitude. While not opposed in principle to the idea of a summer residence, they noted in January 1897 that '. . . it [was] not an expenditure on which [they] . . . were prepared to embark at present . . .'. They also welcomed the news that a temple had been found for 1897.

The battle was not yet over. The Foreign Office was evidently on MacDonald's side, but MacDonald thought that none of them would make much headway, perhaps because of personal animosity at the Office of Works. He wrote to Bertie in May 1897:

> Many thanks for all you are doing about the summer residence. I am afraid it looks like a losing fight – but it is hard to tackle people who don't fight fair. The Autocrat Boyce [of the Office of Works], before whom the entire Diplomatic and Consular Body bow down, has been heard to say that he will see me d—d before he lets me have a summer Residence or sanitarium or whatever I choose to call it.[11]

But though MacDonald did not know it, the Treasury had already decided to give in. While agreeing with the Office of Works' objections, the Treasury wrote on 2 June 1897 that they no longer felt '. . . justified in continuing to oppose the scheme . . . .' Four days later, a telegram – times had changed – went to Beijing conveying this decision. Three days later Beijing replied: 'Our grateful thanks for your successful assistance.' The 1898 Office of

Works' estimates showed £10,400 (perhaps £49,000 in 1999 prices) for a summer residence for Beijing.

When the Office of Works' 'autocratic' Mr Boyce reported on the legation and consular buildings in China in 1898, he noted that the following buildings had been authorized for the summer legation: minister's residence; Chinese secretary's residence; doctor's residence; married attachés' residence; a chancery building with quarters for two assistants; a mess and quarters for two other assistants; stables; and a gate bridge. He added that he suspected that further accommodation would be required in due course, and remarked somewhat disparagingly on the site chosen, which was '. . . about 200 feet above the plain, on an irregular plateau on the side of an utterly bleak and barren hill'. He also noted that the trend in Beijing in the summer was now to go to the seaside at Beidaihe[12] rather than the hills, and that both the inspector-general of the Imperial Maritime Customs, Sir Robert Hart, and the manager of the Hong Kong and Shanghai Bank in Beijing, had villas there. London may have approved the summer legation, but Mr Boyce's scepticisim about the wisdom of the whole enterprise had not gone away.[13]

Whatever doubts remained, however, the building of the new summer legation was already in hand in the summer of 1898. The contractor had promised that all would be ready by the following summer, and by March 1899, authority for the supply of furniture and curtains had been sent to the Works' representative in Shanghai. Mr Bax-Ironsides, chargé d'affaires in the summer of 1899, wrote that the minister's house was usable – Polly Condit Smith, an American girl visiting Beijing the following year, noted the presence of the British minister's 'large, commodious house' in the hills – and sought the Foreign Office's agreement that it could be used by other members of the staff. Sir Claude MacDonald had said before he went on leave that he had no objection to its being used, but according to the chargé, the Works' surveyor would have no part in this proposal. Bax-Ironsides himself did not wish to go to the hills, but two ladies with children did. As far as the rest of the work was concerned, however, the contractor chosen by the Office of Works was both incompetent and practically bankrupt, and most of the work was not finished. From later correspondence, it is clear that a second contractor was brought in and the summer legation was completed in time for the summer of 1900.[14]

We have no details of how it looked or how it was furnished. Lucy Ker, writing long afterwards, noted that it had a veranda,[15] but otherwise nobody seems to have described it. Lady MacDonald, returned from leave, had clearly moved some possessions there, and on 3 June 1900, her sister and the MacDonald children went up to the summer legation. It was an odd time to choose. The Boxer movement (see the following chapter) was well under way and becoming increasingly anti-foreign. On 28 May, groups of foreigners in residence in the Western Hills' temples had seen the small foreign settlement and railway station at Fengtai, the first stop on the Beijing-Baoting line, burning in the distance. The next day, most left the hills for Beijing, travelling in a large convey. Whether it was news of this, or whether it was a more general concern about security around the capital, which prompted him, MacDonald must have thought better of his wife's plans, and the small group of ladies and children was brought back by an armed escort on 4 June. It was a sensible move. On 10 June, Nigel Oliphant, whose brother David was a member of the legation staff, noted that they had heard '. . . that the Summer Legation building near Fengtai had been burnt, and the family of the keeper killed. The place had just been finished, and Lady MacDonald lost a lot of things which could never be replaced'.[16]

For the next year or so, attention focused on other things beside what to do in the summer. The lost summer legation featured in the British government's list presented to the Chinese for compensation for the Boxer 'outrages'. To complicate matters, the contractor who had replaced the first incompetent man and had finished the buildings, and who was believed killed by the Boxers, reappeared, demanding his money. As life returned to normal, however, Sir Ernest Satow, the new minister who had replaced MacDonald in 1900 at the end of the siege, wrote to the Foreign Secretary, Lord Lansowne, in March 1902, seeking help with the hire of temples. The cost of these fell particularly heavily on the junior staff, Satow argued, and he sought support for a Treasury payment of about three-quarters of the cost of such hirings, based on 1898 prices, until a decision was reached on whether to rebuild the summer legation. The Foreign Office was inclined to support the request in principle, but noted that at other posts where financial support was forthcoming for summer accommodation (Washington, Madrid and Bucharest), it was usual to ask for only half the total cost. A similar request was now put in for Beijing, and the Treasury accepted without a murmur.[17]

The following year, the Treasury again accepted the principle, though noting that as prices in China had fallen, its contribution should also be reduced. In 1904, Satow suggested that since it had been decided not to rebuild the summer legation 'at present', and since even the introduction of the 'Diplomatic Quarter' (see below) had not made life more agreeable or less unhealthy, the Treasury contribution should become a regular one. He added that he believed a summer legation was still necessary. He also noted that the Boxer indemnity paid by the Chinese government had included £10,000 for the destruction of the summer legation, with interest of four per cent per annum; the Treasury was thus making £400 a year. The Treasury ignored this, but agreed to contribute not more than £100 per annum towards the cost of temple hirings, adding that this arrangement was to end if the summer legation should be rebuilt.[18]

By the summer of 1905, Satow's views on the desirability of rebuilding the summer legation – or perhaps on the likelihood of it ever being rebuilt – had changed, and he suggested that a more sensible approach would be to build two houses for the use of legation staff at the seaside at Beidaihe. He noted that the Works' surveyor had visited the proposed site and estimated that two houses could be built for Mexican $25,000, or £2500, '. . . just one fourth of the sum charged in our indemnity for the destruction of the Summer Legation in the hills . . .'.[19]

There was no immediate response. Satow wrote to the Foreign Office in October 1905, pointing out that of the £100 sanctioned by the Treasury to pay for temples in the hills, only £40 had been used, yet many staff had gone to Beidaihe and to the neighbouring resort of Shanhaiguan, where the Great Wall met the sea. He asked, therefore, if half the cost of lodging and all travelling expenses for people who had gone to the seaside might be reimbursed, providing the overall limit of £100 was not exceeded. It was not until December that the Treasury replied on both counts. They agreed that two houses could be built at Beidaihe at a cost not exceeding £2500, but said that all payments for temples in the hills must cease. They also agreed that there could be a contribution towards the cost of rents at Beidaihe for the current year, but there could be no question of contributing towards travelling expenses.[20]

The idea of a summer legation in the Western Hills died in 1905, though it was to be three or four years more before the houses at Beidaihe were completed and ready for use. The pattern of work was changing. Satow for one did not think it was possible any longer to transport the chancery to the hills, or for those who remained based in the city to ride fourteen miles to work each day. A weekend, or longer, at Beidaihe was a better arrangement, and Beidaihe appeared in the *Foreign Office List* as the Beijing summer legation until the Second World War. To staff, it was '. . . a good place to get away from summer heat of Peking', and if the sea was not ideal, there were plenty of walks in the hills. Satow's successor, Sir John Jordan, paying his first visit in 1908, wrote that he had

> . . . five clear days at Peitaho and found the rest and change delightful. My impressions of the place . . . are very favourable, and it is hard to realize that a day's journey from Peking can produce such a difference in temperature and surroundings.[21]

Jordan noted that he thought it unlikely that there would be a mass exodus to the Beidaihe summer legation as there had been to the temples, but in fact, after his time some heads of post spent quite long periods there. Life was sometimes enlivened by visits from the naval commander-in-chief, Far East, who would anchor in his yacht off the embassy bungalows.[22] During the time when the head of post was there, a naval frigate would be moored offshore so that telegrams could be dispatched.[23]

There were still those who spent time in the hills. Daniele Varè of the Italian legation recorded a famous meeting with Sir John Jordan about 1912 or 1913 which testified to this. He was staying in a temple at Badachu, while Jordan had rented another nearby. Going over one evening to convey the contents of a telegram to Jordan, Varè reached Jordan's temple and '. . . walked in unannounced'. He found Jordan dining all alone in one of the courtyards and though '. . . on a hot summer evening in a Chinese temple, he was correctly dressed in a dinner jacket with a black tie'.[24] Black tie or no, Jordan regularly recorded his pleasure at being able to escape from Beijing to the fresh air of the hills.

Although perhaps not all went to the extent of Jordan in keeping up appearances, the tradition of extended outings to the hills lingered on, as did the habit of taking large quantities of supplies. A British banker, Evans

Thomas, described an expedition to Tanzhesi (Temple of the Mulberry Pool) in 1912. Starting from the legation quarter before dawn in three rickshaws, he and his servant and their luggage joined others at a station in the west of the city to take the train, and the party reached the temple at noon. They then spent several days exploring, attending Buddhist services – until these got too boring – and eating and drinking. Thomas noted that this was by no means his last visit to Tanzhesi.[25] Perhaps it was the competition from Beidaihe, but prices seemed to have dropped in the Western Hills in the 1930s. Berkeley Gage paid £15 (perhaps £400 in 1999 prices) for the yearly rent of a temple in the mid-1930s, which was looked after for him between visits by some former Imperial eunuchs. He does not give its name, but it was near enough to the city for his servants to bring out dinner. Ann Bridge's novel *Peking Picnic* echoed the reality described in Gage's and other accounts of diplomatic life in Beijing in the 1920s and 1930s.[26]

Beidaihe continued in use until the late 1930s, but after the Japanese occupation of the area in 1937, use tailed away. When the British returned in 1945, the area was in communist hands, and does not seem to have been used again until 1951. Members of the British mission visited in 1951 and 1952, making use of the by now somewhat dilapidated summer legation. Although the Chinese authorities had begun to close off some areas, the resort still provided a welcome break from the capital.[27] Thereafter, although staff could go to Beidaihe until the late 1950s, the Chinese seized the summer legation buildings. Eventually, as part of a comprehensive settlement of claims relating to former embassy and consular property, the British government agreed to accept compensation of some 20% of the estimated value of the property. A little extra was added to the original offer, as compensation for the trees that had been planted around the villas.[28]

Beidaihe continued as a seaside resort patronized by the foreign community, although for a time during the Cultural Revolution it was closed off. Today, it opens each summer and access is allowed by road as well as by train. Many of the early twentieth-century buildings are still in use, though they now belong to the Chinese authorities. It is still a pleasant break from Beijing, but as many more areas of China have been opened up to foreign travel, and as it has become easier to fly to other parts of Asia for short holidays from China, its popularity has perhaps waned a little. It remains favoured by the Chinese, however, and the senior state and party leaders usually spend much of August there, discussing and debating political and economic issues.[29]

Beijing's Western Hills are again accessible, having been closed off for a time during the Cultural Revolution; indeed, some parts of Badachu are still officially closed, though it is usually possible to circumvent the rules. The temples that have survived are now tourist destinations for both Chinese and foreigners, and an easy drive or bus ride from the centre of Beijing. During the 1950s and 1960s, the monks were moved out, but they have returned since the end of the Cultural Revolution. Nobody now stays in the temples, though there are still plenty of picnickers. The few foreigners who do not return to the city stay at the Western Hills Hotel, an award-winning creation by the Chinese-American architect I. M. Pei, or in one or other of the Western-style hotels available to the west of the city. It is all a far cry from the fourteen carts and the cow and her calf, or from Sir John Jordan dining in solitary splendour.

Notes

1 Sarah Pike Conger, *Letters from China: with particular reference to the Empress Dowager and the Women of China*, (London: Hodder and Stoughton, 1909), p. 75.

2 Rennie, *Peking and the Pekingese*, I, 109–20.

3 Mitford, *The Attaché at Peking*, pp. 87, 90; see also W. A. P. Martin, *A cycle of Cathy, or China North and South, with personal reminiscences*, (New York, Chicago and Toronto: Fleming H. Revell Company, 3rd. edition, 1900), 222–223, which gives a similar description of the temple.

4 Mitford, *The Attaché at Peking*, pp. 331–332, 340. The temple, and its continued use, is described in Arlington and Lewisohn, *In search of Old Peking*, p. 306.

5 Fraser, *Diplomatist's Wife in Many Lands*, II, 455 et seq.

6 Lane-Poole, *Sir Harry Parkes in China*, p. 366.

7 FO17/1460, O'Conor to Lord Granville, consular no. 30, 29 April 1885.

8 FO17/1460, especially Treasury to the Foreign Office, 25 July, 30 Nov. 1885, and Granville to O'Conor, consular no. 23, 18 March 1886.

9 FO17/1460, extract from a private letter from O'Conor to Sir Thomas Sanderson, then an assistant undersecretary in the Foreign Office, 6 February 1893.

10 FO17/1460, MacDonald to Bertie, private, 28 April 1896; MacDonald to Lord Salisbury, no. 145, 4 May 1896.

11 FO17/1460, MacDonald to Bertie, private, 8 May 1897. This was the same Mr Boyce who had built the Tokyo compound in the 1870s; see below, pp. 111 et seq.

12 For the background to the development of Beidaihe and other summer resorts used by foreigners, together with excellent pictures of what remains, see Tess Johnston and Deke Erh, *Near to heaven: Western Architecture in /China's old summer resorts* (Hong Kong: Old China Hand Press, 1994), especially pp. 40–53.

13 FO17/1460, Mr Boyce's Report.

14 FO17/1460, Bax-Ironsides to Salisbury, no. 240, 4 August 1899. This series of correspondence stops with this letter, and I have not been able to trace where it begins again. There is a reference to the second contractor in FO17/1715, Legation House, Peking, 1900–1905. For Polly Condit Smith, who wrote under the name Mary Hooker, see Mary Hooker, *Behind the scenes in Peking* (Hong Kong, Oxford and New York: Oxford University Press, 1987), p. 1.

15 Lucy Murray Ker, unpublished ms. 'Lest we forget', vol. II, no page numbers.

16 N. Oliphant, *A diary of the Siege of the Legations at Peking in the summer of 1900* (London: Longmans, Green and Co., 1901), pp. 4, 8; Hooker, *Behind the scenes*, pp. 8–11.

17 FO17/1715, Satow to Lord Lansdowne, no. 55, 2 March 1902; Treasury to Foreign Office, 12 May 1902.

18 FO17/1715, Satow to Lansdowne, no. 239. 4 July 1904; Treasury to the Foreign Office, 3 September 1904.

19 FO17/1715, Satow to Lansdowne, no. 271, 31 July 1905. Beidaihe too had been sacked by the Boxers in 1899, but it had clearly revived: Johnston and Erh, *Nearer to heaven*, p. 41.

20 FO17/1715, Satow to Lansdowne, no. 130 consular, 14 October 1905; Treasury to Foreign Office, 7 and 20 December 1905.

21 FO350/5, Jordan to F. A. Campbell, FO, private, 3 September 1908; in an earlier letter to Campbell, dated 20 August 1908, Jordan noted that the two buildings for the summer legation were still under construction.

22 Berkeley Gage, *It's been a Marvellous Party! The Personal and Diplomatic Reminiscences of Berkeley Gage* (London: privately printed, 1989), p. 57. Gage was appointed second secretary in Beijing in 1935.

23 Conversation in 1996 with Sir Michael Wilford, GCMG. Lady Wilford's father was at one time in charge of one of the ship's so used.

24 D. Varè, *Laughing Diplomat* (London: John Murray, 1938), pp. 120–121.

25 W. H. Evans Thomas, *Vanished China: Far Eastern Banking Memoirs* (London: Thorsons Publishers Ltd., 1952), pp. 75 et seq.

26 Gage, *Marvellous Party*, p. 51; Ann Bridges, *Peking Picnic* (London: Chatto and Windus, 1932). For a more critical account of foreigners and their behaviour in temples, see G N Kates, *The Years that were Fat: Peking 1933–1940* (New York: Harper Brothers, 1952; reprinted Hong Kong: Oxford University Press, 1988), pp. 220 et seq.

27 Peter Lum, *Peking 1950–1953* (London: Robert Hale, 1958), p. 131 et seq.

28 See the list of properties and the expected settlement figures in FO366/ 3167/XCA110/ 4/131, Memorandum by G. D. Crane, 6 May 1960.

29 Johnston and Erh, *Nearer to heaven*, pp. 42–43.

China

$$\boxed{3}$$

The Siege of the Legations and the Boxer Settlement

⬧⟿⟣⟼⬧

The Siege of the Legations

It was not of course just the British summer legation that was affected by the Boxer outbreak in the summer of 1900. Those famous 'Fifty-Five Days at Peking' saw the British legation and its inhabitants playing at the very centre of the conflict, while the aftermath would dramatically change both the British legation and the legation quarter as a whole.

The history of the Boxer movement and the story of the wider siege does not belong here.[1] By way of background, however, it is useful to remember that from late 1899, attacks on foreigners by followers of the movement known in the West as the Boxers, from the rather flowery translation of their title, 'The Society of Harmonious Fists' had increased at an alarming rate. A foreign missionary was murdered in December 1899, many missionary or missionary-related buildings were attacked and often destroyed, and the movement spread nearer the capital in the early months of 1900. As the Boxers enjoyed more and more success, so the court under the Empress Dowager began to favour them, in the hope that they might prove the means of halting the advances of the hated foreigners. By May 1900, imperial troops were openly fraternizing with the Boxers. An all-pervasive anti-foreign movement appeared to be spreading over North China.

The foreign representatives, in their enclave in the city, were slow to take the Boxer threat in and around Beijing seriously. The British legation had as usual celebrated the Queen's birthday on 24 May, with supper served in the small theatre, followed by dancing on the tennis courts to the Chinese band with a Portuguese conductor, maintained by Sir Robert Hart, the inspector-general of customs. Although there were two men to every woman, the sixty guests appeared to enjoy themselves. Hart wrote that little did they think that a month to the day, they would be ten times that number in the legation, living in fear of their lives.[2] A few days later, however, there was sufficient concern among the foreign representatives for them to summon extra forces from Tianjin to protect the legations. These arrived on 31 May, and included British marines. A further sign of troubled times was the number of missionaries who moved into Beijing bringing with them tales of growing anti-foreign feeling in the countryside. But as we have seen, the British minister allowed his children and sister-in-law to go to the Western Hills on 3 June 1900, even though he was aware of the attack on the nearby village of Fengtai. Only gradually did it dawn on the senior foreign diplomats that they were facing a major crisis, and that they might have to defend themselves against a Boxer attack.[3]

The siege itself is deemed to have run from 20 June to 14 August. But even before then foreigners were under attack in Beijing. Britons living in outlying parts of the city began to move into the legation in the early days of June. By 9 June, the Beijing-Tianjin railway line was no longer functioning, and a relief force under the British Admiral Seymour found itself trapped, unable to get to the capital. Next day, 10 June, the telegraph line to Tianjin was cut. Later that same day, the line north to Russia was also cut. According to one of the British student interpreters, Meyrick Hewlett, this was not without benefit, for it reduced the routine work of the chancery to nothing.[4] Beijing was now sealed off from contact with the outside world, and in a further sign that trouble was anticipated, some of the Chinese servants and the language teachers failed to arrive for work. On 11 June, a member of the Japanese legation was hacked to death in the streets. The Chinese authorities claimed it was the work of bandits and nothing to do with general anti-foreign feeling. At night, huge fires could be seen in the city. By day, the various legation guards began clearing lines of fire around the legation area in case there should be an attack. Large numbers of Chinese Christians were rescued from various parts of the city, and were lodged in the Suwangfu, the residence of Prince Su, situated on the other side of the canal from the British compound. Prince Su, given little choice in the matter, quickly agreed to vacate his premises.

On 19 June, the Chinese authorities sent messengers in to the legation area to announce that, as a result of a foreign attack on the Dagu forts near Tianjin, there was now a state of war. All diplomats and other foreigners should therefore assemble the next day and leave the city for Tianjin at three o'clock in the afternoon under a Chinese safe conduct. There was much debate among the foreign envoys about the value of this offer, but most were sceptical. Any doubts about Chinese sincerity were settled as far as the foreign envoys were concerned, on 20 June. That day, Baron von Kettler, the German minister, decided to go to the Chinese Foreign Office to establish what was happening, and was shot dead by an imperial soldier on his way there, and his companion badly injured. That afternoon, at precisely four o'clock, when the ultimatum to leave the capital expired, troops began firing on the legations; at the British legation, the flagpole on top of the main gate was a particular target.[5]

It had not been all gloom during the days before the siege proper began. Those trapped in the city daily expected relief to come from Tianjin and, and in any case, appear to have hoped against all the signs that there would be no attack on the legations. At first, therefore, there was no attempt to save food. The foreign food shops had given up their stocks, and the legations' wine cellars were well supplied. The younger members of the legations, freed from their ordinary work, seemed to enjoy the sense of excitement, and the lack of routine. David and Nigel Oliphant spent the morning of 12 June – the day after the murder of the Japanese chancellor – making a putting green on the lawn at the British legation, '. . . which was well patronized in the evening . . .'.[6] From 20 June, however, the holiday atmosphere, such as it was, disappeared. Things were now serious.

The British was the largest and the most central of all the legations. It was also the easiest to defend of all the legations. It had high walls, good wells, the canal on one side and the Imperial Carriage Park to the north. Its position made direct fire into it difficult. Once the foreign representatives realized the seriousness of the position, they had been decided early on that all foreign women and children should be gathered there if there was conflict. If the situation was desperate, all the foreign community would retreat there for a last stand. After the foreign envoys agreed to this arrangement at one of what seemed to those not party to them their interminable meetings, food, clothing and other supplies began to flow in during the week before onset of the siege. Soon after the first attacks, several male non-combatants also arrived. They included missionaries and the staff of the Imperial Maritime Customs. Before long, there were 500 Westerners, including 73 troops of all nationalities, 350 Chinese and over two hundred horses and mules crammed into the British legation. During a momentary panic on 22 June, it looked as though all those defending the outer legations were about to descend on the British compound, but the crisis passed. In early August, the official number in the British legation totalled 883, of whom the Chinese made up 356. The total number in the rest of the legation area during the siege was estimated at just under four hundred in the garrison, the same number of Chinese servants, and 2700 Chinese Christians.[7] The American doctor, Robert Coltman, felt that the British had not been prepared for such numbers and described scenes of great chaos; others were less scathing.[8]

The British legation staff moved out of their own accommodation to make space for the newcomers. Many moved into the minister's house or camped out in or on the pavilions nearby. Buildings were then assigned to each nationality and to organizations such as the Imperial Maritime Customs. No doubt some rough order of need was worked out, but there were soon grounds for complaint. The Russian minister had a second secretary's house for himself and his community of fifty-one. It was 'in bad repair, and anything but commodious'. In spite of these drawbacks, the Dutch minister slept in one of its cupboards – there seems to be no record of where his colleagues slept, though most of them probably remained in their own legation or else manned the outer barricades. Sir Robert Hart and his customs' staff were allocated an 'inferior house'. Some ascribed this to the fact that '. . . from time immemorial, the British Minister has never loved the Customs people's great power in having control of the huge revenues of China'. More likely in fact, there was little else available. Appropriately, many missionaries and their families were housed in the chapel. It must be a moot point whether their practice of gathering each evening to sing hymns outside the door of the chapel cheered up the rest of the occupants. After the take-over of the chapel, some religious services were held in Sir Claude MacDonald's dining-room.

To keep everybody informed of developments in the siege, the bell tower near the main gate, erected for Queen Victoria's Golden Jubilee in 1887, was used to post notices. Before long, items for sale and other humdrum signs of normality began to appear there as well. Miss Ransome, a British missionary, noted how the siege was forcing everybody to work together; even a first secretary of the British legation was found washing his own socks.[9] Dr Coltman, characteristically, saw it differently:

> One of the most noticeable effects of siege-life has been to bring out into prominence all the mean and selfish characteristics of the individual, as well as the heroic and self-sacrificing.

However, he felt that the missionaries had proved themselves the best of all in the siege.[10]

Clearly, attempts to keep a stiff upper lip in the face of adversity did not impress all. 'Putnam Weale' wrote scathingly of Sir Claude MacDonald's appearance among the assembled refugees on the evening of 21 June, '. . . smoking a cigarette reminiscent of his Egyptian campaign, and clad in orthodox evening dress . . .', which attempt at normality '. . . completed everyone's anger . . .' .[11] Much criticism of the atmosphere in the British legation, which it was felt stifled all initiative, even in the difficult times of June and July 1900, would appear in later published accounts of the siege. Even the legation chaplain felt that it might have been better if the traditional hierarchical approach had been abandoned, so that younger voices could be heard.[12]

Most people were probably unaware of these tensions behind the scenes, and concentrated on the needs of the hour. As well as the existing kitchens, impromptu cooking spots were soon to be found all over the compound. The large numbers to be fed meant that mess eating became common; never less than forty people sat down at Lady MacDonald's table during the siege. George Morrison, the Australian correspondent for the London *Times*, was later to complain that 'no missionary' had been invited to dine at the minister's house during the siege. He ascribed this to snobbery but it may have been the need to feed legation staff which led Lady MacDonald to this course of action. As time went by, horse and mule meat were added to the diminishing supplies of more normal food. Nigel Oliphant noted as early as 6 July that women and children were surviving on a diet of '. . . horsemeat and rice and a little condensed milk'. Most people found horsemeat more palatable than they had expected, though it helped if you did not know which horse or pony you were eating. Towards the end of the siege, however, some became tired of '. . . Chinese rice and pony meat', which were then all that was left for men to eat. Water does not seem to have been a problem; five sweet wells and two brackish ones were available. At some tables, wine, including champagne, and cigars, were still available up to the end of the siege. Indeed, champagne seemed to be less valuable than soda water, which quickly ran out.[13] Other comforts were also catered for; those so minded could use the private library of Henry Cockburn, the Chinese secretary. This, while '. . . not large, was extraordinarily catholic, ranging from law to the art of war, from the classics to yellow-backs . . .' . Every taste could find something 'to amuse and edify'.[14] Others noted impromptu games of cricket and football during quiet periods.

There was soon need of a hospital, not just for those in the British compound, but also to cater for the wounded and dying brought in from the outer barricades. The hospital was set up in the chancery building, with the reading-room serving as an operating theatre. A convalescent ward was later established in the minister's house, and as time passed, more rooms were taken over so that by the end, there were six nursing wards. During the siege, 125 seriously wounded men, one seriously wounded woman, and forty sick were treated in these rooms. Of these patients, seventeen of the wounded men and two of the sick died. (Others died on the barricades, in raids and in other legations.) Two male doctors, one British and one German, managed the hospital, while five women doctors and a small group of women volunteers worked as nurses under the command of the only fully-trained and certificated nurse available, Miss Lambert of the Church of England mission. Two naval sick-bay attendants, one British and one Italian, also worked in the hospital, and were later joined by German and American stewards. This last group had at first given first-aid on the barricades. All worked in what was clearly soon regarded as a hot, dark – no lights were allowed at night – and insect-ridden hovel. There were only a few beds, covered with uncomfortable straw-stuffed mattresses. Before long there were shortages of medical supplies and equipment, though the German doctor, Dr Velde, acquired a reputation for being able to conjur up supplies when everybody else had given up hope. A temporary graveyard was established behind the first secretary's house and here the foreigners were buried. Dead Chinese Christians were buried in the Suwangfu.[15]

During the course of the siege, Chinese troops set fire to the buildings of the Hanlin academy in an attempt to burn out the occupants of the British legation. Sterling fire-fighting work prevented the fire achieving its object, but priceless books and manuscripts were destroyed; many others had already been stolen. A few were saved, and MacDonald sent out a note offering to return them to the Chinese authorities. No answer was received and the rescued material was eventually sent to the British Museum. Thereafter, the grounds and ruins of the academy were incorporated into the legation's defence area.[16]

The relief forces finally broke through on 14 August, a Sikh private being the first, followed by a number of European officers of Indian regiments. Roger Keyes, one of the earliest to reach the British legation, wrote that they expected to find everybody dead. The relief force, close to the city knew that the legation area had been bombarded all night on 13–14 August, and expected that any who had survived the reported earlier massacres would have perished in this last attack. Instead, once they had made their way into the British legation, Keyes reported that they found the majority of the occupants calm and relaxed, and dressed as though for a garden party. The ladies were in 'clean white and light coloured dresses'. While those who were manning the barricades appeared fierce and dishevelled, even the men off duty were dressed for a summer afternoon.[17]

In fact, as Keyes soon realized, the whole legation quarter was in a sorry state. And while the British compound had been spared the worst of the battering, it had by no means escaped untouched. Virtually all the trees had gone, as had the grass, ruined by fires and the trampling of many human and animal feet. All buildings had suffered more or less from shot and shell. The day before the siege ended, two shells had fallen on the British minister's residence, one exploding in MacDonald's bedroom. In the dining room, which had also served as an occasional chapel – there was another chapel in Cockburn's house – a roof-beam hung down into the room, and Queen Victoria's portrait – was it the one which Miss Parkes had mentioned? – was tilted and riddled with bullet holes. Houses in multiple occupancy were dirty and vermin-ridden. Curtains and drapes had gone from all the buildings, joining dresses, night-clothes and other garments, to make sandbags to patch the defences. Furniture had been used as firewood or destroyed. Personal possessions were scattered and stolen; a week after the siege ended, MacDonald enquired of Morrison whether the latter's servant had taken away an inkstand with silver top from the convalescent hospital.

Even as the siege ended, tragedy struck for some. Murray Ker, the infant son of William and Lucy Ker, fell sick with scarlet fever during the siege, and he and his mother spent nearly a month in isolation. He seemed to have recovered as the siege ended, but then took a turn for the worse, and died suddenly. Like all those who had died since the siege began, he was buried in the makeshift cemetery behind the first secretary's house, besides two of the adults, David Oliphant and Captain Strouts, who had played with him in life. Four student interpreters carried him to the grave, wrapped like others who had died, in the Union flag, and all the legation staff, including Sir Claude MacDonald, followed the little coffin.[18]

But the majority were alive, and something like ordinary life soon resumed. Petty international jealousies re-emerged. Young Mr Oliphant, whose brother, David, killed on 5 July while cutting down trees that provided cover for the enemy, lay buried in the same makeshift graveyard as baby Ker, went riding in the west looking for a site for a golf course, successor to the putting green he and his brother laid as the siege began. Once this enterprise was under way, he wrote, he knew he could leave the city '. . . with the pleasing recollection of having introduced at least one branch of civilisation into Peking'.[19]

There is a sad footnote to all this. Once life returned to normal, it was decided that the temporary graveyard in the British legation should be moved outside the city, where other foreign burial grounds were already situated. This was done, and the cemetery became another place for foreigners to visit. Although it survived the upheavals of the warlords and the Chinese civil war, it was destroyed by the Red Guards in the Cultural

Revolution. Today, the local authorities are inclined to deny there ever was such a place.

The Boxer Settlement

During the siege, the foreign missions in Beijing had, for understandable reasons, treated the legation area as being quite outside Chinese control or jurisdiction. Many of the Chinese population were driven out, buildings were destroyed and whole areas formerly under undisputed Chinese control were incorporated into the quarter's defence perimeter. As we have seen, in the British case, this involved the take-over of the grounds of the Hanlin academy and encroachment on the Imperial Carriage Park.

With the end of the siege, it was soon obvious that the foreign envoys were determined to keep what had been obtained. The negotiations which began in late 1900, and which were to end with a protocol signed in Beijing on 7 September 1901, were concerned not only with punishment for those deemed most involved in the anti-foreign movement, and with indemnities for material losses suffered at the hands of the Boxers, but also with providing a safe area for the foreign legations in Beijing so that they would not face the same danger again. There was perhaps also an element of sheer greed:

> Every legation wanted to be as large, or if possible larger than its neighbours, and their extravagant claims were pegged among the ruins of the surrounding Chinese houses[20]

The result was the creation of the Beijing legation quarter, for which no parallel existed elsewhere in the world. It was a small foreign enclave in the midst of an ancient Chinese city, with manifold privileges. After 1900, no Chinese could live in this area. It enjoyed its own system of municipal government. On the south side was the old city wall, while on the other three sides, it had its own walls and gates, with an open space – 'the glacis' – to provide extra protection. As well as these physical barricades, the 1901 settlement allowed for the stationing of large numbers of foreign troops as legation guards in the area; from 1901 onwards, therefore, no legation was complete without its contingent of marines or other protectors. The protocol also made elaborate arrangements to keep open communications to the coast. The foreign diplomatic community was determined never to be cut off again as it had been in 1900.[21]

Thereafter until the Pacific War and the complete Japanese take-over of North China, including Beijing, the legation quarter became one of the sights of the city, at least for foreigners. No guidebook was complete without an account of its splendours. Indeed some devoted as much or more space to the legation quarter as they did to more traditional examples of Chinese magnificence such as the Temple of Heaven.[22]

It can be argued that although the legation quarter was imposed on the Chinese, it was not an alien concept. Like the treaty ports along the coast, the legation quarter was an understandable way for the Chinese to cope with foreigners in their midst. Walled cities within walled cities were a regular feature of Chinese life. Nevertheless, there was much resentment in China at foreign greed during the indemnity negotiations and at the way the Powers grabbed temples and gardens to increase their legation grounds. Some of the smaller Powers sought and obtained compensation far beyond any reasonable estimate of their losses.[23]

After 1901 and the rebuilding of the quarter, the impression the legation quarter created on visitors or new arrivals was of a large area even more cut off from the surrounding population than it had been in the past. Bland's picture of the legations in the 1880s from the vantage point of the 1920s as peaceful havens in a hostile world in some ways became even more true in later years. The Italian diplomat, Daniele Varè, writing later of his arrival in Beijing in 1912, recorded that his first impression of the legations was 'one of astonishment at their size'. He also noted the way in which the legation quarter cut its residents off very completely from the world about them:

> The enormous personnel, civil and military, of the Legations in Peking, gave to diplomatic life there a character all its own. Elsewhere . . . the moment a diplomat passes out of the front door of his embassy, he finds himself in a foreign country and sees only the inhabitants of that country. In Peking, diplomats are surrounded by their own nationals and in constant contact with other foreigners like themselves. They lived a life of complete detachment from the Chinese, in a kind of diplomatic mountain fastness. For the women and children, this was a good thing, if only from the point of view of hygiene. But most of the diplomats were isolated from and out of sympathy with the country they lived in.[24]

Paradoxically, in the last years of the legation quarter, as we shall see, living there was likely to have the opposite effect, as the Chinese constructed alternatives which left most foreigners, and diplomats in particular, even more cut off from the Chinese population. Only in the 1990s did this begin to change.

For the British, the end of the siege and the negotiations which followed allowed them to obtain much extra land. The British legation compound increased to four-and-a-half times its original size. In addition to the Hanlin academy, the Imperial Carriage Park, the Mongolian market, the Boards of Works and War and much of the Court of State Ceremonies were added to the British compound, all at no cost. As the Office of Works noted in a letter to the Foreign Office in January 1901, in which they agreed to new boundaries for the British legation, they assumed there would be no charge since the additional land had been 'acquired . . . by right of war', and justified by the need to give the legation a good defensive area. There were some who had doubts about the justification for this wholesale appropriation of Chinese land, but they were ignored. To emphasize further the defeat of the Chinese, rental payments for the original site ceased; the top-hat was no longer required.[25]

A good proportion of the newly-acquired land was given over to barracks, and the Treasury agreed to the use of funds in the army vote for this purpose. Disputes quickly arose between the civilian and military tenants of the newly-enlarged compound as to whose buildings should go where, and exactly which walls could or could not be knocked down. As early as June 1901, the commander-in-chief of the British expeditionary force, General Gasalee, who had been welcomed as a hero twelve months before, felt constrained to complain to the India Office (he was seconded from the Indian army for duty in China) about attempts by the diplomats to deny land to the legation guard. In February 1903, the then chargé in turn complained to the Foreign Office about the legation guard commander's plan to build his house on the site of the Hanlin academy. The legation wished this to be used for new quarters for the legation's junior staff, but in any case felt that this was not a suitable site for a commandant's house '. . . as it is situated outside the Military enclosure and is immediately contiguous to the Minister's house and to the new offices'. The assumption seems to have been that the commandant was perhaps not quite a gentleman enough to occupy such an important site.[26]

Perhaps there were other reasons; by 1905, the British minister, Sir Ernest Satow, was querying the idea of building large-scale military accommodation when the whole question of the future of the legation guard was under review. Subsequent political developments in China, especially the revolution of 1911, meant that the guard was retained until the 1930s. By then, plans and maps showed about one-third of the total area of the compound as barracks.[27]

Another effect of the siege was to leave several of the buildings with the marks of the fighting, still visible years later, though in time most of the bullet holes were covered with cement. On one of the bullet-scarred outer walls were painted the words 'Lest We Forget'. As Beijing's climate regularly caused this to disappear, it was equally regularly repainted until the late 1940s. In the chapel was erected a brass plaque on which were engraved the names of the Britons killed in the siege, and that of the Kers' infant son. Of the dead, one officer and four men came from the Royal Marines. Four were members of the consular service. The two oldest were aged 24. Two more came from, respectively, the Imperial Customs and the Beijing Imperial University. The plaque is now on the wall of the ambassador's garden. Also in the chapel was a large brass lectern, topped by an American eagle, inscribed: 'This Lectern is given as a Memorial by the Americans sheltered in the British Legation, June–August 1900'. The lectern stood for many years in the entrance hall to the chancery, where it was to survive a later attack.

Notes

1 There is a considerable literature on the Boxers available in English. For a recent examination of the movement, its significance and its treatment by both polemicists and historians, see Paul A. Cohen, *History in Three Keys: The Boxers as Event, Experience, and Myth* (New York: Columbia University Press, 1997. The best popular narrative account of the seige remains Peter Fleming, *The Siege at Peking* (Hong Kong: Oxford University Press, 1986).

2 Sir Robert Hart, 'These from the land of Sinim': Essays on the China Question (London: Chapman and Hall, 1901), p. 11.

3 Much of this is based on Fleming, Siege at Peking, passim. For MacDonald's unwillingess to accept that there was danger, see Robert Coltman Jr., Beleaguered Peking: The Boxer's [sic] War against the Foreigner (Philadelphia, PA.: F. A. Davis Company, 1901), p. 63. Coltman had little good to say about the United States' minister either.

4 W. Meyrick Hewlett, The siege of the Peking Legations, June to August 1900 (Harrow on the Hill: The Harrovian, 1900), p. 2.

5 Fleming, Siege at Peking, chapters 5 and 7. See also C Pearl, Morrison of Peking (Harmondsworth: Penguin Books, 1971), pp. 112–17; Oliphant, Diary of the siege, pp. 30–33; Hooker, Behind the Scenes, pp. 15 et seq.

6 Oliphant, Diary of the siege, p. 9.

7 Oliphant, Diary of the siege, p. 36; Hooker, Behind the Scenes, pp. 63–65; Hewlett, Forty years in China, p. 31; Jessie Ransome, Story of the siege hospital in Peking, and diary of events from May to August, 1900 (London: Society for Promoting Christian Knowledge, 1901), p. 110.

8 Coltman, Beleaguered Peking, pp. 82–83. A more charitable version can be found in an account by another American; see W. A. P. Martin, The siege in Peking: China against the World, by an Eye Witness (New York, Chicago and Toronto: Fleming H. Revell Company, 1900), pp. 80–81.

9 Hooker, Behind the Scenes, p. 50; Fleming, Siege at Peking, pp. 145, 153; p. 77; Ransome, Siege Hospital in Peking, p. 77.

10 Coltman, Beleaguered Peking, pp. 143, 147.

11 Bertram Lennox Simpson Indiscreet letters from Peking: Being notes of an Eye Witness, which set forth in some detail, from Day to Day, the Real Story of the Siege and Sack of a Distressed Capital in 1900 – The Year of Great Tribulation edited by 'B. L. Putnam Weale' (pseud.) (London: Hurst and Blackett; New York: Dodd, Mead and Company, 1907 – reprinted New York: Arno Press, 1970), p. 77.

12 Roland Allen, The siege of the Peking Legations: The diary of the Rev. Roland Allen, chaplain to Bishop Scott, Five Years' Acting Chaplain to HBM Legation (London: Smith Elder and Co., 1901), pp. 87–88.

13 Much of this is based on accounts in Hewlett's diary, Hooker, Oliphant and Fleming. See also Hewlett, Forty years in China, p. 34; Lo Hui-min, ed., The Correspondence of G E Morrison (Cambridge: Cambridge University Press, 1976), I, 763–64; Coltman, Beleaguered Peking pp. 93, 99–100; and Sarah Pike Conger, Letters from China: With Particular Reference to the Empress Dowager and the Women of China (London: Hodder and Stoughton, 1909), p. 113.

14 Allen, Siege of the Peking Legations, p. 177.

15 As well as the references cited in note 13, see especially Ransome, The Siege Hospital in Peking, pp. 5–25.

16 Fleming, Siege at Peking, pp. 121–122; Hewlett, Siege of the Peking Legations, pp. 14–15.

17 Letter of 6 September 1900, from Roger Keyes (Later Admiral of the Fleet and first Baron Keyes), Beijing, to Miss B. Jackson, 1900, now in the possession of Mr Frederic Sharf, Chestnut Hill, Mass.

18 Copy of a letter from W. P. Ker to his mother, 22 August 1900, now in the posession of Ms Kate Ker, Surrey.

19 Lo, Correspondence of G E Morrison, I, 144; Ransome, The Siege Hospital in Peking, pp. 88, 116; Oliphant, Diary of the Siege, p. 217.

20 William J. Oudendyk, Ways and By-ways in Diplomacy (London: Peter Davies, 1939), p. 114.

21 Trouche, Le quartier diplomatique de Pékin, pp. 54 et seq.; Fleming, Siege at Peking, pp. 248–252; US Department of State, Foreign relations of the United States, 1901: Appendix: Affairs in China, (Reprinted in China, 1941), contains much documentation on the negotiations leading to the establishment of the legation quarter. For the British position

during the negotiations, which covered many other matters apart from the question of the legation quarter, see L. K. Young, *British policy in China 1895–1902* (Oxford: Oxford University Press, 1970), pp. 255–266.

22 E.g. K Baedecker, *Russia, with Teheran, Port Arthur and Peking: Handbook for Travellers* (Leipzig: Karl Baedecker, 1914; reprinted Newton Abbot, Devon: David and Charles; London: George Allen and Unwin, 1971), pp. 559–560. The legation quarter is listed first among the sights of Beijing, and has a longer entry than the (then still closed) Forbidden City or the Temple of Heaven.

23 Oudendyk, *Ways and By-ways in Diplomacy*, pp. 114–117.

24 Varè, *Laughing Diplomat*, pp. 84, 86.

25 FO17/1715, Works to FO, 12 Jan. 1901, and related minutes.

26 FO17/1716, Legation Quarter Peking 1901–1905, War Office to Treasury, copy, 30 May 1901; India Office to the Foreign Office, 16 August 1901; FO17/1717, Legation Quarter Peking, 1901–1905, W. Townley, Beijing, to Lansdowne, no. 76, 26 Feb. 1903.

27 FO17/1717, Satow to Lansdowne, no. 151, 3 May 1905. See also Arlington and Lewisohn, *In search of Old Peking*, map no. 3b; Trouche, *Le quartier diplomatique de Pékin*, pp. 107–112.

China

$\boxed{4}$

From the Boxer Rebellion to the
Pacific War

———❦———

The events of 1900 had a deep and long-lasting effect on Beijing's foreign community. In many ways, the siege mentality generated in 1900 would last until the events of 1941 provided the foreign community with other things to worry about, and war swept away most of the legal and social structures created between 1860–61 and 1901. There were periodic alarms and excursions, as China experienced revolution in 1911, and then a long unsettled period as the new republic sorted itself out. The movement of armies and the general air of disorder and violence tended to bring back fears of 1900, even though such developments often had little direct effect on foreigners.

That was in the future. For the present, there was plenty to be done to take people's minds off the harrowing days of the siege. After leave had been taken and the dead moved from the lawns of the first secretary's house to the British graveyard at the edge of the city, the first task was rebuilding. Even before the final Boxer settlement was agreed, the Treasury accepted that restoring the damaged premises would cost more than was available from ordinary funds. A special grant of £5000 towards repairs was accordingly approved in June 1901 and work set in hand.[1]

In the years that followed, buildings were modified or extended and some new ones added, especially as more married officers began to take up positions once occupied by bachelors. With the exception of the military quarters, however, the general layout of the compound seems to have remained the same. A plan to build one house on the old imperial carriage park had to be hurriedly abandoned when it was found that the Chinese military authorities '. . . had a powder magazine right against the wall of our compound . . .'. It was eventually agreed that no buildings would be erected within fifty yards of the wall adjoining the magazine.[2]

Modern amenities gradually arrived. In 1909, the Office of Works noted that 'Heating systems are now generally installed in Peking houses . . .' –

something of a blessing, no doubt, given the coldness of a North China winter The Office of Works issued orders that heating was to be kept on all through the winter, to prevent pipes freezing. The result was that costs on the compound increased dramatically to the chagrin of the minister, Sir John Jordan, who roundly blamed the Office of Works in London for not doing its job properly. He wrote to the Foreign Office that 'Our heating arrangements have proved costly beyond all expectations and were carried out on a scale which excited general wonder'. That was in February 1915, and he returned to the charge in July, claiming that the Beijing legation was '. . . an example of extravagant public expenditure and senior mismanagement' – somehow, Jordan must have felt that he was not part of the senior management, a position difficult to maintain today.[3]

The amenities continued to be installed, however, despite the costs and the inconvenience. New houses had bathrooms incorporated, and they were added to old ones. Mrs Ker, swapping the small house that they had first inhabited on the compound for a new and much larger one in October 1914, was delighted to find that it had 'steam heating', running water and flush lavatories. Writing home, she noted that all these things would be commonplace there, but that they were novelties in China.[4]

By 1916 there were water closets and electric lights in all the main buildings, though not without some resistance. Max Müller, chargé in 1913, noted that '. . . many of the older residents . . . [preferred] the present system of night stools' to water closets, a preference which he did not share. He hoped that the decision on whether or not to include water closets would be decided on the basis of advice from sanitary engineers and the experience of those living in modern buildings rather than by prejudice. Whatever the objections, the work went ahead, causing immense disruption to ordinary life. Sir John Jordan wrote in February 1915 that the trenches in the compound in the summer of 1914 had 'rivalled those in the seat of war', and that the work had still not been finished.[5] Careful rules were drawn up governing matters such as the length of flex supplied for reading lamps and the replacement of worn-out electric light bulbs. Such amenities of course required what the novelist Ann Bridge (and, as Mrs, later Lady, O'Malley, the wife of the secretary of legation, or number two officer), described as '. . . the hideous . . . accessories of the Legation . . . such as a pumping station and a generating plant'. The use of all the facilities was governed by a set of detailed world-wide regulations for government property, together with an additional set of rules for China and Japan.[6]

A sweeping description of the compound as it had developed by the end of the 1920s is provided by the central figure in Ann Bridge's novel *Peking Picnic*, 'Mrs Leroy'.* She obviously felt at home in the 1920s' scene she described, but it could equally have been 1905 or 1935:

---

*Mrs Leroy, who was modelled on Mrs O'Malley, was clearly an exceptional lady among those living in the British legation, for she '. . . spoke Peking colloquial Chinese fluently . . . had sufficient command of Mandarin for social purposes . . . and could only read a bare two or three thousand characters' (!).

'Go in, go in', she cried, waving her hand towards the squat ugly grey gateway of the Legation. The coolie resumed his shafts and trotted obediently through it, past the sentry on the left, past the Constable's lodge with the grey parrot on the right, past the scarlet-pillared *Ting'rhs* of the Minister's house. The Legation compound was clothed with good-sized bungalows and a few larger houses; there were open spaces which would later be grass, there were trees and office-y looking buildings in a network of well-kept roads . . . .[7]

(The 'Ting'rhs' were so named from the Chinese word for a pavilion, *ting*, to which was added the 'r' sound frequently found in the Beijing dialect.)

This grey parrot, or perhaps a close relation, was clearly a noted inhabitant of the compound. Varè, the Italian diplomat again posted to China in the 1920s, recalled diplomatic meetings where it took an active part – and could not resist a sly dig at his diplomatic colleagues, who appeared not to share Mrs Leroy's command of Chinese:

When we met in the British Legation, in warm weather, the windows would be open on the small inner courtyard, where the lilac blossomed in the spring. The Legation parrot used to sit out there and join in our discussions (sometimes very aptly) with a loud guffaw, or a subdued chuckle, or a sudden screech. He was a talking parrot, but he only spoke Chinese, so that his remarks were unintelligible to most of the assembled diplomats.[8]

Whether the supposedly linguistically skilled Mrs Leroy could understand the parrot, or he her, is an interesting point.

Both Ann Bridge and Varè clearly remembered the British legation with affection. So to did Paul Reinsch, the United States' minister around the time of the First World War. He noted that the British legations was the centre of formal diplomatic life, where the regular meetings of the diplomatic corps took place, a position it had held since the siege:

Fortunately, the fine architectural forms of the old structure [the Duke's mansion] had been retained sufficiently to leave this group of buildings justly proportioned, beautifully decorated and free from jarring foreign notes. One passes to the Minister's residence through two lofty, open halls, with tiled roofs and richly coloured eaves. The residential buildings are Chinese without and semi-European within, Chinese decorative elements having been allowed to remain in the inner spaces . . . .

He added that the diplomatic meetings took place in the dining-room, where a '. . . huge portrait of Queen Victoria, from the middle period of her reign, impassively – not without symbolic significance – looked down upon the company'.[9]

Even George Kates, Reinsch's fellow American, but something of a recluse from Western society in Beijing, and a more jaundiced observer of the foreign scene, while not impressed by what he saw as British pretentiousness and rather ordinary buildings, left a not-unfriendly account of the British embassy, as it had become, in the 1930s:

To return to the lordly embassies, the crown of all of course was that occupied by the British. The dinners there, if not the most interesting gastronomically, were the most formal and of course, the best served. The very lion and unicorn on the impeccable gilt-edged Bristol of the place cards guaranteed this. The buildings themselves were nondescript, and the general plan of the irregular large 'compound' methodless. Yet they were well-maintained and comfortable small houses, glossily painted, with small parlors and small stairs, tiled hearths and much chintz, good books and cheerful fires, rear gardens and stables, all clustered about the ambassador's much larger residence. There was daily also a miniature changing of the guard, with British sentries wearing thick hobnailed boots looking properly wooden as they stood motionless before their sentry boxes at the main gate.[10]

'Nondescript' was perhaps a bit hard, but there was certainly a mixture. To the original Chinese buildings had been added a series of substantial Victorian and Edwardian houses, together with some British Indian-style bungalows. The student quarters have been variously described as 'not unlike an African railway station' by one inhabitant, and 'very Indian' by another.[11] (This eclecticism was not uncommon; Kates expressed the view that all the American legation residential properties were based on small town post offices, even down to the counters for receiving the mail! But he may have exaggerated.)

As the nature of the work changed and number of staff grew, the original accommodation was felt to be too small. By 1923, there were twenty staff living on the compound. By 1927, this had grown to twenty-nine, all but one of whom still had accommodation on the compound, often in very cramped conditions. (It is not clear who it was lived off the compound.) The then minister noted that the number of language students had fallen – the first sign of the gradual decline of the British role in China and also a side product of the withdrawal from a number of the smaller consular posts. At the same time, the number of 'executive staff' had grown. These were officers who were members of neither the diplomatic nor consular services, but clerical staff who had begun to take over some of the more routine work of cyphering, decyphering of telegrams, and typing, which had once been done at a higher grade. Now eleven people lived in the student mess, of which only four were students. The chaplain was one of those who suffered from poor accommodation, 'living in one room over the Office of Works' and 'messing' with the students for food and entertainment.

As far as Sir Miles Lampson, the minister, was concerned, it was wrong that the student quarters were not being used for students. At the same time, however, the demands of the work meant that all staff should be available at all hours. An additional argument for increased accommodation was that this was the only way to protect all staff in the event of trouble. The Office of Works agreed that there was need for extra accommodation, but felt that this should be looked at carefully, since two extra houses would cost £6,500. The Foreign Office did not share the minister's concern, believing that the circumstances prevailing in 1927–28 were exceptional, and that it would probably be possible to reduce staff before long, and that Lampson had exaggerated the likely number of students which would be required. Perhaps the move of the capital to Nanjing (see below) persuaded Lampson to change his mind, for in November 1928, he informed the Foreign Office that he had withdrawn his request for more accommodation.[12] Whether it was possible to reduce staff is not clear. The Beijing compound remained the centre of British diplomatic activity in China well into the 1930s, even though the move of capital meant that more time had to be spent at Nanjing. The head of mission continued to reside there, as did most of his staff. Only in the late 1930s did this begin to change.

Despite the stirring events of the 1920s, as warlords fought for control of Northern China and the new Nationalist regime sought to exercise control from Nanjing, the demands of work were not too heavy in Beijing. Duncan McCallum, in Beijing with the East Yorkshire Rifles as part of the legation guard, noted that during the warlord years, life went on very much as it had always done, with drag hunts and polo, and shopping in the markets to fill up spare time. The legation regularly entertained North China's own warlord, Zhang Zuolin, who would stay late to listen to the legation guard band, resisting the temptation to go to play mahjong.[13]

Before 1900, Beijing's foreign community had been small, largely limited to the diplomats, the missionaries and employees of the Chinese, such as the staff of the Imperial Maritime Customs. For some this was one of its attractions, for it allowed more time to study the ways of the Chinese without the distractions of a foreign community and its doings.[14] Post-siege Beijing had gradually become more cosmopolitan, with an influx of traders and bankers on the commercial side, growing numbers of teachers and missionaries, and a small group of resident journalists, as the city experienced an opening up to the outside world. From time to time, there were more exotic groups as well. Just after the First World War, for example, a group of British pilots and aircraft engineers from the British companies Handley Page and Vickers were employed by the Chinese government to start an air force. The confused state of North China politics led the legation to issue warnings about not getting involved. It proved difficult to resist the warlord, Zhang Zuolin, however, and many of the aircraft disappeared from their Beijing base and turned up in Mukden (now Shenyang), Zhang's base in what was then known to foreigners as Manchuria. Meanwhile, the legation learnt of daring feats over the fields of Flanders from aces such as Cecil Lewis.[15] There were also frequent globe-trotting visitors, who seem to have come to see the legation quarter as much as the Great Wall. For members of the community in the British legation, lunches and dinners provided occasions for social chit-chat and diplomatic exchanges, which both Ann Bridge and, in a very different way, Varè described to perfection. Weekend excursions to the hills or to Beidaihe were as popular as always. As more people acquired cars, it was possible to go further afield. In the mid-1930s, some would venture as far as the old summer capital of Chengde (also Rehe, or Jehol in the Wade-Giles' transliteration), by then in the Japanese puppet state of Manzhouguo.[16]

Alcohol seems to have been consumed in large quantities. No description of a picnic or other outing was complete without details of the cocktails drunk and the wine consumed. Not that drinking was confined to recreational expeditions. Sir Hughe Knatchbull-Hugessen, briefly ambassador in the late 1930s, introduced the custom of a daily *vin de midi* for diplomatic staff in the Beijing embassy, at which he served an ice-cold sparkling wine, bought from a monastery near the capital. Those who then needed to cash a cheque at the Hong Kong and Shanghai Bank, and who still felt thirsty, could drink cold bottled beer with the manager.[17]

There were also the prospect of more stirring events than lunch or dinner dates. Reuters News Agency and the London *Times* reported in 1903 that there had been an attempt to blow up the legation while a ball was in progress. This proved to be a somewhat inaccurate account of a burglary during which parts of a gun had been stolen from one of the legation's ordnance stores, but it showed continued nervousness in the wake of the Boxer experience.[18] The 1911 revolution saw the legation quarter again prepared for siege. Mrs Ker, whose husband was now the British commercial attaché in Beijing, wrote to her mother in January 1912, that they were living in 'strenuous and trying times' and describing conditions in the legation quarter. Expecting that the rebels would strike north, in order to capture the 'baby emperor', still of course in Beijing's Forbidden City, and with memories of 1900 close to mind, the denizens of the quarter had prepared themselves for another siege. They laid in supplies of tinned milk, sheep, cows and laying hens, '. . . not to mention flour, butter & sugar & stacks of biscuits in tins'. The danger had passed without any need to use these supplies even by the time Lucy Ker wrote, and her attention shifted to the supply of cotton dresses for the summer.[19]

During uncertain times like this, the foreign representatives would often encourage all foreigners residing elsewhere in the city to come into the legation quarter for safety. In 1911, George Morrison, still correspondent of *The Times*, was pleased to find that Lady Jordan, the wife of the British minister, was kinder to the missionary families than Lady MacDonald had been in 1900. Lady MacDonald's behaviour still rankled with him, for he noted that in 1900, '. . . refuge was given to foreign ladies in accordance with their rank and the missionaries were treated with contempt . . . Now Lady Jordan has every room occupied by missionary ladies and children . . .'.[20] In his vendetta against the MacDonalds, Morrison conveniently forgot that the compound had been much expanded by 1911, and the numbers involved were much smaller. Not that the legation quarter was entirely safe. Shells fell on the British legation during a brief attempt at the restoration of Pu Yi to power in 1917, though fortunately without damage, and soldiers from the Tianjin Volunteers, a largely British force, came up to the capital to stand guard in case the fighting spread. It did not, although the young emperor took temporary refuge with the Netherlands' legation.[21]

Other problems for the legation caused by the events of 1911–12, though less serious than the prospect of a second siege, were nonetheless time consuming. They included the complex question of which Chinese to invite to the King's Birthday Party in 1912. By then, the 'KBP', as it was generally known, was the highlight of the British social year, a time to entertain the British community, the diplomatic corps, and, since the Beijing court had begun to turn itself into something resembling a Western monarchy after 1901, senior Chinese dignitaries. There seems to have been no problem in 1911, either at the KBP in May, or the much bigger coronation celebrations in June. Indeed, on the latter occasion, some 700 people had attended, including many from British India and Chinese ladies.[22]

The dilemma in 1912 was in deciding which Chinese officials to invite. The imperial court had gone, and the post-Manchu republic had not yet been recognized by the Western powers. Jordan solved the problem by inviting only those members of the government who were on his wife's list of callers – in their private capacity. He also noted, however, that, personally, he would have been happy to invite all the government, if it were not for the question of recognition.[23] The need to consider such diplomatic niceties did not end in 1912. Later years were to see the dilemmas posed by the brief attempt to establish a new imperial dynasty in 1916 by the former viceroy, Yuan Shikai, and by warlords contesting jurisdiction in Beijing with representatives of the central government. In protocol terms, it did not make for an easy life.

Another problem thrown up by the confusion of the times was the question of allowing Chinese access to the legation quarter. While large numbers of Chinese lived or worked in the quarter, as teachers and servants, after 1900 the area was formally out of bounds to Chinese unless invited. As time passed, however, when there was fighting in or near Beijing, large numbers of Chinese and Manchus sought refuge in the quarter, despite the treaty provisions. Although many foreigners thought that such influxes only increased the possibility of a Chinese attack, at times of trouble few could resist the pleas of rich Chinese friends and acquaintances even though this often led to complex debates about privileges and immunities. One such refugee was the deposed Manchu emperor, Pu Yi, who continued to reside in the Forbidden City until 1924. In 1922 his British tutor, Sir Reginald Johnston, made arrangements with Jordan's successor, Sir Beilby Alston, to offer the emperor hospitality in the British legation if he was in personal danger. In the event, Pu Yi took refuge in the Japanese legation, later moving to the Japanese concession at Tianjin.[24]

Despite all the fears and political upheavals, the legation quarter remained generally an unaffected haven of peace in the turbulence of China, right up to the outbreak of full-scale Sino-Japanese conflict in 1937. It was not totally without changes. The 1914–1918 war, and the Chinese decision to join the allies from 1915, meant that the German and Austrian legations lost the privileges gained between 1842 and 1901. The new USSR eventually gave up extraterritoriality and related privileges in 1924. The Soviet legation staff still lived on the large compound that had originally belonged to the Russian Orthodox mission. But for most foreigners, life went on as before.

Whereas the widespread breakdown of law and order after the 1911 revolution rarely impinged on daily life, added spice was to be found outside the legation quarter, especially in expeditions to the hills, where warlord armies and bandit groups both operated. From this evolved the plot of the *Peking Picnic*, in which a group of diplomats is kidnapped and held to ransom in the Western Hills. The plot was loosely based on real events of which Ann Bridge was aware and first-hand observations of the places mentioned, though the reader must make considerable allowances for a novelist's license. But the story was not entirely fantastical. Berkeley Gage recalled an expedition to the Mongolian-Manchurian border in the 1930s during which some of the participants were captured by bandits, and a former secretary to the British First World War prime minister and Liberal Party leader, David Lloyd George, was killed.[25] Knatchbull-Hugessen, Gage's ambassador, used part of one summer holiday at Beidaihe to compose a long poem, 'Pricing a Plenipotentiary'. It was a moderately humorous tale about being '. . . carried off by brigands north of the Chinese Wall', and what he imagined would be the less than caring attitude of the Foreign Office and the Treasury.

Fortunately, like many another hero before and since, with one bound across the wall, the poem's ambassador is free and the issue of what would be paid is not put to the test.[26] Knatchbull-Hugessen clearly did not think that it would be much.

A real sign of the dangers foreigners faced occurred at Nanjing in February 1937. Knatchbull-Hugessen's daughter, Elisabeth, was out riding with her father and members of the embassy, when she was hit by a shot fired by a Chinese, apparently aimed at the ambassador. The bullet lodged in her neck, but was extracted by one of her fellow riders, George Young, a second secretary in the embassy, using a latch-key. There was an even more happy ending to the story, for two years later, Elisabeth Knatchbull-Hugessen and Mr George Peregrine Young were married in London at the church of St Peter's, Eaton Square, on 14 February 1939.[27]

A more pleasant development after 1900 was the opportunity for more contacts with the Chinese. Remarkably, soon after the Boxer outbreak, Lady Susan Townley, wife of the chargé who objected to the guard commander's house (see page 48), invited the princesses of the imperial court to lunch at the legation. She noted the irony of the princesses lunching in the minister's dining-room under the same portrait of Queen Victoria that had suffered damage in the siege, though she does not say whether the portrait still carried the bullet holes. A jolly time was had by all, with much amusement at the need to use knives and forks. Afterwards, the Manchu and British ladies sat smoking and drinking coffee while Sir Robert Hart's band played European music in the courtyard outside.[28]

Others recorded frequent dinners and other social occasions with the Chinese. Here alcohol was also much in evidence, for drinking matches between Chinese and foreigners were popular on such occasions. Sir Miles Lampson, British minister from 1927–33, seems to have held the record, having consumed 54 cups of the sorghum-based spirit *maotai* at one session. His Chinese competitors fell out one by one. Whether the record was ever beaten proved impossible to tell, since in the circumstance, few could keep an accurate record. Horse racing also provided opportunities for Chinese and foreigners to mix on an equal basis.[29] Set-piece events such as the 1911 and 1937 coronations provided more formal opportunities for the

British and the Chinese to mix. The latter occasion was marked by the presence of the mayor of Beijing and many other important Chinese. There was a special service at the British embassy on 11 May 1937, followed by a reception hosted by Mr D. J Cowan, the first secretary in charge (the ambassador was in Nanjing), and a buffet supper and a fireworks display in the evening. According to newspaper reports, all nationalities joined in the festivities, and the US embassy's marine guard supplied the music. The celebrations continued well into the night, with British and other buildings illuminated to mark the occasion, and a Coronation Ball at the Wagons-Lits hotel.[30] Though the guests did not know it, this was the end of an era.

For some years, success of the Nationalist forces (the Guomindang – always anglicized in those days as the Kuomintang, or KMT) under Chiang Kai-shek and the move of the capital to Nanjing in 1928 made little difference to the legation quarter. There was growing pressure from the Chinese to end all foreign privileges in China, but these were successfully resisted; the chaotic political state of China made it easy for the foreign powers to reject Chinese demands. Nevertheless, there were some concessions to Chinese demands, with the return to Chinese control of some of the smaller foreign settlements in the 1920s, and the British decision to give back the leased territory of Weihaiwei in 1930.

Such changes affected the foreign community in Beijing hardly at all. Few resident foreigners even bothered to use the former capital's new name, 'Peiping' (Beijing), preferring the long-familiar 'Peking'. Until well into the 1930s, most foreign representatives and their staff remained in Beijing, as did a branch of the Nationalist foreign ministry. In the British case, contact with the government in Nanjing was through a

> . . . Sub-Legation . . . consisting of a single diplomatic officer seconded from Peking for six months or so. This unfortunate, who did not of course speak Chinese and had only a minute staff, did not even have a house of his own, but lived as the guest of the Consul-General, with whom he might or might not be on good terms . . .

To supplement this, the minister in Beijing would periodically arrive in Nanjing with a considerable staff. There was a set pattern to these visits by 'The Circus' as it was known to those on the receiving end: no visit could take place during the hot weather or three weeks either side of Christmas; all circuses had to return to Beijing for the spring and autumn race meetings; and in the case of one head of post, movements of the circus were influenced by the arrival of the sea bass in North China waters.[31]

By the late 1930s, this was no longer enough. Now the visits to Nanjing were more prolonged, and on arrival in September 1936, the new ambassador, Knatchbull-Hugessen, decided that the ambassador's presence was required at Nanjing rather than Beijing, and that his headquarters should be at the latter place. While waiting for a new residence to be built, Knatchbull-Hugessen lived in a modest foreign-style house at the former consulate. There Knatchbull-Hugessen kept up some of the Beijing traditions, for he continued to maintain a fine cellar, and gave dinner parties which were very popular with Chinese officials. Others lived in equally modest style compared with the splendours of Duke Liang's mansion, thought there was consolation in the pink gins and the mixed group of foreign and Chinese officials and military and naval officers available at the Bungalow Club.[32] Almost the last manifestation of the old-style life in Nanjing was the celebration of the coronation of King George VI in May 1937, for which Knatchbull-Hugessen was present. He then went up to Beijing, where the King's Birthday was celebrated with the usual parade at the British embassy. From Beijing he went to Beidaihe, hoping to begin his summer holiday.

That year, however, there was to be no summer holiday and no poetic amusements. Almost as soon as Knatchbull-Hugessen arrived at Beidaihe, there occurred the skirmish at the Marco Polo bridge (Luguoqiao), outside Beijing on 7 July 1937, which proved to be the start of the Sino-Japanese war. As relations between China and Japan deteriorated, the ambassador's place was clearly with the government, and he left for Nanjing.

Knatchbull-Hugessen's ability to do much about the crisis was short-lived. On 26 August 1937, while travelling by road from Nanjing to visit the British community in Shanghai, the cars in which he and his party were riding were strafed and bombed by Japanese aircraft, although clearly marked with the union flag. Knatchbull-Hugessen was hit but survived, though not without many months' convalescence. The Japanese ambassador expressed his regret in person, although he thought that it was unlikely that any Japanese aircraft would have attacked cars bearing the British flag. In fact, the Japanese hinted at their responsibility, in that one of the staff of their Beijing legation flew up to Beidaihe to inform Lady Knatchbull-Hugessen of what had happened. She had already left, on board a British destroyer, and the Japanese official appears to have had a somewhat frosty lunch with other members of the ambassador's family. While the Japanese continued to express regret at the wounding of the ambassador, they were reluctant to admit responsibility, and unwilling to apologize.

The British government, having at one time thought of recalling Sir Robert Craigie, the newly arrived ambassador in Tokyo as a protest (see below, page 140), decided that this would do too much damage to relations with Japan, and instead awarded Knatchbull-Hugessen £5,000, '. . . to show the Japanese the value placed on an ambassador', according to Mr Neville Chamberlain, the prime minister. This struck Knatchbull-Hugessen as a curious way to put things, but the £5,000 was useful since, while convalescing, he went on to half pay. Eventually, Japan admitted that the attack might have been, inadvertently, the work of Japanese aircraft, and therefore expressed 'deep regret' at what had happened. It was enough to defuse the crisis.[33]

With the outbreak of the Sino-Japanese war, it was clearly important for the British ambassador to remain close to the Chinese government, rather than in what became, after 8 August 1937, Japanese-occupied area of Beijing. Ambassadors did from time to time visit Beijing, but it was not now their normal residence. Instead, there began a period when the British embassy followed the Nationalist government from one wartime capital to another. Indeed, even before Knatchbull-Hugessen finally left from Hong Kong, his former colleagues had begun to leave Nanjing, which was now felt to be too dangerous since it was under regular Japanese attack, and were on their way to Shanghai by a somewhat roundabout route.[34] From December 1937, when the Japanese occupied Nanjing, the offices completed the transfer to Shanghai. Theoretically, the chancery remained at Shanghai until the Pacific War began in December 1941. In practice, the British ambassador, like his colleagues, moved first to Hankou and then to Chongqing, to keep in contact with the Chinese government. He was at Chongqing when war broke out, and remained there until 1945. Shanghai after December 1941 was in enemy hands.[35]

Meanwhile, in Beijing, while the war was on the city's doorstep, for most of the time it did not intrude too much on the foreign community or on the inhabitants of the diplomatic quarter. Rumours of fighting of course reached the city even before the Japanese entered it in August 1937, and aircraft from both sides flew over at regular intervals, although they generally only dropped leaflets. After the Japanese occupation, there were moments of tension. Two American marines patrolling on horseback to advise American citizens to go to the embassy compound were shot at on Morrison (now Wangfujing) street on 27 July 1937, and the British were advised that it was safer not to leave the compound. Yet, at other times, the usual round of lunches and tennis continued as before, and there were even expeditions out of the city to some of the old haunts. No doubt those who attended meetings of the British Women's League, or merely went shopping, generally ignored the anti-British campaigns that were regularly organized by the Japanese, and which included large hostile banners on Changan and other prominent streets.[36]

The embassy compound thus remained in use but the number of those living and working there dropped. As in the past, it occasionally served as a safe haven for the British community in Beijing. In the aftermath of the Marco Polo bridge incident in July 1937, all British residents were encouraged to come to the compound, and the American, French, German and Italian embassies all issued similar advice to their nationals. The *Peiping Chronicle* reported that 95 people were in the British compound at the end of July, and all were accommodated in houses or other buildings on the compound. Each person was allowed one Chinese servant. Among these temporary inhabitants was the scholarly recluse – and probable forger – Sir Edmund Backhouse, who was lodged with the embassy doctor and delighted the diplomatic staff with his charming ways. Once the immediate danger passed, he returned to his usual home in the city, though he would return to the compound later.[37]

Eventually, it was decided that rather than leave many of the houses on the compound empty, they should be rented out to a variety of British people in Beijing. These included temporary staff of the embassy not entitled to accommodation, language students from other government departments apart from the Foreign Office, and even some businessmen. The leases drawn up on these occasions were later to be an important element in trying to determine the value of the legation compound. They also show that by the late 1930s, telephones, humidifiers and fire extinguishers were a regular part of diplomatic household equipment in Beijing.[38]

After Pearl Harbor, all the British diplomatic and consular staff in occupied China, together with a large number of non-official members of staff, were interned by the Japanese. The majority of British diplomatic and consular staff were held in Shanghai. The Japanese were somewhat heavy handed in their behaviour in Shanghai. Although they allowed the archives to be sealed and in due course handed over to the Swiss as protecting power, they seized cars belonging to staff, and eventually, despite Swiss protests, the Japanese navy occupied the former embassy premises. The Japanese at first tried to force all the staff of the embassy and the consulate-general onto the latter compound. When this proved too difficult, the consular staff were left there, senior members of the embassy went to the Cathay hotel, and the remainder, and all the women were allowed to stay in their homes. However, the naval liaison officer, Commander Shepperd, was held in a prisoner-of-war camp. He was eventually released and repatriated. The naval staff officer attached to the consulate-general, Commander Wolley, was less fortunate, for the Japanese claimed he was the captain of a Yangzi river gunboat and imprisoned him. When he tried to escape, he was court-martialled and sentenced to ten years' imprisonment. Other staff were questioned by the *kempeitai*, the Japanese gendarmerie, and one, Miss Bernfeld, committed suicide on her release just a few days before repatriation.[39]

In Beijing, as elsewhere in China, detention was not too onerous for diplomatic and consular staff, and most people were allowed to continue living in their houses. Despite protests, the Japanese seized the old legation guard compound, arguing that it was for military purposes, but they sealed the archives and left them alone. There was, however, another problem. From 1935 onwards, the Royal Signals Regiment had been running a wireless listening station at Tianjin, which during the summer months had moved up to the Shanhaiguan-Beidaihe area. Its purpose was to monitor frequencies that could not be covered from Hong Kong. It also provided telegraphic backup for the British embassy either at Beijing or at Beidaihe. As the Japanese occupied more and more of North China, and relations between Britain and Japan deteriorated, it was decided that it was safer to end this operation, and it closed down in the winter of 1939–40. Some signallers stayed on, as members of the British North China garrison. When that was finally withdrawn in August 1940, an even smaller group, six in all, were transferred to the Foreign Office vote, and became the communications section of the Beijing embassy. (Beijing had been for many years one of the few Foreign Office posts with its own wireless communications; most posts used the cable services of the international companies such as Cable and Wireless. The cost of wireless communication at Beijing and other posts was a frequent source of Treasury complaints.[40])

Although this change had been formally notified to all the diplomatic corps in Beijing, and the men were on civilian rates of pay, the Japanese in December 1941 insisted that they were, in fact, members of the armed forces and not entitled to be treated as diplomatic or consular staff. There were a number of exchanges between London and Berne, as the Swiss protecting power tried to persuade the Japanese to change their position. Eventually, the Japanese accepted the argument, and it was agreed that the men could be repatriated. Like all other British diplomatic and consular staff in North China, they were repatriated via Shanghai, in August 1942 on board the Japanese vessel, the *Tatsuta Maru*.[41]

The embassy compound was not left empty. In February 1942, the Swiss consul-general in Shanghai, who was looking after British interests, relayed a request from the staff living on the Beijing compound that any British civilians remaining in Beijing after the repatriation of officials might be allowed to live on the compound. It was agreed that this would be a good idea, if the Japanese would allow it. Rent should be paid if possible, though to whom was not clear). If not possible, then promises to pay should be sought.[42]

It is not clear who stayed on in Beijing. According to the historian of the Society for the Propagation of the Gospel in Foreign Parts, a '. . . small group of aged British and Americans interned in the compound' were able to worship in the embassy chapel. Until his death in 1943, their prayers were led by a medical missionary, Dr W. H. G. Aspland, who in happier days had been the medical officer of the embassy, Dr Timothy Lin, a Chinese Christian who was running the Anglican cathedral in Beijing, was occasionally allowed in to give them communion.[43] Edmund Backhouse was allowed by the Japanese to occupy a single room in the British compound, where he lived with a Chinese servant. For some two years, until illness drove him into the French hospital, Backhouse was often to be found on the veranda of his house, dressed in Chinese scholar's robes, bitterly criticizing the British.[44] In 1946, the Office of Works in Shanghai noted that at the time of liberation from the Japanese in September 1945, there were fourteen unofficial residents on the compound. But Mr Champkins provided no details, and it has proved impossible to find out who they were nor how long they had been there.[45]

Notes

1 FO 17/1715, Treasury to the Foreign Office, 14 June 1901.

2 Works 10/371, Memorandum by H Ashmead, Shanghai, 3 July 1909; memorandum by principal architect, 27 April 1910; report by Ashmead 27 Nov. 1911.

3 FO350/13, Jordan to Alson, Foreign Office, 19 February and 28 July 1915.

4 Letter from Mrs W. Ker, Beijing, to her sister, 31 October 1914. Reference kindly supplied by Ms Kate Ker, Sussex.

5 FO350/13, Jordan to Alson, Foreign Office, 19 February 1915.

6 Works 10/371, copy of Max Müller to Sir Edward Grey, no. 24, 28 Oct. 1910; Bridge, *Peking Picnic*, p. 67; *Foreign Office List*, (London: Harrison and Sons, 1921), pp. 202–209.

7 Bridge, *Peking Picnic*, p. 21. Something of the background to this novel and the characters from it can be found in Ann Bridge, *Facts and Fictions* (London: Chatto & Windus, 1968), Chapter 1.

8 Varè, *Laughing Diplomat*, p. 126.

9 Paul Reinsch, *An American Diplomat in China* (London: George Allen and Unwin, 1922), p.114

10 Kates, *Years that were Fat*, pp. 77–78.

11 W.G.C. Graham, *China Through One Pair of Eyes: Reminiscences of a Consular Officer, 1929–1950* (London: China Society, 1984); conversation with Douglas Hurd, then Secretary of State for Foreign and Commonwealth Affairs, Beijing, 5 April 1991.

12 FO366/851/X457/6/503, Office of Works to Foreign Office 12 Jan. 1928, enclosing Lampson (Beijing) to divisional architect, Shanghai, no. 32 accounts, 13 Sept. 1927, and related papers.

13 Duncan McCallum, *China to Chelsea: A Modern Pilgrimage along Ancient Highways* (London: Ernest Benn Ltd., 1930), pp. 42–43.

14 Clive Bigham, *A Year in China, 1899–1900, with some account of Admiral Sir E. Seymour's Expedition* (London: Macmillan, 1901), pp. 40–41.

15 *Documents on British Foreign Policy 1919–1939* edited by Rohan Butler and J. P. T. Bury, assisted by M. E. Lambert, I st. series, vol. XIV (London: Her Majesty's Stationary Office, 1966), pp. 71–72 contains correspondence between Beijing and London on the issue. See also C. Lewis, *Sagittarius Rising* (London: Peter Davies, 1936).

16 Gage, *Marvellous Party*, pp. 51–52. It remained an adventurous destination even in the late 1980s, but now is connected by a good road and is open to foreigners arriving by road.

17 Gage, *Marvellous Party*, p. 63.

18 FO17/1717, Beijing telno. 237 to Foreign Office, 18 Oct. 1903, FO telno. 169 to Beijing, 19 Oct. 1903, and Beijing telno. 240 to FO, 20 Oct. 1903.

19 Lucy Murray Ker to her mother, 9 January 1912.

20 Lo, *Correspondence of G E Morrison*, I, 762–65, letter to D. D. Braham, 5 March 1912.

21 Reinsch, *American Diplomat in China*, p. 283; Thomas, *Vanished China*, pp. 99–105.

22 FO350/1, F. A. Campbell, FO, to Sir John Jordan, commenting on a letter from Jordan of 24 June.

23 Lo, *Correspondence of G E Morrison*, I, 802, letter from Jordan, 28 May 1912.

24 Reginald Johnston, *Twilight in the Forbidden City* (London: Victor Gollanz, 1934; reprinted Hong Kong, Oxford University Press, 1987), pp. 280–281; 286–287. For Pu Yi's account, written long afterwards, see Asian-Gioro Pu Yi, *From Emperor to Citizen: The Autobiography of Aisin-Gioro Pu Yi* (Beijing: Foreign Languages Press, 1964), I, 149 et seq.

25 Gage, *Marvellous Party*, p. 52.

26 Sir H. Knatchbull-Hugessen, *Diplomat in Peace and War* (London: John Murray, 1949), pp. 250 –261.

27 *Illustrated London News*, 4 September 1937; *Daily Mirror*, 15 February 1939. I am grateful to Mrs Margaret McCallum. Liverpool, for these references.

28 Lady Susan Townley, *My Chinese Notebook* (London: Methuen and Co., 1904), pp. 287 et seq.

29 Gage, *Marvellous Party*, pp. 55–58.

30 Copy of the Order of Service 'for use at the British Embassy in Peking and elsewhere if desired', supplied by Mrs Margaret McCallum. The events were reported in the *Peiping Chronicle*, 12 May 1937.

31 Graham, *China Through One Pair of Eyes*, p. 2.

32 Knatchbull-Hugessen, *Diplomat in Peace and War*, p. 95; Gage, *Marvellous Party*, pp. 63–64.

33 Knatchbull-Hugessen, *Diplomat in Peace and War*, pp. 120–128. The story can also be found, in some detail, in W. N. Medlicott and Douglas Dakin, editors, assisted by Gillian Bennet, *Documents on British Foreign Policy, 1919–1939*, Second Series, Vol. XX1, Far Eastern Affairs, November 1936-July 1938, (London: HMSO: 1984), pp. 268 et seq.

34 Knatchbull-Hugessen, *Diplomat in Peace and War*, p. 126.

35 FO371/35939/F2392/6/23, Lord Clausen to Mr Eden, 6 May 1943, 'Committee of enquiry into the treatment of British subjects in Japanese-controlled territory. Final Report'.

36 Information form Mrs Margaret McCallum, various dates, but especially her ms. Note, 'Memories of my stay in Peking 1936–1938', dated 1990. For anti-British demonstrations, see the photographs and flyers in FO371/23485, which includes a selection from 1939.

37 *Peiping Chronicle*, 29 July 1937; H. Trevor-Roper, *A Hidden Life: The Enigma of Sir Edmund Backhouse* (London and Basingstoke: Macmillan and Co., 1976), pp. 221–222.

38 Works 10/371, copy of Alan Archer, Beijing, no. 86, to Ambassador, Shanghai, 14 April 1939, together with copies of lease.

39 FO371/35939/F2392/6/23, Lord Clausen to Mr Eden, 6 May 1943, 'Final Report of the Committee of Enquiry into the Treatment of British subjects in Japanese-controlled Territory'. (Cited as Clausen report).

40 E.g., FO366/898/X2274/299/505, Treasury to the Foreign Office, 4 April 1931.

41 See papers on FO371/31736/F1320/33/61 of 1942, and the Clausen report. Details of the Royal Signals in North China before 1940 can be found in Peter Elphick, *Far Eastern File: The Intelligence War in the Far East 1930–1945* (London: Hodder and Stoughton, 1997), pp. 65–67.

42 Works 10/371, Berne to FO, telno. 572, 18 Feb. 1942; T. J. W. Wilson, FO, to Works, 20 Feb. 1942.

43 H. p. Thompson, *Into All Lands: The History of the Society for the Propagation of the Gospel in Foreign Parts* (London: Society for the Propagation of Christian Knowledge, 1950), pp. 687–688. For Dr Apsland, see p. 677.

44 Trevor-Roper, *A Hidden Life*, pp. 225–33.

45 Works 10/117, T. G. Champkins, architect, Shanghai, 'Report on the Peking Legation', 24 Aug. 1946.

China

$\boxed{5}$

Last Years of the Old Legation, 1945–59

⟡

With the defeat of the Japanese in 1945, the British returned to the old legation quarter in Beijing, still officially Beiping, and the Nationalist capital was again at Nanjing. Despite the war and the Japanese occupation, the legation compound, now to be used for the Beijing consulate-general, was in surprisingly good repair. The first Office of Works survey after the war, carried out by the resident architect in East Asia, reported in August 1946 that the grounds were in first-class condition, and the trees had been well looked after. While the houses were all in need of decoration and a number of urgent repairs were required, most of the buildings except for the quarters for the legation guard and officers, were usable. The furniture in all the houses was also in good shape and the ambassador's furniture had been particularly well looked after. Even the fire engine was in working order. There were then four official residents on the compound, including two Chinese who had looked after the premises during the war, and fourteen unofficial residents. The latter included a number of Royal Air Force language students. There was also much property belonging to Britons and British-protected persons that had been brought to Beijing from all over China. To those returning, it was almost as though nothing had changed since their departure in 1941.[1]

Such appearances were deceptive, however, for the war had caused a major change in Sino-British relations. For many years after the establishment of the Nationalist government in 1926, steadily increasing Chinese pressure had been to reverse the nineteenth century 'unequal treaties' and the system of extraterritoriality and foreign settlements in China. Negotiations had begun at the time of the Washington Conference of 1921–22, but made little progress in the face of the disunity of China. Following the Nationalist reunification campaign that had officially ended the warlord period, the new government could argue that disunity was no longer a factor and that negotiations should begin in earnest. Whatever their doubts about the degree of Nationalist control, the powers agreed to begin the process. For a time, the Chinese seemed near to success in the early 1930s, but the intensification of Sino-Japanese conflict over Manchuria in 1932, and the full-scale war that developed from the 1937 clash at the Marco Polo bridge, pushed the issue from centre stage.[2] Both the US and the British governments, however, publicly undertook in 1940 to look at the issue again when peace was restored. They also raised the issue of the end of extraterritoriality with Japan, the other major power concerned, but made little progress, although in the US case, discussions only ended in November 1941.[3]

Following the attack on Pearl Harbor and the outbreak of war between Britain and the US on the one hand and Japan on the other, attitudes among the allies changed. In October 1942, the British and US governments told the Chinese that they were ready to negotiate new treaties to sweep away the hundred-year-old extraterritorial system and its special privileges. In fact, the negotiations were speedily concluded, and Britain and the United States conceded Chinese demands in 1943 as a gesture to a wartime ally. It could be no more than a symbolic gesture, for many of the old centres of foreign residence were under Japanese control. As one historian of the end of extraterritoriality put it: 'It was not until extraterritoriality had lost its practical usefulness that Britain and the United States finally agreed to give up their rights.' Nevertheless, the Chinese government and press were pleased that the old humiliation had ended and were prepared to be generous in their praise for the action.[4]

Although at the time it did not seem to matter, since Beijing was under Japanese occupation, the new treaty which Britain had signed had consequences for the future of the Beijing compound. Under the terms of article 3 of the British treaty, signed at the war capital of Chongqing (Chungking) on 11 January 1943, Britain relinquished all extraterritorial rights in China. Specifically, all rights under the Boxer protocol of September 1901 and related agreements were surrendered. Britain also undertook to cooperate with the Chinese government to persuade other governments to negotiate the end of the special status of the legation quarter. This undermined the basis on which the Beijing embassy compound was held, but at the same time, the treaty provided for the compound's continued use by Britain. Article 3(iii) laid down that:

> The Government of the Republic of China shall accord to His Majesty's Government in the United Kingdom a continued right to use for official purposes the land which has been allocated to [it] in the diplomatic quarter in Peiping, on parts of which are located buildings belonging to His Majesty's Government . . . .

Britain still had the use of the compound but was now clearly dependent on the goodwill of the Chinese government to be able to continue doing so.[5] By 1943, it had also become clear that it would be difficult to prove the British title to the pre-1900 holdings. There apparently never had been a formal lease for the minister's house, acquired in 1860, while leases to the other plots of land purchased or otherwise obtained before 1900 were all lost in Shanghai in 1941.[6]

In 1943, that did not seem to be a problem. Neither did it loom large in 1945, when the compound was reoccupied. Instead, there were practical issues to consider. With the majority of embassy staff re-established in Nanjing, there was plenty of spare space on the Beijing compound. This was rented out to various people and organizations. During 1946 and 1947, for example, the inhabitants of the compound continued to include Royal Air Force language students, the British Council, and a company of United States marines. The Office of Works main interest in these groups was in making sure that they paid rent. When the Air Ministry confirmed that the language students were nothing to do with the work of the consulate, for example, they became eligible to pay rent, which was duly collected.[7]

The US marines occupied what had been the British legation guard premises. When it became clear that these would leave in May 1947, concern arose about Britain's entitlement to the land occupied after 1900. In the case of the military compound, it was clear that it was no longer being used for the purpose for which it had been obtained, and there was some worry that the Chinese authorities might demand the return of this section of the compound. In fact, the Chinese did nothing, and the guard area continued as part of the British compound. In other ways, however, the Chinese made it clear that times had changed. They indicated that they reserved the right to assume control over compounds and concessions, although they did not move immediately on this issue as far as the British were concerned. They also indicated that they were not happy with reminders of foreign triumphalism after the Boxer rebellion. In October 1947, the ambassador in Nanjing agreed that all Boxer memorials should be moved inside the Beijing compound. It was also accepted that the words 'Lest We Forget', painted on a bullet-scarred section of the north-east corner of the compound wall since c. 1901, might be obliterated. As the ambassador noted, this was not the original inscription but one which had been repainted many times. Now it was time to abandon such reminders of the past.[8]

By then, China was again in political turmoil as the uneasy relationship between the Nationalist government and the Chinese Communist Party (CCP) degenerated into civil war. The communists began their final attack on the Beijing-Tianjin area in early December 1948, and the People's Liberation Army (PLA), as the CCP's Red Army was renamed in 1947, captured the former capital on 31 January 1949. In the following months, Beiping, which was still the official name of the city, began to take on the role of the capital, a role confirmed when the CCP leader, Mao Zedong, formally proclaimed the establishment of the People's Republic of China on 1 October 1949 from the rostrum of the Gate of Heavenly Peace (Tiananmen).

Until then, though aware of what was happening all around them, those in the former legation quarter, including the British, continued very much as before. The area escaped the bombardment of the city during the civil war, and was not at first directly affected by the communist takeover. An enterprising member of the staff allowed the Shell manager to store his petrol, held in small cans, on the embassy lawns. When the manager left, the embassy sold off the petrol, making a handsome profit. Before long, however, it was obvious that things would not remain the same as in the past. As they carried all before them in the north-east of the country, the CCP had shown that they regarded themselves as not bound either by existing codes of international practice or by treaties signed by past governments. Consular officers, especially but not exclusively Americans, in areas which came under communist control, were treated with scant respect. The PLA's arrival in Beijing was therefore awaited with some anxiety by the British and other diplomats as success in the civil war swept them forward in the summer of 1949.[9]

Mao's declaration of the establishment of the PRC on 1 October 1949 posed a complicated problem for Britain, involving its relations with the United States and its large economic interests in China. After much internal debate, now chronicled in great detail as the archives have been opened,[10] the British government announced its recognition of the PRC on 6 January 1950. The expectation was that this act of recognition would immediately lead to the establishment of normal diplomatic relations, a delusion which would persist for some time, though communist behaviour at the time of the *Amethyst* incident in May 1949 had shown that while they were willing to deal with British diplomatic officials, they would do so only as negotiating agents, not as an embassy.[11] As late as October 1950, for example, the Foreign Office still thought that Sir Esler (Bill) Dening, who had been selected as ambassador to Beijing, might be able to take up his post.[12] Instead, the new Chinese government 'took note' of the act of recognition, but made it clear that they would require more. In particular, the British decision to retain a consular post on Taiwan, where the Nationalist government was now established, proved a major sticking point for the Chinese. The official British position was that the post at Tamsui, north of the island's capital, Taipei, was merely accredited to the local authorities, and had nothing to do with the central Nationalist government. The Chinese professed themselves unconvinced, and were to remain unconvinced for another twenty-two years.[13]

The British embassy staff in Nanjing were allowed to travel to Beijing, now again the capital, and John Hutchison, the commercial counsellor, who was appointed chargé d'affaires to handle negotiations with the Chinese, moved there with his colleagues on 13 February 1950. Despite Hutchinson's formal position as chargé d'affaires, they were received as negotiators, not as a fully fledged diplomatic mission. Talks now began on those issues the new government wished settled before it would agree to diplomatic relations, including Taiwan. The atmosphere was not good. Britain's announcement of recognition had been accompanied by a statement that indicated this did not mean approval; this statement, while no doubt an accurate reflection of British views, tended to dissipate any goodwill created by the early recognition. With long gaps and little progress, the dialogue continued until June 1950. Then came the Korean war. The talks were suspended indefinitely and the British mission in

Beijing, once again established on the old legation site, entered a half-world which was to last until 1954.[14]

Even before Hutchison moved from Nanjing to Beijing, there were signs that the new government had plans for the legation quarter. When Walter Graham, then HM consul-general in Beijing, delivered the formal note of Britain's recognition of the new government, he returned to the compound to find that the PRC's Military Control Commission had posted notices on the British, US, French and Netherlands compounds that stated that, as a result of the abolition of unequal treaties, all foreign military compounds were to be taken over. The Chinese moved in immediately on the last three. The British, however, received a further note, saying that in view of the notice of recognition, there would be no immediate action.[15]

It was only a short respite. Only two military compounds now remained, the British and the Soviet. On 3 March, the latter gave theirs up, following a Sino-Soviet exchange of notes. This left only the British as holders of a 1901-linked military compound. A month later, this was taken over, without protest. Before long, the Ministry of Public Security, the Chinese police authority, had established itself on the site, where they remain to this day.[16]

With the military quarters went the tennis courts, though what was left of the compound was still substantial and a new set of courts appeared near the site of the Hanlin academy. In this somewhat truncated compound, the British embassy staff, now described as 'The Office of the negotiating representatives of the British government' sat, studiously ignored by the Chinese. Although the British were allowed certain diplomatic privileges, the Chinese made it clear that they were not, in their view, an established diplomatic mission. British diplomatic notes, for example, were received but generally not acknowledged. On practical matters such as entry and exit visas and the importing of duty-free goods, Chinese behaviour indicated that the notes had been received and acted upon. It was less clear on other matters, where the mission often had to listen to Chinese radio or to scan the pages of the Chinese press in the hope that they could discern some statement that could be constituted a reply. In most cases, there was none, to the exasperation of Hutchinson's successor as chargé, Leo Lamb. Lamb's claims to represent US and some Commonwealth countries' interests in China were also ignored.[17] On a more individual level, the mission, like others in the legation quarter, had to suffer the prevailing voice of the new China. All around loudspeakers broadcast revolutionary music, and the Chinese reasserted control over the old legation area by building in the former glacis. No wonder that Humphrey Trevelyan, arriving as chargé d'affaires in 1953, thought that he had '. . . been admitted to a superior mental home provided with every comfort, but having no contact with the outside world beyond the limits of the British Embassy compound'.[18]

Throughout the 1950s, the whole legation quarter remained under constant threat. Regular hints were dropped about new roads through the British compound, though they all came to nothing. But it was obvious that the Chinese intended to close down the quarter. As Beijing's diplomatic community grew, new embassies appeared. These were not sited in the old legation quarter, however. At first, they were scattered about the city, but it was clear that the Chinese did not like this arrangement either. Instead, they were busily constructing a new diplomatic enclave to the east of the city, outside the city walls. The legation quarter might be disliked but it was a useful precedent for isolating the barbarians. As the Chinese gradually snipped away bits of other diplomatic compounds, and as grandiose plans emerged for the development of Beijing, Trevelyan was told by the Chinese in 1954 that they intended to repossess the legation quarter. Trevelyan and his colleagues viewed this with some trepidation for they felt that the new area was a 'new diplomatic ghetto . . . on an unattractive site among the factories on the east side outside the city walls . . .'.[19]

That would be some way in the future. In the meantime, something like the traditional way of life continued in the British compound. The Duke of Liang's mansion, the head of post's house in former days, and the acknowledged centre of the compound, had fallen on evil times. While the public rooms were sometimes used for functions, nobody now lived there. Hutchison had not used it when he arrived in 1950, preferring the house he had occupied pre-war as commercial counsellor.[20] Trevelyan chose to live in what had been the number four, or Chinese secretary's, house, which at least one consul had occupied in recent years. (Other accounts say that Trevelyan lived in the number three house.) As for Duke Liang's mansion, Trevelyan gave no clear reason why he did not live there, though he noted a lack of chair covers and hinted at other things which made it unusable. He also felt that it had lost its character because of additions made to accommodate the European way of life. The chapel still functioned, with the American eagle lectern in full display, though there was no longer a chaplain. The head of post regularly read the Anglican service of Matins to such Protestants as would come, while reading the lesson fell to a second secretary. Once, the 'Red Dean of Canterbury', the Rev. Hewlett Johnson, a firm supporter of the 'New China', was prevailed upon, despite much resistance, to take a service in the chapel. In the summer, there was tea on the lawns and barbecues. At Christmas, there were carol parties around the British and other compounds, while all 'friendly' missions joined in such entertainment as Scottish country dancing or the occasional film show.

Some found this life oddly civilized in the midst of confusion, and welcomed tea and Madeira cakes on the lawns. Others were less sure. The British journalist, George Gale, who accompanied a Labour Party delegation to China in 1954, wrote scathingly of a party that he attended at the British mission. Hearty attempts to organize a barbecue struck Gale as bizarre, but hardly less so than the treasure-hunt which followed. Noting that probably all diplomatic or journalist life abroad was somewhat unreal, Gale opined that in Beijing '. . . the unreality had always the element of fantasy'. It was no doubt a view with which Trevelyan, his formal host at the barbecue, might have sympathized.[21]

People no doubt felt somewhat beleaguered. Chinese staff appeared and disappeared at whim. In the British case, at least one interpreter/assistant was arrested during the '100 flowers campaign' and charged with counter-revolutionary activities because of his embassy work. It did not make for easy relations.[22] The Beijing foreign community had once again shrunk, so that there were few foreigners apart from diplomats. The missionaries had virtually all gone by the mid-1950s, as had the representatives of foreign banks and trading houses. Cold war hostilities meant that the British diplomats had little to do with the majority of their diplomatic colleagues or 'foreign experts' living in the capital, who were of Eastern European or Soviet origin. There were a small number of non-official Westerners in Beijing in the 1950s, some of whom would remain, despite all difficulties, until the 1980s. They included some Britons, engaged mostly in translation or polishing texts for the New China News Agency and similar bodies. In general, they were strong supporters of the new Chinese regime and wanted little to do with their official representatives.

Although isolated both from the Chinese and from this wider foreign community, however small. Those on the British compound could survive in relatively cheerful fashion because they themselves remained a relatively large group. In December 1954, for example, 37 people were living on the British compound, including four children. In September 1955, there were 38, including seven children.[23] Among these two groups were five future heads of post in Beijing (Denson, Addis, Youde, Evans and Donald), one future Foreign and Commonwealth Office political director, (Fretwell), and one future foreign secretary (Hurd). Several of the others also became ambassadors.

From mid-1954, the position of the mission in Beijing was put on a more regular basis. The Chinese remained unwilling to move to full diplomatic relations, but Sir Anthony Eden, then foreign secretary, and the Chinese premier and foreign minister, Zhou Enlai, agreed in the margins of the Geneva Conference on Korea and Indo-China in April 1954, that, despite continued differences, there could be an improvement in relations. This led to the establishment of substantive (*en titre*, in diplomatic jargon, rather than *ad interim*) chargé d'affaires' offices in their respective capitals. According to a minute by John Addis, this improvement in relations was hailed by a Chinese diplomat at a private dinner held by British and Chinese officials in the margins of the conference, when he described it as the 'one great achievement' of the conference.[24]

Although these new arrangements still left the British in Beijing at the bottom of the diplomatic pecking order, together with the Netherlands representative, who was also chargé d'affaires *en titre*, it was undoubtedly an improvement on the previous position. Now they could function more normally. Work began to resemble the patterns established before 1949, though on a much smaller scale. From 1954 on, occasional political delegations arrived from Britain, and there was more British trade with China, both of which gave work to the mission.[25] There was always political reporting, of course, which could be fleshed out a bit more as members of the chargé d'affaires office now began to come into more frequent, and occasionally more productive, contact with Chinese officials. There continued to be a heavy reliance on reading the runes as they could be discerned from the pages of the *Renmin Ribao*, the official party newspaper, or in the bulletins of the New China News Agency, practices which would persist long after other sources of information became widely available.

This improvement in the mission's status did not solve all problems. Despite a large compound in what generally seemed reasonable condition, frequent concerns were expressed to London. Con O'Neill, who would later play a prominent role in negotiations for Britain's entry into the European Economic Community, was chargé in late 1955. His worry was that if the mission in Beijing became a fully-fledged embassy – a most unlikely prospect in 1955 – there would not be enough space for all the new staff required. There was concern that the buildings occupied by the more junior diplomatic staff did not give them sufficient room for studying and entertaining. Many of the buildings were badly affected by damp. O'Neill himself, living in the number four house, formerly that of the Chinese secretary, fought hard against being compelled to move back into the old number one house, which was steadily deteriorating through lack of use and damp. Despite these problems, in O'Neill's view, it would be best converted into students' quarters.

In December 1955, the Foreign Office decided that Beijing's worries needed investigation, and sent an inspector to Beijing. He confirmed that there were problems. Some of the buildings were crammed with goods either from the now closed former consular posts all over China or else belonging to long-departed British subjects. Some of this material dated back to the Pacific War, some to the communist takeover in 1949–1950. In keeping with the spirit of new China, much of the former stableyard was used as a coal dump. The inspector tended to agree with O'Neill that the former head of post's house was better converted into students' quarters since it was unlikely that any future ambassador would wish to live in what he described as '. . . a monstrous and wildly expensive piece of Chinoiserie'. (An interesting contrast with Trevelyan's apparent belief that it was because the building had become too Europeanized that it was not suitable.) Even with such a change, however, there would barely be sufficient accommodation for all those who needed to be housed on the compound. An additional argument in support of this position was the Chinese refusal to allow new British staff to use the very limited hotel space available, since they took the view that the British had a compound that should be sufficient for all their accommodation needs.[26]

There was clearly scepticism in the Ministry of Works about some of these claims. Faced with a series of letters from the Foreign Office which were seen as 'masterpieces of inconsequence', the Ministry of Works reached the conclusion that it was necessary for its own staff to examine the problems on the ground, for there was growing suspicion in the Ministry of Works about some of the claims coming out of Beijing.[27] In May 1956, therefore, an architects, Mr Tough, was instructed to go from Singapore, by then the Ministry's far eastern headquarters, to look at the question of accommodation in Beijing.

Mr Tough's visit turned out to be a most unhappy experience. He found himself faced with an adamant refusal by the head of post to consider anything except the conversion of the number one house into student flats. Attempts to discuss the matter were thwarted by O'Neill's refusal to deal with Tough directly. The latter had to talk to the head of chancery, Mr Alan

Campbell, who in turn relayed his views to O'Neill. O'Neill would then summon Tough to deliver his views while refusing to hear any counter-arguments. O'Neill himself never made plain the reason for this vehement opposition to the use of the old house, but Mrs O'Neill hinted that she and her husband were terrified at the expense of trying to run what had by now become a dilapidated wreck as a head of mission's house. Tough felt that he could not trust the Beijing secretarial staff to type his report and confided his real views to a private letter written from Hong Kong. It was not what his colleagues in London had expected, and they were not best pleased. Some within the Ministry of Works felt that the post had '. . . behaved like spoilt children throughout'.[28]

By mid-1956, however, such discussions of future housing needs on the compound were becoming somewhat irrelevant, for it was increasingly obvious that the days of the legation quarter were numbered, as more and more diplomatic missions opened in Trevelyan's 'ghetto . . . outside the city walls'. Although the British were not asked to go and view these new premises, they learnt of them from other missions. Thus in 1956, the Finns told of a visit to the new site, where they had been shown a soundly built house. Unfortunately, the Chinese idea was that the ambassador would have the ground floor, with a drawing-room and dining-room, while upstairs counsellors and other staff and their families would live on a dormitory basis. The Finns reported that they, the Bulgarians and even the Albanians had all said that this would not be suitable for Western missions.[29]

By mid-1958, the pace of development of the city quickened even further, with extensive rebuilding of the centre to mark the tenth anniversary of the Communist victory in 1949. The chargé d'affaires' office, busily collecting all the town plans it could and sending them back to London, was convinced that this rebuilding must involve the end of the legation quarter. In London, the wisdom of trying to hang on in the old compound, which all agreed was more comfortable and convenient than anything likely to be offered by the Chinese, had to be balanced against the possibility of being left with little choice in the accommodation available if the Chinese suddenly insisted on a move. The Foreign Office was 'in favour of masterly inaction', a phrase with Daoist connotations that no doubt appealed to those in the know, but which would subsequently be thrown back at them with some contempt.[30]

The blow fell on 21 January 1959. Both the British and Soviet missions received diplomatic notes from the Ministry of Foreign Affairs demanding that they vacate their existing premises by 31 May 1959.[31] In notifiying the British and the Soviet missions at the same time, the Chinese could argue that they were being even-handed, The fact was, however, that the Soviet embassy had been constructing a new embassy on the site of the old Russian Orthodox mission in the north-east of the city for some years, while the British had done nothing.

There was consternation in London at this failure of 'masterful inaction'. The post received instructions to argue that no move could be made before October 1959 at the earliest, though quite what good three extra months would do was not clear. Beijing's view was that unless some threat – and they were unaware of any – could be used against the Chinese, nothing could be done to stop the eviction process. In London, much energy went into examining the legal basis on which the compound was held and whether there were grounds to oppose the Chinese action. The conclusion of the various meetings was that the title to the compound rested solely on the basis of article 3(iii) of the 1943 treaty and that it was '. . . not so clear that we could take a firm stand . . . even if it were considered politically desirable to adopt this basis at all.'[32]

Officials and ministers at both Works and the Treasury were unhappy at the Foreign Office's unwillingness to fight, especially since the legation compound had on it assets worth at least one million pounds (perhaps £11–12 million in 1998 prices), and the alternatives on offer seemed so poor by comparison. Despite this continued soul-searching, nobody could in the end see any way of fighting the Chinese demand.

There followed frantic activity to obtain premises in the new diplomatic quarter and to dispose of the lumber of years in the legation compound. The Chinese for their part offered 'for use as temporary accommodation', a newly-built two storey-house opposite the Albanian embassy as offices, and another next door for the head of post's residence. Rent for these premises would be renminbi 1150 per month, or £2000 per annum, each. Other senior staff would be accommodated in blocks of flats fronting the main east-west road and junior staff in other blocks behind. The office and residence were described as rather severe in appearance, '. . . representing a somewhat semi-public building of UK pattern'. (They had, indeed, been designed by a British-trained Chinese architect, although nobody either in London or in the Beijing mission at the time seems to have known this.) While they were considered unsatisfactory for the long term, these arrangements would do for the present. For the future, the Chinese were asked to provide a twelve-acre site for eventual development. There was a reluctance to finalize the arrangements for a new site, since there was a general dislike of the area where the new office and residence would be, and it was thought better to wait until new diplomatic areas would be developed. Quite what length of time it was envisaged this might take was never spelled out, but the British embassy in Beijing still in 1999 operates under these 1959 arrangements. The twelve-acre site never seems to have materialized.[33]

It was planned to take over the new premises at the beginning of May to allow work on necessary structural alterations. In the meantime, a huge clear-out began. Volumes of diplomatic and consular archives, some dating back to the earliest days of the mission, were shipped back to the Public Record Office in London. Among the papers were found large quantities of Chinese documents, some 77 boxes in all, including the archive of the Guangzhou local government papers captured in 1858. Some of this material, now highly valued by scholars, had lain neglected for years in the roof of the chapel.[34] (The Chinese government occasionally sought the return of these papers, without success. In 1988, however, as a gesture of friendship, Mr Nicholas Ridley, then secretary of state for the environment, who was on an official visit to China, presented the Chinese Number Two

Archives in Beijing with a microfilmed set of the Guangzhou archive collection.) The Royal Coat of Arms was shipped to Hong Kong, where it adorned the ballroom at Government House until the British departed from Hong Kong in 1997.[35]

There were also various commemorative plaques in the chapel, some in remembrance of former ministers and ambassadors, a custom that seems to have dated from Sir Thomas Wade's departure in 1883. Others related to former prominent members of the British community, together with a number assembled from all over China from the 1920s onwards as the various consular posts closed. While it was the intention that a chapel would be included on the new site where these mementos might find a home, for the moment there was nowhere to put them. In some cases, surviving relatives were approached, to see if they would like the relevant plaque. This did not always produce the hoped for results. Sir Ernest Satow's great nephew said he did not care what happened to the monument, as long as it was not sent to him. In the end, Satow's former parish church at Ottery St Mary in Devon agreed to take it, and it is now displayed there.

Those plaques for which no home could be found were moved to the new premises, and stored away, as was the baptismal font and the eagle lectern given by the United States legation to mark the Boxer siege. Eventually, a home would be found for them in the new residence garden.[36] Among other items to be disposed of were two brass cannons, with two extra barrels, and a stone monolith commemorating the Boxer siege. The cannon had once stood outside the main house, but Hutchison had them removed in 1950 as being too provocative and militaristic, and they had been added to the growing collection of miscellania that now had to be dispersed. Works declined to have anything to do with either the cannon or the monolith, saying it was up to the Foreign Office to dispose of them. After some debate, the cannon were sold to the Chinese. In London, it was noted that scrap metal was fetching a good price in China, as the Great Leap Forward encouraged the development of backyard furnaces! Other goods were either destroyed, where owners or relatives indicated that they wanted this, or sold, since Chinese export regulations were very strict. Some goods went to the Chinese and some to Beijing's small foreign community. What could not be sold was given away. Many books went to the Beijing library. The sisters of the Sacred Heart Convent were given the late Dr Apsland's 'large and ancient gramophone' and were reported to be very pleased. The post retained Sir Edmund Backhouse's Patent of Baronetcy.[37]

By 31 May 1959, the British legation compound should have been no more, but there was a reprieve. Having begun so late, it was clear that the new premises could not be got ready in time, and the Chinese, who were carrying out the work, agreed to an extension of the deadline for moving to October 1959. In the end, it was in late September 1959 that the compound was finally given up. When the moment came to leave, there was some sadness, but also a hope that the move might be the start of a new and better relationship. Meanwhile, negotiations began to secure compensation for the loss of the buildings on the old site. These were not easy, and dragged on until payment of £250,000, half of what had been asked, was made on 14 July

1961. Since neither the post nor Works could produce title deeds for most of the property, and since the Chinese payment was almost double their first offer, the mission in Beijing clearly felt that they had not done too badly in the negotiations. In addition, the Chinese waived the rent for the new residence and offices while negotiations continued.[38]

Notes

1 Works 10/117, Champkins' report, 24 Aug. 1946. See also D. Jacobs-Larkcom, *As China fell: the experiences of a British Consul's Wife 1946–1953* (Ilfracombe, Devon: Arthur H. Stockwell Ltd.; 1976), p. 20.

2 The most detailed account of this subject in English remains Wesley R. Fishel, *The End of Extraterritoriality in China* (Berkeley, California: University of California Press, 1952; reprinted Taipei: Rainbow-Bridge Book Co., 1974).

3 Fishel, *End of Extraterritoriality*, pp. 207–208.

4 Fishel, *End of Extraterritoriality*, pp. 208–210. The quotation comes from p. 220. A good recent account of the British negotiations, and the considerations that affected the decision to end extraterritoriality and all that went with it, can be found in Li, Shian, 'The extraterritoriality negotiations of 1943 and the New Territories', *Modern Asian Studies*, vol. 30, part 3 (July 1996), pp. 617–650, especially pages 617–640.

5 Parliamentary Papers House of Commons, 1943, China No. 1 (1943) (Cmd. 6417), *Treaty for the Relinquishment of Extra-Territorial Rights in China*.

6 Works 10/110, Letter from A. Miller, Works to S. K. Millar, FO, DC16/124644, 19 November 1942; letter from T. Terrance, repatriated from Shanghai, to G. Howard-Jones, 14 December 1942.

7 Works 10/117, G. M. Patrick, Works, to H. W. Walsh, Air Ministry, red. DG16/796, 16 Dec. 1946; F.O.B. McDermott, FO, to J. E. Winter, Works, 19 March 1947; M. C. Gillett, Beijing, to Chancery, Nanjing, no. 61, 26 April 1947.

8 Works 10/117, copy of M. C. Gillett, Beijing, to Chancery Nanjing, no. 61, 26 April 1947; no. 76, 17 May 1947; copy of ambassador, Nanjing, to consul Beijing, no. 144, 31 Oct. 1947.

9 Graham, *China Through One Pair of Eyes*, pp. 11–12; Jacobs-Larcom, *As China Fell*, passim. The Shell story comes from Sir John Morgan: interview 5 May 1993.

10 See, for example, James Tuck-Hong Tang, *Britain's Encounter with Revolutionary China, 1949–54* (Basingstoke and London: Macmillan Press Ltd., 1992; New York: St. Martin's Press, 1992); Zhong-ping Feng, *The British Government's China Policy, 1945–1950* (Keele, Staffs.: Ryburn Publishing/Keele University Press, 1994); and Peter Lowe, *Containing the Cold War in East Asia: British policies towards Japan, China and Korea, 1948–1953* (Manchester and New York: Manchester University Press, 1997).

11 Zhai Qiang, *The Dragon, the Lion and the Eagle: Chinese-British-American relations, 1949–1958* (Kent, Ohio: Kent State University Press, 1994), p. 15.

12 Tang, *Britain's Encounter*, pp. 92–94. Instead, Dening went on a wholly abortive mission to try to enter China to discuss the problems between the two sides.

13 Lowe, *Containing the Cold War* , p. 148.

14 Graham, *China Through One Pair of Eyes*, pp. 12–13; B. Porter, *Britain and the People's Republic of China, 1949–74* (Basingstoke and London: The Macmillan Press, 1976), p. 35; Tang, *Britain's Encounter*, chapter 3; Wenguang Shao, *China, Britain and Businessmen: Political and Commercial Relations, 1949–57* (Basingstoke and London: Macmillan Academic and Professional Ltd., 1991), pp. 34–35.

15 Letter from Walter Graham, 18 Feb. 1994.

16 Works 10/117, Nanjing to FO, telno. 41, 7 Jan. 1950; FO to Beijing, telno. 54, 3 March 1950; Beijing to FO, telno. 247, 5 April 1950. See also *The Times*, 13 April 1950 and H. Trevelyan, *Worlds Apart: China 1953–5; Soviet Union 1962–5* (Basingstoke and London: Macmillan London Ltd., 1971) p. 23.

17 Shao, *China, Britain and Businessmen*, pp. 58–59. Lamb had been a member of the China consular service, and had much experience of China in war and peace. See the obituary in *Daily Telegraph*, 7 Aug. 1992.

18 Trevelyan, *Worlds Apart*, pp. 22–23. This account was partly based on a despatch, classified 'Secret', on 'The life of a diplomatist in Peking'; FO371/11492/FC1018/50, Trevelyan to Mr Macmillan, no. 119, 11 May 1955. For life in the compound 1950–53, see Peter Lum (Lady Crowe), *Peking 1950–1953* (London: Robert Hale, 1958).

19 Trevelyan, *Worlds Apart*, p. 24; Works 10/372, McAdam Clark, FO, to A. W. Cunlifee, Works, 6 Sept. 1954. A New China News Agency announcement of 13 April 1953 had in fact already indicated that the Chinese government planned major redevelopments, some of which were bound to affect the legation quarter.

20 Letter from Walter Graham, 18 Feb. 1994.

21 Nicholas Wollaston, *China in the Morning: Impressions of a Journey through China and Indo-China* (London: Jonathan Cape, 1960) pp. 30–31; George S. Gale, *No Flies in China* (London: George Allen and Unwin, 1955), pp. 62–65.

22 This was the half-French, half-Chinese Bao Ruo-wang whose father was Corsican. Arrested in 1957, he was released in 1964 as a gesture to France on the establishment of diplomatic relations between the two countries. In his autobiography, Bao does not say for which foreign mission he was working when arrested, but a number of British diplomats have confirmed that it was the British. See Bao Ruo-wang (Jean Pasqualini) and Rudolph Chelminski, *Prisoner of Mao* (London: Andre Deutsch, 1975), pp. 9, 22–23, 27–28.

23 Trevelyan, *Worlds Apart*, pp. 24 et seq.; Works 10/372, Memorandum by W. I. Combs, 17 Dec. 1954; letter from Brigadier C. D. Steel, FO, to Works, 10 Sept. 1955.

24 Lowe, *Containing the Cold War* , p. 261.

25 Shao, *China, Britain and Businessmen*, provides a useful account, especially of the revival of British trade with China after 1954.

26 Works 10/372, J. McAdam Clark, FO, to R. B. Marshall, Works, 30 December 1955; C. D. Steel, FO, to R. B. Marshall, Works, 28 March 1956.

27 Works 10/372, Minute by J. R. Gibbs, Works, to senior architect, 1 December 1955.

28 Works 10/372, A. Tough to Mr Alexander, superintending architect, and to Mr Chamkins, senior architect, confident., 23 July 1956; private letter from Tough to Alexander, 26 July 1956. For the spoilt children comment, see minute by J. R. Gilbin to Mr Jenkins, 10 April 1957.

29 Works 10/372, copy of J. M. Addis, Beijing, to C. T. Crowe, FO, 11 January 1956.

30 Works 10/374, extract from Mr Williams to Brig. Steel, secret, 20 June 1958; A. C. Many, Beijing, to P. G. Dalton, FO, 30 Sept. 1958. I am grateful to my colleague David Coates for pointing out the Daoist ring about 'masterly inaction', which I had missed.

31 Works 10/374, Beijing to FO, telno. 32, confid. and private, 21 Jan. 1959.

32 Works 10/374, Memorandum 'Peking Embassy', 30 Jan. 1959.

33 Works 10/374, Beijing to FO, telno. 99 confid., 18 Feb. 1959; Works 10/372, memorandum 'British Legation Compound', by C. C. Libby, 30 June 1959. The information about the architect comes from Sir Robin and Lady McLaren, who found themselves sitting beside him at a dinner in Beijing. He had been trained in Liverpool, on a British Council scholarship.

34 P. D. Coates, 'Documents in Chinese from the Chinese Secretary's Office, British Legation Peking 1861–1939', *Modern Asian Studies*, vol. 17, no. 3 (1983), pp. 239–255.

35 Letter from Lord Wilson of Tillyorn, 12 June 1995.

36 See below, p. 86.

37 Letter from Walter Graham, 18 Feb. 1994; Works 10/374, D. McD. Gordon, Beijing, to P. Jenkins, Works, 10 April 1959; FO366/3167/XCA1101/4/5, 'Disposal of private property stored on the Embassy Premises', chancery Beijing to consular dept., 11 Feb. 1960, and a supplementary letter written the same day on FO366/3169/XCA1101/4/5. For Dr Apsland, see above, p. 63.

38 FO366/3169/XCA1101/4–8/61, includes various papers relating to the issue of compensation.

China

$\boxed{6}$

Outside the Walls: The British Mission
in Beijing Since 1959

———————◆≈◇≈◆———————

It was a much smaller world that the British now inhabited. Even after the loss of the military land, the old compound had covered many acres. Now the offices and residence occupied but one-and-a-half acres each. The flats where most staff now lived were in a nearby compound, shared with many other nationalities, and very different from the legation quarter. Winifred Stevenson, one of those forced to move in 1959, wrote that '. . . the new flat is far smaller than the old house and servants on top of one . . . [i]t's not beautiful, more or less Council house within and without . . . The Chinese have obviously tried to build European flats, copying without understanding half the arrangements'.[1]

Mrs Stevenson noted that she had not liked the old compound, which cut its inhabitants off from the Chinese, and would have liked to have lived out in the city. Because of lack of space in the new diplomatic enclaves, a few privileged diplomats were able to do just this. In the British case, there were two courtyard houses, one at Beishuaifu, the other at Ganyu in the Beijing *hutong* (lanes), whose inhabitants much preferred them to the ghetto-like diplomatic compound. Not only were they living in the city, but, it could be argued, they were more in touch with the real China. The houses, so different from the standardized apartments, were also important social centres.[2] This practice ended for the British with the Cultural Revolution. Other embassies managed to hold on to *hutong* houses and even offices for a few years longer, and at least one embassy, Luxembourg, did so until the 1990s.

For the most part, staff and their families settled down to the new arrangements. Since most postings were for a maximum of two years, there was a rapid turnover of staff, and the numbers of those who had known the old compound gradually diminished. By mid-July 1961, the then head of post, Michael Stewart, noted that most people accepted the new arrangements, though there was some unhappiness over the supply of

furniture. He was told that some £4000 of furniture was on order for junior
staff and £400 for senior, and seemed to think that would soon end any
complaints. The fact that the Chinese had agreed that a swimming pool
could be built was also likely to help staff morale. Asked whether staff
would like new cookers, Stewart replied that this would make little
difference, since everybody had a Chinese servant and he saw no likely
problems with servants in the future. Since the servants '. . . were all used to
cooking on the existing cookers which were the normal Chinese type, and
no European used a cooker, why waste money changing them?'[3]

Some of the well-liked features of life in the old compound quickly reappeared, and while facilities for entertainment were more cramped in the
new quarters, there was, as before, no lack of it. The Stevensons, newly
established in their quasi-council flat, found social life in the autumn and
winter of 1959–60 exhausting.[4] The mission grew larger, with a commercial
counsellor added in 1964. The resident foreign community also increased,
which helped the social life. Film shows, Scottish country dancing and
Christmas carols were still a major feature of the new diplomatic enclave as
they had been of the old. By all accounts, there was much music, with one
future ambassador providing Gilbert and Sullivan on the piano. Other staff
also displayed abilities as singers or performers. Then as now, if there was a
special occasion, the public rooms of the head of post's residence could be
used by other members of the mission for official entertaining. This
provided a more spacious venue than the flats, and sometimes would attract
a higher rank of guest. On a more everyday level, there remained the
Beijing restaurants, and the antique shops. Until the worst period of the
Cultural Revolution, it was still possible to visit some of the scenic spots
around the city and the seaside resort at Beidaihe. The Chinese had also
created an International Club, then at the edge of the old legation quarter,
hoping to satisfy foreigners needs for entertainment and their own wish to
keep control over foreigners' movements. Closed during the Cultural
Revolution, it would re-open about 1970, complete with new tennis courts
and, perhaps more surprising at that stage, with Chinese professional tennis
trainers ready to give advice. It would later move to new premises on
Jianguomenwai street.[5]

From a work point of view, there was no doubt that after the move it was
more difficult to keep in touch with what was happening. In the opaque
world of Beijing, it had been important to watch the cars arrive at the
Beijing Hotel, or to see who was visiting the Communist Party headquarters.
The fact that the few non-diplomatic foreigners resident in Beijing who
wanted to keep up links with diplomats, such as Western journalists, and
most visiting businessmen, tended to stay in the Beijing Hotel, encouraged
the diplomats back into the centre but regular observation was more
difficult. Another useful point of contact with a different aspect of Chinese
life could be gleaned from the foreign students, whose presence added an
interesting dimension to the foreign community, and who could sometimes
be prevailed upon to talk to diplomats. Most were African or Asian, but
there was also a smattering of British and other Europeans. Growing
restrictions on foreigners following the failure of the Great Leap Forward

limited the value of such contacts, as all foreigners were more and more isolated from the Chinese. Eventually, the Cultural Revolution led to the departure of virtually all foreign students.

There was also a small group of foreigners resident in Beijing during the 1950s and 1960s, known to the Chinese as 'the foreign friends', and to others as the 'Three hundred per centers' for their fervent support of the Chinese position on most subjects. Most of these normally refused all contact with their countries' diplomatic representatives, except when absolutely necessary, such as to renew a passport. Many of them found themselves in trouble during the Cultural Revolution. As a result, from about 1972 onwards, they generally tended to re-establish contact with their embassies. The Great Leap and the resulting famine in many parts of the country also lay behind the increasing growth of travel restrictions. Diplomats who had once been able to move with relative freedom around Beijing now found that more and more areas were off limits. For some time, the Ministry of Foreign Affairs organized expeditions for diplomats to various parts of the country. These were, in the words of one participant, '. . . very much part of the system for managing foreigners – distinctly uninformative but in their way hilarious'.[6] They stopped with the Cultural Revolution, but were later revived.

The tours were not all that was affected by the onset of the Cultural Revolution in 1966. Before long, what had begun as an attempt by Mao Zedong to reassert his authority in the party and the state had become a much bigger movement to eradicate old ways and old thinking. In the process, life became a constant struggle for most Chinese, and eventually, the relatively even tenor of life in the British mission was rudely shattered. At first, however, these events had little effect on foreigners. The diplomats, cut off from real sources of information, viewed the events 'only darkly and fragmentarily', with little understanding of what was happening within the party where the major struggles were under way.[7] Few thought that it was likely to have much to do with foreigners. There was distress at the increasing evidence of the destruction of China's cultural heritage, and concern at the growing violence that marked the movement. Destruction of things old was extended to things foreign, and Chinese staff hastened to return small gifts which they had once been happy to take. For many foreigners, however, the most distressing development was the take-over of the small international school ran by the Franciscan nuns of the Sacred Heart – the same nuns who had take Dr Apsland's gramophone only a few years before. Now, as representatives of a foreign religious power, they became the target of the Red Guards, the young people who were Mao's chosen method of attacking his erstwhile party companions. The foreign nuns were handcuffed and beaten, and then thrown out of the country. The Chinese nuns were also beaten. Some died, the rest were sent back to their places of origin and an unknown fate.[8]

Although this was a sign that foreigners might not be immune from the Cultural Revolution, the general view was that these were internal Chinese matters, and were unlikely to have much effect on foreigners. Stray incidents occurred involving diplomats, but until January 1967, they were

small and were not accompanied by violence. Then an incident involving
Chinese students in Moscow led to three weeks of massive demonstrations
outside the Soviet embassy – the days of Sino-Soviet friendship were by
then long past. The Soviet authorities decided to withdraw women and
children from China. When they came to leave, they were spat upon and
struck at the airport. Other embassies, too, were targeted, with the
Yugoslavs, Burmese and Indians being the subject of particularly fierce
demonstrations.[9]

It was, therefore, not surprising that eventually the British would be the
subject of demonstrations. Anti-British demonstrations were not unknown
in post-1949 China. Middle Eastern issues, in particular, had frequently led
to protests outside the compound in the 1950s. The fifteen foot (4.6 metre)
high walls had provided 'a superb target for the posters and whitewash of
'spontaneous' demonstrators',[10] but these were to be as nothing to the anti-
British fury which erupted in 1967. This time it was not the distant Middle
East but Hong Kong which set the fuse.

It began in May 1967, when a labour dispute in Hong Kong led to the first
demonstrations against the British in Beijing. An effigy of the then British
prime minister, Harold Wilson, was burnt outside the mission. On 15 May, a
million demonstrators paraded in the street in front of the British mission,
and other rallies and further parades took place in the following weeks. In
the west of the city, the Reuters correspondent, Anthony Grey, whose office
was then the only other permanent British presence in Beijing, found his
house decked with anti-British slogans. There, Wilson was hanged in effigy.
When the British foreign secretary, George Brown, summoned the Chinese
chargé d'affaires in London to protest at these actions, the Chinese retaliated
by announcing the closure of the Shanghai branch office of the Beijing
mission – the Chinese had always refused it the formal status of a consulate-
general after 1950 – on 22 May.[11]

The first demonstrations were followed by a quiet spell of about a week,
but they then began again. Flats where British diplomats lived were
plastered with slogans and some had their windows whitewashed. Paint
was thrown at staff vehicles, and Chinese staff at the British mission went on
strike. The Arab-Israeli Six Day War in June led to further Chinese
demonstrations, and to an attack on the mission itself by Arabs living in
Beijing, probably encouraged by the Chinese. A few Britons joined in. The
demonstrators broke into the office and damaged a picture of the Queen.
The Queen's Birthday Party, held on 9 June, saw another demonstration
designed to prevent visitors attending. Only the Danish chargé d'affaires,
Arne Belling, was able to outwit the demonstrators and attend.

As the summer progressed, the office stood with broken windows and
mouldering placards and posters, but there followed a lull in major
demonstrations as Chinese fury shifted elsewhere. A few acts of
discrimination against the British continued, nevertheless. (Hopson, the
chargé d'affaires, a former wartime commando and ambassador to Laos,
decided in early August that some of the effigies outside the office should
come down, and launched a largely successful 'Operation Effigy' to have
them removed despite the watchful eye of the Chinese police.[12]) By mid-

July, however, as tensions mounted again in Hong Kong with clashes in the streets and on the border, so the British again became the Red Guards' target. On 21 July, following the passing of a prison sentence on a New China News Agency journalist in Hong Kong two days before, Anthony Grey was placed under house arrest that was to last some two years. During the next three weeks, the conditions under which Grey was confined steadily deteriorated, despite diplomatic protests in both Beijing and London. When Percy Cradock returned from leave in early August, he found things much worse than they had been on departure. There were protests under way at the Mongolian, Soviet, Kenyan and Sri Lankan embassies. Some related to incidents in Beijing, such as traffic accidents. Others were the result of alleged insults to Chairman Mao; the Sri Lankan authorities, for example, had somehow insulted a contingent of Mao badges. The British mission was sure that, because of Hong Kong and the continued disturbances there, it would not be long before they once again became targets.

On 17 August, three Hong Kong Communist newspapers were suspended from publication, pending criminal proceedings against members of their staff who had been arrested on 9 August. On 19 August, Hong Kong police supported by troops raided the offices of the three newspapers. On 20 August, Hopson was summoned by the Foreign Ministry at 22.30 to a meeting at the International Club – the Foreign Ministry itself was apparently undergoing its own internal problems, and could not be used. Hopson received a Note of Protest, which demanded the lifting of the ban on the three newspapers, together with the release of detained Chinese journalists and the newspaper executives within forty-eight hours, and the abandonment of the lawsuits. Otherwise, in a standard phrase '. . . the British Government must be held responsible for the consequences'. This would have been a total surrender, and there was no question of compliance. Hopson indeed refused to accept the Note, but the deputy director of the Western European department insisted that he take it, laying great emphasis on the importance of the time-limit. The mission prepared for the worst. In London on 21 August, the Chinese chargé d'affaires, Shen Ping, was told that the British government held the Chinese government responsible for the safety of the British mission.[13]

The Chinese ultimatum was due to expire at 22.30 on 22 August. During 21 August, some 200 unarmed Chinese soldiers surrounded the two houses which made up the British mission, while Chinese press organisations held demonstrations outside. The British staff gathered food and bedding in the two buildings, prepared for a siege, and occasionally went out to receive the latest protest. On the morning of 22 August, most staff came to work normally. As they did so, a small crowd of Red Guards began gathering outside the mission. The Chinese office and domestic staff belonging to the mission managed to persuade Hopson and senior members of the staff to gather on the ground floor terrace, cut off their retreat back into the offices and then engaged them in some three hours' argument as the August sun beat down. They demanded that Hopson should 'bow his head and admit his guilt' to the demonstrators at the gate. Eventually, they departed after

Hopson had agreed to receive a protest. By then the gates were shut, and nobody could get in or out. As the day wore on, the eighteen men and five women gathered in the offices realized that they would have to spend the night there. As the crowd grew noisier outside, the destruction of classified papers got under way.[14]

It was realized that the expiry of the ultimatum was likely to see the crowd in a frenzy, and plans had been made to retreat to the strongest part of the offices if necessary. In the meantime, some intended to play bridge, others to watch a film. Fifteen minutes after the expiry of the ultimatum, at 22.45, the attack came, with a furious onslaught that lasted about an hour and a half. Those inside the building were forced to retreat into the safe area and eventually forced to leave the building altogether. In doing so, they were physically manhandled, beaten and kicked. Their Chinese attackers yelled 'Sha, sha [kill, kill]', the same cry that had been heard at night during the Boxer Rebellion. Eventually, around 02.30 on 23 August, all those who had been in the burnt-out building were rescued from their attackers by police and People's Liberation Army (PLA) men, and taken to safety. During the course of the night, other British diplomats were threatened with attack in the diplomatic apartment compound nearby, but the PLA and other diplomats intervened to prevent this. The attack left one first secretary in bed for two weeks with concussion. All had bruises and many had lost watches and other possessions in the attack. The Japanese news agency Kyodo reported that ten fire engines had arrived too late to save the burning building. The New China News Agency, which said that ten thousand Red Guards had demonstrated against the British, reported that 'The enraged demonstrators took strong actions against the British chargé d'affaires office'. By the time that dawn broke on 23 August, the office was a burnt-out shell and the residence was looted and empty.[15]

There followed a period in which the British mission in Beijing gradually pieced itself together, with an office operating out of one of the flats. Various items of equipment were rescued from the ruins, and they do not seem to have been as badly off as the Indonesian embassy, which had found itself compelled to assemble a telephone from various broken bits and a teapot. More of a problem was that while the strong room in the office was intact, the papers still had to be destroyed. A clever device designed to do just this produced a collection of paper neatly charred at the edges, but at the same time creating a gas-chamber effect in the strong room. Science having failed, the mass of papers was burnt in more traditional fashion.[16]

The Chinese did not interfere. Having burnt the mission, they now left its inhabitants alone for a few days. Gradually, Chinese office and domestic staff returned to work, which allowed the office to function again. Sir Percy Cradock believes that this was to allow the Chinese to devise a scheme to put the British in the wrong, and thus justify controls on the staff in Beijing. Immediately after the attack, Britain had imposed tight movement restrictions on the Chinese mission in London. On 29 August, in two separate incidents in London, Chinese diplomats spilled on to the streets wielding axes against protesters, and a number of Chinese officials and London policemen were treated in hospital. The Chinese summoned

Hopson to the MFA at 02.00 on 30 August, later changed to the even more inhospitable 03.00, to receive a protest. In the light of what had happened to Anthony Grey, and the apparent collapse of all normal diplomatic standards, Hopson and his companions were not sure whether they were to be treated as diplomats or prisoners. In the event, it was the former, though the Chinese retaliation for the alleged attacks on Chinese personnel in London was to limit all movement of the British in Beijing to the area between the offices and residence and their apartments, and the cancellation of all existing exit visas. Later that same morning, there was a demonstration at the flats where the British were now operating, in protest at the alleged atrocities in London.[17]

After a personal plea from Hopson, five schoolchildren who had been spending the summer with their parents were allowed to leave on 10 September; later, the Chinese agreed to issue occasional visas on medical grounds, but the rest of the mission including family members remained, clearly as hostages. To emphasize the new restrictive relationship, the office in Shanghai was formally taken over on 12 September 1967. Some of the Chinese constraints on the movement of British diplomats in Beijing were eased in November 1967, following relaxations in London. But the battle continued. Like others caught in similar circumstances, Hopson and his colleagues on the spot found it hard to understand the tactics employed in London, and there were complaints that not enough was being done. Percy Cradock claims that this led him to formulate 'Cradock's First Law of Diplomacy: It is not the other side you need to worry about, but your own'. Twenty-five years previously, Sir Robert Craigie, fretting in Tokyo over an evacuation policy which seemed to make little sense from so far away, might have used the same formula.[18]

In the meantime, the strains of confinement told in terms of short tempers and minor ailments. London and Beijing exchanged tough telegrams, each bringing different considerations to bear on the issue. In some ways, relations between Britain and China continued to deteriorate. Several Britons were arrested, mostly on spying charges, and the mission could do little to help[19]. One slight improvement came in April 1968, when consular access was allowed to Anthony Grey – though for Grey, this first visit in nearly a year, which lasted but twenty minutes, was not an easy one. Finally, in July 1968 the Chinese ended the restrictions on the issue of exit visas, and Donald Hopson was at last allowed to leave.[20] Cradock took over as acting chargé d'affaires from August 1968 until John Denson replaced Hopson in March 1969. The British mission now operated out of the first floor of the residence. The chargé continued to live in a flat on the nearby compound, the Wajiao Dalou. Consular work took up much time, and although Grey remained under house arrest, there was some progress in other cases.

The attack on the British in August 1967 seems to have been a turning point in the Cultural Revolution, as far as foreign affairs were concerned. In domestic terms, it was only after there was much loss of life following factional fighting a year later that Mao agreed that things had gone too far. Then the army restored order. Later in 1971, when relations between Britain and China had improved, Premier Zhou Enlai used a call by John Denson, who was about to go on leave, to blame the attack on the British on 'extremist elements', and to indicate that the Chinese government would pay for repairs. Zhou claimed that it had never been official policy to behave in this fashion, and that he had opposed the attack and had tried, together with Jiang Qing, Mao's wife, to stop it.[21] The official Chinese line was that control of the Foreign Ministry had fallen into the hands of fanatical Red Guards, with the principal instigators of the 22 August attack a diplomat returned from Indonesia, Yao Dengshan, anxious to prove his revolutionary credentials, and Wang Li, leader of the '516 [16 May] Group. There were rumours Yao had been tried and executed for his role in those days.[22] Some are sceptical of claims of innocence from the leadership, which reflect a general change of line as attempts were made to curb the more violent aspects of the Cultural Revolution. As for Yao and Wang Li, whatever criticisms they may have gone through, neither was executed. Yao was interviewed about his role in the Cultural Revolution in the late 1980s, while Wang Li, released from prison in 1982, still claims that he was made a scapegoat, though admitting that he might have stirred up some trouble at the Foreign Ministry in August 1967.[23]

From 1967 until 1971, the burnt-out office building stood as a reminder of the violence of the Cultural Revolution. During this time it was used as a somewhat dusty storehouse once the worst of the damage had been removed. In the process of clearing up, the brass lectern given by the Americans in 1902, which had been thought destroyed during the violence, was found and proved reparable. A picture of the Queen was rescued from the attack, and ever since has occupied pride of place in the office of the head of the department dealing with China in London. A portrait of Queen Victoria was lost, however, though it is not clear if it was that which had survived the Boxer siege.[24]

In February 1970, the walls of the residence and the offices were cleaned of their Cultural Revolution slogans, as were those of other embassies still so adorned. There was no announcement, and the clean-up was described as part of a health campaign. Eventually, the Chinese rebuilt the office building exactly as before, and it was re-occupied, the brass eagle again taking up residence in the entrance hall (until banned by a recent ambassador – in 1998, it had moved to the ambassador's residence.). The residence then reverted to its former use. Now, the events of 1967 have generally slipped from view in both China and Britain. When in 1997, a group of those who had lived through the experience met for dinner in the Locarno rooms at the Foreign and Commonwealth Office in London, it attracted little attention.[25]

Although some internal modifications have been made to the residence over the years, both the house and the garden remain basically as they were in 1959. One small change took place in 1978. The plaques from the old legation chapel, and those which had been brought from elsewhere in China as the former consular posts closed in the early 1950s, had hitherto been stacked behind the offices. Now the ambassador, Sir Percy Cradock, had them assembled and re-erected in the residence garden, thus creating a small remembrance corner.[26]

In 1972, full diplomatic relations were finally established between Britain and the People's Republic of China, some 22 years after Britain had formally recognized the new government. Sir John Addis, once a language student and later a junior member of the mission, became the first ambassador. This was followed by the first ever visit of a British foreign secretary, Sir Alec Douglas-Home, and the Great Hall of the People echoed to the strains of the 'Eton Boating Song'. In subsequent years, the new embassy grew larger, and new sections were added; the first of the new arrivals was a military attaché and his staff. This expansion required new building on the office compound, in particular a set of offices for the British Council, which operated the cultural section of the embassy. These were opened in 1983. Another development was an earthquake shelter, erected at the rear of the compound. This was deemed necessary after the extensive damage to buildings in Beijing at the time of the 1976 Tangshan earthquake. The shelter also served as an 'amenities' hall', equipped with a stage and a lighting room. Here took place film shows, Scottish dancing and amateur dramatics, as in the old compound. There was a vigorous choir. There was also an annual pantomime, which occasionally fell foul of Chinese political correctness. Other staff amenities included an outdoor swimming-pool, two tennis courts built by the Chinese out of marble clippings, and a squash court. The embassy pub, 'The Bell', which still has Queen Victoria's jubilee bell as its inn-sign, was moved to new premises attached to the amenities hall in 1983; these had originally been a furniture store and were converted by staff to their new role in 1972. Until well into the 1980s, it was a recognized landmark for foreigners in Beijing, even receiving some – unwanted – occasional notices in guidebooks. Other outlets were more limited than in the past, although it was still possible to visit Beidaihe, taking one's own cook and a certain amount of supplies. Nobody knew whether they were staying in what had once been British houses, but few cared. It was the escape from the capital that mattered.[27]

The years after the Douglas-Home visit saw Britain's relations with China improve dramatically. There were still occasional problems, for example, over air services and flights to Taiwan, but in time these were sorted out. In 1985, a consulate-general was opened in Shanghai; the Chinese were of the view that this was a new office, not a re-opening of that closed in 1967. The old premises were not made available either. Life for all foreigners living in China, including diplomats, became easier as Western-style hotels and shops began to appear. Domestic travel restrictions also eased, though limitations remained on how far foreigners could drive. Tianjin was possible, and Beidaihe in the summer, but it was not entirely clear, for example, whether travel by road to the old Manchu summer capital of Chengde was permitted. Some went without trouble; a few found themselves escorted back. For the Britons, negotiations over the future of Hong Kong resulted in the 1984 Joint Declaration, which seemed to settle the issue. In 1986, the Queen and Prince Philip visited China. There were fraught moments, but the visit was clearly a success and much enjoyed. For the occasion, the residence received new lavatories and some splendid new wallpaper depicting birds and bamboo for the dining-room. One remarkable feature about the latter was that it incorporated in discreet fashion, a picture of the then ambassador's pet duck, the one-footed Ping.[28]

The events of 1989 led to a dramatic downturn in China's relations with Britain, as with most Western countries. For a brief moment in Beijing, foreigners feared that they might again come under attack in the aftermath of 4 June and the killings carried out by the PLA in the vicinity of Tiananmen Square. There was widespread international condemnation of this action, to which China reacted angrily. Once again, embassy staff found themselves destroying papers in a hurry; as always, the lessons of the past had not been learnt and it took days to destroy what should have only taken minutes. It was not that foreigners were a prime or probably a secondary target, but when there are convulsions in a big city and it is placed under a form of martial law, as happened in Beijing in May 1989, nobody can escape.

Tension rose after the Chinese nuclear physicist, Fang Lizhi and his wife, both well-known political activists, took refuge in the United States embassy in the Jianguomenwai district, and there were clear signs of a willingness to intimidate the foreign community. Tanks, with guns uncovered and pointing at the diplomatic compound nearby, took up position on the Jianguomenwai flyover, although it quickly became apparent that there was no military requirement for such a move. From 5 June onwards, lorry loads of troops periodically swept through the area of the Jianguomenwai diplomatic enclave, site of the British and probably more important, US diplomatic missions, firing warning shots at anybody who ventured on to the streets. Again, there seemed to be no obvious military requirement for this behaviour, but it meant that all embassies, not just the British, exercised a high degree of caution. On 7 June, troops entering the city from the east fired on the Jianguomenwai compound and other buildings associated with foreigners. They would later claim that they had come under sniper fire, although nobody else noticed this. Some British embassy property was hit by bullets, though nobody was injured. Staff in the British Airways office, on the first floor of a building opposite the Jianguomenwai complex, looked out to find a tank gun trained on their plate glass windows. A Japanese bus taking tourists to the airport was fired upon and stopped by troops, who mounted roadblocks at various points in the city. For most embassies, including the British, such incidents were a major factor in confirming the decision to evacuate some staff and dependants from a city where all shops and petrol stations were closed and the military appeared on the verge of being out of control.[29]

During the crisis, consular work took up most time. Many British students were studying in China at the end of the 1980s, and it seemed best to evacuate them since it was feared that the army might begin an attack on universities. There were also thousands of Hong Kong people in China and some hundreds had taken part in the demonstrations in Tiananmen Square. Few of them had registered with the embassy, but many now turned to it for help. Some complained that they were not allowed to take refuge in the embassy, others that they were told to take taxis to the airport where these were available. In fact, all Hong Kong people who wished to do so got away safely, and much embassy effort went into helping those who appeared to be in real danger. These included the trade unionist Lee Chuk-yan, who was forcibly removed from a Hong Kong-bound flight on 5 June. Lee admitted that he had brought funds from Hong Kong to help the student demonstrators, thus, in Chinese eyes, aiding and abetting them in their anti-state activity. After many hours of negotiation, he was handed over to the author at Beijing airport on 8 June, and allowed to fly to Hong Kong, though his funds were confiscated. Although widely reported, such activities failed to counteract the belief that the embassy had failed to help people from Hong Kong, and complaints continued into the summer of 1989.[30]

There was one other complaint, from those stalwarts of British diplomatic life, the Queen's Messengers or couriers. For many years, Beijing received its confidential mail via Moscow and the Mongolian capital, Ulan Bator, brought by train by the Queen's Messengers. The international train was inevitably late in arriving in Beijing, and it had been the custom for many years to send embassy drivers to check possible arrival times before sending an escort to the station. In the confused circumstances of 5–6 June 1989, this was not possible. The army occupied the streets and appeared to be firing at anything that moved. The Ministry of Foreign Affairs was not operating, and in any case could not have guaranteed the safety of British diplomats roaming the streets. Nobody answered the telephone at the railway station, and so it was impossible to find out if international trains were arriving. They were, and so did the Queen's Messengers. When they found no escort, they decided not to wait until morning, but to make their own way to the embassy, thirty bags and all. With the help of a couple of bicycle rickshaws, they succeeded, and were greeted with great enthusiasm. (The enthusiasm was dampened a little later when they put in a formal complaint about not having been met. Not surprisingly, no action was taken in the circumstances.)[31]

The immediate crisis passed with the appearance on television on 9 June 1989 of Deng Xiaoping, China's paramount leader. Yet there was sporadic firing in the city until the autumn. For several months, the People's Armed Police (PLP), who in recent years have guarded embassy buildings, patrolled the streets in steel helmets and carried automatic weapons. There was much speculation among the foreign community as to whether these weapons were loaded. The consensus was that they were not, since the rather bored young men who carried them frequently appeared to 'fire' them at each other, and as time passed, seemed only too happy for foreign children to play with them. Eventually, following a protest by former US President Richard Nixon, the PLP ceased to appear in quite such martial attire. Yet martial law continued in force until January 1990, and there were frequent police roadblocks in the city. Most of those manning these had little regard for diplomatic niceties – the author found it somewhat disconcerting to be ordered from the balcony of his flat in July 1989 by a pistol-waving officer in charge of a roadblock on the ring road 14 floors before! There were, for foreigners at least, occasional comic opera touches to 1989, but once again, the sense of being under siege returned to haunt them. As before, however, while there was no Chinese apology for what happened on 7 June 1989 in and around the diplomatic compounds, the

Foreign Ministry later paid bills for redecorating and dry cleaning without demur.

By 1990, the compound was clearly too small and a decision was made to outhouse the cultural section. This moved in June 1991 to the new Landmark Centre on the third ring road, near the Sheraton Great Wall Hotel, one of the many major Western-style hotels to have opened in Beijing in recent years. This move freed space to better house the consular and visa section and allow other sections of the embassy more space to expand. Although at first the British Council was reluctant to go, fearing that the costs of the move would outweigh any possible advantage, it was soon apparent that the move away from formal diplomatic premises meant that it was much easier for ordinary Chinese to gain access to the Council's offices and facilities. Meanwhile, staff housing has moved beyond the original compound. During the 1970s, the Chinese developed new diplomatic housing at the Jianguomenwai intersection, slightly further in towards the centre, and many staff have been housed there over the years. In the late 1980s, another new diplomatic housing development saw staff moving to Tayuan, some two miles to the north. Finally, in 1990, two counsellors were rehoused in joint venture housing at East Lake Villas, the first move out of officially provided housing since the early 1960s. Although many other embassies have long since decided to build for themselves, and the Chinese appear to have accepted that they can no longer house all diplomats, it is only at the end of the twentieth century that the British seem finally to accept that they will have to move out of their 1959 'temporary accommodation'.

Today, the old legation quarter is still recognizable despite the new building all around it, though its future cannot be certain. From time to time, it has looked as though the Chinese might preserve it as part of their history as well as a symbol of the West's aggression, but economic pressures to exploit a prime city centre site seems overpowering.[32] Some of the former diplomatic compounds are accessible, but the former British compound is still used by the Ministry of Public Security, or police force, and remains firmly off limits. Various requests by visiting former residents to see inside the gates have always been politely refused. Occasional glimpses are possible from the road, and the Museum of Chinese History sometimes allows an overview. In the latter case, however, over-zealous custodians will swiftly draw the curtains on anybody showing too obvious interest. It still retains many of the old features, but much new building has also gone up and even the old structures tend, as so often in China, to have rather ramshackle new bits tacked on. The main gate is recognizable, but is always firmly closed, and the current occupants use a new concrete entrance on Changan Avenue. By autumn 1998, it had been cleaned up and a shop, selling security equipment, installed in the archway.[33] Few occupants probably know that it once was the British embassy.[34]

Maybe one day, it will be possible to wander across the lawns of the former British embassy. Until then, the nearest most people will get to that bygone era is a look at the small monument corner in the residence garden or at the photographs which hang in the chancery building.

Notes

1 Beryl Smedley, *Partners in Diplomacy* (Ferring, West Sussex: The Harley Press, 1990), p. 100.

2 Letters from Sir John Boyd, 21 February 1994, and from Lord Wilson of Tillyorn, 12 June 1995.

3 FO366/003187/XCA110/4/5/61, minute by C. D. Steel, 25 July 1961, recording a conversation with Mr M. Stewart, 19 July 1961.

4 Smedley, *Partners in Diplomacy*, p. 134.

5 A. Winnington, *Breakfast with Mao: Memoirs of a Foreign Correspondent* (London: Lawrence and Wishart, 1986), p. 198; letters from Sir John Boyd, 21 February 1994, and from K C Walker, who was a first secretary in Beijing in 1971, 2 July 1994; Percy Cradock, *Experiences of China* (London: John Murray, 1994), pp. 22–28, 35–36.

6 Letter from Sir John Boyd, 21 February 1994.

7 Cradock, *Experiences of China*, p. 37. For the Cultural Revolution in general, see Roderick MacFarquhar and John K. Fairbank, eds., *The People's Republic Part 2: revolution within the Chinese Revolution, 1966–1982* (Cambridge, England: Cambridge University Press, 1991) (Cambridge History of China, vol. 15).

8 Letter from Sir John Boyd, 21 February 1994; Cradock, *Experiences of China*, p. 40–41.

9 Cradock, *Experiences of China*, pp. 53–56.

10 XCA1101/4/186, G. F. Rodgers (for M. Stewart), to Mr Selwyn Lloyd, no. 117, confid., 9 November 1959. The original of this file has apparently been 'destroyed under statute', as being of no long term interest, and there is therefore no full reference number. However, copies do exist.

11 My original account of the events of 1967, which appeared as J. E. Hoare, 'Building Politics: The British Embassy Peking, 1949–1992', *Pacific Review*, vol. 7, no. 1 (1994), 67–78, was largely based on that given in Anthony Grey, *Hostage in Peking* (London: Weidenfeld and Nicholson, 1988), pp. 60–69. Grey witnessed some of the early developments but was then under house arrest. However, he appears to have been given an account of what happened after his house arrest by a member of the British mission. Since then, Sir Percy Cradock, who was in 1967 Political Counsellor and Head of Chancery in Beijing, has published his account – see Cradock, *Experiences of China*, pp. 56 et seq. The official papers have also become available – see 'Envoys besieged: Claret and bridge as Beijing Red Guards storm British Office', *The Guardian*, 1 January 1999. I have drawn on all these sources for this account.

12 FCO21/34/FC1/14, Mr Hopson to Mr Brown, no. 23, restricted, 8 August 1967. See also 'Britain's tough diplomat in Peking', *The Times*, 23 August 1967, which gives a brief account of this incident.

13 Keesing's *Contemporary Archives* (1967), p. 22267; Cradock, *Experiences of China*, p. 61.

14 Letter from Sir Percy Cradock, 10 March 1993; see also Cradock, *Experiences of China*, pp. 61–62.

15 Cradock, *Experiences of China*, p. 61 and letter from Sir Percy Cradock, 10 March 1993. For a contemporary newspaper account, see Jean Vincent, 'Red Guard attack as Ultimatum Expires', *The Times*, 23 August 1967. Keesing's *Contemporary Archives*, (1967), p. 22267 reproduces part of the British Foreign Office statement on the incident issued on 23 August. The Japanese Kyodo News Agency report, and the New China News Agency statement can be found in BBC, *Summary of World Broadcasts*, Far East, 24 August 1967. Hopson gave an account in a letter to his wife of 28 August 1967, reproduced in Denise Hardy, *En Chine avec Lady Hopson* (Paris: André Bonne, 1969), pp. 53–57. Grey, *Hostage in Peking*, pp. 120–32, is based on an account by one of those present. Finally, Ray Whitney, one of the first secretaries in the mission, published his account as 'When the Red Guards stormed our embassy [sic]', *Sunday Telegraph*, 23 November 1980. Hopson's official account of that night can be found in FCO21/34/ FC1/14 'The burning of the British office in Peking', Hopson to Brown, unnumbered, confidential, 31 August 1967. All the accounts are more or less in agreement.

16 Cradock, *Experiences of China*, pp. 60, 66–67.

17 Cradock, *Experiences of China*, pp. 69–70. For a contemporary Chinese account of the incidents in London, see *Peking Review*, 14 August 1967.

18 Cradock, *Experiences of China*, p. 78. For Craigie, see below, p. 152.

19 For one such case, see George Watt, *China 'spy'* (London: Johnson, 1972). Watt was an engineer working at Lanzhou when he was arrested in 1967; he was released in 1970.

20 Cradock, *Experiences of China*, p. 80. See also Keesing's *Contemporary Archives*, (1968), pp. 22268–69; Grey, *Hostage in Peking*, pp. 129–30. For the visit, See Grey, *Hostage in Peking*, pp. 234–239.

21 A. M. Rendel, diplomatic correspondent, 'China to pay for sacking of British mission', *The Times*, 23 March 1971; letter from Sir Percy Cradock, 10 March 1993.

22 For the hints that he had been executed, see J. Van Ginneken, *The Rise and Fall of Lin Piao*, (Harmondsworth: Penguin Books, 1976) pp. 115–117, 233.

23 Letters from Sir Percy Cradock, 10 March 1993 and Professor Michael Schoenhals of the University of Stockholm, 20 April 1994. The latter pointed out that Yao was still alive, after I had repeated the story of his 'execution' in 'Building Politics', pp. 67–78. Wang Li's defence appeared in Patrick E. Tyler, 'A Red Guard Leader seeks His Rehabilitation', *International Herald Tribune*, 12 April 1996.

24 Stephen Markbreiter, 'In Search of an Identity: the British Legation at Peking, 1861', *Arts of Asia*, vol. 13, no. 3, (May-June 1983), 129.

25 Raymond Whitaker and David Usborne, 'Peking embassy siege veterans recall Red Guards' summer of hate', *The Independent on Sunday*, 17 August 1997. Ray Whitney, now Sir Ray Whitney, was the moving force behind the commemoration.

26 Letter from Sir Percy Cradock, 10 March 1993.

27 Information supplied by Alan Waters, former management officer, Beijing 30 June 1995, and letter from Sir John Boyd, 21 February 1994.

28 Some of this paragraph is based on personal experience and observation. For the Hong Kong negotiations, on which there is a considerable literature, see Cradock, *Experiences of China*, pp. 162 et seq.; James T. H. Tang, 'Hong Kong's transition to Chinese rule: The fate of the Joint Declaration', in Judith. M. Brown and Rosemary Foot, editors, *Hong Kong's Transitions, 1842–1997* (Basingstoke, and London: Macmillan Press Ltd., 1997), pp. 149–66.

29 'Britons advised to flee for their safety', *The Independent*, 7 June 1989; 'Chaos as thousands of foreigners converge on airport', *Daily Telegraph*, 9 June 1989. There are numerous accounts of June 1989, from journalists and academics. See, for example, Timothy Brook, *Quelling the people: The Military Suppression of the Beijing Democracy Movement* (New York, Oxford: Oxford University Press, 1992). For a Chinese official account, see Che Muqi, *Beijing turmoil: more than meets the eye* (Beijing: Foreign Languages Press, 1990).

30 'Police seize Hong Kong activist in Peking', *Daily Telegraph*, 6 June 1989; 'Fears for detained Hong Kong trade unionist', *The Independent*, 6 June 1989; 'Peking frees Hong Kong activist', *The Independent*, 9 June 1989.

31 The story is told, though without reference to the subsequent complaint, in Terry Coleman, 'True Brits pack up their bags', *The Guardian*, 28 May 1994.

32 Liu Jie, 'Occidental slice of Oriental Life', *China Daily*, 15 March 1989. The messages are mixed. Despite its fame as the home of the most famous modern Beijing Opera star, Mei Lanfang, the capital's Jixiang theatre was pulled down in 1994 to make way for office blocks: Ian Johnson, 'China sacrifices history for profits', *The Guardian*, 27 October 1994; this piece originally appeared in *The Baltimore Sun*. The official line remains that real relics are protected: Wei Liming, 'Relics protection in Beijing', *Beijing Review*, 5–11 May 1997.

33 The BBC's then Beijing correspondent, James Miles, gave a good account of the old compound and its current occupants, in a despatch about the expulsion of Andrew Higgins, a fellow British journalist, which was broadcast on the BBC World Service on 16 September 1991 (transcript in author's possession).

34 A conversation with a young Chinese official in January 1999 revealed that his wife worked in the police headquarters. He clearly had no idea of its former history. Another Chinese living in Britain, who was born on the compound and lived there in the 1960s refused to discuss it, saying that there was nothing to say; it was just a set of buildings.

Part Two

<u>Japan</u>

Japan

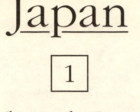

The Early Days, 1859–72

PROLOGUE

Today, the British embassy in Tokyo sits proudly on the edge of the Imperial Palace moat, with an address, 'Number 1, Ichiban-cho, Chiyoda-ku', the Japanese equivalent of 'Number One, London'. Visitors flying over central Tokyo can easily pick out the compound, a smaller green oasis next to its neighbour the Imperial Palace; lungs in the urban sprawl. It lies in an area, Kojimachi, which at the end of the Meiji period (1912), was regarded as the social centre of the city and which contained most of the embassies and legations. Only the German and the British embassies occupied prime positions on the inner moat. The former, once deemed grander than the British, has long since gone, and today, only the British embassy occupies such a favoured position.[1] In some ways, of course, it has been left behind by the subsequent development of the city. Yet enough of the Japanese bureaucracy is still to be found relatively nearby, as are the Diet and the Imperial Palace itself. Any move would be to a lesser site, however more convenient that may be given the horrific traffic conditions of present-day Tokyo.

As this account will show, the British embassy has had a not uninteresting history, even if it did not all take place on today's site. It may not have had quite so stirring times as that in Beijing, or share in the architectural splendours of Duke Liang's palace. It certainly lacks the historical continuity of Seoul. Its older buildings, interesting enough in a city which has relatively few monuments from the Meiji period, are, in fact, somewhat false friends since the oldest only dates from the late 1920s. That is why the present buildings, somewhat mockingly described as 'earthquake proof Queen Anne',[2] are nowhere mentioned in Dallas Finn's monumental study of 'Victorian' buildings in Japan.[3] It all began, however, in a very different setting.

Tozenji

Britain's first legation in Tokyo, or Edo, as the city was known before 1868, was in a temple called Tozenji, a temple of the Rinzai sect of Zen Buddhism, which has its headquarters in Kyoto.[4] Tozenji still stands today. It lies not far from Shinagawa station, and a few minutes walk from Sengakuji, the famous temple of the 47 ronin. Many people visit Sengakuji, though it was much damaged in the war and has been heavily rebuilt. Few visit its near neighbour. Tozenji has changed since it was the British legation. It has lost its main gate, and like many Tokyo temples, its grounds have shrunk. It escaped damage in the 1923 earthquake and the bombing raids of the Pacific War, but there are a number of new buildings, including a pagoda, which were not there in 1859. Yet even today, the buildings used by Britain's first minister and his staff can still be seen, and the pond which so pleased the British in 1859 still bears a resemblance to that shown in early photographs.

Like their fellow East Asians, the Japanese were not familiar with the concept of a resident envoy. The idea of a diplomatic mission was well-established.[5] There were periodic visits from Korea to Japan, and the Japanese also sent envoys to Seoul. There had been Japanese embassies to China and even return missions from China, though over a thousand years before. But these were non-permanent missions, whose leaders carried out their tasks and departed. Buildings might be set aside for their temporary use, not for long-term residence. The Westerners who came to Japan in the 1850s had very different ideas. Their diplomats were to be resident and, it soon emerged, it was as important that they were to be resident in the capital. By the time of the 'opening of Japan', the Western Powers had become fixed on this concept, especially after nearly twenty years of being kept out of the Chinese capital and what were regarded as the negative consequences of that arrangement.

It was true that the early treaties, drawn up by naval officers with the need for coaling stations and sources of food in mind rather than political imperatives, had not insisted on such a residence.[6] Townsend Harris, the first US and the first Western diplomatic representative in Japan, resided at Shimoda, some distance away from Edo. But even he insisted on the right to visit and reside in the capital.[7] By the time the negotiations began for the later American and British treaties, those concerned, including Harris, were determined that the Japanese should concede the right of residence at Edo. With this in mind, the British negotiator, Lord Elgin, insisted on negotiating in Edo rather than at Nagasaki which the Japanese would have preferred. The Japanese officials involved in the negotiations were very much opposed to such residence. They feared that the close juxtaposition of foreigners and hostile Japanese would inevitably lead to clashes and they knew what had been the consequences of such clashes in China. There were also practical worries about the feeding and protection of foreign envoys. But their objections proved unavailing, and the foreign negotiators had their way. Harris's treaty of 29 July 1858 and Elgin's of 26 August 1858 both contained clauses which allowed the stationing of diplomatic agents at

Edo. (Much of Elgin's treaty derived directly from Harris's, but by including a 'most favoured nation clause', the British treaty allowed other powers to gain the same benefits when they came to negotiate treaties.) The Japanese asked Elgin to request London not to exercise the right to station a diplomatic agent in Edo until 1861. He did, but with little expectation that London would agree.[8]

Elgin was right. There was no disposition in London to agree to the Japanese request for postponement. The Foreign Office had been preparing for a separate establishment for Japan since the first treaty in 1854 and now approached the Treasury for formal approval. At this stage, with few expectations of the Japan ports except for resorts for whalers, London intended only to appoint a consul-general to Edo, but it was to Edo that he would go.[9]

Rutherford Alcock was the first official appointed to represent Britain in Japan. He had been an army surgeon and later served in China as one of the first British consular officers appointed after the Treaty of Nanjing (Nanking) in 1842. He had gained a good reputation in China, serving as consul in both Shanghai and Guangzhou. Now, in 1858, he became the British consul-general for Japan, and in that capacity arrived in Edo bay (modern Tokyo bay) in July 1859, one year after the signing of Lord Elgin's treaty. He was nothing if not self-confident. Discovering that his fellow diplomats were ministers plenipotentiary, he decided to give himself the title plenipotentiary, on the grounds that it would be wrong for the British representative to be outranked by the representatives of other Powers. The Foreign Office approved and went one better, appointing him minister plenipotentiary and envoy extraordinary, though warning him that this advancement was not to give him a claim to any further appointment outside East Asia.[10] Despite the caveat, Alcock had started a process which was to lead Sir Harry Parkes, Sir Ernest Satow and Sir John Jordan to diplomatic status from a consular background.

He aroused strong feelings, and his career in Japan remains controversial to this day. To his staff, he was a long-winded and indecisive man, who never used one word when he could find three. He could be snobbish and had a rather exalted view of his own position and authority. He fell out with the British merchant community at Yokohama for a number of reasons, the chief of which was that its members had allowed the Japanese to develop a settlement at Yokohama rather than at the official treaty port of Kanagawa nearby. As a consequence, British officials were banned from the merchant-organized clubs of Yokohama until after his departure.[11]

It was Alcock who selected the first legation site. Lord Elgin had been accommodated in a temple. As in China, there was a general lack of public buildings in Japan which could easily be converted for Westerners' use. Ernest Satow noted that the only really suitable buildings were the palaces of the feudal lords, and there was little likelihood of those being made available for foreigners' use. Temples, with their many rooms and spacious grounds, were relatively easy to adapt. They also frequently had special apartments set aside for visitors which could be adapted for more permanent use. Indeed, before the arrival of the Westerners, they were often used for the reception of envoys from Korea or the Ryukyus. Thus many a group of Buddhist monks found themselves forced to share their quarters with foreigners. Such objections as they may have had related to the fact that their new guests were foreigners rather than the mere fact of having guests thrust upon them.[12] The Japanese had made considerable efforts to ensure that Elgin and his party were comfortable in their temporary quarters. Officials had been sent to Shimoda, to take note of and to copy Townsend Harris's furniture and fittings before he had made his first visit to the capital, and these provided the model for the use of Elgin and his party.[13]

Alcock's arrival saw the same dearth of suitable accommodation, and so he, too, was forced to settle for a temple. The *bakufu* officials supplied him with a selection of four from which to choose. He did not like the first one he was shown feeling that it was '. . . but ill adapted for the accommodation of Europeans.' The second was Tozenji, '. . . one of the largest and best endowed in Yeddo' and here he decided to stay. He noted that it was still not ideal since it was far from the centre of government i.e. the shogun's palace. Harris was much nearer. But it was convenient for the bay and therefore for easy access to the ships. This was useful both for communications and as a means of escape at times of danger. Tozenji was also not far off the Tokaido, the great eastern road which connected Edo with Kyoto, and now also connected the newly opened treaty port of Kanagawa with the capital.[14]

The temple itself was situated in well-kept grounds, with plenty of shady trees, no bad asset in a hot Japanese summer. There was also a pool, stocked with carp, and an imposing gateway. Alcock clearly liked the temple gardens, which he thought '. . . as beautiful a specimen of Japanese garden as can be conceived.' He also enjoyed the view over the bay given by a large platform in front of the temple – a view now, alas! replaced by some nondescript office blocks and the outskirts of Shinagawa station.[15] Bishop Smith, visiting from Hong Kong, thought that it was the '. . . finest location conceded by the Japanese Government to a foreign official', and was much impressed by the interior arrangements. Indeed, much work had been done to make the temple suitable for its new occupants, with kitchens and outhouses added to the original structure.[16] Laurence Oliphant, erstwhile secretary to Lord Elgin, who returned to Japan in June 1861 as first secretary of the legation, was less impressed and found the legation building somewhat flimsy. What he described as 'sugar icing architecture' and sliding paper walls made for comfortable rooms but was unlikely to give a great deal of protection at a time when most foreigners lived in daily fear of assassins. There was also the problem of the resident priests, who seemed to resent their uninvited guests. Yet he liked the general quaintness of the surroundings and wrote favourably of the gardens.[17]

Others also felt that it was not the safest of places, for reasons apart from the flimsy nature of the buildings. Tozenji was surrounded by shady trees because it was situated in a hollow and well-wooded dell, which might make it easy for an attacker to approach unseen. According to one of Alcock's colleagues, it was also unsafe because it was in an area of brothels and saké houses, much frequented by young samurai hostile to foreigners.[18]

Others had doubts about Tozenji for different reasons. Ernest Satow found the rooms small and uncomfortable. Neither was he over impressed with the heating arrangements. There were a couple of stoves in the principal rooms, but elsewhere the occupants had to make do with charcoal in a *hibachi*.[19] Like all the buildings assigned to foreign diplomats in Edo, Tozenji had a squad of guards, numbering some 150, provided by the *bakufu*. Their main task, however, seemed to be to watch the doings of their charges, rather than to protect them, and they showed an alarming tendency to disappear at the first sign of trouble.[20] In addition, most members of the legation began to experience earthquakes for the first time. All in all, Japan was not a restful country, however delightful the legation gardens.

Oliphant's fears about the safety of the legation were not an abstract concern. During the early years after the opening of Japan, a regular pattern of attacks on foreigners, some of them fatal, had become established. According to Ernest Satow such attacks were premeditated and unprovoked, and there was little or no defence against them. Men carried revolvers, but attacks from behind or when least expected meant that such precautions were of little use. The first of these attacks took place in August 1859, when two Russian sailors were hacked to death in Yokohama. In November 1859, a Chinese servant of the French vice-consul in Yokohama was killed. Early the following year, the Japanese interpreter of the British legation was killed outside the legation. (That same night, the French legation caught fire, and the inhabitants arrived seeking sanctuary for the remainder of a night already thrown into confusion by murder.) Shortly afterwards, two Dutch shipmasters were attacked and killed in Yokohama. Later in 1860, there was an attack on an Italian servant of the French minister just outside the French legation in Mita. In January 1861, Henrik Heusken, Townsend Harris's Dutch interpreter, who had been in Japan since 1855, and who had played a major role in many of the early treaty negotiations, was killed as he rode home from the Prussian legation.[21]

For most of the small number of diplomats then in Edo, this last attack proved the last straw, and they withdrew to the relative safety of Yokohama. From then on, until the site of the present embassy was acquired in the early 1870s and the legation moved permanently to Edo (or Tokyo as it became in 1868), there were to be in effect two British legations, one at Edo and one at Yokohama.

Although it had been his colleague and companion who had been killed, the US minister refused to leave Edo, arguing that to do so would mean that the foreign envoys would never be able to return and that the Japanese claims that they could and would protect the legations should be tested.[22] His colleagues did not remain away long. Their action in quitting their posts was not highly regarded in the treaty ports, being seen as panic rather than a wise action in the face of Japanese hostility. There was little support for the idea put forward by the British and French ministers of turning Yokohama into a fortified foreign enclave. The Dutch and Prussian ministers returned to Edo first, and eventually the French and British were persuaded to do likewise. The incident created a rift between Alcock and Harris, previously good colleagues, and they did not speak to each other again.[23] Before long, however, those who had returned to the capital must all have wondered whether they had done the right thing, for the next major attack was on the British legation itself.

Alcock had been away travelling in the south of Japan, and returned to Edo from Nagasaki at the beginning of July 1861. Mr Morrison, the consul at Nagasaki, was with him and was staying in the legation. After much conversation in the garden – there had been a comet and some time was spent discussing this as well as Alcock's travels – the minister retired to bed about 11 pm on the night of 5 July. The rest of the group stayed talking and singing until after midnight, and then they too retired. It was hot, and the sliding screens facing the garden had been left open. As well as the *bakufu*'s 150 guards, there were porters at the entrance and two night watchmen to patrol the grounds. Nobody was expecting trouble and no special precautions were in place.

Oliphant, the newly-arrived secretary of legation, was woken by the sound of his dog barking. He soon became aware that things were not as they should be. The watchman's rattle sounded and there was the sound of scuffling in the yard outside. His revolver case was locked, so he seized his hunting crop and went to investigate. In the long passage from his room, he encountered a sword-wielding Japanese. The Japanese struck at him twice, but failed to hit him, and Oliphant struck back with his whip. A third blow from the sword cut Oliphant's shoulder. His life was only saved by Morrison, who shot the attacker. Morrison was in turn attacked by a second swordsman, receiving a cut to the head. Together Morrison and Oliphant retreated to the dining-room where they found the rest of the Britons gathered. On the way, Oliphant stepped on what he thought was an oyster, but which turned out to be a human eye. Safe in the dining room, Oliphant's wounds were patched up by Alcock, thus saving his life. From outside came sounds of fighting and eventually, their Japanese guards succeeded in driving off the attackers, killing and capturing several in the process.

For the rest of the night, there were comings and goings, and great fires burned in the grounds. Morrison and Oliphant were both badly hurt, but the wounds were not life threatening. The rest of the British staff had escaped with nothing worse than a fright. The events were recorded in both words and pictures by Charles Wirgman, and his account appeared in the London *Illustrated London News* in October 1861. The London *Times*, too, carried an account, probably also from Wirgman.[24] Examining the damage next day, Alcock noted that the legation '. . . looked as if it had been sacked after a serious conflict'. There was blood everywhere, with slashed screens, mats and furniture all over the place.[25] When the *bakufu*'s foreign affairs representative came to call bearing a basket of ducks and a jar of sugar, Alcock was not best pleased. Refusing to rely on the Japanese guards, who were asleep when the attack began, Alcock sent a message to Yokohama for a protective naval guard to be sent up to the legation, and by midday on

6 July, twenty sailors and their officers had arrived. After some delay, it was arranged that the legation would be supplied with a guard on a more permanent basis from British forces in China. The Japanese, meanwhile, increased their guard to 500 men. Oliphant, more seriously wounded than Morrison, was taken to Yokohama and placed on board HMS *Ringdove*, then the only Royal Navy vessel in Japan. There he made a sufficient recovery to be able to take part about a week later in the first of many meetings with the Japanese at which Alcock demanded compensation for the attack. In the process, he nearly became the victim of another attack, as he crossed in front of a daimyo procession on the Tokaido. Despite his wounds, he was forced to run for the legation gates to escape his assailants.[26]

When news of the attack on Tozenji reached London, instructions were sent to Alcock to seek the capture and punishment of those involved in the attack, redress for those injured, and to secure a better site for a legation. At the very least, the latter should have as security from further attacks, '. . . a site defensible by walls, ditches, and stockades'. There was also a vague threat that the Japanese might be asked to meet the costs of the British guard now deemed necessary to protect Alcock and his staff.[27] These demands were to lead the *bakufu* to agree to construct a new diplomatic quarter in Gotenyama, which included a new British legation.

Alcock spent the next few months moving between Edo and Yokohama, heavily involved in negotiations. But he was never to reside permanently at Edo again, and eventually went on leave in March 1862. He was replaced as chargé d'affaires by Lt Col. St John Neale, appointed secretary of legation in place of the unfortunate Oliphant, who arrived a few days before Alcock's departure. Alcock and Neale had known each other in Spain, but according to Satow, were not particularly friendly. There seems no truth in Dr McMaster's claim that Alcock picked Neale as chargé because he wanted a weak man running the legation while he was away; Neale was the number two, and as such took charge on Alcock's departure. Neale, in Satow's words, 'had great command of his pen', and he could be genial, but he lacked both political judgement and an understanding of the situation in which he found himself. It was not long before his capabilities were to be tried.[28]

Neale decided that he should re-occupy Tozenji, and went up from Yokohama on 12 June 1862, accompanied by several members of his staff and an escort of twelve British soldiers. These were soon joined by a marine guard of thirty men. On arrival at the temple, they found some 535 Japanese guards also assigned to them, provided, on the *bakufu*'s orders, by the daimyo of Tamba. The British and the Japanese shared sentry duty, and an incident seems to have occurred which either involved one of the marines kicking a samurai, or some other mark of disrespect. The result was another attack on the British legation on 26 June. The insulted man first cut down one of the British marines on sentry duty with a Japanese. The alarm was raised, bringing the occupants from their beds. The attacker fled through the garden, where he met a marine corporal and attacked him too. The corporal, though mortally wounded, was able to draw his pistol and wounded his attacker before dying. The assassin made his escape, but, knowing that he could be identified, killed himself before he could be caught. It was reported that he was the friend of one of those killed in the 1861 attack.[29]

The *bakufu* officials produced the body of the dead assassin, and replaced the Tamba men with their own soldiers. Neale sent for more British guards, and HMS *Renard* provided an additional twenty-one men and three officers. But even before this incident, the admiral on the China station, Sir James Hope, had already expressed unwillingness to supply more men, and had suggested that it would be better if the legation should return to Yokohama. After some delay, during which the sleep of the legation's inhabitants was regularly broken by diligent Japanese and British sentries shouting 'All's well', Neale withdrew to Yokohama on 11 July 1862, just a month after his arrival. The Tozenji legation was beginning to seem a dangerous place. But as Willis, the legation doctor, noted, the new legation building being erected at Gotenyama, commissioned after the 1861 attack, was expected to be ready by October 1862, and they might return to Edo then.[30] Events were to prove otherwise.

Gotenyama, Sengakuji, and Yokohama

Gotenyama

The second British legation in Edo was built at Gotenyama, also in Shinagawa and therefore relatively near to Yokohama. Gotenyama was an area of ancient temples and pine trees. It was famous as a spot where Tokugawa Ieyasu held court when he made Edo the capital, and where his immediate successors had met the daimyo on their journey to Edo. In more recent years, it had become popular as a site for viewing the cherry blossoms.[31] Although the area was much in decline by the 1860s, and large amounts of earth had been taken from it to build forts, there was much Japanese opposition to foreigners being allowed to occupy such a site. To the foreign envoys, its main value was that, like Tozenji, it allowed quick access to the sea. In times of danger, therefore, the occupants would be able to escape to Yokohama.

Here work began in 1862 to construct a proper legation, with office and residential accommodation, to British designs, but at Japanese expense. By the time of the second attack on Tozenji, the work was already well-advanced, and so Colonel Neale's decision to withdraw from Edo was not regarded as anything more than a temporary measure. There was to be a large two-storied house, overlooking the sea, for the head of post. It would have spacious reception rooms, with lacquered floors and attractive Japanese paper on the walls. Behind the main house was a bungalow for the Japanese (i.e. Japanese-speaking) secretary, and other bungalows were planned for other staff and students. On the south side of the compound were stables for forty horses, with quarters for the legation guard above.[32] To protect the area, as demanded by London, a deep trench would be dug around the whole enclosure, and a wooden palisade erected on its inner side. By the end of 1862, the British legation had made considerable progress, although the French and Dutch legations had scarcely begun.[33]

But even before the building could be occupied, it was burnt down by hostile samurai from Choshu in January 1863. Among the attackers were the future prince and constitutional reformer, Ito Hirobumi, and Inoue Kaoru, later foreign minister. Perhaps, as one of Ito's biographers implied, they were so outraged that foreigners should be allowed to desecrate such a sacred spot, or perhaps an empty building, with apparently only one watchman, provided an easy target. Whichever it was, the point was taken, and the building was abandoned by the British.[34] The French and the Dutch, perhaps thankful that their buildings had not got as far as the British, also abandoned the area, although there was no attempt to attack their buildings. When the foreign envoys again established themselves in Edo, the Gotenyama area, though planned by the Japanese as a diplomatic enclave, was not used.[35]

Sengakuji

For the next two years, the old temple at Tozenji continued to be used on the occasions that the British minister wished to reside in Edo. Without permanent residents, however, the quarters assigned to the British steadily deteriorated. It was also felt, after two attacks, that Tozenji was perhaps not a very safe spot. By the time of Sir Harry Parkes's arrival as minister in 1865, Tozenji was no longer regarded as usable and on his first two visits to the capital, Parkes found himself obliged to stay with the Dutch consul-general.[36]

The *bakufu*, having tried and failed to provide new accommodation at Gotenyama, had up until then refused to do more than offer alternative temple sites in the area of Tozenji. One was at Daichuji, next door to Sengakuji, and for a time letters were dated 'HM Legation Sengakuji'. Daichuji also seems to have been used by the Russians for a time. The British were not there long, and nothing now remains of the temple. Dr Willis, the archivist of the legation, who clearly spent a lot of time there, did not find it very congenial. He was tall, and the relatively low ceilings forced him to walk bent over to get around the passages which connected the various buildings.[37]

Parkes, for his part, who knew at first hand the battle there had been in China to secure the right of residence in the capital, found these temporary arrangements unsatisfactory, but was determined that he should be able to live in Edo. He, together with a large part of his staff, was regularly travelling back and forth to Edo, which was both expensive and time-consuming. As he told Algernon Mitford, his secretary of legation, he intended to stop this, for it was most undignified and anomalous that the British minister could not live in the capital of the country. He therefore persuaded the Japanese government to erect a temporary legation, which seems to have been situated in the grounds of

Sengakuji. The Japanese authorities were willing to do this on condition that the building should be made of relatively simple materials and easy to construct. The result was a new legation building situated in a courtyard in front of the Sengakuji temple, in which the British took up residence early in November 1866.[38]

The new legation was '. . . [a] long, straggling, one-storied building, consisting of two blocks with shorter wings at right angles, containing a number of large and lofty rooms communicating with each other'. In addition, there was a cookhouse and a lavatory, and a house at the gate, where the 9th Regiment of Foot provided a guard. Willis thought that it was a considerable improvement on what had gone before. He particularly liked the fact that the new buildings provided sufficient accommodation for all the staff.[39] To others, however, it was not very satisfactory, even though the cost of the finished buildings was high. The house was mostly of ill-seasoned wood and badly constructed. Mitford noted that the buildings furnished 'a miserable lodging'. Nothing fitted and the stoves either got red-hot and smelt of burning iron, or gave off no heat at all. The wind whistled through 'long passages and chilly rooms', and he rather felt that they would have been better off in the open since they would have at least avoided draughts.[40]

These views found an echo in the opinion of Major Crossman, of the Royal Engineers, who was sent in 1866 by the Foreign Office to examine all British official buildings in China and Japan. In his view, the Edo legation quarters were only suitable for use by bachelors and then only in the summer. He felt that the Japanese authorities had only provided temporary quarters which were likely to need such frequent repair that it would be best to pay rent for it, and to demand that repairs should be the responsibility of the owner. He also suggested certain alterations in order to make the house usable in the winter, but was clearly worried by the risk of fire. Parkes was sensitive to Crossman's criticisms. He pointed out that he had little choice in the matter, but that he had improved both the safety and the total accommodation available by acquiring the use of a small hill, overlooking the legation building, and the temple situated on it, as additional accommodation. Here lived Satow and Mitford, glad to escape from the confines of the official buildings, and technically out of the bounds of the legation area, though unable to escape the attentions of the Japanese guards.[41]

This temple was tiny, 'not much bigger than a doll's house', according to Mitford, but 'pretty and snug'. It was also vulnerable to attack. Mitford, left alone there on one occasion while Satow was in Nagasaki, put cockle-shells on all the walks in the garden. In this way, he hoped to be alerted to any intruder. He was not disappointed, for one night he heard the crunching of the shells and found some five or six attackers in the gardens. A rifle and a revolver helped to persuade them to leave.[42]

Whatever the drawbacks, the collection of buildings which made up the temporary legation was to serve as the British base in Edo until 1874. No wonder that Parkes, writing in 1871, noted that the British legation could be said to be 'hutted' rather than 'housed' in that city.[43]

Yokohama

Although Parkes was determined to establish the right of residence in Edo, for most practical purposes the British legation remained in the treaty port of Yokohama. Strictly speaking, nearby Kanagawa, not Yokohama, was the official treaty port. To the Japanese authorities faced with the influx of foreigners in 1859, however, Kanagawa had seemed too dangerous a place to allow the unrestricted residence of foreigners. It was situated on the Tokaido and seemed likely to bring foreigners and anti-foreign *daimyo* and their samurai into far too dangerous proximity. It also provided few opportunities for controlling foreigners. The Japanese authorities proceeded, therefore, to erect a foreign settlement on the reclaimed land which formed the village of Yokohama. The foreign merchants, offered accommodation with no upset costs, were only too happy to agree to these arrangements. The foreign envoys protested at what they considered a flagrant abuse of the treaties, but to no avail. Yokohama was the foreign settlement by the mid-1860s, even though some foreign missions would date their communications from 'Kanagawa' for the next twenty-five years.[44] (A number of foreign missions, again including the British, also continued to date despatches from 'Yedo' long after the Japanese had changed the name to Tokyo; here, the argument was that 'Yedo' was the name used in the treaties, and that the Japanese had no right to change it without the agreement of the foreign envoys. By the mid 1880s, however, it was clear that the Japanese had no intention of reverting to 'Yedo', and the use of Tokyo was gradually introduced, even among the conservative British.)

Whatever the theory, in practice, foreign envoys who felt compelled to leave Edo set up their establishments in Yokohama and the British were no exception. Captain Neale rented two houses in Yokohama in 1862 to serve as a temporary legation after the withdrawal from Edo; these two houses had, it seems been used in earlier days as temporary accommodation for the legation.[45] One of these buildings, according to Ernest Satow, who arrived in Japan as a student interpreter in 1862, occupied the site later occupied by the Grand hotel, known as No. 20 Yokohama. It was a rambling building, mostly used for offices, but also occasionally for living quarters, and here Satow lived for a time on his arrival. Mitford, too, in his early days in Japan, was lodged in the legation building, which he described as '. . . a rather rickety but comfortable bungalow on the bund'.[46] However rickety the building, it must have been reasonably large, for both Alcock and Winchester, chargé d'affaires after Alcock's final departure from Japan, managed to give large parties on occasions such as the Queen's birthday, with music supplied by the band of the British garrison.[47]

Other houses were rented in the town to provide additional accommodation and offices. By 1866, Satow, Mitford, Willis and Siebold all lived in small Japanese houses on the edge of the Japanese town rather than in the settlement itself. That same year, Parkes, dissatisfied with the accommodation available for him and his family, rented one house as his residence and another as a residence for the secretary of legation, who also had a family with him. These additions doubled the cost of renting the various buildings, to Mexican $12,320 a year. Parkes, feeling it necessary to defend this expenditure under the examining eye of Major Crossman, argued that while the rents were high, they were '. . . not in excess of the ordinary rates of Yokohama and the houses were by no means of a superior description'.[48] Several of the rented buildings, including the small Japanese houses, were swept away in the great fire which broke out in Yokohama on 26 November 1866. Much of the Japanese town and about one-third of the foreign settlement were destroyed, together with much loss of life. The British consulate was also destroyed. The legation building on the bund was spared, only to be destroyed in another fire in late November 1867. On this occasion, Parkes lost everything. Underinsured, he found that he had but '. . . four or five thousand dollars to replace property worth more than double that amount', which had to be replaced immediately. A couple of years later, Parkes reported to his wife, then back in England, heavy rains damaged various legation houses at Yokohama, including the residence. Three bathing tubs had to be placed in the drawing-room to catch the water flowing from Lady Parkes' bedroom on that occasion.[49]

Even before the fires, however, Parkes had decided that there was a need for a more substantial establishment at Yokohama. Although he remained determined to establish himself and his staff in Edo, he still felt that 'Japanese shortcomings' meant that they might be required to live at Yokohama from time to time. He therefore began a battle – one feels that most things with Parkes were a battle! – to persuade the Japanese authorities that it was their duty to '. . . erect at Yokohama a range of buildings sufficient for the accommodation of the whole Legation at a cost not to exceed sixty thousand dollars, and to let these buildings to the British Government for such time as the latter might require, at a rental of ten percent upon the outlay'. The buildings to be provided would be on the hill to the south of the existing settlement, known as the Bluff. They were to be built to foreign specifications and Parkes undertook to supply the plans himself.

Parkes's scheme envisaged a considerable complex of building, although as he pointed out, this would provide accommodation and offices for all staff at half the cost of the buildings previously rented. There were to be houses for the minister, the secretary of legation and for two married assistants, or for one married and three unmarried assistants. By the time Major Crossman arrived in Yokohama in the autumn of 1866, plans had been drawn up for these buildings by an American architect, Mr Bridgens – later to design Shimbashi station[50] – and work had begun on the minister's residence. In addition, although the plans were not ready, Parkes intended to add accommodation for an officer and twenty men of the 9th Regiment of Foot, who provided the legation guard, another building for the captain and eight men who made up the minister's escort, and stables and other outhouses. Crossman modified the plans for the minister's house, and made various suggestions for economies – the legation guard, for example, could be housed at the British camp, some ten minutes walk away. Parkes bridled somewhat at what he saw as criticism of his arrangements, but accepted most of Crossman's proposals. In the end, two houses were built, providing accommodation for the minister and for other staff and their families, together with reception rooms and offices. They were ready for occupation by midsummer 1867. The only people to miss out in these arrangements were the student interpreters, for whom no accommodation was provided at Yokohama. Parkes noted that they would probably be able to learn more in Edo anyway.[51]

The completed buildings were handsome and much admired. They featured in a splendid *ukiyo-e* by the second Hiroshige, which appeared in 1869 (see cover). In front of the two houses, is an attractive Japanese-style garden. In the foreground a white-coated military band and a group of red-coated soldiers and their officers march by, watched by a Japanese couple and child, a European lady with two children and two Chinese men. The union flag flies over all from an enormous flag staff. The buildings also featured in two photographs in John Reddie Black's *Far East*, in 1870 and 1873.[52]

But as the *Far East* noted as early as 1870[53], the Yokohama legation was underused, and work was more and more concentrated at Tokyo. The secretary of legation's house was rarely occupied by that officer, who spent most of his time in Tokyo, and there was some talk of making it available for Sir Edmund Hornby, the chief justice of the British court for China and Japan. (Crossman had opposed an earlier plan to build a bungalow at Yokohama for Hornby, on the grounds that it would at best be used only for three months in the year.) The students lived in Tokyo. The minister expected to go there several times a week, which involved much riding. The accommodation was growing more and more unsatisfactory and dangerous to health. By 1871, Parkes was adamant that for all possible reasons, it was time to move from Yokohama to Tokyo.[54]

Notes

1 Edward Seidensticker, *Low City, High City: Tokyo from Edo to the Earthquake: how the shogun's ancient capital became a great modern city, 1867–1923*, (London: Allen Lane, 1983), pp. 232–33, 235.

2 Sir Hugh Cortazzi, 'The First British Legation in Japan (1859–1874)', *The Japan Society of London Bulletin*, No. 102, (October 1984), p. 49. This was not the first use of the term, which seems to have crept in when Sir John Pilcher was ambassador.

3 Dallas Finn, *Meiji Revisited: The Sites of Victorian Japan* (New York and Tokyo: Weatherhill, 1995). Oddly enough, however, Finn does give an account of the British consulate-general at Yokohama, although this, too, was destroyed in 1923 and rebuilt in the late 1920s.

4 Much of the following account is based on Cortazzi, 'The First British Legation in Japan (1859–1874)', and Kawaseki Seiro, 'Edo ni atta gaikoku kokan' (Foreign missions in Edo), *Gaimusho choso geppo*, 1987 / No. 1, pp. 45–59. I visited Tozenji in January 1996.

5 For traditional East Asian diplomacy as it applied in the Japanese context, see Ronald P. Toby, *State and Diplomacy in Early Modern Japan* (Stanford, CA: Princeton, NJ: Princeton University Press, 1984; reprinted Stanford, CA: Stanford University Press, 1991, and W. G. Beasley, *Japan Encounters the Barbarians: Japanese Travellers in America and Europe* (New Haven, Conn., and London: Yale University Press, 1995), Chapter One.

6 W. G. Beasley, *Great Britain and the Opening of Japan* (London: Luzac and Co., 1951), pp. 87–144; reprinted Sandgate, Folkestone: Japan Library 1995.

7 William L. Neumann, *America encounters Japan: From Perry to MacArthur* (Baltimore, MD: The Johns Hopkins Press, 1963), pp. 83–84.

8 Laurence Oliphant, *Narrative of the Earl of Elgin's Mission to China and Japan in the years 1857, '58 and '59* (New York: Harper Brothers, 1860), p. 356; Beasley, *Opening of Japan*, p. 188–191. For an example of Japanese objections and the text of Harris's treaty, see W. G. Beasley, translator and editor, *Select Documents on Japanese Foreign Policy 1853–1868* (London, New York and Toronto: Oxford University Press, 1955), pp. 170–72; 183–189.

9 Beasley, *Opening of Japan*, p. 192.

10 Alexander Michie, *The Englishman in China during the Victorian Era* (Edinburgh and London: William Blackwood and Sons, 1900), II, 14. For the background to this issue, see J. E. Hoare, 'Britain's Japan Consular Service', in Ian Nish, editor, *Britain and Japan: Biographical Portraits* vol. II, (Richmond, Surrey: Japan Library, 1997), pp. 94–106.

11 For the passion which Alcock can still arouse, see John McMaster, *Sabotaging the Shogun: Western Diplomats open Japan 1859–69* (New York: Vantage Press, 1992), passim., and Hugh Cortazzi, 'Sir Rutherford Alcock, the First British Minister to Japan 1859–1864: A Reassessment', *Transactions of the Asiatic Society of Japan*, Fourth Series, Vol. 9 (1994), pp. 1–42.

12 Ernest Satow, *A Diplomat in Japan: An inner history of the critical years of the evolution of Japan* (London: Seeley Service, 1921, reprinted Tokyo and Rutland Vt: Charles E. Tuttle Co., 1983), p. 63

13 Oliphant, *Narrative*, pp. 374–375.

14 FO46/3, Alcock to Malmesbury, no. 3, 9 July 1859. See also his published account of the temple in Rutherford Alcock, *The Capital of the Tycoon* (London: Longman, Green, Longman, Roberts and Green, 1863), I, 102–106.

15 There is a fine picture of the viewing platform, now long gone, in Kawaseki, 'Edo ni atta gaikoku kokan' p. 47.

16 George Smith, *Ten Weeks in Japan* (London: Longman, Green, Longman and Roberts, 1861), pp. 280–285; Cortazzi, 'First British Legation', pp. 26–27. The well-known photographer, Felix Beato, took some pictures of the temple entrance and grounds, probably in 1862. See Rijkisuniversiteit Leiden, *Herrinnergen aan Japan, 1850–1870 – Yomigaeru Bakumatsu – Foto's en Fotoalbum in Nederland Bezit* ('s-Gravenhage: Staatsuitgeverij, 1987), pp. 182–83, 200; Yokohama kaiko shiryokan/Yokohama Archives of History, *F. Beato Bakumatsu Nihon Shashinshu* ('Collection of Felix Beato's photographs from the Bakumatsu period') (Yokohama: Yokohama shiryo kaikan, 1988), p. 108.

17 Cortazzi, 'First British Legation', p. 27; Philip Henderson, *The Life of Laurence Oliphant: Traveller, Diplomat and Mystic* (London: Robert Hale Ltd, 1956), pp. 97–98. For a brief sketch of Oliphant's life, see Carmen Blacker, 'Laurence Oliphant and Japan, 1858–88', in Nish, *Biographical Portraits*, II, 35–47.

18 C. Pemberton Hodgson, *A Residence at Nagasaki and Hakodate in 1859–1860* (London: Richard Bentley, 1861), pp. 80–81. Hodgson, however, also liked the garden – see p. 76.

19 Satow, *Diplomat in Japan*, p. 64.

20 See the description of Harris's guards at Shimoda, in McMaster, *Sabotaging the Shogun*, p. 11.

21 See the lists of such attacks in Michie, *Englishman in China*, vol. II, pp. 34–36 and Satow, *Diplomat in Japan*, pp. 46–47.

22 McMaster, *Sabotaging the Shogun*, pp. 46–47.

23 McMaster, *Sabotaging the Shogun*, pp. 48–49.

24 There are many accounts of the attack. This is largely based on Henderson, *Laurence Oliphant*, pp. 1–4, which in turn draws heavily on Wirgman's account in the *Illustrated London News*, 12 October 1861; see also *The Times* 3 October 1861. For Wirgman, see John Clark, 'Charles Wirgman, (1835–1891), in Sir Hugh Cortazzi and Gordon Daniels, editors, *Britain and Japan: Themes and Personalities* (London and New York: Routledge, 1991), pp. 54–63.

25 Cortazzi, 'First British Legation', pp. 32–34.

26 Henderson, *Laurence Oliphant*, pp. 99–102.

27 Confidential Memorandum by Rutherford Alcock, 14 February 1862, in Beasley, *Select Documents*, pp. 211–16.

28 Satow, *Diplomat in Japan*, pp. 29–30; McMaster, *Sabotaging the Shogun*, p. 64.

29 Hugh Cortazzi, *Dr. Willis in Japan: British Medical Pioneer 1862–1877*, (London and Dover, New Hampshire: The Athlone Press, 1985), pp. 22–28.

30 Cortazzi, *Dr. Willis*, p. 27.

31 Edward Seidensticker, *Low City, High City: Tokyo from Edo to the Earthquake: how the shogun's ancient capital became a great modern city, 1867–1923* (London: Allen Lane, 1983) p. 129; Satow, *Diplomat in Japan*, p. 65.

32 A copy of a plan of the proposed legation, based on the original in the Tokyo University historical archives, was reproduced in the Yokohama Archives of History's 1986 exhibition about the life of Ernest Satow. See Yokohama shiryokaikan, 'Ernest Satow Exhibition File', Vol. 1. See also FO46/29, Memorandum by Sir Rutherford Alcock, 7 November 1862.

33 Satow, *Diplomat in Japan*, pp. 64–66.

34 Kengi Hamada, *Prince Ito* (London: George Allen and Unwin Ltd, 1936), pp. 28–29. Ito's own account can be found in *Ito Hirobumi den* (Biography of Ito Hirobumi), (Tokyo: Sumpoko Tsuishikokai, 1940), I, pp. 70–71.

35 Seidensticker, *Low City, High City*, p. 12.

36 Parliamentary Papers, House of Commons, 1867–68, vol. xlviii, pp. 373–403 (315), *Reports from Major Crossman and correspondence respecting the Legation and Consular Buildings in China and Japan* (cited as Crossman, *Report*), 'Remarks', by Sir Harry Parkes.

37 Cortazzi, 'First British Legation', p. 46; Cortazzi, *Dr. Willis in Japan*, p. 70.

38 Lord Redesdale (A. B. Mitford), *Memories* (London: Macmillan 1915), I, 383; Grace Fox, *Britain and Japan 1858–1883* (Oxford: Clarendon Press, 1969), p. 190.

39 Cortazzi, *Dr. Willis in Japan*, p. 74.

40 Redesdale, *Memories*, I, 383; this was, of course, not Mitford's first complaint about draughty legations! See above, p. 21.

41 Crossman *Report*; Redesdale, *Memories*, I, 384–85.

42 Redesdale, *Memories*, II, 411–415, 471.

43 Records of the Office of Works (cited as Works) 10–35/1, Part 1, E. Hammond, Foreign Office to Office of Works, 20 November 1871, enclosing Parkes, 'Memorandum on Legation and Consular Buildings in Japan', 18 November 1871.

44 J. E. Hoare, *Japan's Treaty Ports and Foreign Settlements: The Uninvited Guests 1858–1899* (Sandgate, Folkestone: The Japan Library, 1994), pp. 6–7.

45 Cortazzi, 'First British Legation', p. 39.

46 Satow, *Diplomat in Japan*, pp. 29, 56; Redesdale, *Memories*, I, p. 375. A picture of it appeared in *Illustrated London News*, 29 October 1864.

47 Hugh Cortazzi, *Victorians in Japan: In and around the Treaty Ports* (London and Atlantic Highlands, NJ: Athlone Press, 1987), p. 76.

48 Crossman *Report*, remarks by Sir H. Parkes.

49 For accounts of the great fire at Yokohama, see *Illustrated London News*, 9 February 1867, which also has an engraving showing the fire, and J. R. Black, *Young Japan: A narrative of the settlement and the city, from the signing of the treaties in 1859 to the close of the year 1879* (Yokohama: Kelly and Walsh; London: Trubner and Co., 1880–81), II, 17–26. Parkes described his losses in a letter to Marcus Flowers at Edo on 1 December 1867, in Dickins and Lane-Poole, *Parkes*, II, 78, and the flooding of 1869 in a letter to his wife of 20 August 1869, in Dickins and Lane-Poole, *Parkes*, II, 122–23.

50 Finn, *Meiji Revisited*, pp. 18, 46.

51 Crossman *Report*, Crossman's notes and remarks by Sir Harry Parkes.

52 T. Tamba, *Meiji tenno to Meiji jidai* ('The Meiji emperor and the Meiji period'), (Tokyo: Asahi Shimbun, 1966), p. 82; *Far East*, vol. I, no. 5, August 1870 (full view of both houses), and vol. IV, no. 2, August 1873 (rear view of the minister's residence, showing the gardens.)

53 *Far East*, vol. 1, no. 5, August 1870.

54 Works 10–35/1, Part 1, E Hammond, Foreign Office to Office of Works, 20 November 1871, enclosing Parkes, 'Memorandum on Legation and Consular Buildings in Japan', 18 November 1871.

Japan

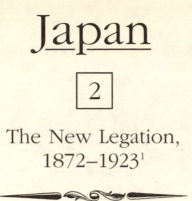

The New Legation, 1872–1923[1]

I n May 1872, in the absence of Sir Harry Parkes on leave, the chargé
d'affaires, F. O. Adams, signed the lease for a plot of land outside the
Hanzomon gate in Kojimachi in Tokyo. Parkes had been searching for a
site for the British legation in the city proper since at least 1867, although
the disturbed state of the city at the time of the Restoration meant that little
was done about the project between 1868 and 1871. (It also meant that all
Parkes's diplomatic colleagues had moved to Yokohama – perhaps by
moving back to Tokyo quickly, he hoped to get ahead of them?) In the
spring of 1871, he found what he had been looking for, close to what had
now become the Imperial Palace in Tokyo. As he explained in a
memorandum drawn up in November 1871, while he was home on leave,
rather than lose this site he had undertaken to lease it, even though he did
not have Treasury approval.[2]

He also provided a description of the site, prepared in May 1871 by Mr
Boyce, the assistant surveyor at Shanghai, which perhaps showed less
enthusiasm than Sir Harry, but nevertheless indicated that the site would
do. Boyce noted that it was close to the '. . . official offices and residences
of the Native Government' and to the palace. He assured his readers that
Parkes's only motive for selecting the site was on public grounds, '. . . for
this site except that it is high and dry possesses none of the natural
advantages that made the site on the Tokaido so desirable for private
residences'. But the rental asked, at Mexican $5 per 100 *tsubo*, giving a total
rent of Mexican $900 or £200 a year was fair and, he said, reflected the
usual rate. (Parkes noted that this was 'Not the usual rate, but an unusually
modest one in Japan'.) Finally, on the assumption that Parkes's actions
would be approved by the Treasury, he had begun drawing up plans for
the buildings, and was '. . . happy to say that they have one and all
received the approval of the Minister and officers more immediately
concerned'.[3]

The temporary lease which Mr Adams signed in 1872, and which replaced Sir Harry Parkes's 1871 'option', was in turn to be replaced by a permanent one in 1884. The lease made just over 10,833 *tsubo* of land available for the legation (one *tsubo* equals 3.96 square yards, so the total area was some 42,898.68 square yards) '. . . and for no further use free of any charge whatsoever except the rent'. The rent was to be six silver yen – the yen now having replaced the Mexican dollar as the general currency in use among foreigners in Japan – per 100 *tsubo*, which gave a total of yen 652.32, or some £200, payable on 1 July each year. The lease also contained a clause, never invoked, which allowed for the reversal of the land to the Japanese government should it ever be needed '. . . for the purpose of defence against a foreign or a domestic enemy'. This seems to be the origin of the story that the Japanese government retained the right to station troops in the legation if required.[4]

Boyce's preliminary drawings of May 1871 proved acceptable in London, and the plans were finalized by November 1871, again with Parkes's involvement. Parkes's main wish for his own house was that it should have a veranda on the north side, and that there should be a tower attached to the house. This would serve 'as a cool retreat on summer evenings', and equally important, as a lookout point over the city. Boyce was of the opinion that the proposed two-storey house for the minister, built with bricks and bounded with hoop iron, would be well able to withstand '. . . the slight shocks of earthquake occasionally felt', since the palace gates and walls nearby had evidently done so for a long time. The estimated building cost was £8, 000 for the minister's house, and a further £18, 000 for the other buildings. These would include the chancery or office building, single-storied residences for the secretary of legation, the Japanese secretary, a doctor, the interpreter (the assistant Japanese secretary), accommodation for the students and the escort, and outhouses, stables and all the other requirements of such a compound.[5] With slight modifications, and the instruction to adhere to 'the strictest regard to economy' – the use of local wood, for example, and wood instead of iron for verandas – these plans were approved. There was also sanction for Parkes's tower. This would carry a flag, and could 'serve as a general lookout in case of emergency'.[6] The flagpole and its flag on top of the tower, and its post-1923 successor, have always been clearly visible from the Imperial Palace; Mrs Fraser claimed that for this reason, the flagpole on the tower was never used, and was moved elsewhere in the compound. Nothing in the archives indicates that the Japanese ever formally raised the issue, in Sir Harry Parkes' day or after, but apparently the Ministry of Foreign Affairs may have contemplated doing so in the 1960s.[7]

To return to the building. Work should have begun in the spring of 1872. Boyce was detained in Shanghai, however, and when he returned to Tokyo in August 1872, he found the site quite unready for building. Brushwood and weeds covered it, and these had to be cleared before any work could begin. He was also concerned about finding suitable contractors. He wrote to London:

1

'Legation Court at Leong-Koong-Fu' 1861. From: D. F. Rennie, *Peking and the Pekingese during the first year of the British Embassy in Peking* 2 vols., (London: John Murray, 1865).

2

Beijing legation under snow, 1899. Photographed by George W. W. Pearson. Reproduced courtesy of the Public Record Office, Kew, ref. Copy 1/495

Beijing c. 1902. Lady Susan Townley leans on a lion, while her dogs watch. From Lady Susan
Townley, *My Chinese Notebook* (London: Methuen and Co., 1904)

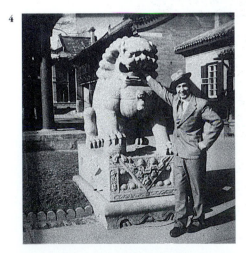

And Harry Lester does the same some 50 years
later. Reproduced courtesy of Tom Sharp, London

■ C H I N A ■

Beijing c. 1895. Looking towards the main gate, on a quiet winter's day. Photographed by George W. W. Pearson. Reproduced courtesy of the Public Record Office, Kew, ref. Copy 1/495

Beijing c. 1902. A busier scene, as sedan chairs leave through the main gate, watched by the mounted guard. From: Lady Susan Townley, *My Chinese Notebook* (London: Methuen and Co., 1904)

The Beijing embassy side gate c. 1937, with the 'Lest We Forget' Wall (see pp. 48, 68). Reproduced courtesy of Mrs Margaret McCallum, Liverpool

■ C H I N A ■

8

Beijing main gate, outside view from across the Imperial Canal (see pp. 19–20), at the end of the siege August 1900 – note the sandbags. Reproduced courtesy of the Peabody Essex Museum, Salem, MA

9

Today, the gate is recognizable, but the Royal Arms have gone, and security equipment shop occupies the front. The compound behind houses the Ministry of Public Security. Photographed by Michael Preston, summer 1998. Reproduced with permission.

■ C H I N A ■

10 Siege 1900: sandbagged verandas. Reproduced from an album held in the British embassy, Beijing

11 Siege 1900: manning a gun. Reproduced from an album held in the British embassy, Beijing

12 Siege 1900: reinforcing the outer wall. Reproduced from an album held in the British embassy, Beijing

13 Siege 1900: the temporary graveyard. Reproduced from an album held in the British embassy, Beijing

14 Siege 1900: badly damaged student quarters. Reproduced courtesy of the Peabody Essex Museum, Salem, MA

15

16

17

18

19

20

21

15 Registry stool and desk. 1920s. Reproduced from HBM Office of Works Beijing ordering catalogue formerly in the British embassy Beijing.

16 Office arm chair, 1920s. Reproduced from HBM Office of Works Beijing ordering catalogue formerly in the British embassy Beijing.

17 Beijing 1991: the lectern in the offices, a link with 1900 (see pp. 48, 71, 76, 86). Photograph by J. E. Hoare

18 Beijing 1937: a small member of the British community sits, with sola topee, between the Boxer cannons, later sold off in the 1959 Great Leap Forward (see p. 76). Reproduced courtesy of Mrs Margaret McCallum, Liverpool

19 Beijing 1950s: third secretary Douglas Hurd (later Secretary of State for Foreign and Commonwealth Affairs, and now (1999) the Rt Hon Lord Hurd of Westwell CH CBE PC, author of the foreword to this book), and colleagues at the Great Wall. Reproduced courtesy of Tom Sharp.

20/21 New Beijing 1991: the residence from the gardens and the offices. Photographs by J. E. Hoare

1 Entrance to Tozenji temple, site of Britain's first legation in Japan c. 1860. Courtesy of the Japan Times

2 Tozenji today. Photograph by J. E. Hoare, 1996

3 Sir Rutherford Alcock (1809–97), Britain's first minister to Japan, and later minister to China.

4

5

4 British legation Yokohama c. 1867 (Compare Hiroshige print on the dust jacket). Photograph reproduced courtesy of Yokohama Archives of History

5 Sir Harry Smith Parkes (1828–85), British minister to Japan (1865–83), to Beijing (1883–85), and to Seoul (1884–85).

6 Tokyo: British embassy, c. 1905. Baroness Albert D'Anethan, Fourteen Years of Diplomatic Life in Japan, (London: Stanley Paul and Co., 1912)

6

■ J A P A N ■

Tokyo minister and staff early 1870s: Sir Harry Parkes in front row, second from left, seated. Lady Parkes ('Fanny'), seated fourth from left, Ernest Satow, third from left standing, with tall bowler hat. Photograph reproduced courtesy of Library and Records Department, Foreign and Commonwealth Office

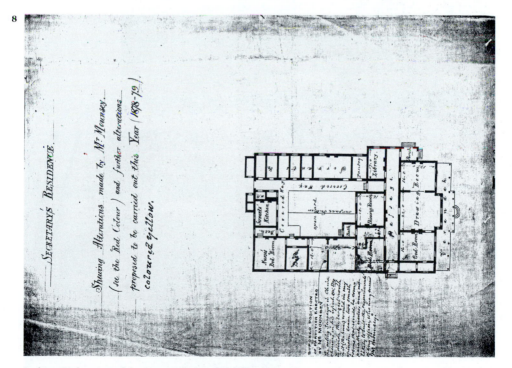

Architect's drawing of the house of secretary of legation (the second in command), as modified in the late 1870s. From Works 10–35/1, Part 4. Reproduced courtesy of the Public Record Office, Kew

9

10

11

9 'The Minister at Chuzenji'. From Osman Edwards, *Residential Rhymes* (Tokyo: T. Hasegawa, n.d. [1900]) Reproduced courtesy of the library of the School of Oriental and African Studies, London

10 Chuzenji in the 1930s. From Sir Robert Craigie, *Behind the Japanese Mask* (London: Hutchinson and Co. Ltd, 1945).

11 Chuzenji today. Photograph courtesy of Sir John Boyd

12 The ruined residence 1923. From Works 10/641. Reproduced courtesy of the Public Record Office, Kew

13 The new gateway 1931. From Works 10/641. Reproduced courtesy of the Public Record Office, Kew

14 The completed residence 1931. From Works 10/641. Reproduced courtesy of the Public Record Office, Kew

15 Sir Robert Lindley in his new study 1931. From Works 10/641. Reproduced courtesy of the Public Record Office, Kew

■ JAPAN ■

16 Sir Robert and Lady Craigie, and embassy staff during internment 1942. (Compare numbers with no. 7) From Sir Robert Craigie, *Behind the Japanese Mask* (London: Hutchinson and Co. Ltd, 1945)

17 Long-serving member of the residence staff, Yonebashi Shinichi, photographed in 1967 (see page 153). Photograph courtesy of C. E. Ripley

18 Sir Oscar Morland, with Col. John Figgess, military attaché, behind his right shoulder and Vere Redman, information counsellor, to the left of the representative of the Japanese Imperial Household Agency, prepares to present his credentials, 1959. Photograph courtesy of C. E. Ripley

19 Mr Adachi, long-serving butler at the Tokyo residence poses with his wife in front of the portrait of HM The Queen, at his retirement party, 1995. Photograph courtesy of Sir John Boyd

20 HM Ambassador, Sir John Boyd, greets TRH Prince and Princess Takamada arriving for an embassy ball, 1995. Photograph courtesy of Sir John Boyd

1

Seoul, the original buildings. Walter Hillier collection, reproduced by courtesy of Michael Hillier.

2

Walter Hillier, consul-general Seoul, with diplomatic colleagues, late 1880s. Walter Hillier collection, reproduced by courtesy of Michael Hillier.

3 The consul-general sets out on a call, c. 1890. From A. E. J. Cavendish, *Korea and the Sacred White Mountain, being a brief account of a journey in Korea in 1891,* (London: G Philip and Son, 1894)

4 The new buildings under construction c. 1890. A Chinese labourer watches the camera. - Walter Hillier collection, reproduced by courtesy of Michael Hillier.

5 Copy of the foundation stone, laid by Mrs Hillier on 19 July 1890, replacing the much damaged original, now preserved inside the residence. Photograph by J. E. Hoare

6 The residence completed 1892. Walter Hillier collection, reproduced by courtesy of Michael Hillier.

THIS STONE WAS LAID
BY
M^{RS.} WALTER C. HILLIER
ON TH 19 DAY OF JULY 1890
BEING THE   YEAR OF THE REIGN OF
HER   GRACIOUS MAJESTY
QUEEN VICTORIA
TH   YE R OF KUANG HSÜ
AND
THE 499 OF THE COREAN ERA

7 Relaxing in the grounds, 1890s. William Ker (see pages 182, 183), nearest the steps. Walter Hillier collection, reproduced by courtesy of Michael Hillier.

8 In the grounds, 1890s. Bishop Corfe (see pp. 186, 187), Walter Hillier (second from right), and two naval officers. Walter Hillier collection, reproduced by courtesy of Michael Hillier.

9 Seoul's foreign diplomatic and missionary ladies, c. 1890. Mrs Hillier in the centre. Walter Hillier collection, reproduced by courtesy of Michael Hillier.

10 William Ker as a young man. Courtesy of Kate Ker

11 Arthur Hyde Lay, consul-general Seoul 1914–27 (see p. 193n). From A. C. Hyde Lay, *Four generations in China, Japan and Korea* (Edinburgh and London: Oliver & Boyd, 1952)

12 The legation guard c. 1905. From A. C. Hyde Lay, *Four generations in China, Japan and Korea* (Edinburgh and London: Oliver & Boyd, 1952)

■ KOREA ■

15

13 The Seoul British community on St George's Day 1939, in the grounds of the bishop's palace. Acting consul-general Arthur de la Mare first on left at the back. Courtesy of Miss A. J. Roberts OBE

14 Ambassador to Tokyo Sir John Tilley in Seoul in 1929, with the third Anglican bishop of Korea, Mark Trollope, and Oswald White, consul-general Seoul 1927–31. From a contemporary newspaper, courtesy of Miss A. J. Roberts OBE

15 Ambassador Jeffrey Petersen together with embassy staff and contractors at the ground-breaking ceremony for the new office buildings in 1974. From an album in the British embassy Seoul

16 Ambassador Nicholas Spreckley presents his credentials to President Chun Doo Hwan, May 1983. The author is first on the left of the picture. Photograph courtesy of the Blue House (Presidential Palace), Republic of Korea

17 New entrance gate c. 1974. From an album in the British embassy Seoul

18 The number two house (foreground) and the residence, from the office building, winter 1984. Photograph by J. E. Hoare

19 The new offices, 1992. Photograph by Mrs Y. S. Park, information section, British embassy Seoul

I will endeavour to enter into contract for all works that admit it, but at present, except for one or two foreigners who only take contracts to make fifty or one hundred per cent out of them, and give a great deal of trouble into the bargain, I do not know a single contractor for such work as the Minister's house but will try.[8]

Boyce loyally did not admit that he now had another problem, for his attempts to push on with the work were being hampered from a new quarter. R. G. Watson, who had replaced Adams as chargé when the latter had a nervous collapse, was beginning to have doubts about the project. In July 1872, he wrote privately to the permanent under secretary in London, E. Hammond, suggesting that there should be no further work on the proposed legation site since circumstances had changed since Parkes had gone on leave. Before Parkes's departure, it had taken three to four hours riding to get to Tokyo from Yokohama. Now that the railway between the two cities was functioning, it was but an hour door-to-door from the Yokohama residence to the offices in Tokyo. He felt that the chancery and the language students should stay in Tokyo, but the residence could remain in Yokohama, because

. . . Yokohama . . . must always be a more attractive place for a lady; and I am convinced that were the Legation house here given up, the Minister would have to hire one here on his own account, for the community, who are numerous and hospitable, would be very ill content to see the English representative take up his abode elsewhere.

A few days later, Watson also argued that there was no need to supply accommodation for the escort, since Japan was now much safer following the disarming of the samurai. He added that despite the provision on the plan for a house for the Japanese secretary, the current holder of that position, Ernest Satow, would prefer to live off the compound. Satow argued that Tokyo was now a much safer city and that it was better for his job if he did not live with his colleagues, since many Japanese would hesitate to call upon him if he lived in a foreign enclave. (It may also have been that Satow, who was living with a Japanese woman by whom he had two sons, preferred to conduct his private life away from the eagle eyes of Sir Harry Parkes.) Finally, Watson gave it as his general opinion that Japan would never amount to much, and there would be a falling demand for staff accommodation.[9]

Parkes, asked to comment in London on these documents, was adamant that considerations such as the wishes of ladies or the British community at Yokohama should not interfere with the far more important principle that the British minister should be established in the capital of the country, with the staff of the legation gathered in one place. This was also more economical. Neither was he impressed by Satow's wish to live off the compound. He pointed out that Satow had had ample opportunity to express his views earlier and had made no objection to the proposal that he should have a house on the compound. In any case, even if Satow did not want the house, his successor might. Parkes suggested that three members of staff, Satow, his assistant, W. G. Aston, and the vice-consul/chancelier, Martin Dohmen, should be asked to see if they could find suitable housing off the compound and to report to him on his return to Japan. It was eventually decide to postpone work on the escorts' quarters until Parkes returned, but everything else should go ahead.[10]

Parkes returned to Japan early in 1873. The result of the trawl of officers about living off the compound was that it was agreed that Satow could do so, and would receive a rent allowance in lieu of accommodation. To his earlier arguments, Satow added that the house proposed for him was really only suitable for a single man '. . . as it has only four habitable rooms, the fifth being more of the nature of a large cupboard'.[11] The other two had claimed to be unable to find suitable housing and, in any case, preferred to live in a Western-style house. However, one of the diplomatic service officers, Mr Laurence, had also expressed the wish to live off the compound, thus freeing his house for Aston, while Dohmen could be accommodated in the modified student quarters. Parkes argued that there was still a clear need for the escort. Not only had the men concerned signed new five-year contracts in 1872, but they might still be needed as before, as the head of post's personal escort – the dangerous times might not yet be over – and they could perform useful messenger and other tasks for the legation.[12] (In the event, the escort lasted until the 1890s, and its last commander, Inspector Peter Peacock, MVO, formerly of the London Metropolitan Police, died in 1906 aged 67, still working for the embassy, though in later years as a clerical officer. Another former member, George Hodges, who had joined with Peacock in 1867 was also a long-time employee of the embassy, and died in 1916.[13])

Work began in March 1873. In August, Boyce reported that it was still going ahead on some parts of the site, although not on the houses of the Japanese secretary or the assistant Japanese secretary. He had modified the proposed student quarters to provide accommodation for the vice-consul. But he was unhappy about the rate of progress. All his calculations were thrown into disarray by the '. . . unreliable and worthless character of the natives, from the principle man downwards and there is practically no redress for breach of contract'. By October 1873, he was somewhat more optimistic. He now had two of his Shanghai staff supervising the works, Mr Bennett acting as clerk of works on the southern side, while Mr Hooper concentrated on 'the Minister's house and other buildings of importance'. He hoped therefore, that '. . . the Chancery, Vice Consul's residence and the students' quarters will be ready for occupation by the close of the present financial year'.[14]

Whether Boyce kept to his timetable is not clear, but work continued during 1874. Then one small cloud appeared on the horizon. Although Parkes had been closely associated with the designs of all the buildings, including his own house, he now suggested that the new residence might be better if an additional 'pavilion' or ballroom were attached to the drawing-room. Boyce agreed, and asked for the extra £200 which would be required to be included in the estimates for 1875–76. He also asked for more funds for a general storage building, trees and shrubs for the compound and money for the internal roads.[15] He received funds for the latter works, but the Treasury refused to supply funds for a ballroom. None of those concerned knew that a long saga was about to begin.

The new legation was largely occupied by January 1875, although Parkes's family remained at Yokohama for a little longer. Then on 3 April 1875, the *Japan Mail* reported the end of the Yokohama legation:

> The transfer of H B M Legation from Yokohama to Yedo [foreigners were still reluctant to use the new name for the capital] took place today, and the buildings on the Bluff were formally handed over to the Japanese authorities. The departure of Sir Harry and Lady Parkes is a source of deep regret to the foreign residents of Yokohama, and many pleasant memories of hospitalities and kindnesses will long cling to the old and now desolate mansion.[16]

Most of the buildings of the old legation had in fact been given up to the Japanese by early 1871, and the only building which now passed back to their control was the minister's residence. What happened to the buildings subsequently, or how long they survived, is not clear, and all trace of the Yokohama legation has long disappeared. Henceforward, Tokyo was the site of the British legation.

Despite the confident tone of the *Japan Mail*, however, the compound was not completed and Parkes does not seem to have taken up residence in his new house in April 1875. And of those who did, most had complaints. Indeed, when Mr Boyce wrote to London in July 1875, he had to list a catalogue of such complaints and a list of changes which had been necessary to overcome them. The fact that Parkes and his colleagues had all been involved in the drawing up of the earlier plans proved to be no protection against either changes of mind or changes of staff.

The most complex of the changes involved the house of the secretary of legation, the number two in the legation. Boyce wrote that he had been assured by 'H. M. Chargé' – it is not clear whether this was Adams or Watson – that there would never be a married secretary of legation in Japan. Then there arrived F. R. Plunkett, who was indeed married. Plunkett's house was similar to that to which Satow had objected. It was single storey, with a drawing-room, dining-room and three bedrooms, one quite small, a kitchen and various servants quarters, with a large open yard to the rear. Water came from a well in the garden. This house Plunkett refused to accept unless it was adapted to include an additional bedroom, a wine cellar, storeroom and quarters for European servants, work which Boyce seems to have carried out. He had also been forced to modify the rooms prepared for the vice-consul, who had wanted his own yard apart from that of the students and a room for 'native servants'. The escort men, too, sought modifications to their quarters so that they might have individual kitchens rather than being compelled to mess together.

Parkes was also dissatisfied with his house. Some problems were minor. Boyce noted that '. . . The Minister's residence is ready for occupation but his Excellency requires a better description of wallpaper than I can provide for his principal rooms', and therefore he had asked Parkes to find his own. But that was not all. Parkes wanted extra servants' quarters, and he also required '. . . water tanks, force pumps and water closet apparatus to be introduced throughout his house'. Boyce, therefore, sought financial sanction for the changes for both houses. It must have been forthcoming for at least some of them, for we hear no more of Plunkett's house, though a plan shows the modifications introduced, and Parkes and his family were firmly ensconced in their house, presumably with water closets and all, by 1877.[17]

The new legation can just be discerned, soon after its construction, in an indistinct photograph in the monthly magazine *The Far East*, which has subsequently been frequently reproduced.[18] Little can be seen in this picture, taken from across the moat. Parkes's tower, later to be regularly the subject of comment, is nowhere in sight. With the photograph is a short account of 'The English Legation, Tokei' – most foreigners remained confused as to the correct reading of the capital's name in Japanese, and both 'Tokyo' and 'Tokei' are found until the late 1870s.

The Far East noted the inconvenience of the previous arrangements, which involved much travelling for those concerned, and also involved buildings scattered over two cities. Now all were brought together on the one site, with the British consulate for Tokyo (in fact, the consular offices remained in the foreign settlement at Tsukiji for some years) and the consul's residence alongside. All this was most welcome. But the writer was less impressed by the buildings themselves:

> These buildings covering a large area of ground, cannot be given in a photograph so as to exhibit them photographically. Indeed, with due respect for the designer, we confess that we have never seen public buildings of a less imposing appearance . . . .

The main impression is of roofs and chimneys of ordinary suburban villas. Another photograph, from the early 1890s, of the residence alone, shows a solid brick two-storied house, with the three-storey tower, which would have fitted well into any of the new suburbs growing up around London.[19]

Perhaps that was the aim. British visitors clearly found the new legation to their satisfaction, and remarked on the homeliness of it all. Lady Brassey, sailing around the world with her husband, the Liberal MP Thomas Brassey in their steam yacht, *Sunbeam*, recorded a visit in 1877 in her journal. The 'English Embassy', she noted, '. . . is a nice brick house, built in the centre of a garden, so as to be as secure as possible from fire or attack'. There she and her husband were entertained to lunch, and shown Lady Parkes's second collection of curios, the first having been lost in the fire that had destroyed the legation building in Yokohama.[20]

In the following year, 1878, Isabella Bird, who already had a well-established reputation as a traveller, visited Tokyo at the start of her tour of Japan. She stayed with Sir Harry Parkes at the beginning and end of her visit and appears to have found the newly built legation more congenial than she did many other British official buildings in Asia. She noted that it was in

Kojimachi, '. . . on very elevated ground overlooking the castle'. This was a good location. It was near to the Foreign Office, several other government departments and the residences of several Japanese ministers. (These last, she wrote, were chiefly of brick 'in the English suburban style'.) The legation compound itself had a brick archway with the Royal Arms upon it for an entrance, the minister's residence, the chancery, two houses for the secretaries of legation, and quarters for the escort. Within the minister's house, Parkes maintained 'an English home', though with all Chinese servants, apart from a nurse for his children.[21] Isabella clearly liked Parkes, whom she described as bringing 'sunshine and kindliness' into a room, and leaving it behind him.[22] It was a description few of his staff would have recognized, though in the contemporary *Japan Punch*, written and illustrated by Charles Wirgman, chronicler of the attack on Tozenji, Parkes often appeared as the genial character 'Sir S. Smiles'. Whatever Parkes's merits, the homeliness of the compound and its buildings were to be a constant theme. In 1889, the visiting British artist, Sir Alfred East, found the red brick and the hedges, together with an 'English drawing-room . . . with its hundred-and-one little knickknacks' a pleasant interlude in his travelling schedule.[23]

There is no doubt that there were some defects. The lack of a ballroom, or any other large room for entertaining, was quickly felt. Parkes described what sounds like the Queen's Birthday Party from hell in letters to his wife, then in England, in May 1879. Despite her absence, he felt that he could not avoid giving a ball, so sent out invitations and expected some 200 people. They included the Queen's grandson, Prince Henry of Prussia. The day began fine, and, in the absence of a ballroom, two large pavilions were erected on the lawn, one for the band and one for supper. At 12.00 noon, it began to rain and it continued heavily all afternoon. The pavilions proved useless against the weather, and the visitors retreated to the verandas, designated as sitting-rooms. These promptly flooded and the guests had no choice but to move into the cramped quarters of the house. The following year, despite stronger pavilions, rain also drove guests into the house.[24]

Parkes moved to Beijing in 1883, dying there two years later. His successor was the former secretary of legation, Francis Plunkett, who seems to have been more popular than his predecessor from the beginning. Satow, who had known them on their first posting to Tokyo, met the Plunketts in London in November 1883, and wrote to Parkes that they had persuaded the Foreign Office and the Office of Works to furnish the ground floor of the residence, no doubt on the grounds that this was the area used for public functions. Satow also noted that Mrs Plunkett was taking her two girls with her, and a governess. The British legation would still have a young air about it.[25]

The only notable change during the Plunketts' time was a decision in 1885 to abandon a separate Tokyo consular office. Instead a room for the Tokyo vice-consulate would be provided at the legation. This was deemed to work well, although there was apparently some confusion about which establishment's servants were which.[26] Plunkett also raised the question of a ballroom, but was told firmly that since Sir Harry Parkes had told the

Treasury when the legation was under construction that the plans contained all that he required, the matter was closed.[27] As in Parkes' day, many major functions were held on the lawns, and smaller ones crammed into the limited space available.

The Plunketts left in 1889. Francis Plunkett was succeeded by Hugh Fraser, who died *en poste* in 1894. His wife, Mary, left an account of their life in Tokyo in a series of letters which she published after his death. They retain a freshness and a sense of fun over a hundred years later.[28] She barely described the compound in her letters, yet it emerges from her incidental descriptions and the illustrated version of her book contained pictures of the residence and 'a corner of the drawing-room'.[29] She clearly enjoyed its privacy and its spacious grounds, with great banks of flowers brought from all over Japan, even if she also enjoyed escaping to the hills in the heat. The wide verandas provided welcome coolness in the summer She was gently mocking about the watch tower. She claimed that it was never used for its original purpose since, with a flag on it, it would have been higher than the Imperial Palace. The flagstaff was moved elsewhere in the grounds. The tower, much bound about with iron bands as a result of earthquake damage, was used to store water until it collapsed in an earthquake in June 1894.[30]

Mrs Fraser's other great delight in her residence was the splendid views it gave of Mount Fuji, in those days before pollution prevented more than an occasional glimpse of the mountain. Otherwise, she said little about the buildings on the compound, except to note that 'the present Chancery' was a 'strong little building' well away from the main gate. She also noted that it lay between the building which the now much reduced legation guard occupied and the residence. From this account, it seems clear that the building in use as the chancery by 1889 was not the original one of 1874.[31]

From Mary Fraser we also learn that by the early 1890s, the total population of the compound was around two hundred people. She seems to have had no difficulty with this, and was especially fond of the Japanese children, who held her in some awe, as well they might, given her exalted rank.[32] Cecil Spring-Rice, briefly a second secretary in the legation between 1892 and 1893, noted on arrival that all the staff and their servants made the legation 'quite a settlement in itself'.[33] Added to the British occupants were Japanese servants, writers, teachers and their families, down to the vice-consul's jinrikisha man's grandmother. This lady appeared at the children's Christmas party carrying a small child who turned out to be motherless son of the aforesaid functionary.[34] The Christmas party for all the children on the compound seems to have been a custom started by Mrs Fraser, who delighted in the preparations and the surprise which resulted when the first one was held in January 1890, it having proved impossible to fit it in around Christmas itself. There was a decorated tree, to the astonishment of the Japanese children, and presents for all. (There had been Christmas trees at the British legation in Lady Parkes's day, too, though it was unlikely that Japanese children were invited to see them.[35])

When the day came, the lack of knowledge of what was meant by 'children' caused endless problems, as a doll had to be hurriedly substituted for a toy sword, or a map of Europe replaced by a rattle. Since the fifty-eight young guests ranged from one to nineteen, it was not surprising that there were difficulties. It was a party that was special in other ways too. Mrs Fraser's helper in purchasing presents was J. H. Gubbins, then Japanese secretary to the legation, a noted Japanese scholar and chief negotiator of the revised British treaty of 1894. On the day itself, she was assisted by Sir Edwin Arnold, traveller, poet and newspaper editor, then visiting Japan, and the recently appointed Anglican Bishop of South Tokyo, Edward Bickersteth.

Parties and children clearly played an important part in Mrs Fraser's life. She gave two Christmas parties the following year, one for the legation children, and one for all their foreign and Japanese friends. This was also judged a great success, except that most of the visitors subsequently went down with influenza. On that occasion, there were some two hundred children to receive presents. The adults ate downstairs and the children in the long gallery on the first floor – one of the few descriptions of the house which Mrs Fraser includes.[36] That she got on well with small children is indicated not only by her delight in the Japanese children on the compound but also by General Piggott's story of how, as a small boy attending the Queen's Birthday Party at the residence, he had a long discussion with her about his shiny patent leather shoes.[37]

Mary Fraser's other great delight was to escape from the city to the hills. She made it clear that she did not like to do this during the Christmas season, as did many foreigners. But in the summer, it was a different matter. Then she fled the heat and established herself in the area around Karuizawa, a summer resort made popular by missionaries, which was well established by the 1890s.[38] Here the Frasers had a Japanese-style, two-storied house, which she called 'the Palace of Peace'. It is not clear if this was rented, or purchased, but clearly she thought of it as her own. It, too, had deep verandas, tatami floors, and an elaborate system of bamboo pipes to bring water from the hills. They also acquired a protective policeman, who proved useful in dealing with a local drunk. Hugh Fraser clearly spent part of the summer there, as did Gubbins, though the latter stayed in another house. Mrs Fraser lamented that pressure of work sometimes forced them both to return to the city.[39]

The Frasers' years in Tokyo saw the revision of the treaties of the 1850s in Japan's favour. This was achieved in 1894, but not before there had developed much acrimony between foreigners and Japanese, with much talk on the British side of the '. . . good old days and Sir Harry Parkes.'[40] From the Japanese came the first real signs of anti-foreign feeling since the 1870s. Foreigners were jostled and insulted in the streets. Nationalistic young men, known as *soshi*, became a particular concern. They were seen as direct descendants of the hostile samurai of the 1860s, but made worse by a leavening of modern Western freethinking. The British legation was not spared their attention, for at least once, an excited young man wished to debate the merits of treaty revision with Hugh Fraser in person but was turned away at the gates.[41]

Fraser was followed as minister by P. Le Poer Trench, a bachelor, and something of a stopgap appointment, who in turn gave way to another bachelor in early 1895 when Sir Ernest Satow, then minister in Morocco, was appointed minister to Tokyo. This was a case of local boy made good. Satow had been a most successful Japan secretary, and had established a reputation both as a diplomat and a scholar. The former had been rewarded by his transfer to the diplomatic service, and by appointments as minister in Siam (Thailand), Uruguay and Morocco. Even if these were not the plum postings in the diplomatic service, Satow's appointment to them represented a major breakthrough for a member of one of the consular services. His appointment to Japan in 1895 was, therefore, very much a personal triumph, for the post had been held, since Parkes had moved to Beijing in 1883, by a succession of diplomatic service officers.[42]

The clever young man of the 1860s, confidant and drinking partner of Willis and Wirgman, and father of a Japanese family had, however, become a somewhat different character by the time of his appointment to Tokyo. He was now somewhat austere and aloof, even to those who had been his colleagues in earlier days. Perhaps he enjoyed the triumph of occupying what had once been Parkes's house, but it rarely showed. His main pleasure in the house seems to have been the room which he turned into his library. He enjoyed showing it to appreciative visitors, one of whom remarked that it seemed to be the best room in the house.[43]

His other great pleasure, and which set a pattern for the future, was a summer cottage which he regularly rented at Lake Chuzenji. He used it for the first time soon after his arrival, and noted in a letter to an old friend, F. V. Dickins, that '. . . [v]ery probably I shall fix my residence here during the summer months for the rest of my stay in this country'.[44] This proved to be the case. Satow appears to have purchased the original villa, and employed the well-known British architect, Josiah Conder, to redesign whatever original building was there.[45] There Satow would normally spend July and August, taking part in picnics and other open air activities with his colleagues from other legations, and in 1899, he lent it to the visiting Prince Henry of Prussia.[46] This retreat, and the scholarly interests of its occupier, were gently mocked by Osman Edwards in his *Residential Rhymes*, published in 1899.[47]

Satow left Japan in 1900, to become minister in Beijing. In March 1900, when he was first approached about the post, Beijing was still seen as the more important of the two posts, and such an appointment was therefore clearly a promotion.[48] His successor was Sir Claude MacDonald, hero of the siege of the Beijing legations (though his appointment to Tokyo had been considered before that event). MacDonald arrived in Tokyo late in 1900, having declined Lord Salisbury's offer to return to Britain to recuperate after the siege, and was to remain until 1912. When, following the Russo-Japanese War and the conclusion of the second Anglo-Japanese Alliance in 1905, it was decided to raise the Tokyo post to an embassy, MacDonald became the first resident ambassador.[49]

The MacDonalds had been great entertainers in Beijing. They were both, therefore, dismayed on arrival in Tokyo to find that the embassy offered only limited facilities for entertaining. Proposals to provide Tokyo with such a facility had clearly once again been turned down, and in private letters to the head of the Office of Works, Lord Esher, they made plain their dissatisfaction, perhaps playing a little on their reputation as the heroes of Beijing.

MacDonald's letter followed on the heels of an official despatch asking that a ballroom be constructed as soon as possible as recommended by Mr Boyce – now head surveyor in Shanghai – in Satow's time but turned down in London. The official despatch provided a dismal account of what happened at the Queen's Birthday Party if it rained and guests were forced to take refuge in the corridors and spare rooms of the residence, '. . . to the discomfort of hosts and guests alike'. In the private letter, he said that he knew that Works were 'friendlies' and the real problem was the Treasury, but something must be done. The Treasury's previous responses had all pointed out that Sir Harry Parkes had approved of the plans for the residence, but

'. . . times have changed.' When Sir Harry Parkes was satisfied, Japanese society went about with two swords and their hair à la Gilbert and Sullivan.

Now they expected to be entertained in proper fashion. The lack of proper dancing facilities had not mattered to his two predecessors, since they were bachelors. And in passing, and no doubt in sorrow, he noted that he had heard that Satow intended to turn the Beijing legation's 'charming little ballroom' into a library. He also noted that Satow – and he had every reason 'to believe him a brave man' – had not dared to tell Lady MacDonald of this plan.[50]

For her part, Lady MacDonald also had a number of issues to raise. Foremost again was the ballroom. In Beijing she wrote: '. . . the British legation had the pleasant reputation of being hospitable and a cheery meeting ground for all our friends during the winter months'. They had, of course, hoped to acquire the same reputation in Tokyo, but found themselves limited to a double drawing-room which seated twenty-eight and was full with thirty. To make matters worse, the floor of this room was of 'unstained deal' which was no good for dancing, even if they were prepared to turn their household out into the compound so that dances could be held. Not only were the main rooms unsuitable for dancing, but they did not even communicate, and beyond lay a dreary corridor, her husband's study, '. . . which should be sacred from intruders', a waiting-room, and an '. . . unfurnished "library" which we have been obliged to turn into a schoolroom' – it would appear that neither of the MacDonalds had much time for Sir Ernest Satow's interest in books. All in all, the layout of the house and the lack of suitable facilities meant that the British minister would have to retire into the background, '. . . and entertain on a par with the representatives of Siam & Corea!'. In addition, she went on to note that she was not a discontented person, but that '. . . one always suffers by following bachelors', and the house was dirty and the wallpaper either hanging off the walls – in the billiard-room – or such that she would '. . . not attempt to describe the drawing-room paper chosen by Mr Trench'.[51]

Whether it was the strength of these private pleas, or whether there happened to be money available, is not clear, but, whatever the reason, money was found for the required construction and work was due to begin before the end of the 1901–02 financial year. However, when the MacDonalds were informed, they began to drag their heels over the project. In particular, they seem to have been worried that the works, once commenced, would drag on and interfere with their lives too much. So they first of all sought a postponement, and then suggested that the construction of a ballroom was no longer necessary, since they had been able to arrange for the drawing- and dining-rooms to be opened up so that they could now entertain up to 130 guests.[52] The ballroom saga then fades from the records.

Apart from the drawbacks of his own house, MacDonald was not over impressed by what he saw as the inefficiency of the waste of space on the compound, which was bigger than Beijing had been before the siege. Yet the Beijing compound had accommodation for forty, of whom twenty were students, while the Tokyo compound only held five, of whom two were students. The growth of telegraphic traffic, and therefore the need for diplomatic service officers to be on hand for decyphering, had led him to cancel the arrangements hitherto in force whereby, apart from the secretary of legation, the senior members of staff sorted out among themselves who would and who would not live on the compound. Instead, he had insisted that the second secretary take over the assistant Japanese secretary's house and had found room for that officer in two rooms not used in the students' quarters. But, as he reported to London in 1903, the number of new student interpreters was to be increased from two to four, which would put a strain on the existing accommodation. He proposed that at least additional student quarters should be built, which London seems to have accepted.[53]

MacDonald was a genial boss, who may not have been the most active of men, but took an interest in those who worked for him which had not always been the case of heads of mission in Tokyo. He sought new furniture for the students, for the first time since the new quarters had been built in the 1870s. Hitherto, the students had been caught by rules which said that nothing could ever be replaced until the absolute necessity of doing so had been demonstrated, and a reasonable time had elapsed since the original purchase. As he noted, by 1905, when he made his second application on the students' behalf, the furniture which they were using had been in use for some thirty years and had been '. . . gradually eaten away by the tooth of time'. So bad was it that when the latest batch of students had arrived, they had been forced to buy '. . . bedsteads, mattresses, cupboards, washing stands, tables, chairs, earth-closets (Sir Harry Parkes' wish for water closets having not apparently extended as far as the students' quarters) and the like', out of the '. . . not excessive pay which they receive in their first years'. He got his way.[54]

He also got his way in the matter of the plate. This was ordered and supplied in 1907. There was a problem almost immediately since access to the strong-room constructed in 1906 to hold it lay through the chancery offices. In order to put the plate away each night as instructed, he would need to ask 'one of [the] chancery gentlemen' to be on duty each night the plate was in use, in order to open the doors. In any case, the strong room was far too damp, for the plate. Instead, he announced that he was going to keep it in the residence. Then he reported that he would be going to Chuzenji and that the house would be shut up from 1 July to 15 September. He therefore intended to put the plate in the strong room and lock the keys away. Instead – and this was no doubt the intention all along – instructions came from London to put the plate in a bank at public expense.[55]

Despite MacDonald's concerns about the growth in telegraphic traffic, others found the pace of life still relatively easy-going. When George Sansom joined the embassy as the ambassador's private secretary in 1907 – he had already spent three years as a student interpreter – he found that it was a leisurely life which he was expected to lead. Years later, he noted that the younger members of the embassy were expected to take an interest in things Japanese, presumably by going out and looking at them, since it was '. . . even thought rather priggish to attend the Chancery in the afternoon'. There was plenty of time. Although the telegram was indeed beginning to be the dominant feature of embassy work, a lot of business was still done by letter, and since the bag only left once a month, there was little point in writing the necessary despatches until just before the it closed.[56] In Sansom's case, the leisure time enabled him to read and to begin to publish the scholarly papers which laid the foundation for his major books. He also got on well with the scholarly Sir Charles Eliot, ambassador from 1920 to 1926, who praised his work highly.[57]

Others perhaps preferred the sporting opportunities which were on offer. A set of 'Hints for newly appointed Student Interpreters proceeding to Japan',[58] produced by Sansom in 1912, laid stress on the need to bring clothes for sporting activities: Lawn tennis and squash rackets are to be played in Tokyo; cricket, football, baseball, hockey, roller skating and golf can be had at Yokohama and Kobe. There is some shooting and skating up country, boating and bathing at most ports. The Capital offers poor opportunities for riding, but there is a race-course at Yokohama. Tennis racquets, preferably strung with black gut, should certainly be taken. Golf clubs, riding kit, saddlery, fishing tackle, guns, etc., may be taken if already possessed, but with the possible exception of a golf club or two, should hardly be specially purchased. A bicycle is a great convenience in Tokyo. It is best bought in England, though Government does not pay carriage to Japan.

Eliot's period as ambassador was marked by the end of the Anglo-Japanese Alliance, a matter of personal regret to him, and one which he fought hard to prevent. When it proved impossible to reverse this decision, Eliot continued to work hard for good Anglo-Japanese relations, even though the climate was less favourable. He opposed the proposal to build a naval base at Singapore, seeing it as provocative to Japan. But in London he was seen as too pro-Japanese, and he was retired in 1925, despite his strong protests and insistence that he could still do many other jobs. He remained in Japan, living at Nara and writing a monumental study of Japanese Buddhism. This remained unfinished at his death, and was completed by

Sansom. Eliot's only biographer describes it as a 'complex and frankly imperfect' work.[59]

His time as ambassador was also a period when the technological changes of the early twentieth century began to produce new requests from staff. Thus Eliot supported an unsuccessful attempt by the Tokyo consul in 1920 for official assistance in running a motor-car. The consul, C. J. Davidson, argued that since there was no accommodation for him near the consulate, he was forced to live out – clearly the arrangement from Parkes's time whereby the Tokyo consul or vice-consul lived on the embassy compound had ceased – and that led to transport problems. Trams were hopelessly crowded and in any case '. . . trams are rarely used by the better class Japanese'. Rickshaws were no longer in use and the poor condition of the roads made the use of bicycles difficult and, in any case, '. . . no persons of any position uses them'. So Davidson, with Eliot's support sought assistance with a motor-car. He was unsuccessful, although the ambassador was soon using one, even if he did not do so in 1920.[60]

In the meantime, the embassy compound continued to supply the safe haven of a corner of England in central Tokyo. Frank Ashton-Gwatkin, arriving as a student interpreter in 1913, described the compound as '. . . like a slice of Wimbledon flown out to Tokyo on a magic, green carpet'. Within this little kingdom, the ambassador's house '. . . looked suitable for a late Victorian tycoon', and there were also houses for the counsellor, the Japanese secretary, the first secretary and the second secretary. The five student interpreters shared a house and messed together. They had two rooms each, and were supplied with basic furniture.[61]

Another account, published some eight or nine years later, but which related to the years just after the Russo-Japanese War (1904–05), made the same point about the suburban nature of the compound, and how little it owed to Japan, though the author, Lord Frederic Hamilton, a visiting former diplomat and Member of Parliament, seems to have got a little confused by it all! He wrote in his memoirs:

> The interior of our Embassy at Tokyo was rather a surprise. Owing to the constant earthquakes in Tokyo and Yokohama, all the buildings have to be of wood. The British Embassy was built in London (I believe by a very well-known firm in Tottenham Court Road), and was shipped out to Japan complete down to its last detail. The architect who designed it unhappily took a glorified suburban villa as his model. So the Tokyo Embassy house is an enlarged 'Belmont', or 'The Cedars', or 'Tokyo Towers'. Every familiar detail is there; the tiled hall, the glazed door into the garden, and the heavy mahogany chimneypieces and overmantels. In the library, with its mahogany bookcases, green morocco chairs, and green plush curtains, it was difficult to realise that one was not in Hampstead or Upper Tooting.

He conceded that it was comfortable, despite its air of suburbia, and also noted that there were few Japanese about.[62] And if he was wrong about the nature of the building, he was right about the danger of earthquakes.

On 1 September 1923, just before noon, on a warm, wet day, Tokyo was struck by a huge earthquake. Then, or in the next forty hours as fires raged throughout the city, much of old Tokyo disappeared.[63] With it went the British embassy. Reporting the event in his review of the year 1923, Eliot noted that the shock of the 'terrible earthquake' had been less in Tokyo than in Yokohama, but that even in Tokyo things had been very bad. While only one of the embassy houses, that belonging to Harold Parlett, the Japanese secretary, was totally destroyed, all had been rendered uninhabitable, either by the shock itself or in the fires which followed, and had eventually to be pulled down.[64] Again, while only one member of the British community had been killed in Tokyo, over 120 died at Yokohama. This total included a vice-consul (William Haigh) and a shipping clerk (James Percy Lyes) from the Yokohama consulate-general, together with two members of the Tokyo embassy, the acting commercial counsellor (Hugh Archibald Fisher Horne) and the embassy accountant (David Waddell). All had been killed in the collapse of the Yokohama consulate-general buildings.[65] The Tokyo compound was left in a state of ruin, without even a protecting wall standing. All around, too, were signs of destruction, for the Kojimachi area was one of the worst hit in Tokyo.[66]

Eliot was on leave in Britain when this great catastrophe occurred. On his return, he worked hard for substantial British aid for relief work, but without much success. He did, however, persuade the British government to give £25,000 to Tokyo Imperial University to help it to restore the library which had been lost.[67]

Notes

1 The broad outline of story told in this and the next chapter appears in J. E. Hoare, 'The Tokyo embassy 1871–1945', *Japan Society Proceedings*, no. 129, (Summer 1997), 24–41.

2 Works 10–35/1 Part 1, copy of E. Hammond, Foreign Office, to the Treasury, 20 November 1871, enclosing a memorandum by Sir Harry Parkes, 18 November 1871.

3 Works 10–35/1 Part 1, copy of E. Hammond, Foreign Office, to the Treasury, 20 November 1871, enclosing a memorandum by Sir Harry Parkes, 18 November 1871, together with an attachment 'Extract from Mr Boyce's Report to the Secretary to the Treasury', 1 May 1871.

4 Cortazzi, 'First British Legation,' p. 49. The draft text of the 1884 lease can be found in Works 10/636, Foreign Office to the Treasury, 30 June 1884. In 1939, the Tokyo Taxation Control Bureau, which was anxious to see a revision of the rent paid, sent a translation of the final Japanese text of the lease to the embassy – see F)366/1052/K.7309/877/503, Sir Robert Craigie to Mr Eden, no. 467, 21 June 1939. The original British copy has not been found.

5 Works 10–35/1, part 1, E. Hammond to the Office of Works, 20 November 1871, enclosing H. S. Parkes, ' Memorandum on Legation and Consular Buildings in Japan', 18 November 1871; R. H. Boyce, Shanghai, to Office of Works, 27/71, 30 November 1871.

6 Works 10–35/1, Part 2, Works to Boyce, 26 January 1872.

7 Letter from P. L. Finch, 19 August 1996, recalling a conversation with MFA officials; for Mrs Fraser's account, see below.

8 Works 10–35/ 1 Part 2, Boyce to Works, 81/72, 9 September 1872.

9 Works 10–35/1, Part 2, copies of Watson to Hammond, private, 16 July 1872 and Watson to Lord Granville, no. 15 consular, 29 July 1872.

10 Works 10–35/1 Part 2, Memorandum by Sir Harry Parkes, 28 September 1872; Works to Treasury, 5 December 1872, no. 4404/72.

11 Works 10–35/1, Part 2, Copy of Satow to Parkes, 18 April 1874.

12 Works 10–35/1, Part 4, Foreign Office to Office of Works, 7 May 1874, forwarding a copy of Parkes to Granville, no. 6 consular, 8 March 1874,

13 *Eastern World*, 2 June 1906. See also Patricia McCabe, *Gaijin Bochi: The Foreigners' Cemetery, Yokohama, Japan*, (London: British Association for Cemeteries in South Asia, 1994), p. 326, where the date of Peacock's death is wrongly given as 1908. For Hodges, see *Japan Weekly Mail*, 3 June 1916.

14 Works 10–35/1, Part 3, Boyce to Office of Works, 28 August 1873, 23 October 1873.

15 Works 10–35/1, Part 4, Boyce to Office of Works, 15 August 1874.

16 *Far East*, vol. 6, no. 7, January 1875; *Japan Weekly Mail*, 3 April 1875.

17 Works 10–35/1, Part 4, Boyce to Office of Works, 9 July 1875. One of the plans in this file claims to be of works carried out for Mr Plunkett in 1873, but this seems to be a mistake. Another plan, dating from 1878–79, is also in this file, and shows further works carried out or planned for Plunkett's successor, A H Mounsey.

18 *Far East*, vol. 6, no. 7, January 1875. For a recent reproduction, see Yokohama kaiko shiryokan/Yokohama Archives of History, *Meiji no Nihon: Yokohama shashin no sekai*, (Meiji Japan: The World of Yokohama Photographs'), (Tokyo: Yurindo, 1990), p. 73.

19 Mrs Hugh Fraser, *A Diplomatist's Wife in Japan: Letters from Home to Home*, (London: Hutchinson and Company, 1899), I, 7.

20 Lady Brassey, *A Voyage in the Sunbeam: Our Home on the Ocean for Eleven Months*, (London: Longman, Green and Co., 1878, reprinted London: Century Publishing House, 1984), p. 315.

21 Isabella L Bird, *Unbeaten Tracks in Japan: An Account of Travels in the interior Including Visits to the Aborigines of Yezo and the Shrine of Nikkō*, (London: John Murray, second edition 1911), pp. 13–14.

22 Bird, *Unbeaten Tracks*, p. 8. See also the account of Parkes's helpfulness in Anna M. Stoddart, *The Life of Isabella Bird (Mrs Bishop)*, (London: John Murray, 1908), p. 105.

23 Sir Alfred East, *A British Artist in Meiji Japan*, edited, with an introduction, by Sir Hugh Cortazzi, (Brighton: In Print, 1991), p. 60.

24 Dickins and Lane-Poole, *Parkes*, II, 273–76.

25 Parkes Papers, University of Cambridge, Satow to Parkes, 25 November 1883. I owe this reference to Mr Ian Ruxton.

26 FO97/582, Salisbury to Plunkett, draft no. 32, consular, 19 October 1885; Plunkett to Salisbury, no. 11 consular, 15 February 1886.

27 See the reference to a reply to Plunkett from the Office of Works of 21 March 1885, referred to in Works 10–35/2, Sir Claude MacDonald to Lord Esher, private, 23 January 1901.

28 In 1995, the then ambassador arranged for a dramatized version of her account to be performed in the present residence. Conversation with Sir John Boyd, 15 July 1996.

29 Fraser, *Diplomatist's Wife in Japan*, I, 7, 403.

30 Mrs Hugh Fraser, *A Diplomatist's Wife in Japan: Letters from Home to Home*, (London: Hutchinson and Company, one volume edition, N.D.), pp. 19–20. For the collapse of the tower, see Harold S. Williams, *Shades of the Past: Indiscreet Tales of Japan*, (Tokyo and Rutland, Vt: Charles E. Tuttle Company, 1959), p. 182.

31 Fraser, *Diplomatist's Wife*, p. 136.

32 Fraser, *Diplomatist's Wife*, pp. 56–57.

33 Stephen Gwyn, editor, *The Letters and Friendships of Sir Cecil Spring Rice: A record*, (London: Constable and Co. Ltd, 1929), vol. 1, 122.

34 Fraser, *Diplomatist's Wife*, p. 143.

35 Clara Whitney noted in 1876 that a friend described the Whitney's tree as 'finer than Lady Parkes's' – Clara Whitney, *Clara's Diary: An American Girl in Meiji Japan*, (Tokyo, New York and San Francisco: Kodansha International, paperback edition, 1981), p. 112.

36 Fraser, *Diplomatist's Wife*, pp. 292–94.

37 F S G Piggott, *Broken Thread*, (Aldershot, Hants.: Gale and Polden, 1950), p. 4. Piggott, later defence attaché in Tokyo, was the son of a legal adviser to the Japanese government.

38 Hoare, *Japan's Treaty Ports*, p. 48.

39 Fraser, *Diplomatist's Wife*, pp. 232–33, 253–55, 360–63.

40 Fraser, *Diplomatist's Wife*, 2 vol. edition, vol. 1,199. For the background to the revision of the treaties, see Hoare, *Japan's Treaty Ports*, pp. 97–105.

41 Fraser *Diplomatist's Wife*, pp. 42–43.

42 For some of Satow's personal considerations in taking the Tokyo post, see Nigel Brailey, 'Sir Ernest Satow and *A Diplomat in Japan*', *Japan Society Proceedings*, no. 131 (Summer 1998), pp. 56–69.

43 Bernard M Allen, *The Rt. Hon. Sir Ernest Satow, GCMG: A Memoir*, (London: Kegan Paul, Trench and Trubner, 1933), p. 114.

44 Satow to F. V. Dickins, 21 August 1895, in Sir E. M. Satow, *The diaries and letters of Sir Ernest Mason Satow (1843–1929), A Scholar-Diplomat in East Asia*, selected, edited and annotated by Ian C. Ruxton (Lewiston, N. Y; Queenston, Ontario; Lampeter: The Edwin Mellon Press, 1998), p. 209.

45 Conder was identified as the designer of Satow's Chuzenji villa, which is virtually the same today, apart from the garden, at an exhibition held in Tokyo in 1998: letter from Lady Wright, Tokyo, 25 January 1999. For Condor, see Dallas Finn, 'Josiah Conder and Meiji Architecture', in Cortazzi and Daniels, editors, *Britain and Japan*, pp. 86–93. He is also mentioned in Finn, *Meiji Revisited*, passim. However, neither of the last two works mention any link with Chuzenji.

46 Allen, *Ernest Satow*, p. 114

47 Osman Edwards, *Residential Rhymes*, (Tokyo: Hasegawa, [N.D] (1899)). For Osman Edwards and the publisher, Takejiro Hasegawa, see Fred Sharf, *Takejiro Hasegawa: Meiji Japan's Pre-eminent Publisher of Wood-Block-Illustrated Crepe-Paper Books*, (Salem, Mass: Peabody Essex Museum Collections, 1994), especially p. 41.

48 Allen, *Satow*, p. 117.

49 Ian Nish, 'Sir Claude and Lady Ethel MacDonald', in Ian Nish, editor, *Britain and Japan: Biographical Portraits*, (Folkestone, Kent: Japan Library, 1994), pp. 133–145.

50 Works 10–35/2, MacDonald to Office of Works, 23 January 1901; MacDonald to Lord Esher, private, 23 January 1901.

51 Works 10–35/2, Lady MacDonald to Lord Esher, private, 20 January 1901.

52 See various papers and letters on Works 10–35/2 relating to the estimates for 1901–2.

53 Works 10–35/3, MacDonald to Lansdowne, no. 26 consular, 31 July 1903.

54 Works 10–35/3, MacDonald to Lansdowne, no. 10 consular, 16 February 1905; Works to Foreign Office, draft, 22 April 1905.

55 Works 10/399 contains the relevant papers from 1907–8.

56 Katherine Sansom, *Sir George Sansom and Japan: A Memoir*, (Tallahassee, Florida: The Diplomatic Press, 1972), pp. 5–6.

57 Eliot was appointed ambassador in August 1919, but did not in fact arrive in Japan until April 1920). Dennis Smith, 'Sir Charles Eliot (1862–1931) and Japan', in Cortazzi and Daniels, *Britain and Japan*, p. 187.

58 'Hints for newly appointed Student Interpreters proceeding to Japan' 31 March 1912, Confidential Print 10025, in FO369/484/16134, G B Sansom to Lampson, 2 April 1912.

59 Smith, 'Sir Charles Eliot', p. 196.

60 FO369/1685/X4738/887/503, Sir Charles Eliot to the Foreign Office, no. 572, 16November 1920, enclosing C.J. Davidson to Eliot, no. 22, 10 November 1920.

61 Frank Ashton-Gwatkin, 'The meeting of John Paris and Japan', *tsuru*, vol. 3, no. 1, (September 1973), p. 3. Details of the messing arrangements come from 'Hints for newly appointed Student Interpreters proceeding to Japan' 31 March 1912, Confidential Print 10025 – see note 25.

62 Lord Frederic Hamilton, *Vanished Pomps*, (London: Hodder and Stoughton, 1920, reprinted 1932), p. 287. I am grateful to Lady Wright, British Embassy Tokyo, for this reference.

63 There is a brief account in Edward Seidensticker, *Tokyo Rising: The City since the Great Earthquake*, (New York: Alfred A Knopf, 1990), pp. 3–11.

64 For a detailed account of the condition of all the buildings on the compound, see Works 10/638, Julius Bradley, Shanghai to chief architect, London, 16 November 1923. Although not everything was rendered uninhabitable in the first shock, aftershocks, and a further earthquake in January 1924 (see below), completed the destruction.

65 Works 10/638, Tokyo tels to FO no. 139 and 146, 10 and 19 Sept. 1923. See also Annual Report 1923, Sir Charles Eliot to Mr MacDonald, no. 164, 19 April 1924, in Archive Research Ltd., editors, *Japan and Dependencies: Political and Economic Reports 1906–1960*, (Farnham Common Slough: Archive Research Ltd., 1994), (Cited as *Japan and Dependencies*), vol. 2, p. 8. Those who died are commemorated by a memorial in the Yokohama Foreign Cemetery. See McCabe, *Gaijin Bochi*, p. 269.

66 *Japan Weekly Chronicle*, 6 September 1923.

67 Smith, 'Sir Charles Eliot,' p. 192.

Japan

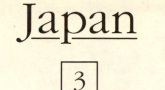

After the Earthquake, 1923–40

Once it was established that all staff in Tokyo were safe, the immediate need was to organise some form of temporary office and to provide housing. It was some three weeks before it was announced that a temporary British embassy office had been established in the Imperial hotel, which had survived the earthquake.[1] The temporary office was a makeshift affair, mainly concerned with consular matters. Most of the embassy papers had been destroyed – with the usual increase in efficiency, according to Sir George Sansom twenty years later.[2]

Housing was not easy. In the immediate aftermath of the earthquake, a temporary wooden structure was erected on the lawns to provide some degree of protection. This was of the most primitive kind. As the Office of Works representative in Shanghai reported:

> . . . the Embassy staff are being accommodated in a temporary wooden shelter on the public lawn. This shelter has bee hastily constructed of light boarding and comprises 14 cubicles separated by matting and curtains. The sanitary arrangements & water supply have broken down and latrines of a primitive nature have been contrived as an emergency measure.

In the writer's view, there should be no attempt to send families to Tokyo, especially as it was likely to be difficult to arrange winter accommodation.[3] (Neither the Foreign Office nor the Office of Works were very pleased when both the Admiralty and the Air Ministry began to insist that they had to have additional staff in Tokyo.) A series of aftershocks, which were still being experienced in November, made life difficult for those living in temporary structures, and also made the remaining structures on the compound increasingly unsafe. A further earthquake in 1924 not only damaged some of the temporary buildings on the compound but completed the destruction begun in 1923, and made certain that there was no possibility of using any of the old buildings.[4]

This is to run ahead. As the autumn progressed, work began to convert the makeshift building on the lawn into temporary accommodation for the ambassador. In the meantime, when he returned from leave, Sir Charles Eliot moved into a rented house in Omote-cho, Akasaka, which later became the Brazilian embassy.[5] Others were forced to share whatever they could find. Major Piggott, the military attaché, was fortunate. He was at Chuzenji when the earthquake struck and although the shocks caused the house there to sway, there was no hint of the devastation that had struck on the coast. Only gradually did news filter through of the seriousness of the disaster. He found on return to Tokyo that his wooden house remained standing and habitable, though it had suffered some damage. All the surrounding houses had been burnt down. Piggott attributed the survival of his to the damp atmosphere created by a ginkgo tree which stood next to it. Alas, however, while the house stood, the tree died. For a time, he shared his house with various other members of the embassy, now made homeless. Eventually, as winter began, houses were rented for staff at what seemed extravagant rents by pre-earthquake standards.[6]

Sir Charles Eliot was moderately content with the bungalow erected for his use on the devastated compound. As his successor noted later, he made some alterations to the original design but on the whole, he accepted it as it was, though he did complain to London that it was very hot in summer and very cold in winter. As a bachelor, he perhaps had little need of a large establishment. Such grand entertainment as was required took place at the Imperial hotel or in the grounds of the compound, as weather and other circumstances dictated. His only complaint, made towards the end of 1924, was that the rubble from the damaged buildings was still strewn about the compound. This was not only unsightly, but was likely to delay work on rebuilding.[7] His successor, Sir John Tilley, who arrived in Tokyo in 1926, was less happy.

Sir John Tilley had no East Asian background. He recounted in his memoirs that he had been appointed to the Tokyo embassy without even being consulted; it had seemed easier to somebody in London to seek *agrément* before informing Tilley.[8] But, as a former Chief Clerk (head of the Foreign Office administration), he was used to the ways of the office and did not object. He reached Japan in January 1926, and was joined in May by his wife and son, who was appointed an honorary attaché of the embassy. Soon after his arrival, he enquired rather plaintively about the proposed rebuilding, noting that '. . . the bungalow is quite comfortable as bungalows go', but the bedrooms were small and '. . . the compound is a horrible wilderness of ruins & shanties'.[9] By that stage, most of the earthquake damage in the city had been cleared away, and only the British and one or two other embassy compounds were still desolate.[10] All that remained of Sir Harry Parkes' legation was a double avenue of cherry trees along what had been the outer wall. The compound was still generally open to the world. There were no walls when the Tilleys arrived. Instead, there were barbed wire fences, which offered little protection. In November 1926, a visiting

Office of Works representative, sent to report on a proposal that a strip of land at the back of the compound should be surrendered to the Japanese government, noted that there had been two recent examples of intruders gaining easy access to the compound. In one case, a dagger was thrown at the ambassador's son. In another, a man had tried to set fire to the Office of Works godown (warehouse) on the compound, which was full of furniture, but had been stopped in time.[11]

Tilley clearly continued to have a low opinion of the accommodation which had proved sufficient for Sir Charles Eliot. He wrote that he understood that Eliot had been content to live in a building made out of 'something called Canadian wood pulp'. The main – Tilley clearly felt the only – merit of this building was that there would be little damage if there was another major earthquake. Otherwise, it was not very successful. There was a large dining-room and an equally large drawing-room, but no other sitting-room apart from the ambassador's study. The bedrooms were small – in supporting the plea by the commercial counsellor and the Japanese secretary for better accommodation, Tilley noted that the officers had been reluctant to raise the issue of the size of their bedrooms, '. . . since they are at least better than the bedrooms provided for the Ambassador and his family'.[12]

According to Tilley, Eliot had had the verandas glassed in, with the result that the house was hot and airless in summer. In the winter, Tilley claimed, the glass prevented what little sun there was from penetrating the house. (In fact, Eliot, too, had raised this as an issue.) More accurately attributed to Eliot was the growth of the rat population, which had moved into the British embassy compound after the earthquake. Eliot had refused to allow the embassy cat into the bungalow, after it had produced kittens in the study. As a consequence, when the Tilleys arrived, the house was infested with rats. As well as dead rats under the floorboards, rats raced around the frieze of the dining-room. Unwilling to tolerate this intrusion at their dinner table, the Tilleys persuaded the houseboys to swipe the rats down with long-handled brooms. Once on the floor, the Tilleys' dog made short shrift of them. It must have been a somewhat unnerving addition to dinner parties.

In addition to the residence bungalow and a makeshift office building, there was a small guesthouse in the grounds when the Tilleys arrived, providing 'very modest shelter' for distinguished guests. The Tilleys also persuaded the Office of Works to build a bungalow for two of their British servants, though they had a battle to persuade the Office's representative to include a Western bath rather than a Japanese one. Tilley was of the view that any self-respecting British maid would promptly give notice if expected to use a Japanese bath. Another small house was occupied by a Japanese lady, the widow of a former gatekeeper. She apparently lived in dread that the rebuilding works now underway would lead to the cutting down of the large cherry tree which overshadowed her house, for she believed that her husband's soul resided there.[13]

In his memoirs, Tilley indicated that there were no other buildings on the compound at the time of his arrival. By 1927, there was at least one other bungalow, constructed after the earthquake, and apparently known as the Japanese secretary's house. In November 1927, George Sansom, now commercial counsellor, and C. J. Davidson, the Japanese secretary, submitted a memorandum to the ambassador, protesting at the idea that either of them should be expected to live in this house in its existing condition. They noted that others had lived there since the earthquake. They had tolerated this since they had expected that it would be a temporary arrangement. But four years on, they thought that it was not suitable for use by senior officers without considerable modification. It was half the size of the original house on the same site, and half the size of the houses projected for counsellor-rank officers. They also had been led to believe that there was little chance of more permanent accommodation 'for at least ten years'. They noted that their situation was different from diplomatic service officers, who spent '2 or 3 years at the most' in Japan, while both Sansom and Davidson had a long period of service before them. It had been ten years since they had had permanent housing, and they '. . . naturally felt discontented with the miserable accommodation provided' in Japan, especially in the light of that which officers enjoyed in China. It was the same story as the ambassador's: a too small house, hastily constructed in the first place, and after four years, quite inadequate for the purpose to which it was now being put. Large stoves and zinc chimneys took up to much space, and the whole was surrounded by rubble. Sansom and Davidson asked that one or both of them should be allowed to rent accommodation off the compound. If one of them did have to live in the house, then a series of relatively inexpensive works should be undertaken to make the house more pleasant.[14]

The consular department of the Foreign Office noting that, while housing for Davidson was their responsibility, Sansom's accommodation was in fact the responsibility of the Department of Overseas Trade, since he, as the commercial counsellor was regarded as a member of the Overseas Trade Service. On the assumption that Davidson would occupy it, the Foreign Office sought Treasury sanction for work on the bungalow. In the end, however, Sansom seems to have ended up living in it, for it was there that he was married in May 1928.[15] How the change came about remains a minor one of the many minor mysteries hidden by the Works' archives.

Meanwhile, and after many complaints about the slowness of the work – though the US embassy was equally slow – plans were being prepared in London for the new buildings for the compound. They were based on a memorandum drawn up in the Foreign Office with advice from Sir Edward Crowe and George Sansom, which indicated what buildings would be required and where they should be placed. This in turn was approved by the ambassador.[16] The plans themselves were mainly the work of Sir Richard Allison, then chief architect of the Office of Works, who had designed, *inter alia*, the British legation in Stockholm, and, nearer to home, the new Stationery Office building at Cornwall House in 1912 and the main facade of the Science Museum in 1913. (Cornwall House was the home of a number of Foreign Office departments, including parts of the then research department and library and records department, for many years from the mid 1960s.)[17] Two Office of Works officials, J. Cumming Wynnes and Roland Unwin, were sent to supervise the work at the local level during the actual construction of the buildings, and were responsible for some local modifications to Allison's work.[18]

Allison, conscious of the need for economy, especially after the Great Slump of 1929, grasped the nettle of who should or should not live on the compound. Apart from the residence, his plans provided for detached houses for the counsellors and for the (diplomatic) first secretary, four semi-detached residences for the second and third secretaries, four other smaller semi-detached houses for junior staff, servants 'barracks', outhouses, garages and gate lodges. Above the office block, or chancery, were provided rooms for three language students and the embassy archivist. There was also a squash court and two tennis courts. Each residence would have its own lawn surrounded by low hedges, with the general effect aimed at giving the sense of a collection of buildings in a large garden. The buildings were designed to be earthquake proof, and to this end, a Swedish consultant with much experience of work in earthquake-prone areas, was involved with the planning.

The basic structure of all of the buildings was steel and concrete, each building being divided into a series of earthquake-resistant sections, with expansion joints from 4″ to 12″ wide, designed to provide maximum flexibility during an earthquake. The external walls were backed with pumice concrete for soundproofing and to cope with temperature changes. Externally, the buildings were coated with layers of a Japanese artificial stone, *jinzoseki*, (lit. 'artificial stone') which, when set, resembled granite, and which was grooved to resemble granite blocks. (The *jinzoseki*, which has ever since fooled more than one resident of the compound into thinking that they were living in granite houses, was regarded as a great success. There was a certain degree of satisfaction recorded in 1938 when the US embassy, built about the same time, but using concrete facings, had to undergo a major repair programme because the concrete had become discoloured. It was noted in London that the British embassy looked as clean as the day it had been finished.[19]) Japanese copper was used for the roofs, gutters and rainwater pipes. Teak from the East Indies (now Indonesia) was used for windows and doors, and Japanese woods were used for internal woodwork and floors. Ornamentation of the buildings were also in *jinzoseki*, while most of the internal fittings came from Britain. Whatever style later inhabitants have thought the finished works resembled, to contemporaries, it was 'English renaissance, almost without ornamentation'. To British commentators at home, the new compound seemed an excellent combination of the private and the public, the residence '. . . a gentleman's house to which a number of public offices have been attached'.[20]

Tilley saw what must have been an early version of the plans when home on leave in 1927. Though he never lived in the new residence, he claimed in his memoirs that he was able to suggest some major changes which made it a more usable and safer house than the one originally designed. The need for a ballroom was now finally conceded, though not without a rearguard action from the Treasury, which suggested that since there had not been a ballroom in the former residence, there was perhaps no need for one now. The ballroom had large French windows, which made it open on one side, thus making it safer in the event of an earthquake, and the kitchen was brought nearer the dining-room.[21]

Meanwhile, the grounds were still available for grand parties. Lady Sansom recalled a particularly fine one when the Duke of Gloucester visited Japan in 1929 to present the Order of the Garter to the Emperor of Japan. The ambassador determined to invite as many of the British community in Japan as possible to meet the Duke. Indian ladies from Yokohama mingled with Boy Scouts and teachers from distant outposts, while the Salvation Army girls concentrated on reforming the sailors and midshipmen from HMS *Suffolk*. Presumably none of them realized that it had been the Office of Works' intention to begin digging the foundations of the new buildings just before the arrival of the mission, and that only a heartfelt plea from the ambassador had led to postponement![22]

During his period as ambassador, Tilley revived the use of the summer quarters at Chuzenji. He claimed that Sir Charles Eliot did not care about 'the simple life' – Katherine Samson wrote that Sir Charles had enjoyed nothing better than riding around in a big car – and one of the embassy secretaries had occupied the Chuzenji villa in his time. Now Tilley went there regularly, to stay in the two-storied Japanese-style house, with shutters instead of doors and windows, looking across to mount Nantai, (8000 ft). Hitherto, access had been by foot from the railway station at Nikko, but the Tilleys began to use a car. There were some protests from other ambassadors who also had houses there but these did not last, and before long there was also a public service of cars to the resort. Sailing, walking and fishing were popular pastimes at Chuzenji.[23]

Tilley left in late 1930, noting that there were sinister new developments in Japan, with the growing strength of extreme nationalist forces. But not only had Japan begun to change during the years he served in Tokyo, but the nature of the embassy's work did too. The leisurely pace which Sansom had noted over twenty years before had gone. Chancery hours were now longer as the growing use of telegrams demanded instant responses in the way that the traditional despatch had never done. In other ways, too, a new form of diplomacy was coming into existence. The British dominions were beginning to move towards independent representation. In 1927–28, Tilley found that he had to negotiate with the Japanese on behalf of the Canadian government, which wished for independent representation in Tokyo.

This was not the first time that the issue had been raised. As early as 1906, the Canadians had shown signs of wishing to break away from dependence on Britain for diplomatic representation. In that year, the Canadian government had nominated a trade agent to visit China, Japan and Korea, but, in the Japanese case at least, had failed to notify the British embassy or the Japanese government. When this official arrived in Tokyo, he had apparently began a campaign against the foreign community and the foreign-language press, claiming that both were anti-Japanese – not an inaccurate assessment. The ambassador, Sir Claude MacDonald, had interviewed the offending agent, a Mr Preston, and had warned him that this had to stop. Fortunately, the Canadian government had also taken a dim view of Mr Preston. He was removed, and his successor seems to have behaved himself. Sir Claude had then raised the whole question of dominions sending independent agents with the secretary of state for the colonies, but had been told that there were objections to any attempt to rule against such a practice. There the matter had rested until the Canadians raised it again in the late 1920s.[24] Agreement was reached in January 1928. In his official correspondence and in his memoirs, Tilley noted the arrival of a Canadian legation in Tokyo in somewhat disparaging terms. He could concede the need for a Canadian trade mission but failed to see the value of a diplomatic one given Canada's relative lack of power. He also noted that the Japanese government was rather puzzled at the development, and seemed unsure what a Canadian legation would do which the British embassy was not able to do. Nevertheless, the Canadian mission opened in 1929 and Tilley got on well with its first head, Mr Herbert Marler.[25] Until the Second World War, Canadian consular interests elsewhere in Japan, like those of the other dominions and the Irish Free State (Eire after 1937), continued to be handled by British officials.[26] Australia followed Canada with its own separate diplomatic representation in August 1940, having had a separate trade commissioner from 1935.[27]

Tilley's successor was Sir Francis Lindley,* who had served in Tokyo before the First World War. Not surprisingly, his first reaction was to note

---

*After Lindley's death, the following was found among his papers:

'Form of Daily Service to be used in Government Departments'

Let us pray
O Lord, Grant that this day we come to no decision, neither run we into any kind of responsibility, but that all our doings may be ordered to establish new departments, for ever and ever, Amen.

Hymn
Oh Thou who seest all things below,
Grant that Thy Servants may go slow,
That they may study to comply
With regulations till they die.

Teach us, O Lord to reverence
Committees more than common sense;
Train our minds to make no plan,
And pass the baby when we can.

See when the tempter seeks to give
Us feelings of initiative
Or when alone we go too far,
Chastise us with a circular.

May war and tumult, fire and storms
Give strength, O Lord, to deal out forms.
May Thy servants ever be,
A flock of perfect sheep for Thee.

Benediction
The Peace of Whitehall, which passes all understanding, preserve your mind in lethargy, your body in inertia and your soul in coma, now and for evermore. Amen.

the major changes in Tokyo since his departure. He also found himself
homeless, for the new residence was still not complete when he arrived in
July 1931. But the new Canadian legation came to his rescue. The minister,
Mr Marler, was due to go on leave about the time of Lindley's arrival, and he
kindly made his own house available for the interim period, without charge
for accommodation or servants. Perhaps for this reason, Lindley was more
positive than his predecessor on the question of the need for a Canadian
legation in Tokyo! He noted too that the Japanese had decided to appoint a
military attaché in Ottawa, which seemed to indicate that the Japanese too
were reconciled to the change.[28]

Lindley moved from the Canadian legation to Chuzenji for most of the
summer, where his wife joined him. He could have occupied the
'ambassador's bungalow', which was still standing, while the final touches
were added to the new residence, but his decision not to allowed work to
begin on the last of the planned buildings, the 'diplomatic counsellor's
house'. When he returned to Tokyo in September 1931, the residence was
ready and the Lindleys moved in on 17 September. Although Lindley liked
the new house, for a time he was worried that it would prove too expensive
to run, and he wrote to London suggesting that he might be forced to take
over one of the smaller houses on the compound.[29]

In the event, he decided that none of the other houses would be large
enough, and accepted that he would have to manage. The new residence's
capacities were soon amply tested. In October 1931, Lindley entertained
some 450 people on the occasion of a major naval visit. He noted that 'the
accommodation as regards bedrooms' was not lavish, but that the living and
reception rooms were '. . . remarkably fine and suitable for their purpose'.
He and his wife liked the ballroom, where they had hung such royal
portraits as they had – he asked for one of Queen Victoria – and '. . . which
is really a very fine room and a charming one, now that the little courtyard
at the back has been arranged as a Japanese garden'. They changed some
other things; Lindley had the ceiling fans taken out of the dining-room and
the two drawing-rooms since '. . . [t]hey completely ruined the appearance
of the rooms and are, in my opinion, quite unnecessary'. The Office of
Works had no picture of Queen Victoria, and expressed some surprise that
there was not one already in Tokyo, but Lindley found he had engravings of
the Winterhalter pictures of the Queen and Prince Albert, bought in Lisbon,
and used those.[30]

Lindley recorded with some pride that Viscount Massey, former Canadian
minister at Washington, felt that the Tokyo residence was '. . . superior for
entertaining purposes to Sir Edward Lutyens' palace' – the British residence
in Washington, designed by the architect of the central buildings in New
Delhi. Another unsolicited opinion in favour of the new residence, and of
its new occupants, was quoted by Sir Edward Crowe of the Department of
Overseas Trade, and himself a former commercial counsellor in Tokyo, in a
letter to the Office of Works in March 1932. A Russian resident of Tokyo, a
'very talented man', had written to Sir Harold Parlett, former Japanese
counsellor, comparing the new, and traditional-styled British embassy to its
US counterpart:

Another event was the opening of the new British Embassy, although Mr Raymond (a well-known architect) and other people whose taste is founded on such examples of art as our Imperial Hotel, were disgusted by the absence of modernity in it. They found it beautiful, very comfortable, very homely and at the same time very imposing. Here I must say that though I always make the defence of the old residents, and declare that the new ones cannot be compared with the old, I must confess that the more I see of the Lindleys, the more charming I find them.

The writer found the new US embassy, which attempted to '. . . combine comfort with, luckily restrained, modern ideas' somewhat less successful, It was, he said, '. . . a kind of Ritz with Corean roof'.[31]

The new chancery building was completed and in use before the residence. The staff flats and new offices had been occupied since the middle of 1930. The chancery was, in Lindley's opinion, the 'most imposing and complete' such building that he had seen anywhere – though privately he was somewhat concerned at the cost of heating and lighting the chancery, which he had to meet. He also noted that a number of other houses were still under construction. When they were finished, all the staff would be able to live on the compound.[32] (Although he presented this as a positive development in 1931, in 1933 he would claim that he did not think it was a good idea, and that diplomatic staff should have been compelled to find and pay for their own accommodation, 'as they do elsewhere'.[33]) Not all were as taken with the new compound as the ambassador. Piggott, returning in 1936 for a further spell as military attaché, noted that '. . . the British Embassy was entirely new, but it would be idle to pretend that old hands though it an improvement in appearance or architecture on the original building'.[34] The rebuilt Yokohama consulate-general also reopened in 1931.

The rest of the buildings were finished, and the compound fully in use by December 1932. The Office of Works took much pride in its handiwork, which, as we have seen, had received praise from the trade press and from individuals. There was one other source of praise, at least as far as the residence was concerned. On 31 January 1931, the Treasury wrote to the Office of Works noting that the estimate of the '. . . total cost of the scheme, excluding furniture' had again been reduced, from £205,000 to £180,000, and that '. . . Their Lordships desire to record Their satisfaction at the way this important undertaking is being handled by your Department'. The Office of Works was amazed, and it was suggested, tongue-in-cheek, that this unexpected and unusual testimonial might be framed and presented to Mr Wynnes, who had supervised the work on the spot. Alas! Others felt that to do so would ignore the contribution made by the rest of the team, and the light-hearted thought gave rise to much solemn minuting. In the event, nothing was done, and the testimonial was locked away in the confidential safe until 1958. By then, all concerned had retired, and it was thought safe to downgrade it.[35]

How long the new compound could contain all staff is not clear, but it was not very long. There had never been any intention to accommodate the service attachés on the compound, and Piggott, on his return in 1936, certainly found that he was expected to provide his own housing. Arthur de la Mare, a newly arrived student interpreter in 1937, at first lived in the student quarters above the chancery. He did not enjoy it much, especially when he found that the student interpreters were expected to provide gin each lunch-time for any members of chancery who felt in need of a drink. The result was a procession of '. . . Third Secretaries, cypher clerks, accountants, archivists, Naval, Military and Air Attachés, and their respective satraps, and all manner of other creatures all claiming both a right and a thirst'.[36]

This apparently could be dangerous; de la Mare tells with relish the story of a chief cypher clerk who hid the code books, brought to the drinks party for safe keeping, only to find a week later that he could not find them. This would have mattered little, except that the Foreign Office, having sent a cyphered telegram on Monday, was expressing concern by Friday that it had not been answered. Fortunately, however, the Japanese maid remembered that the code books had been concealed inside the gramophone on the previous Friday. They seem to have been safely recovered, and nobody was told of their disappearance. De la Mare, who claimed to dislike gin, was pleased when he was forced at the end of his first year to leave the student quarters and find a house off the compound. He found a Japanese house, in a Japanese quarter and, after his marriage in 1940, he continued to live off the compound in another Japanese house.[37]

Lindley left Japan in 1934. He and his wife had been popular with their staff, and both were regarded as genial and friendly. George Sansom apparently thought him the best ambassador he had known, and was particularly pleased by Lindley's willingness to take on the Foreign Office.[38] Lindley's successor was Sir Robert Clive, of whom the *Dictionary of National Biography* notes that he held a series of 'difficult and frustrating posts' including Tokyo and Brussels. Why Brussels was so frustrating is not clear, but Clive's time in Tokyo coincided with the events which were to lead Japan to full-scale war in China in 1937, and the consequent deterioration in Anglo-Japanese relations. His own lack of an east Asian background may partly account for his frustration in Tokyo. Like Lindley, Clive was popular with his embassy colleagues, as was his wife, whom Lady Sansom found particularly witty and amusing.

It was Lady Clive, however, who caused joy in the Office of Works with the saga of her teapots. In a private letter written in January 1936, to Sir Patrick Duff, permanent secretary at the Office of Works from 1933, Lady Clive drew attention to the poor condition of the embassy's plate. The plate had been purchased in 1907 and it had not worn well. The knives were old-fashioned and needed elaborate cleaning. But worst of all were the teapots, which were such bad pourers that they could not be used. In reporting this, she claimed that she did not wish to be a nuisance, but that she thought it was right that Sir Patrick should know about the condition of his property.[39]

Sir Patrick replied promptly, and in the nicest possible fashion. Far from taking offence, he was delighted to be able to help. Times were hard, however, and he could do little about the plate. But if Lady Clive returned the teapots, then he would see what could be done. The teapots were duly returned, under cover of a letter from Sir Robert Clive, on 3 April. On 15 June, Sir Patrick wrote to Clive:

> We duly received the two teapots . . . and they have now been examined. Both, as you say, poured badly, but do you know what was the matter? Just an accumulation of tea leaves and tannin, and when they had been removed by means of hot water and a little strong soda they poured quite easily! As a matter of interest, I had them both brought up to me to see, one of them treated and the other before it had been cleaned. There is, therefore, nothing for us to do but return them, and we will start them back on the long trail by this week's bag.

Lady Clive replied on 18 July:

> Your letter of June 15th to my husband about the teapots really must have cheered you up and relieved some of the tedious side of your correspondence! I must say I felt shocked and scandalized & offer you my sincerest apologies. It is the old story of believing what one is told instead of looking to every detail oneself.
>
> When I arrived in Tokyo & the silly things poured so badly I spoke to the head servant who said that they had always been like that & that Lady Lindley could not & did not use them. He even declared that they had been to a silversmith here who had been unable to improve them. I never dreamt of the accumulation of 30 years & took what the servant said to be a fact. I am so sorry. Such a thing shall not happen again if I can help it.

No doubt it made a pleasant interlude in what was generally rather a glum year.

In 1937, Clive in turn was succeeded by Sir Robert Craigie. Like his predecessors, Craigie, although familiar with some of the problems of East Asia – he and General Piggott, who was now to be his military attaché in Tokyo, had worked together at the 1921 Washington Naval Conference[40]- did not speak Japanese and was not an East Asian expert. It was his misfortune, to put it no higher, to find himself in the middle of a set of circumstances which seemed destined to lead Britain and Japan into conflict.[41] To the Sansoms, stern assessors of ambassadors, at least in private, both Craigie and his wife were uncongenial from the start. Lady Sansom described the new ambassador as '. . . experienced as a committee sort of man . . .

. . . [who] seems to have no idea what people are really like, let alone oriental ones'. She found Lady Craigie equally wanting: '. . . she is an American from Georgia who means well but acts entirely autocratically'.[42] Craigie was to make little use of Sansom's knowledge and experience, preferring to rely on Piggott, which perhaps partly explains the lack of rapport between the men.

The Craigies had arrived in Yokohama on 3 September 1937. It was not an auspicious time. In early July, there had occurred the clash between Japanese and Chinese forces at Luguoqiao, or the Marco Polo bridge, south west of Beijing, which was to develop into the full-scale Sino-Japanese War. Even though the full consequences of that incident were not obvious by late August, it was clear to all that events in China had moved into a new stage. On 26 August, the British ambassador in China, Sir Hughe Knatchbull-Hugessen, was wounded when his car was bombed and machine-gunned by aircraft with Japanese markings. The Japanese locally and in Tokyo expressed their regrets about the incident, but denied that Japanese forces were necessarily involved. Anglo-Japanese relations were thus at a very low ebb. The chargé d'affaires in Tokyo had received instructions to seek an apology from the Japanese government, and to warn that if no apology was forthcoming, Craigie would be withdrawn as soon as he arrived.[43]

Craigie, still at sea, was not aware of these exchanges, but claimed that he seriously wondered whether he should disembark at Yokohama. But he did, and having endured what he described as the 'penance' of the eighteen-mile drive to Tokyo, something which he and his wife clearly never enjoyed during their years in Japan, he arrived at the embassy and was welcomed by all the staff. But so uncertain was Craigie of his future in Japan that he and his wife did not unpack their trunks for a fortnight.[44] In due course, Britain received from the Japanese government an acknowledgement that an unfortunate incident had occurred, and an undertaking that everything would be done to ensure that no similar incidents should occur. It was less than Britain had demanded, but seemed all that it was likely to get, and so was deemed acceptable.[45]

Once in Tokyo, and safe within the grounds of the embassy, the Craigies were more pleased with their new appointment. They were delighted with the welcome which they received from the residence staff, who were to serve them loyally even after the outbreak of war. They were less impressed with their new house. Craigie wrote:

> The Embassy was comparatively new, having been constructed on the site of the old buildings which had been damaged beyond repair in the 1923 earthquake. The house, built in the Georgian style, is comparatively well proportioned and commodious. But the furniture and furnishings left much to be desired, both as regards quantity and quality. The bleak appearance of the rooms, the suffocating damp heat and the mosquitoes combined to produce a depressing effect at the outset. But this soon wore off. In our desire to leave nothing undone which might help to promote relations at this critical time, we had brought with us some of our best furniture, rugs and pictures. So we were consoled by the thought that we could make these rooms quite different.

They also succeeded in obtaining new candelabras from London, which, Craigie thought, would help him in his policy of putting up a good show to the Japanese, in spite of difficulties.[46] Whatever the Craigies did, however, the photographs in his book show the embassy's public rooms in his time as being remarkably dreary, at least by current standards, and far less pleasant than those which had adorned the pages of *The Builder* in 1933.[47]

In 1937, however, it would require more than rugs and pictures to help improve Britain's relations with Japan. By the late 1930s, anti-British feeling was strong in many parts of the Japanese empire and in those parts of China under Japanese control. There had been a few anti-British demonstrations outside the embassy in the past. In 1932, for example, a group of 'ill-kept youths' had staged a protest at the embassy in favour of Gandhi, which eventually led to the arrest and imprisonment of the leader.[48] In those days, any sign of anti-foreign hostility had been met by a an increased police presence and instant action against those involved.

By 1937, it was different. That November, as Sino-Japanese relations deteriorated following the Marco Polo bridge incident and the growing Japanese belief that the British were pro-Chinese, the embassy reported a series of anti-British demonstrations which culminated in the presentation of petitions at the embassy gates. The embassy also noted a large and hostile postbag.[49] In 1938, as the Japanese became more and more embroiled in China, there were frequent incidents involving the British, which did little to improve relations. In any case, despite repeated reassurances from the Japanese government that there was no intention on its part to interfere with foreign interests in China, there was growing scepticism in London as to Japanese motives and ultimate intentions. By the summer of 1939, the embassy was regularly reporting both the hostile tone of some sections of the Japanese press, the receipt of anti-British petitions – the *Hochi Shimbun,* a newspaper generally regarded as a pro-German, was seen behind many of these – and, increasingly, the appearances of demonstrating mobs outside the embassy gates. There were threats to the Japanese staff, and some British officials found it difficult to get served in restaurants. The embassy's view was that none of the demonstrations were really spontaneous and that on the whole those in Tokyo were not really dangerous; the occasional impolite group usually ceased to be so once reminded of the normal standards of behaviour.[50]

In many ways, normal embassy life continued. General Piggott, always one to look on the bright side, wrote enthusiastically many years later of a dinner and film evening given by the embassy in May 1939 at which senior Japanese military officers were present. The King's Birthday Party on 8 June 1939 was another occasion when the Japanese military turned out in force. The Japanese foreign minister was also present.[51] Yet despite Piggott's optimism, and the embassy's generally low-key assessment of the threat, Sansom, revisiting in 1940, noted a great outpouring of hostility in the press and the open expression of anti-foreign feeling on the streets and in the newspapers.[52]

For the Craigies, escape from this tension-filled atmosphere was provided by the embassy summer residence at Chuzenji. There, in the house reconstructed by Sir Ernest Satow, to which '. . . modern European comforts have been grafted on to the original Japanese structure without spoiling its original design', the Craigies kept in touch with Tokyo by telephone, and went sailing or fishing with colleagues from the British and other embassies who rented or owned houses in the hills around. In addition, they rented a house at Hayama, a seaside resort some 50 minutes by train from Tokyo, which was also useful for weekends away and more accessible than Chuzenji. Transformed with new curtains and cushions, and the removal of all 'Victorian excrescences', with a backdrop of Mount Fuji, it was a useful place to entertain Japanese friends who might have been embarrassed to visit the embassy. Among those who visited it were Prince and Princess Chichibu.[53]

Notes

1 *Japan Weekly Chronicle*, 20 September 1923; see also Works 10/638, Michael Palairet, chargé d'affaires, to Lord Curzon, no. 458, 11 September 1923.

2 Sansom, *Sir George Sansom*, p. 127.

3 Works 10/638, Julius Bradbury, Shanghai, to Chief Architect 21 September 1923.

4 Works 10/638, Tokyo telno. 17, 15 January 1924; Works Shanghai tel. to London, 18 January 1924.

5 Piggott, *Broken Thread*, p. 192.

6 Piggott, *Broken Thread*, pp. 182–83, 191; papers about renting of accommodation from November onwards can be found in Works 10/638.

7 Works 10/638, Eliot to Ramsey MacDonald, no. 420, 28 October 1924.

8 Sir John Tilley, *London to Tokyo*, (London, New York and Melbourne: Hutchinson and Co. Ltd., N.D. [1942]), p. 135.

9 Works 10/639, private letter from Tilley to Sir L. Earle, 27 February 1926.

10 Tilley, *London to Tokyo*, pp. 138–9, 172.

11 FO369/1977/K441/441/223., Tilley to the FO, no. 562, 22 November 1926, enclosing Memorandum by Julius Bradley, 14 November 1926.

12 FO369/1978/K17020/17020/223, Tilley to Sir A. Chamberlain, no. 596, 22 November 1927.

13 Piggott, *Broken Thread*, p. 183.

14 See the memorandum, unsigned, but attributed to Davidson and Sansom, enclosed in Tilley to Chamberlain no. 596, 22 November 1927 in FO369/1978/ K17020/17020/223.

15 Sansom, *Sir George Sansom*, p. 18.

16 In fact, papers in Works 10/638 show that both Eliot and Tilley had let London know at regular intervals their views on what was needed for new buildings in Tokyo. Both, for example, had very clear – and accurate – ideas of what could be done in terms of providing relatively earthquake-proof buildings.

17 See references to Allison in Nikolaus Pevsner, *The Buildings of England: London except the cities of London and Westminster*, (Harmondsworth, Middlesex: Penguin Books, 1952), pp. 258, 280; *Who's Who 1947*, (London: Adam and Charles Black, 1947), p. 42. Allison's whole career was with the Office of Works. For the Foreign Office involvement in the plans, see Works 10/641, Memorandum of 20 October 1931; this paper notes that the Foreign Office paper was not on file.

18 'New Embassies in Tokyo: Buildings of Character', *The Times*, 8 February 1932.

19 'US embassy scene of $35,000 repairs', *Japan Advertiser*, 14 July 1938, and minute on it by J C Wynnes, Office of Works, 31 August 1938 in Works 10/641.

20 'New Embassies in Tokyo: Buildings of Character', *The Times*, 8 February 1932; *The Builder*, 17 November 1933. Both articles carried photographs of the new compound, and *The Builder* included plans of the residence.

21 Tilley, *London to Tokyo*, pp. 171–72. For Treasury doubts about the ballroom, see Works 10/639, Treasury to Works, S.22140/01, 28 May 1925.

22 Sansom, *Sir George Sansom*, p. 35. It was also mentioned in Tilley's Annual Report for 1929, though in more restrained terms. See Tilley to Arthur Henderson, no. 150, 26 March 1930, *Japan and Dependencies*, vol. 2, p. 383. For the Office of Works plans, see Works 10/ 640, Tokyo telno. 72, 2 April 1929.

23 Tilley, *London to Tokyo*, pp. 149–50, 154–55.

24 Annual Report 1909; Sir Claude MacDonald to Sir Edward Grey, no. 22, 28 January 1910, in *Japan and Dependencies*, vol. 1, p. 133.

25 Annual Report 1928; Tilley to Sir Austen Chamberlain, no. 100, 13 March 1929, *Japan and Dependencies*, vol. 2, pp. 306–07, 311–12; Tilley, *London to Tokyo*, pp. 194–95. For the background to the establishment of an independent Canadian mission, see Klaus H Pringsheim, *Neighbours across the Pacific: Canadian-Japanese Relations 1870–1982*, (Oakville, Ontario: Mosaic Press, 1983), pp. 27–34. Many Canadians objected to the move, for similar reasons to those Tilley advanced.

26 See, for example, the correspondence relating to the estate of R L Hancock, who died intestate at Yokohama in 1931, in FO369/2273 of 1932.

27 Tokyo embassy political diary no. 1 of 1935 (16 May–5 June), *Japan and Dependencies*, vol. 3, p. 217; Tokyo embassy political diary no. 10, August 1940, *Japan and Dependencies*, vol. 4, p. 496.

28 Annual Report 1931, Sir F. Lindley to Sir John Simon, no. 1, 1 January 1932, *Japan and Dependencies*, vol. 2, p. 522.

29 Works 10/641, Lindley to Sir L. Earle, 19 September 1931.

30 Works 10/641, Lindley to Sir L. Earle, 19 September 1931; 25 November 1931.. The Japanese garden virtually disappeared for many years, but was rediscovered, much overgrown, by Lady Wright in the mid-1990s.

31 FO369/2272/K532/223, Sir E. T. F. Crowe to H. N. de Norman, Office of Works, private, 15 March 1932. In fairness, the US ambassador, Joseph Grew and his wife Alice, who arrived a couple of months later, were very much taken with their house and the US embassy. See Joseph C. Grew, *Ten Years in Japan*, (London: Hammond, Hammond and Co. Ltd, 1944), p. 17.

32 Annual Report 1931, Sir F. Lindley to Sir John Simon, no. 1, 1 January 1932, *Japan and Dependencies*, vol. 2, p. 519; for the chancery as a charge on the ambassador, see Works 10/641, Lindley to Sir L. Earle, 19 September 1931.

33 Works 10/641, Lindley to Sir Patrick Duff, 29 May 1933.

34 Piggott, *Broken Thread*, p. 261.

35 Works 10/641, Treasury to Works, E.18810/01/2, 31 January 1931, and related minuting.

36 Sir Arthur de la Mare, *Perverse and Foolish: A Jersey farmer's son in the British Diplomatic Service*, (Jersey, Channel Islands: La Haule Books, 1994), p. 63.

37 de la Mare, *Perverse and Foolish*, pp. 63–64, 66, 72.

38 Sansom, *Sir George Sansom*, pp. 51–52, 95.

39 Works 10/399, Lady Clive to Sir Patrick Duff, 10 January 1936. All the correspondence in this little saga comes from this file.

40 Piggott, *Broken Thread*, p. 138.

41 For Craigie, see Peter Lowe, 'The Dilemmas of an Ambassador: Sir Robert Craigie in Tokyo, 1937–1941', in Gordon Daniels and Peter Lowe, editors, *Proceedings of the British Association for Japanese Studies*, Vol. II, (1977): *History and International Relations*, pp. 34–56; Anthony Best, 'Sir Robert Craigie as Ambassador to Japan 1937–1941,' in Nish, *Britain and Japan: Biographical Portraits*, pp. 238–251.

42 Sansom, *Sir George Sansom*, p. 96.

43 The details relating to the attack on Knatchbull-Hugessen and the subsequent diplomatic exchanges can be found in W. N. Medlicott and Douglas Dakin, editors, *Documents on British Foreign Policy 1919–1939*, Second Series Vol. XXI 'Far Eastern Affairs November 1936-July 1938', (London: HMSO, 1984), Chapter 3. See also page 60–61 above.

44 Sir R. Craigie to Mr Eden, no. 1 confidential, Annual Review 1937, *Japan and Dependencies*, vol. 3, p. 591; Sir Robert Craigie, *Behind the Japanese Mask*, (London: Hutchinson and Co, N. D. [1945]), pp. 42–43.

45 Tokyo to Foreign Office, telno. 420, 21 September 1937; Foreign Office to Tokyo, telno. 334, 22 September 1937, *Documents on British Foreign Policy 1919–1939*, Second Series Vol. XXI, 333, 335–36. The exchange was published in *The Times*, 23 September 1937.

46 Works 10/399, Craigie to Sir Patrick Duff, office of Works, 4 November 1937.

47 Craigie, *Behind the Japanese Mask*, p. 44. The photographs appear opposite page 64.

48 Sir F. Lindley to Sir John Simon, Annual Report for 1932, no. 1, 1 January 1933, *Japan and Dependencies*, vol. 3, pp. 21–22.

49 Political Diary no. 11 (1 –30 November), 1937, *Japan and Dependencies*, vol. 3, p. 565.

50 Political Diary No. 7, July 1939, *Japan and Dependencies*, vol. 4, p. 287; similar material can be found in *Documents on British Foreign Policy*, Third Series, vol. IX, edited by E. L. Woodward and R. Butler (London: HMSO, 1955), p. 378. Arthur de la Mare's neighbours staged a demonstration outside his house on one occasion, but called around in the evening to apologise, claiming that the military police had forced them to demonstrate. On another occasion, students shouting anti-British slogans broke off to help put back a crashed car onto the road. Only then did they continue their demonstration. de la Mare, *Perverse and Foolish*, pp. 66–67.

51 Piggott, *Broken Thread*, p. 318–19.

52 Sansom, *Sir George Sansom*, pp. 114–15. For a discussion of the question, see Peter Lowe, 'The Dilemmas of an Ambassador', pp. 38–41, and two works by Anthony Best, 'Sir Robert Craigie as Ambassador to Japan 1937–1941,' in Nish, ed., *Britain and Japan: Biographical Portraits*, pp. 238–251 and *Britain, Japan and Pearl Harbor: Avoiding War in East Asia, 1936–41* (London and New York: Routledge, 1995).

53 Craigie, *Behind the Japanese Mask*, pp. 63–66, 94–98.

Japan

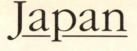

War, Detention, and Repatriation, 1941–42

The Day War Came

There was no hiding the steady deterioration in Anglo-Japanese relations, and in Japan's relations with the West in general. Whatever the optimism of General Piggott and, with qualifications, the ambassador, the embassy increasingly had to accept that war was likely. During 1940 and 1941, the embassy and the consulates throughout Japan and the Japanese empire were preoccupied with issues such as the supply of gas masks and the evacuation of as many Britons as possible from the danger areas. Japan itself seemed more dangerous, with assassination in the air. Anti-British demonstrations continued from time to time. Arrests of British subjects by the Japanese authorities in Tokyo, Seoul (Keijo) and elsewhere pointed to other dangers. The detention and apparent suicide of M. J. Cox, the Reuters' correspondent in Tokyo in July 1940 caused considerable alarm in the foreign community.[1] The American ambassador began to carry a gun after the attempt on the life of Prince Konoe in September 1941, though there is no evidence that his British colleagues did the same.[2]

By the end of April 1941, some 1,040 British subjects, including abut 140 Indians, had already left the Japanese empire and Manzhoukuo. Soon after, British and American shipping ceased to call at Japanese ports. After the freeze imposed on Japanese assets by Britain, the Netherlands and the United States in July 1941, in retaliation for the Japanese seizure of bases in Indo-China, Japanese shipping in turn ceased to operate except to areas within the co-prosperity sphere, and the evacuation of British and other allied subjects became even more difficult. Eventually, the only route available was through Shanghai. Even that became difficult, as Japanese companies began to discriminate against people from what it regarded as hostile countries. Yet efforts to get people out continued, with special ships chartered from China to take foreigners to Shanghai and then onwards. By autumn 1941, all British subjects who were willing to go had done so. The remainder totalled just over a thousand people, of whom 733 were in Japan, 278 in 'Manchukuo', 58 in Korea, 10 in the Kwangtung Leased Territory, and 1 in Taiwan.[3] The world of the foreign community was now a smaller and more dangerous place.

At the same time, of course, life went on. Within the embassy compound and the reduced British community, it was much as before. The embassy was large, and as international tension increased, more and more busy. Paul Gore-Booth, arriving in early 1938 from Vienna, found it all much harder work than he had been used to. Gone were the leisurely days when chancery officers were not expected to attend in the afternoons. Now chancery officers were expected to work from 09.00 to 13.00 and from 14.30 to 19.00, with no time for tea, never mind gin. New work needed to be done. It was only after the outbreak of the war in Europe, for example, that the embassy began to do any form of information work. This eventually led to the appointment of the *Daily Mail* Tokyo correspondent, Vere Redman, as press and information officer, to organize the somewhat amateur enterprise which the embassy itself had set up. Curiously enough, Craigie claimed that he learnt of this addition to his staff from the Japanese press before London informed him. He was not best pleased. Sansom, visiting from London in the summer of 1940, wrote to his wife that '. . . The Chancery is lousy with Ministry of Information staff, most of whom (not their fault) are ineffective and expensive'.[4] But there was still time for that favourite of British embassies and British expatriates everywhere, amateur dramatics. There were also two weddings in 1940; those of Arthur de la Mare and Paul Gore-Booth. Perhaps all was not completely sweetness and light in the compound, and old divisions between diplomats (Gore-Booth) and consuls (de la Mare) may have still been strong; both bridegrooms wrote memoirs and neither mentions the other's existence, never mind wedding.

Practical issues did not go away, either. In the middle of the anti-British demonstrations of 1939, the embassy began to receive enquiries from the Tokyo Tax Bureau about the rent paid for the compound. The French, United States and German embassies, all of which seemed to be held on similar terms, received similar enquiries. Only the leasehold properties had been approached, Craigie noted in reporting this.[5] The post clearly felt that the Japanese had a point, since the rent had remained unaltered since 1884. London was less convinced, and the Treasury view was that the original arrangement was intended to be perpetual. There was therefore no obvious reason why there should be any change. The Foreign Office tended to agree, but accepted that if the US embassy was to agree to a change to its lease, then Britain should follow. Replying, the post indicated that the US attitude was robust, querying the right of the Taxation Bureau rather than the Ministry of Foreign Affairs to raise the issue, and arguing that it had been settled in the 1890s. This stiffened Foreign Office resolve, and a telegram instructed Craigie to say that in the British view, the lease was perpetual, and HMG would prefer that the issue was not raised. Nothing more was heard before the outbreak of war.[6]

War came to the Tokyo embassy at 7.45 on what Lord Gore-Booth described as '. . . the singularly weird morning of Monday 8 December 1941'.[7] That was the time at which Craigie received a telephone call summoning him to call on the Minister of Foreign Affairs at his official residence. In fact, by then the embassy had been functioning for several hours, since Vere Redman had arrived at 0500 hours to begin the radio watch which enabled the embassy to put out up-to-the-minute public bulletins about the progress of the war. Redman reported that according to broadcasts from Lisbon and Ankara, the Japanese had attacked Pearl Harbor. Such reports had been heard before and nobody paid much attention. In any case, reception was bad and it was not certain that the news had been properly received.

There followed a busy day. At the minister's house, Craigie was told that negotiations in Washington had broken down, but although the import of this was clear, the Japanese did not announce that war had begun. When Craigie returned to the embassy, however, he was told that the Japanese radio had announced that 'warlike operations' had begun against Britain and the United States. Having heard this news, the embassy staff began to destroy the remaining cyphers and confidential papers. They also sent out messages to those not on the compound to come in with their families. By 08.20, the telephone was cut and it was then difficult to contact staff.[8]

Later that morning, Craigie was able US ambassador to see Grew. At the British embassy everything seemed relatively normal, with no extra police, but the scene was quite different at the American embassy, where Japanese police were out in force and controlling access. Craigie saw Grew, though not without some difficulty. When he returned to his own embassy, however, normality had disappeared. Extra police were everywhere and the gates were closed. He was allowed in, and the gates shut behind him.[9]

Craigie was able to send a telegram reporting his early morning call on 8 December, but it was to be the last normal function of the embassy. Telegrams were still sent, but they now went via the Argentine embassy, since Argentina was the British protecting power, and tended to take a relatively long time. It was through this channel that Craigie was able to report in early January 1942 that, according to the MFA, all diplomatic and consular staff throughout the Japanese empire and occupied territories were safe – although the Japanese claimed to have no information about the condition of British officials in the independent state of Manzhoukuo.[10]

Soon after the beginning of the war, the government of Japan issued a statement in which it claimed that all foreigners detained in Japan were being carefully looked after, but protected in their own interests. In the case of diplomats, the statement said that

> . . . the Japanese Government does not spare its efforts to concede them, in accordance with international practice, the greatest possible facilities to enable them to continue in a normal manner their daily life, allowing them to leave their domiciles with the previous consent of the officer of the Ministry for Foreign Affairs appointed in the Embassy or Legation concerned. With regard to the purchase of foodstuffs and indispensable articles these diplomats will also enjoy every possible facility.

To make sure that this happened, the note went on, the Chief of Police of Tokyo had visited each diplomatic mission on 9 December 1941, asking its head to communicate with him if there were any problems.[11]

The reality was perhaps a little different. When Craigie returned to the compound on 8 December 1941, he found an MFA official waiting to deliver the notice of the outbreak of war, and demanding to search the compound for a wireless transmitter. Despite pressure, the staff had managed to persuade him that nothing should be done until Craigie's return. Craigie first of all requested a formal call on the Minister of Foreign Affairs to ask for his passports, but this was refused on the grounds that there could be no question of an immediate departure because of the lack of transport. Instead, the official, Mr Ohta, head of the British section of the MFA, asked for the handover of the wireless transmitter which he claimed was known to be on the premises. (In fact, there was no transmitter; at that time, only the residual mission in Beijing had its own wireless facilities among British diplomatic posts.) When Craigie denied that there was a transmitter, Ohta announced that he was going to search the compound, but eventually agree not to search the residence. He took away all the short -ave radio receivers – or at least those which he could find – with vague, and eventually unfulfilled, promises that they would be returned. Meanwhile, the burning of the remaining confidential papers went on in Chancery; the Japanese made no attempt to interfere with this exercise.[12] (Paul Gore-Booth noted that twelve years later, when he was ambassador in Rangoon, Mr Ohta became the Japanese ambassador, and sent a note looking forward to '. . . renewing our old friendship'; it was a nice touch from '. . . the person who has in effect declared war on you'.[13])

In the meantime, other members of the embassy who lived off the compound and who had been uncontactable earlier, were being brought in by the Japanese police. Although they were treated in rather a rough-and-ready fashion, perhaps by rather worried policemen who were not sure how the Japanese population would react, there were no real complaints about their treatment, except the case of Mrs Redman, the wife of the embassy's information officer. She managed to pass a message to the embassy which said that she was being prevented from coming to the compound because she was being held as a hostage to ensure her husband's return from the embassy, preparatory to his arrest. It required much effort, including an unsuccessful expedition by Lady Craigie, to effect her release, and was to prove only a temporary victory in the battle with the Japanese over Redman. Others outside the compound included the embassy chaplain, Mr Simonds, who was held for several days before he, too, was released and allowed to join the detained group.[14]

Internment December 1941–July 1942[15]

By the end of 8 December 1941, the expatriate population of the compound had tripled, with some sixty additional people being brought in. (The Foreign Office in London in late December estimated that there were 43 men, 15 women staff members, 16 wives and 'perhaps 9 children' on the compound.[16]) There followed a major logistics exercise to fit the new arrivals into the existing space. Many had arrived for work on the morning of 8 December without realizing that war had begun and now found themselves with only the clothes they were wearing. Every available source of additional clothing was raided. There were not enough beds to go round, but the wife of the Danish consul-general arrived with a supply of camp beds, which she managed to get in despite the efforts of the police to prevent her.

Food was another problem, solved again by pooling all resources – interestingly enough, neither the embassy nor the Japanese authorities appear to have given much thought to this issue in advance, and on neither side had proper stocks of food been built up. There were a few domestic caches which individual officers had accumulated, and these the embassy as a whole was able to use. A supply of food which had arrived at Kobe for the embassy just before the outbreak of war was eventually released by the Japanese. It not only provided some variety in a monotonous diet, but allowed the embassy ladies to make three-quarters of a ton (!) of marmalade, most of which was sent to prisoner-of-war camps. But for most food, the embassy was dependent on Japanese supplies, which were erratic at first. Even when they became more regular, they were often barely sufficient for those detained. Craigie placed the control of food supplies in the hands of Mrs Mason, the mother of John Mason, the vice-consul. She ruled with a rod of iron, was never accused of unfairness, and received an OBE for her efforts. Later, after the war, when she continued to live in Japan, she would attend the Queen's Birthday Party. Lording it over lesser mortals and acquiring the title 'Queenie' – though perhaps not to her face.[17]

Much effort was devoted to negotiations with the Japanese. The Japanese police, charged with supervising the detainees, were at first very intrusive, insisting on periodically visiting the various houses on the compound. After a series of meetings with the MFA and the Tokyo Metropolitan Police chief, the intrusions stopped just before Christmas. Much of the day to day handling of the police was left to two Japanese-speaking officers, H. R. Sawbridge and John Mason, who often had to engage in long and complex negotiations over relatively simple matters, usually in the vicinity of the embassy main gate.

Issues that could not be handled at the gate level, as it were, involved the protecting power. At the outbreak of war, this was Argentina, but the efforts of the Argentine chargé, Senor Vila, to help the British were complicated at first by the refusal of the Japanese to accept that Argentina was the protecting power. In order to establish that all the British diplomatic and consular staff were safe, Vila got around the Japanese restrictions by conducting a conversation with Craigie at the gates, but this was not a very satisfactory nor reliable way of doing business. After vigorous protests and allegations that their behaviour was contrary to international law, the Japanese relented, and Vila was able to visit Craigie. For a time the Japanese insisted that a liaison officer had to be present during these meetings, which led to further protests; eventually that too stopped. The Japanese continued to keep a tight control over the detainees, who, apart from the ambassador, were only allowed out to visit the doctor.[18] Early in 1942, the Swiss government took over as protecting power. This was not, as de la Mare says, because Argentina had been persuaded by the United States to declare war on Japan,[19] but because the Swiss were already the protecting power for Japan in Britain and the British empire, and it was administratively more convenient to have the same country handling both sides. All agreed that the Argentine officials had done everything possible to help, despite the severe restrictions which the Japanese placed on their activities.

The most serious incident involving the protecting power, and one which it was believed by the British that the Japanese were wholly in the wrong, was the arrest and detention of members of the embassy, and of consular officers at Yokohama. At Yokohama, three members of staff were arrested in late December, interrogated and maltreated, and imprisoned until repatriated in July 1942. R. Hawley, director of the cultural and information library in Tokyo, was also arrested, and accused of espionage. He, too, was detained in prison until repatriated.

But the most serious case was that of the head of the information department and press attaché, Vere Redman.[20] That Redman was viewed with particular suspicion was obvious from the Japanese behaviour towards his wife on 8 December, but they had never been happy about the appointment of a former journalist as press attaché. There was a further complication in that the ambassador had not sought to list Redman as a diplomat until October 1941, although he had been appointed in early 1940. When war broke out, negotiations as to his status were still in train. In December 1941, therefore, he was listed only as a member of the clerical and support staff of the embassy. Craigie expected further moves against Redman, and this proved to be the case. The Japanese informed Vila on 11 December 1942 that they intended to arrest Redman and asked for Craigie's agreement. Craigie believed that this move was made at German and Italian prompting, for the Axis powers had disliked Redman's news bulletins. Craigie refused to cooperate, on the grounds that no charge had been laid against Redman, and that as far as he was concerned, Redman had kept strictly to his allotted task, which was to counter German and Italian propaganda. None of Redman's work had been directed against the Japanese. However, Craigie moved him and his wife in the residence, in the hope that being under the ambassador's roof might provide extra protection.

This proved to be in vain. The chief of the MFA's protocol department, Mr Kiuchi, called on Craigie and asked him to reconsider his refusal. Craigie declined to do so, and on 13 December, Mr Kiuchi called again, this time in top hat and tails. He announced that Redman would be taken by force. As soon as he left, a party of Japanese gendarmes burst in and Redman was taken. The Japanese assured Craigie that they were fully aware of Redman's medical condition – he was diabetic – and that he would receive proper treatment. Instead, he was deprived of insulin for long periods, severely interrogated and confined to a small cell until released in July 1942 just prior to repatriations. During this period, he received one visit from the Swiss minister and one from his wife.

For most in the compound, the period of internment was one of monotony and boredom. Some regular work remained to be done; political reports were compiled on the basis of Japanese media reports, and the events of early December were carefully chronicled. Paul Gore-Booth and a colleague compiled an inventory of British business and personal property in Japan. As usual on such occasions, there were strenuous efforts to provide entertainment of one sort or another. There were classes in various languages and skills, including Scottish dancing on the squash courts. Tennis and squash helped some, gardening and woodcutting others. Craigie welcomed the chance to put the compound gardens in order. Various publications appeared, aimed at a variety of readers. There was much music, including an embassy orchestra, and occasional parties. It was possible to get outside for medical and other treatment, and, in Lady Craigie's case at least, even for shopping, which meant that the King's Birthday dinner took place in a room bedecked with paper Union Jacks carefully sorted out by her police escort in one of the shops. The orchestra played, and there was even a film sent by the Japanese MFA.

Although not known to most, a concealed short-wave receiver provided news of the outside world in addition to that which could be gleaned from the Japanese press and radio. The information received in this fashion could only be disseminated in very roundabout way but it helped to put Japanese claims into some perspective. Not that the news was particularly good in early 1942, as the Japanese swept all before them, but it was thought better to have it from non-Japanese sources. The first of the 'Doolittle raids' in April 1942 not only provided a welcome test for the embassy's ARP staff, but also a sign that perhaps Japan would not have things all its own way.

As spring gave way to summer, there arose the possibility of the whole embassy moving to Chuzenji. This fell through, mainly because most of the staff did not want the expense involved, and the Japanese were adamant that all or none had to go. Craigie, who fell ill, was allowed to go with his wife to Miyanoshita in early July, where he found many other diplomatic detainees. When he returned, the final preparations were under way for the repatriation of all the staff.

Repatriation[21]

From the very beginning of the internment, the diplomatic staff expected that they would eventually be repatriated. It was a well understood principle of international law that diplomatic and consular officers would be allowed to return to their own countries once normal diplomatic relations have given way to the abnormal conditions of wartime.

The first move came from the Japanese. On 7 January 1942, the Japanese proposed through the Argentine government that negotiations should begin for the repatriation of all officials, non-permanent residents, and women and children among permanent residents in Japan, Manzhouguo and occupied China. This proposal was received at the Foreign Office in London on 10 January 1942. After some discussion, it was agreed that such an exchange should take place. There then followed a long period of internal negotiations which threw up a series of complications involving British colonial officials and the British communities throughout Japanese occupied territory. Meanwhile, the United States (and Canada) were working on a set of separate but parallel proposals. Since any exchange would include representatives of the Allied powers and the Dominions, their governments also had to be consulted. It was not until mid-April 1942, therefore, that a reply was finally sent agreeing to an exchange, providing that those such as Redman who had been arrested by the Japanese, were included.

There then followed complicated negotiations with the US about coordination of movements, and with the Dominions and allies about numbers and categories. There were also exchanges with neutral countries and with other British government departments over the provision of shipping, no easy task in wartime. Perhaps the most difficult of these negotiations was with the British Ministry of War Transport, which was reluctant to make shipping needed for the transport of men, food and other necessities of war, available for the repatriation of civilians, however exalted. Because of the lack of cooperation from the Ministry of War Transport, there was no definite ship available by the time the reply was sent to the Japanese on 17 April. Another complication was the attempt to keep the US and British exchanges simultaneous. In the end, this had to be abandoned.

While these exchanges were taking, Craigie sat in Tokyo, vaguely aware of what was going on, but increasingly concerned at the slowness of it all and the apparent success of the US in getting their detainees out ahead of the British. Petulant telegrams arrived through the protecting power, which the Foreign Office could do little about. There was some gritting of teeth, but Craigie's stress was understood, and soft answers were returned.[22]

Eventually, in July 1942, all was ready. There were last minute hitches at both ends, as people failed to appear on lists, or, in the case of one group of Japanese, were discovered still detained after the evacuation ship had sailed. (The ship returned to Liverpool to take them off.) In the Tokyo case, however, London was relieved to receive a Note from the Swiss Legation in London on 1 August 1942 announcing that the *Tatsuta Maru* had left Japan at 6 am Tokyo time on 31 July.[23] In what was an unusual lapse of courtesy as far as the diplomats were concerned, the Japanese declined to provide help with hand baggage, and the final departure from Japan for many involved a difficult struggle with their own and other peoples' belongings.

The formal exchange took place at the Portuguese colony of Lourenço Marques, with the British going down one gangplank as the Japanese went up another. From there, Craigie sent more telegrams, complaining now more openly about Japanese behaviour during the repatriation process, and causing numerous complications by intervening in matters he inevitably did not understand.[24] But before long, he and his colleagues moved on to London and other destinations, and new jobs.

Epilogue – The Embassy in Wartime

From the moment of the departure of the British, Swiss officials became responsible for the compound. A number of Japanese servants continued to live there, right through the war. When the Swiss first assumed responsibility, there were fifteen heads of household and their families on the compound, but this had been reduced by 1945. A list compiled in 1945 gave the names as follows:[25]

Yonebayashi Shinichi
Kedoin Hiroshi
Kato Yokichi
Kamada Chozo
Aizawn (sic) – Aizawa Manzo
Kobayashi Masakichi
Kanai Heiji
Yasui Takeo.

All of these had been employed before the war, and in some cases had long service. Kamada, for example, had been a janitor for thirty-seven years, and Kanai a groundsman for twenty-three years. During the war, they had kept a general watch over the grounds and buildings, and had helped to construct air-raid shelters. Two of staff, Kato, who had been employed for twenty years, and who had been the head servant in pre-war days, and Yonebayashi Shinichi, employed for sixteen years, had some access to the houses during the war. In general, however, the Japanese staff seem to have entered the houses only when accompanying Swiss officials, who visited regularly to air the buildings and supervise the cleaning.

At first this work was carried out by Swiss diplomats. Alfred Kunz did the job from 29 July 1942 until October 1944. From September 1944 until the end of the War, Paul Zimmerlin, a former Swiss-American businessman, was employed as custodian, a post he held until the British resumed control in 1946.[26]

Notes

1 Embassy Tokyo, Political Diary No. 9, (July 1940), No. 11, (August 1940), *Japan and Dependencies*, vol. 4, 477–78, 490–91.

2 Grew, *Ten Years in Japan*, p. 306.

3 FO369/2732/K5158/10/250, Craigie to Eden, no. 431, 21 October 1941 (received 29 April 1942), and enclosure; FO371/31736/F217/33/61, Minute by T E Barnely, 19 December 1941. By way of comparison, ten years previously the numbers had been as follows: Japan proper, 2,500; 70 in Taiwan; 283 in Korea; and 43 in the Kwangtung Leased Territory. See Lindley to Simon, no. 1, 1 January 1932, in *Japan and Dependencies*, vol. II, p. 520. 'Manchukuo' did not exist in 1931.

4 Paul Gore-Booth, *With Great Truth and Respect*, (London: Constable, 1974), pp. 79, 89–90; Sansom, *Sir George Sansom*, p. 116. For an account of Vere Redman, see Sir Hugh Cortazzi, 'Sir Vere Redman, 1901–1975' in Nish, *Britain and Japan: Biographical Portraits*, vol. II, 283–300.

5 Works 10/636, Craigie to Halifax, no. 467, 21 June 1939.

6 Works 10/636, Treasury to Works, 20 October 1939; FO to Works, 27 January 1940, and related papers; some of the papers are also on FO366/1052 of 1939. In 1942, the Tokyo embassy, awaiting repatriation, drew up a memorandum suggesting that if the issue was raised with the protecting power, the matter should be refereed to London. In practice, nothing happened during the war.

7 Gore-Booth, *With Great Truth and Respect*, p. 104.

8 Gore-Booth, *With Great Truth and Respect*, p. 105–6; Craigie, *Behind the Japanese Mask*, pp. 134–36. The account in de la Mare, *Perverse and Foolish*, pp. 77–8 is characteristically more racy, and emphasises the important role of the author; it is, perhaps, a little less accurate than the other two.

9 Craigie, *Behind the Japanese Mask*, pp. 134–36. Grew's account of the call is in Grew, *Ten Years in Japan*, p. 425.

10 FO371/3176/F116/33/61, Buenos Aires to Foreign Office, telno. 11, 3 January 1942.

11 FO371/3176/F1408/33/61, Sir E. Ovey, Buenos Aires, to Eden, no. 288, 22 December 1941, enclosing Argentine MFA to British Embassy, 18 December 1941.

12 Craigie, *Behind the Japanese Mask*, p. 136. A similar, if less precise account, is given in de la Mare, *Perverse and Foolish*, pp. 77–78, which implies that various radio sets were concealed from the Japanese.

13 Gore-Booth, *With great truth and respect*, p. 108.

14 Craigie, *Behind the Japanese Mask*, p. 136–7.

15 Most of what follows is based on published accounts of the internment period: Craigie, *Behind the Japanese Mask*, pp. 138–51; Gore-Booth, *With Great Truth and Respect*, pp. 109–114; and de la Mare, *Perverse and Foolish*, pp. 77–80. Readers will make up their own minds, but the first two seem to me more reliable than the third.

16 FO371/31736/F217/33/61, minute by T. E. Barnley, 25 December 1941.

17 Letter from Sir Hugh Cortazzi, 16 July 1996.

18 FO371/31737/F1924/33/61, Buenos Aires telno. 225 to FO, 26 February 1942.

19 Argentina did not in fact declare war on Japan (and Germany) until 1945. See R. A. Humphries, *Latin America and the Second World War*, (London: Athlone for the Institute of Latin American Studies, University of London, 1982), II, 197.

20 Apart from the three published accounts (see note 11), all of which deal with Redman's case, there is also the report of the official committee appointed in October 1942 by the Foreign Secretary, Anthony Eden, to enquire into the treatment of British officials and other subjects in Japanese controlled territory, which examined Redman's case in some detail. This committee, under Lord Clauson, reported in May 1943. See FO 371/35939/F2392/6/23 of 1943.

21 Much of the following is based on papers in FO371/31749, especially F6634/33/61, G. P. Young, 'History of the negotiations of the Anglo-Japanese exchange'. Some idea of the complexity of the issue is given by the fact that this was the 1000th entered paper on the subject.

22 E.g., see FO371/31741/F4151/33/61, Berne to FO, telno. 1939, 2 June 1942, and the minuting thereon.

23 FO371/31747/F5471/33/61, Swiss Legation, Special Division for Safeguarding Japanese Interests, Note J. D. D.1. a/313, 1 August 1942.

24 E.g. FO371/31748/ F6134/33/61, Lourenço Marques to FO, telno. 190, 29 August 1942, and F6347/33/61, Lourenço Marques telno. 267 to FO, 8 September 1942.

25 Works 10/399, Chancery Tokyo to FO Consular Department, no. 75, 28 December 1945.

26 Works 10/399, Chancery Tokyo to FO Consular Department, no. 75, 28 December 1945, testimony of Alfred Kunz, 6 December 1945; testimony of Paul Zimmerlin, 7 December 1945.

Japan

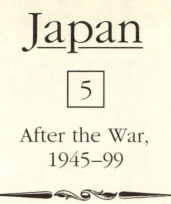

5

After the War,
1945–99

The war in the Pacific had been expected to last well into 1946. The capitulation of Japan after the bombing of Hiroshima and Nagasaki, therefore, found the allies, including Britain, unprepared for the occupation. Wartime planning for what would be required after the Japanese surrender had not developed very far. The same was perhaps true of the United States, but the difference was that the United States had vast resources available in the Pacific, which could quickly be switched to occupation duties. Britain had few resources available, and the main British interest was to secure the colonies. Japan was fairly low down the list of British priorities. One of the few areas to which the British had given some attention was the question of the Emperor; on the whole British officials, especially those who had served in Japan, thought that the Emperor should be retained.[1]

As a consequence of this lack of relevant planning, and the US dominance in the Pacific, British involvement in the initial occupation of Japan was severely limited. Following the surrender, a United Kingdom Military Liaison Mission, under the command of Lt General Gairdner, was appointed to the headquarters of the Supreme Commander for the Allied Powers (SCAP) in Japan. General MacArthur was SCAP, and Gairdner had been acting as the British prime minister's personal representative with General MacArthur during the last period of the Pacific War. Appointed to General Gairdner's staff was a solitary British diplomat, Dermot MacDermot, a pre-war member of the Japan consular service, who had already re-opened the consulate-general in Manila. He arrived at Yokohama on 1 September 1945, and took part in the ceremony which formally reopened the British embassy compound on 16 September 1945.[2] He was eventually joined by another former member of the Japan consular service, Oscar Morland, later to be ambassador, who had married Sir Francis Lindley's daughter, Alice, in 1932. They remained the only British diplomats in Japan for some months, though by the end of the year, other staff were beginning to arrive.

On the whole, MacDermot was pleasantly surprised by what he found when he first arrived in Japan.[3] He went ashore at Yokohama in some trepidation, carrying a revolver and escorted by two Royal Australian Navy officers, only to find that the proud and arrogant Japanese policemen of pre-war days were now so terrified of their new masters that they did not reply unless spoken to in polite fashion and with a friendly smile. Yokohama he found badly damaged, but a '. . . magnificent example of what concentrated incendiary bombing can do'. Yet the damage was patchy, with the Bund surviving intact. Most of the Bluff, the chief area of foreign residence in pre-war days, was also in reasonable condition, though the Anglican Christ Church had sustained some damage. The British consulate-general and residence were undamaged, '. . . and all their contents intact, which includes Austin's furniture and Bromley's gramophone records'. This good news was duly passed on, though Mr Bromley noted that he had three boxes of personal effects in the Yokohama garage, about which he was also anxious. By early September 1945, the consulate-general was in use as the shore establishment of the Senior Naval Officer, British Pacific Fleet, Tokyo area, whose staff lived in the residence. Later, many former naval staff would call, anxious to see again where they had once slept.[4] Technically, of course, it was still under Swiss control, as the protecting power, but the Royal Navy had reached an informal agreement with the Swiss representative. MacDermott stayed there too at first, but only as a member of the liaison staff; he reported to London that he had not hoisted the consular flag nor broken the seals on the safes and the archives.[5]

On 5 September 1945, MacDermot visited Tokyo and the embassy compound. Although much of the surrounding district lay in ruins like the rest of Tokyo, the compound had survived the war intact. One window frame in the ambassador's residence was burnt 'and that was the extent of the damage'. More damage had, however, been done to the garden, with trees scorched and most areas overgrown. He noted that the Swiss, acting as protecting power, and the Japanese staff had done a good job of fire fighting. He reported that various Japanese members of staff who had fled the city during the bombing had returned, and complained that they were getting much higher wages than in pre-war days. He expected salary rates to go even higher since the Americans were paying vastly inflated rates because '. . . they have nothing to spend their money on'. Although MacDermot did not mention any of the Japanese staff by name, they included several who had given long service to Britain.[6] In passing, MacDermott noted that the US embassy and the Canadian legation had also emerged unscathed from the bombing.

The formal re-occupation of the embassy compound as the British (Military) Liaison Mission took place on 16 September 1945, with the flag being hoisted by Admiral Sir Bernard Rawlings. The hoisting of the colours was accompanied by a changing of the guard ceremony performed by a joint Royal Marine and a Royal Navy guard, and there were many naval officers in attendance. MacDermot noted that both he and the Swiss representative were concerned lest this move should somehow affect the re-opening of the compound as embassy premises, but they decided that as it was a purely military occasion, to mark the entry of British naval and military officers into Tokyo, no harm had been done. The Swiss minister, whose own legation had been burnt out in the last days of the war, also asked for permission to use part of the British premises. This was agreed.[7] (When former members of the embassy learnt that it would be used by the British military, some expressed concern that private property would be less well looked after than the Swiss and the Japanese had done. Esler Dening, then at Singapore, sent a telegram about his grand piano, left behind in 1942. There seems to have been no further reference to it, so presumably it survived.)[8]

By mid-September 1945, the occupants of the compound were made up of General Gairdner and other officers, comprising the British Staff Section, and occupying the first secretary's and the number 7 house – where presumably MacDermot lived as part of that staff; junior naval officers in the Japanese counsellor's house; the communications team in the former Ministry of Information house; and the marine guard in the chancery flat. A small Royal Navy detachment, under the title HMS *Return* were responsible for day-to-day administration of the compound until they were paid off in May 1946. At that time, the guard and other duties were taken over by the Australian Infantry Force and then by the British Dorset Regiment.[9]

A member of the naval detachment may have been responsible for the theft of some of the embassy's silver plate, though the case was never proved. In December 1945, Brigadier Profumo of the British Liaison Mission (later Minister of War, and the centre of the Profumo affair), sought the assistance of the US provost marshal's office to investigate a theft that had come to light on the compound. When the inventory of the embassy silver was checked, several pieces were found missing. Extensive investigations including interrogations of the Japanese staff who had lived on the compound during the war, as well as the Swiss officials who had looked after the embassy and who had also periodically checked the plate, proved inconclusive, though they did reveal widespread suspicions of Kato, the pre-war senior man. Both MacDermott and some of his Japanese colleagues expresed the view that he had been 'squeezing' the Japanese staff in the past. Enquiries of Japanese silver traders also failed to reveal any illegal sales of silver. Eventually, however, the discovery of some of the missing plate hidden under a Royal Navy towel, and evidence from 'a naval source' pointed to a British rather than a Japanese or Swiss thief. The investigations stopped, and the losses were written off.[10]

The embassy compound was only used by General Gairdner and his staff for residential accommodation. Their offices were with MacArthur in the Dai-Ichi Life Insurance Building just across the moat from the Imperial Palace. Meanwhile, the Swiss continued to occupy the east end of the compound. MacDermot noted that the British were 'setting a high standard of comfort', with more generous accommodation than most US officers, who were crammed into the Imperial and the Dai-Ichi hotels. The compound and its occupants were consequently a magnet for every British officer who happened to pass by. The staff lived on US army rations, supplemented by supplies from the fleet, and the Royal Navy supplied crockery, cutlery and bedding. They also had their own wireless communications established at both Yokohama and Tokyo. To complete the scene, MacDermot noted that the marine guard made the place seem like Buckingham Palace. In the following months, various naval teams from Britain and the Dominions undertook such rehabilitation work as was required around the embassy compound. Men from the Australian navy ship, HMAS *Bataan*, restored the embassy flagpole, for example, and a commemorative plaque recording this event is still standing in the grounds of number 9 house.[11] Although supplies of the 'Scotch spirit' were short, they were clearly more readily available at the British embassy compound than at most other places in Tokyo, and two receptions in early 1946 for MacArthur's staff clearly went down well with those attending. Empire Day, in May 1946, was also a great success, with a mixture of military and civilian celebrations, culminating in a reception on the compound for 250 people, including General and Mrs MacArthur.[12]

While the Foreign Office found it useful to have MacDermot on the spot in Tokyo, they clearly hoped to re-establish something more like a normal diplomatic mission in Japan as soon as possible. As early as October 1945, the US embassy in London reported that Ernest Bevin, the foreign secretary, had written to enquire when it would be possible to send a political representative to Japan. The State Department response was prompt and unforthcoming. Such a move must await the establishment of the planned Far Eastern Commission which it had been agreed at the 1945 Yalta conference should be established to oversee the allied occupation of Japan. The appointment would also need to be cleared by MacArthur, who would require details of the proposed function of whoever was appointed and the size of his staff.[13]

It was to be several months before the Foreign Office got its wish, but there was progress. In November, at the suggestion of the Swiss minister, a degree of control of the compound in Tokyo and the consular premises in Yokohama passed to MacDermot, although they both continued to be used by military staff.[14] And, as mentioned, in the meantime a number of foreign service personnel, both career and non-career officers, were added to General Gairdner's staff in line with recommendations which MacDermot had made at the beginning of his time in Tokyo. By December, MacDermot, who in September had complained that he would be unable to engage in normal reporting, was in a position to put in a large stationery order to London, including duplicating paper, stencils and typewriters, a sure sign that normal business was under way.[15]

Early in 1946, the *ad hoc* Foreign Office presence, which MacDermott had represented, gave way to the formal establishment of the 'United Kingdom Liaison Mission', which it was intended should behave more like a normal diplomatic mission. More staff continued to arrive, including Vere Redman, who resumed his pre-war role as information officer, with the additional portfolio of education adviser. Finally, in June 1946, Alvary

Gascoigne was appointed United Kingdom political representative in Japan, a post he was to hold until February 1951.[16] Gascoigne had been in the army during the First World War, and had later joined the diplomatic service. He had served in China in the 1920s, and in Japan between 1931 and 1934. From 1934 to 1936, he was head of the Foreign Office's far eastern department. He was 'bluff and reasonably direct', no intellectual but a man of 'shrewdness and common-sense'.[17] He found that despite MacArthur's reputation as a difficult man to deal with, he was able to get on well with him. Indeed, Gascoigne claimed on his departure in 1951, that he had all along been treated as a member of MacArthur's inner circle or 'Court'.

The work of the liaison mission was unlike that of a normal diplomatic post. While some of the traditional functions, such as gathering and reporting information and the handling of visitors, were undertaken, many others were not. It was not until late 1946, for example, that the mission undertook regular consular work. Until then, as a state of war technically continued to exist in the absence of a peace treaty, the Swiss continued as the protecting power, though they were quite eager to rid themselves of the task. The Swiss clearly found the task of looking after the 300 or so British civilians in Japan in late 1945-early 1946 a heavy one. The majority of this group were wives of Japanese origin and their children, although there were also some members of religious communities. In theory, these were fed by the Japanese, but in practice either the Swiss, the Red Cross or the British naval authorities supplied them with food. For those who wanted it, there was free repatriation to their place of origin.[18]

Much of the mission's time was taken up with contacts with SCAP rather than with the Japanese. Indeed, it was not until the signing of the San Francisco Peace Treaty on 8 September 1951 that SCAP authorized official contacts between the various diplomatic missions, including the British, and the Japanese government. (There had, of course, been informal contacts since the mission was first established.) By that time, Gascoigne had been replaced by Sir Esler Dening, a former language student and member of the Japan consular service. After a brief period as head of the liaison mission (August 1951-May 1952), Dening became the first post-war ambassador, presenting his credentials on 6 May 1952.[19]

With the coming into force of the Japanese Peace Treaty in April 1952, the newly constituted embassy took on once again all normal diplomatic functions, though the British role in Japan was now much reduced from pre-war days. Yet that June, the Queen's Birthday Party was celebrated in something like the old style, with a garden party in the afternoon of 5 June for some 800 guests. It was also noted that an Imperial messenger had called in the morning to express the Emperor's good wishes on the occasion. The Queen's Coronation the following year saw 1500 guests assembled for a garden party, followed by a ball.[20]

The resumption of normal diplomatic life meant that soon old problems reappeared. Although for a time it was possible to accommodate most staff and functions on the compound, this arrangement, as in the past, did not last very long. Soon staff numbers were again such that many people had to be outhoused, and the old problem of the cost of Japanese housing once again began to bedevil the lives of the British embassy. By 1953, the consular, trade, Hong Kong and cultural sections were all outhoused, and those working on the compound often did so in very cramped conditions. The air attaché's clerks, for example, were housed in what had been in pre-war days the student interpreters' pantry, '. . . a room totally unsuited for use as an office'. The layout of other offices was distinctly odd. Despite the security implications, all the Japanese staff except the messengers and an administration assistant worked in the attics. The commissariat, established in December 1952 because of the difficulty in getting Western foods in Tokyo and used by some 250 British and Commonwealth diplomatic and support staff, was scattered in a number of buildings on the compound.[21]

One solution was to convert one of the house into offices, while some of the servants' quarters were taken over for the commissariat. Another was the use of a number of houses which had belonged to the German embassy in pre-war days, and which were now available as part of the post-war settlement. At least one of these, used by the naval attaché, was still in use until the early 1970s, and was eventually sold for a good profit. If there had been funds available, all of them could have been purchased. But there were no funds, and the opportunity passed.[22]

A more contentious question was that of the revision of the lease. From 1945 until 1952, Japan, forbidden by the occupation authorities from formal contact with foreign missions, was in no position to reopen the question that had been raised in 1939. No rent was paid for the war or occupation years; in theory, rent should have resumed in 1952, but this did not happen. With the post-war fall in the value of the yen, the 1884 rent had become almost valueless. The £200 of 1884 was, in 1952 terms, worth 6/8d (perhaps 30 pence in 1999 values). However, when the Japanese authorities raised the issue on Japan's resumption of sovereignty, suggesting that a more realistic rent might be yen 2.75 million (£2,750 in 1952 prices; perhaps £36,000 in 1999), the attitude in London remained as it had been in 1939–40; HMG could see no reason why there should be any increase in the rent. Thereafter, the Japanese regularly raised the issue, and the British just as regularly declined to discuss it – although not without some internal qualms. These arose from the belief that the Japanese might be able to revoke the lease, rather than from any belief in the justness of the Japanese claims. Only in 1968 did the embassy send a note to the foreign ministry accepting the principle of a rent increase. The terms, however, were not acceptable to the Japanese, and the offer was refused. By that stage, the Ministry of Public Building and Works noted, no rent had been paid since 1941. It was to be another two years before a change of mind led to an offer to pay yen 971,000 backdated to 1 January 1968.[23]

In 1959–60, the embassy purchased a property nearby in Sanbancho, with a view to building staff apartments. Nothing came of this proposal, but for some years, the administration officer/vice-consul lived in the old wooden house on the site. When land prices began to increase sharply in the late 1960s, it was decided to sell the land. Within months, the value of the property had more than doubled. From the occupation period, there was a 'Ladies' Mess' in Nogizaka where all the single ladies of the embassy lived together, taking their meals communally. By the late 1960s, most staff no longer wished to partake in such communal life. It was difficult to entertain, and according to the embassy's medical adviser, the arrangement was having a bad effect on some members' health. It was also unpopular with more senior members of the embassy, since the need to use the officially provided transport to return home in the evening had led '. . . to an unhealthy clock-watching method of working in the office'.[24] The ladies' mess thus gave way to individual apartments. The building was used for a time as an embassy club and for general storage, until it too was sold off to take advantage of the rise in land prices and the fall in the value of sterling. Other property in Tokyo and Yokohama was sold for the same reason. The loss of the ladies' mess, with its convenient concentration of female staff, was apparently much regretted by many of the younger male members of the embassy.[25]

There were also major changes in the office accommodation. During the 1950s and 1960s, the consular section was located in the Sankei Building, close to Tokyo station. In the late 1960s, as prices rose in Japan, it was decided to relocate this section to the compound. Accordingly, the ambassador's tennis court was moved from the area directly in front of the residence to a place behind number three house. On the vacant site, there was erected a temporary two-storey building for the consular and commercial sections, which was ready for use by August 1967. As is often the case, that temporary structure lasted some twenty years. But the expansion of the embassy did not stop. Commercial section, regarded since the mid-1950s as the most important part of the embassy,[26] pushed out consular section during the 1970s into the Kinokuniya Building near to Kojimachi police station. Later, the information, science and technology, and atomic energy sections moved to the Diamond hotel annex just behind the compound. Another change which marked the more busy world of the late twentieth century was that in Sir John Pilcher's time (ambassador 1967– 72), the ambassador finally moved his office, and that of his private secretary, from the residence to the chancery building. This was at first a temporary arrangement, although it was of concern to more than one set of inspectors, but it was eventually to become permanent, and clearly suited the more intensive working practises of the 1970s. Now the ambassador came to his staff and the papers, rather than they coming to him.[27]

There were also other changes during this period. Electric fans were first supplied from official funds to Tokyo in 1928, and they appear in some of the illustrations of the new buildings erected after the earthquake.[28] The Tokyo embassy first raised the possibility of installing air-conditioning in the residence in April 1941, arguing that since the political situation made it difficult to get away, air-conditioning units should be installed in some parts of the residence. This was turned down, on the grounds that since Tokyo was on an island and near the sea, its climate was not too bad, and even the embassy in Washington did not have this facility. The Pacific War intervened, and it was not until 1951 that the issue was again raised.

By then, much had changed. While air-conditioning had been a rarity in East Asia before the Pacific War, it had rapidly spread in the post-war period. This innovation seems to have been accepted by the Ministry of Works without difficulty in South East Asia, but further north proved more of a problem. Clearly air-conditioning was not required in winter, but in the Treasury view, climatic records indicated that it was not justifiable in summer either. A Mr Macauley wrote in June 1951 to the Office of Works, in considering Tokyo's case for air-conditioning in the cypher room that he understood that 'the climate of Tokyo is very similar to that of London', and asked if Works would consider air-conditioning for such a room in London. No action seems to have been taken then, but the post re-opened the question in 1953. This time the argument was accepted as far as the cypher room was concerned. The room had been moved from the basement to the attic, and the post had recorded temperatures of up to 115 degrees Fahrenheit in the day, which was hotter than Singapore. This small victory prompted the post to return to the charge, seeking air conditioning for the offices and, eventually, for the houses. The battle was fought every inch of the way. Sir Oscar Morland persuaded London that he needed air-conditioning for his wife's health in 1959. In October 1963, the Treasury agreed that the main bedroom, the guest bedroom, the study and the upstairs sitting-room in the residence might be air-conditioned; two years later, all offices were air-conditioned, but not staff bedrooms. (Sir Hugh Cortazzi has recorded how uncomfortable houses on the compound could be without this facility, especially with trams still running along the road outside the embassy.[29])

In 1968, the then ambassador, Sir John Pilcher, wrote an impassioned letter to London, arguing that Japanese, who, he claimed, referred to the British embassy as the 'unair-conditioned embassy', were declining to visit the residence during the hot months. His plea failed, but the following year, he used the forthcoming visit by Princess Margaret and Lord Snowdon to argue for an increase in the number of residence' bedrooms that were air-conditioned. There was much reluctance in London, but Sir John got his way. Finally, in the 1970s, it became increasingly difficult to argue the case against air-conditioning. All rented office and residential accommodation had it, and so, after some twenty years, it was installed in the houses and offices on the compound.[30]

The compound continued to play an important social role for members of the embassy, especially in the years before Tokyo had fully recovered from the effects of the war. There continued to be a number of tennis courts on the site, and it was a regular centre for the outdoor events which mark the British social calendar, such as Guy Fawkes Night. So enthusiastic were the bonfire builders on one occasion in the 1970s that the nearby Kojimachi fire brigade turned out in force and unsolicited when they became aware of a huge blaze practically on their own doorstep. They retired, assured that all was safely in hand. In fact, years before, the late 1950s, to meet such dangers as fires getting out of hand, a large number of staff turned out to create an emergency water supply, which, by a happy coincidence, proved to be eminently suitable as a swimming pool, and has retained its dual function to this day. Vere Redman, the then the information counsellor, was a moving power behind the work.[31]

The embassy could not escape the side effects of the rapid development which was the hallmark of post-war Tokyo. The burst of activity which marked the preparations for the 1964 Olympics, in particular, caused much disruption to the normal life of the compound. When it was all over, the then ambassador, Sir Francis Rundall, commented that:

> This Embassy was not the least sufferer, for the Compound was for years surrounded night and day by noisy and dusty construction work. This included the building of a large new hotel and of an underground section of the high-speed road which temporarily converted the park before the Embassy into what one journalist, only a few months before the games began, described as 'the appearance of the aftermath of a tank battle' . . . .

He conceded that Tokyo was much improved, but '. . . it imposed great inconvenience at the time'.[32]

Nor did the embassy escape the political ferment of post-war Japan. Britain's Middle East policy was not popular and led to occasional protests. More serious were the demonstrations against Britain's nuclear tests. The dates for these were announced in January 1957, and there followed a series of rallies and demonstrations outside the embassy. On 1 March 1957, 1500 people attended one rally, including the Egyptian ambassador, the Indian chargé d'affaires and senior officials from both the Japan Socialist Party and the Japan Communist Party. The protests reached a climax in May 1957, following the explosion of the first British hydrogen bomb on Christmas Island, when for two days, large crowds gathered outside the embassy gates, and anti-nuclear petitions were presented. As in pre-war days, however, the demonstrators generally remained good natured. The second explosion, in June, saw much smaller demonstrations, and the protests then abated.[33] (One minor curiosity to emerge during the demonstrations was the police refusal to go onto the strip of land between the front of the embassy and the road, so allowing the demonstrators to approach right up to the front gates. On enquiry, it emerged that the police believed the embassy's land ran to the road, and that they should not venture onto it for fear of violating diplomatic immunity. The police eventually accepted that they were mistaken.[34]) Thereafter, protests and demonstrations were virtually non-existent until hostile comment in the British tabloid press as the Emperor lay dying in 1988 brought the loudspeaker trucks favoured by right-wing groups to the area day and night. It was a short-lived nuisance, which disturbed the sleep of some.[35]

From the 1960s onwards, there were various suggestions about the future use of the embassy compound. More and more staff were now forced to live off the compound. Some welcomed this, others did not. But the cost of such accommodation grew steadily as Tokyo became the most expensive capital in the world. It was suggested that part of the compound be sold off, to finance other building, but it was soon realized that this was not possible since Britain did not own the land. Other proposals, such as the replacement of some of the compound's houses by blocks of flats, were also considered.

There was a general feeling in London that the Tokyo compound was out of date and should be the subject of major changes. One first secretary, who remained nameless, was quoted as saying that the Japanese talked of the British embassy in disparaging tones as the 'British museum'. A 1964 inspection had proposed a major redevelopment of the compound. Another inspection in 1968 came to the conclusion that there was nothing worth saving on the compound, and all the buildings should be replaced. The only possible exception was the residence, which might be kept as an historical curiosity, to be used as a guest house and for special exhibitions. Some would have gone further, and got rid of the residence as well.[36]

There was, however, a warning voice from the ambassador, who clearly did not share the views of either the Ministry of Public Building and Works, or the Foreign Office, or his subordinates. Sir John Pilcher, who according to one letter, '. . . admits to having aspired to architecture in his youth', made it clear that in his view, the compound could continue in use, with the existing houses turned into flats. He did not want high-rise blocks replacing the houses and overlooking the residence. Neither did he display much enthusiasm for the idea that the residence should be replaced by a penthouse flat. Sir John also argued that there was a danger in trying to develop the site too much, since this might attract Japanese attention and '. . . the Japanese might feel that in view of the less important place in world affairs which Britain occupied, we had too grand a compound and [they] might want to take it from us'.[37] How important the ambassador's views were it is now impossible to say, but he was clearly prepared to put up a fight. In the end, the British economy intervened with the result that it was decided to leave things as before as far as the compound was concerned.

Eventually, in the late 1980s, it was decided to undertake the construction of new commercial, information and consular offices. When this was put out to free tender to both Japanese and British firms in 1989, there were protests from British construction companies, who argued that there was no such thing as a free tender in the Japanese construction industry. Despite the protests, the British government stuck to its position.[38] Although the final building programme was less grandiose than originally proposed, by 1987, there was a handsome new office block, very much in keeping with the general style of the compound yet also representing modern architecture, which brought back into the compound all the outhoused sections. As part of the same programme of improvements, all of the counsellors' houses were upgraded in the following years.[39]

Of course, the post-war years saw some old problems re-occur. Few ambassadors were happy with their predecessors' choice of decor or pictures. An ambassador whose taste reflected the best in modern art could easily be followed by one of a more conservative bent. Indeed, pets and pictures were almost guaranteed to produce tensions. There were also problems over the supply of equipment. While one ambassador, or one ambassador's wife, might avoid the kitchen areas like the plague, and not care what happened as long as dinner was on the table at the required time, another might expect up-to-date equipment. Gradually, however, the kitchens at least were dragged into the twentieth century.[40]

Today, the Tokyo embassy is one of the biggest, with numerous sections covering the whole range of British interests in Japan. In any given year, thousands of guests will be entertained, while a string of British VIPs will stay at the residence. No doubt there will be further plans to change and alter the Tokyo compound, and to squeeze more buildings onto the site. Many clearly share Sir Claude MacDonald's view that it was much underused. For the present, however, the compound has a sense of completeness that it would be a pity to destroy. There is a charm in the lawns, little gardens and the trees – some of the latter marking events of historical significance – and interesting corners which together make up the compound. There are monuments which are worth preserving.[41] For many Japanese, coming from cramped accommodation far out in the suburbs, there is pleasure in visiting the relatively spacious building so the British embassy, with its links back to the 'good old days of Sir Harry Parkes' and the opening of Japan.

Notes

1 Roger Buckley, 'Britain and the Emperor: The Foreign Office and Constitutional Reform in Japan, 1945–1946'. *Modern Asian Studies*, vol. 12, no. 4, (1978), pp. 553–570.

2 Roger Buckley, *Occupation Diplomacy: Britain, the United States and Japan 1945–1952*, (Cambridge: Cambridge University Press, 1982), pp. 34–35.

3 The following account is mainly based on MacDermot's 'Circular Memorandum' of a 'gossipy informality' sent home at the end of September 1945, to give an impression of what occupied Japan was like. It was addressed to the far eastern department of the Foreign Office, and copied to some of MacDermot's former colleagues in the Japan consular service. It is reproduced in *Japan and Dependencies*, vol. 17: *Political Reports 1945–1953*, pp. 15–24. His formal reporting telegrams can be found in FO369/3223 of 1945.

4 Undated letter from Sir Michael Wilford, 1996.

5 FO369/3223/K19258/15777/223, MacDermot to the FO, no. 1, secret, 8 September 1945.

6 Works 10/399, Chancery Tokyo to FO. no. 75, 28 December 1945; letter from Ian Lindsay, British embassy Tokyo, 26 April 1996, enclosing a memorandum by C. E. Ripley, dated 7 March 1996.

7 FO369/3223/K15777/15771/223, Tokyo telno. 1 3 September 1945; FO telno. 7, 12 September 1945.

8 FO369/3223/K16261/15777/223, Supreme Allied Command, South East Asia to FO, telno. 479, 12 September 1945.

9 British Liaison Mission Tokyo, Periodic Report No. 5, (May 1946), *Japan and Dependencies*, vol. 17, 223.

10 Works 10/399, Chancery Tokyo to FO. no. 75, 28 December 1945; O. Morland to FO, no. 72, 19 March 1946.

11 Letter from R. Cummins, British embassy Tokyo, 12 April 1996.

12 British Liaison Mission, Tokyo, Periodical Reports No. 3, (March 1946) and No. 5 (May 1946), *Japan and Dependencies*, vol. 17, 158, 223–24.

13 Telegram US embassy London to the State Department, 4 October 1945; telegram State Department to US embassy London, 13 October 1945, in *Foreign Relations of the United States 1945*, Vol. VI, *British Commonwealth/Far East*, pp. 735-56, 751; see also Buckley *Occupation Diplomacy*, pp. 36–37

14 FO369/3223/K18257/15777/223, MacDermot to Consular Dept., FO, no. 9, 29 September 1945; FO to Tokyo telno. 64, 9 November 1945.

15 See the exchanges on FO369/3223/K21903/15777/223.

16 FO371/92521/3/FJ1019/5, 'Trend of Events in Japan from July 1946 to February 1951', Gascoinge to Bevin, no. 41, secret, 2 February 1951. See also British Liaison Mission Tokyo, Periodic Report No. 1 (January 1946), and Periodic Report No. 2 (February 1946), *Japan and Dependencies*, vol. 17, 105, 139.

17 Peter Lowe, 'Sir Alvary Gascoigne in Japan, 1946–1951', in Nish, *Britain and Japan*, pp. 279–294.

18 Lt. Gen. Gairdner to the Secretary of the Cabinet, Periodical Report No. 1, January 1946, *Japan and Dependencies*, vol. 17, 115.

19 Tokyo to FO, telno. 25 saving, confidential, 11 May 1952, *Japan and Dependencies*, vol. 17, 551; Roger Buckley, 'In proper perspective: Sir Esler Dening (1897–1977) and Anglo-Japanese relations 1951–1957', in Cortazzi and Daniels, editors, *Britain and Japan*, pp. 271–276.

20 Tokyo to FO, telno. 34 saving, confidential, 10 June 1952; telno. 22 saving, confidential, 13 June 1953, *Japan and Dependencies*, vol. 17, 560, 677.

21 FO 366/3011/XC01/23D/3053, copy of a report by R. Whittingham, April–May 1953; F. J. Gaunt, FO, to Mrs M. G. Bradley, Works, 15 July 1953.

22 Letter from Sir Hugh Cortazzi, 16 July 1996.

23 Most of the papers relating to this issue up to 1968 are available on Works 10/643 or 10/644. The latter includes a copy of a Note Verbale of 12 January 1970 offering to pay from 1 January 1968, and appears to be the last paper in the public domain. See also Works 10/636, beginning with D.F. Mann, Works, to T. Willson, FO, 12 February 1952. Some enlightenment came from a conversation with Sir Hugh Cortazzi, 11 June 1996.

24 Works 10/643, note for the record by G. S. Knight, 15 January 1965, recording a meeting at the Foreign Office, 13 January 1965.

25 Letter from Ian Lindsay, British embassy Tokyo, 26 April 1996, enclosing an undated memorandum by C. E. Ripley, first secretary.

26 R. T. D. Ledward to A. L. Mayall, Foreign Office, personal and confidential, 8 June 1955, *Japan and Dependencies*, vol. 18, 117.

27 Letter from Sir David Wright, HM ambassador, 13 December 1996; letter from Sir Hugh Cortazzi, 16 July 1996. For Pilcher, who was a somewhat larger than life figure, see Hugh Cortazzi, 'Sir John Pilcher, GCMG (1912–1990)', in *Britain and Japan: Biographical Portraits*, III, edited by J. E. Hoare (Richmond: Japan Library, forthcoming).

28 FO369/2040/K6067/2143/233, Works to FO, 15B/13205/28, 8 May 1928.

29 Hugh Cortazzi, *Japan and back, and places elsewhere* (Folkestone, Kent: Global Oriental, 1998), p. 88.

30 Papers on this saga are conveniently grouped together on Works 10/635. They also reveal that the buildings on the compound in Seoul were air-conditioned in 1965, 'because of the smallness of the rooms'; letter from K. M. Cartwright, works, to P.S. Dimoine, Diplomatic Service Administrative Office, 13 June 1965. Further details are provided in a letter from Sir Hugh Cortazzi, 16 July 1996.

31 Letter from Ian Lindsay, British embassy Tokyo, 26 April 1996, enclosing an undated memorandum by C E Ripley; conversation with Sir Hugh Cortazzi, 11 June 1996.

32 FO371/176045/FJ1802/27, Sir Francis Rundall to Mr Gordon Walker, no 92, restricted, 30 October 1964.

33 Tokyo embassy Diary, entries for 10–23 January, 20 February- 6 March, 6–19 May, and 20 May–2 June 1957, *Japan and Dependencies*, vol. 18, 321, 334, 358, 363; *The Times*, 17 May 1957

34 Works 10/642, Chancery Tokyo to FO Library, no. 9053/2/57 of 30 May 1957.

35 *Observer* 15 October 1988.

36 Works 10/643, R. Slater to C. L. Reeves, Senior Estate Surveyor, 25 April 1968; Report by Mr Peter Murray, June 1968; J. C. Cloake, FO, to G. S. Knight, Ministry of Public Building and Works, 2 August 1968.

37 Works 10/643, R. Slater to C. L Reeves, Senior Estate Surveyor, 25 April 1968; Works 10/644, Record of a meeting at the Foreign Office 28 April 1969.

38 'UK row over work on embassy in Tokyo,' *Financial Times*, 2 November 1989.

39 Letters from Ian Lindsay, British embassy Tokyo, 26 April 1996, enclosing an undated memorandum by C. E. Ripley, and from Sir David Wright, HM ambassador, 13 December 1996.

40 Letter from Sir Hugh Cortazzi, 16 July 1996. See also his memoirs Cortazzi, *Japan and back*, p. 190.

41 They are listed in *The Work of the Embassy*, (Tokyo: British embassy, 1995).

Part Three

Korea

Korea

1

Beginnings

Introduction

The British had been aware of Korea from the beginning of the seventeenth century, but little came of this awareness until the 1790s. Even then, although Captain Broughton surveyed the area around Pusan in 1797[1], and thus became the first known Briton to visit Korea, it was not for another fifty years that the British became regular visitors in Korean waters. In the 1870s, British interest in the peninsula quickened, especially under the influence of Sir Harry Parkes, then minister in Tokyo. Parkes pressed in particular for the occupation of the islands of Port Hamilton (Komundo in Korean), widely seen in British naval and diplomatic circles as likely to be a useful link in a chain of coaling and other stations between China and the rest of the world. Parkes, however, was unable to persuade the Conservative government in London that it would be a wise move to occupy territory claimed by another country.[2]

Nevertheless, the British watched closely as Japan and the United States pressed in on Korea. When it seemed clear that the latter would follow the Japanese example and conclude a treaty, the British government instructed the commander-in-chief of the China station, Vice Admiral George Willis to follow the American Commodore Shufeldt to Korea; If he deemed it necessary, he was also to conclude a treaty. When Shufeldt's negotiations were successfully completed in May 1882, Willis felt that he should indeed follow the American example. He began negotiations immediately, taking Shufeldt's treaty as his model, and in June 1882, the first British treaty with Korea was signed on the beach at Inch'on, the port of Seoul.

By all accounts, the admiral was pleased with his work, but few others were. It did little to open Korea for trade, the main British interest in East Asia, and it was at best ambiguous on the difficult question of Korea's relationship with China. The British chambers of commerce in the Chinese and Japanese treaty ports were loud in condemnation, and their complaints were taken up in London. Sir Harry Parkes in Tokyo was also opposed. Rather than seek modifications to a flawed document, Britain decided to renegotiate the treaty from scratch. This time, the negotiations were entrusted to Parkes, who in turn sent one of his most experienced consular officers to Seoul to carry out the day-to-day dealings with the Korean foreign ministry.

This was William George Aston, already skilled in Japanese, and well on the way to acquiring a comparable standard of Korean.[3] Aston engaged in detailed negotiations with the Koreans, so that by the time Parkes, now transferred from Tokyo to the Beijing legation, arrived in Seoul in November 1883, there was relatively little to do, and a new treaty was signed on 26 November of that year in Seoul's Kyongbok Palace. Parkes signed for Britain, and Min Yong-mok for Korea. The new treaty came into force in April 1884, when Parkes returned to Seoul to exchange ratifications.

As soon as negotiations began to replace the 1882 treaty, Sir Harry Parkes instructed Aston, in March 1883, to find a suitable site for official premises, not just in the capital but also at possible future open ports. Today, the British embassy compound in Seoul is the only piece of land owned by the British government in Korea. Offices are leased at Pusan, and Britain also leases the small plot of land on Komundo (Port Hamilton), which began as a graveyard during the British navy's occupation of the islands from 1885 to 1887, and where two graves are still visable.

Once the British had other property. There was a consular post at Chemulp'o, now a suburb of Inch'on, from the 1880s, and an office and residence for the consul was completed in the 1890s; extensive plans for both buildings survive in the Office of Works' records. Early hopes of trade proved unfounded, however. The post was closed in 1915 and the office site sold in 1925. From then until 1940, a British merchant, W. G. Bennett, was the British consular agent at Chemulp'o, operating from the former residence, which he rented for fifty yen a month. When the post was inspected in 1928, the inspector noted that Mr Bennet, then aged sixty-one, was a great talker, who had lived thirty-one years in Korea without a break, and who had previously lived nine years in Japan. He was popular with the Japanese officials – he spoke good Japanese – and with the Chinese community. Indeed, during anti-Chinese demonstrations the previous year, large numbers of Chinese had fled to Mr Bennett's compound, and he still continued to receive presents of fruit and dried ginger by way of thanks. He seemed '. . . a very good type of consular agent'.[4]

The site continued to be known as 'British consulate hill' long after it had ceased to be leased by the British. After the Pacific War and the liberation of Korea, the former consular residence was used as a community centre in the 1940s, for Mr Bennet had not returned after the war. It survived until 1950, when it was one of the targets for the troops coming ashore during General MacArthur's 'Operation Chromite', the amphibious landing exercise which succeeded in capturing Inch'on in September 1950. Whatever remained after that disappeared with the building of the Olympia hotel on the site in the 1970s.[5]

But to return to Mr Aston. While he had been instructed to find a site for offices and residence in Seoul, he was to make no financial commitment initially, but was to try to obtain first refusal on the sites he secured, and to indicate that the British would be willing to pay similar amounts to those paid by the Japanese, who had opened a consulate in Chemulp'o in January 1883, and were expected to open a legation at Mapo, then just outside Seoul, in August 1883.[6]

Aston set about his two tasks at once. He found that the Korean authorities were not interested in getting involved in negotiations over house purchases for foreign diplomats, and they suggested that he might deal with estate agents – a surprisingly modern concept, but one which failed to deliver. Aston then decided that the house in which he was lodging, which also happened to be for sale, would do well enough. He therefore returned to the Korean Foreign Office, where an old friend whom he had met in Tokyo was working, This was Kim Ok-kyun, who had returned to Korea on the same boat as Aston. From Kim, Aston obtained a promise that the house would not be sold to anybody else until the British decided whether or not they wanted it.[7]

The house which Aston had selected was '. . . within the walls of the city, betwen the south and the west gates, and about a mile from the Palace, the Foreign Office and the Japanese Legation'. He felt that it was a bargain. It occupied some 700 square yards/0.0006 square kilometres, and was on a '. . . rising ground sloping off on three sides'. On the fourth side, where the entrance was, it sloped gradually down to the street below. The hill commanded a fine view of the city spread out below it. Aston was not blind to some of the problems attached to his chosen spot. It was, of course, a Korean-style house, with numerous small buildings arranged around a courtyard, mostly in poor repair. Aston did not think that the buildings would be much use, except as temporary accommodation, and he noted that the surrounding wall would provide little protection. The alleyways around were also somewhat unsanitary, and it would be necessary to sink a deep well. There were wells on the site which produced water which was clear, and pleasant to drink, but since there were 'fetid gutters' nearby, Aston felt that these could not be producing safe water. (So it proved, and a new deep well was dug on the compound, which provided good water for nearly twenty years, until it, too, became polluted.[8]) Despite all the drawbacks, Aston thought that the house, if it could be secured, would be a bargain. House prices in Seoul in 1883 were low, following a military revolt in 1882, and he had been offered the house at '7,500 nyang', or some Mexican $860. Since one Mexican dollar was then worth approximately two shillings and six pence in Britain's pre-decimal currency, this equalled slightly more than £100 at the then rate of exchange.[9]

The area where Aston had secured lodging, and where he now proposed to buy, had long been an important area of the city. Indeed, the house stood on the site of the temporary tomb of the consort of King T'aejo, the founder of the Chosun or Yi dynasty.[10] By the 1880s, however, it was in decline. The area was originally royal land, but most of it had slipped out of royal control into the hands of courtiers, and the whole area had become much run down. Nevertheless, it contained pleasant small hills, and some evidence of its former grandeur lingered on. It was also convenient. After the signing of the various treaties with Western Powers in the 1880s, it was to benefit greatly from the king's decision to allow foreigners to dwell inside the city walls. From being a run-down part of Seoul, Chong Dong was soon to become the heart of the city's foreign quarter.[11] And if Chong Dong, in the Korean phrase, was the egg at the centre of the city, the compound where the British were now established was the yolk at the heart of the egg.

Mr Aston's judgement was therefore a shrewd one, and was approved by both Parkes in Tokyo, and, eventually, by the Foreign Office in London. Parkes was able to judge for himself, for he went to Seoul from Beijing, where he was now minister,. in November 1883 to negotiate the final stages of the new British treaty. In letters to his daughters, he recorded his days of hard work at the Korean Foreign Office, supported by Aston and two members of the Beijing legation whom he had brought with him. One of them, Walter C. Hillier, of the China consular service, will feature again in this story. Parkes recorded arriving soaking wet and raiding Aston's wardrobe for dry clothes, and then days of hard work preparing final texts, in English and Chinese, of the new treaty, even while still negotiating the finer details.

At night, however, they relaxed in the dining-room which, though it was a good room, '. . . is something like our dining-room in Peking – too public to be comfortable'. The reason was plain from the sketch map which accompanied this letter, for the dining-room was the central room of five, and anybody wishing to pass from the office to the drawing-room, for example, had either to go out into the cold night, or else pass through the dining-room. But Parkes felt that whatever the disadvantages, the four of them enjoyed fair dinners: '. . . always a soup three entrées – one sweet – plenty of wine, with the feast of reason and the flow of soul for desert'. Those who had to work on Sunday – 'a couple of Chinese writers' – were kept going with champagne and quinine.[12]

Unfortunately, the Treasury in London did not share the positive view of Aston's possible bargain. Indeed, the Treasury had grave doubts about the whole Korean enterprise. To them, Korea was 'this wretched place', scarcely worth any expenditure, and it was only with the greatest difficulty that they were persuaded to agree to even a temporary British establishment in Korea, never mind a long-term commitment implied both by the treaty negotiations and, on a lesser scale, by Aston's efforts over accommodation. In the end, they gave reluctant agreement to the establishment of a temporary presence. Accordingly, it was agreed in 1884 that Mr Aston should be acting consul-general, and should be assisted by Mr W. R. Carles of the China consular service as vice-consul. (Carles would later achieve some degree of notariety for his actions during the legation seige in Beijing.) The British minister in Beijing would be side-accredited to Seoul, as the minister plenipotentiary and envoy extra-ordinary to the court of Korea. It was an understandable decision given the doubts about the value of Korea as a trading partner, but it was to create additional ambiguity as to the real British view of the international status of Korea.[13]

Perhaps the Treasury had a point, for it was true that the work in Seoul does not seem to have been particularly arduous during the 1880s and indeed, the 1890s, although it could be dangerous on occasions. Consular duties were light, and the British community small. There was some work in aiding British merchants, and the interests of the British employees of the Korean government had to be carefully watched. These tasks scarcely filled the days, and there was much time for tennis, balls and dinner parties, as the foreign community became more established. There was also plenty of time to go travelling, and several consular officers produced detailed accounts of visits to the more remote parts of Korea. This was of course true of most British posts in China and the smaller ones in Japan. At the same time, Britain was sending out ambiguous signals over both the status of Korea, and its apparent belief in the strategic impotance of the Korean peninsula by its occupation of Port Hamilton/Komundo, a small group of islands off the southernmost coast of Korea. Nobody seems to have drawn the contradictions in policy to the attention of the Treasury.[14]

It was as well that Aston had Parkes's support over the house in Seoul, for when he tried to put the temporary arrangement onto a more formal footing, he found the owner unwilling to stick to his original price. His reports hint of an additional problem. In a letter to Parkes, he said that he had not felt able to insist on the original price because the man who had acted as a go-between was a Christian. Mixing too openly with foreigners might well draw the authorities attention to him, and he was, presumably, liable to persecution if his belief was to become public knowledge. But with this one mention, the story disappears.

Aston now negotiated directly with the supposed owner of the land, who appears in Aston's letters as 'Shin Hyop-hi', but as 'Sin Syok-hwi' in the English translation of the lease. Shin was described as an official of the first rank, which fits in well with what we know of those owning land in the area, and was perhaps a little unsure of his title, for he obtained from the governor of Seoul a certificate which stated that he was entitled to sell the land.

The new asking price was 10,500 ryang, or Mexican $1200 – about £200 at the then rate of exchange. This was still a bargain. Parkes noted in his report on the transaction, drawn up after his return to Seoul in 1884 for the ratification of the 1883 treaty, that prices in the area were on the way up, with the arrival of more foreigners. The first United States' envoy, who had purchased a property nearby the year before, had paid Mexican $3200 for a similar plot. The Germans, Russians and Italians were expected to arrive shortly, and that would push prices even higher. Perhaps mindful of the Treasury's doubts, Aston nevertheless did offer to pay the difference in price himself, an offer not taken up.[15]

Now that he and Parkes had decided to buy the house, Aston sent a fuller description of it back to London:

The site . . . is occupied by six separate buildings at some distance from each other, offering in all accommodation which may be considered equal to twelve European rooms. There is also stabling for six or seven horses with a tolerably large godown [warehouse], and a number of smaller houses suitable only for nativeservants. All the buildings are of wood, old, and in an indifferant state of repair.[16]

Surviving photographs show a pleasant Korean-style compound, with a series of low buildings connected by open verandas.

It was soon obvious that more money would need to be spent on the buildings. The Office of Works in London agreed that the site itself was a bargain, and therefore was willing to undertake the extra work required to make the buildings more comfortable for Europeans. In particular, they agreed that some attempt should be made to link the buildings, so that there would be no need for the inhabitants to go outside to move from one room to another. That this was dangerous, especially in the winter, and that there were other drawbacks to the compound became abundantly clear in the winter of 1884–85.

In December 1884, there occured the 'Post Office coup', when a group of Korean reformers, including Aston's friend Kim Ok-kyun, tried to overthrow the royal government. In the resulting uncertainty, Aston and his family were forced to flee in the dead of night from the British legation, which was undefendable in its dilapidated condition, and had to take refuge with the Americans on the hill just behind.[17] It was later agreed that these night excursions, and the general need to keep going outdoors on winter nights, damaged Aston's health beyond repair, and ultimately led to his early resignation from the Japan consular service in 1889.

At least one of Aston's successors in Seoul suffered from poor health because of the buildings. As a result, and despite regular attempts to patch them up and keep them in use, it was eventually decided that the original Korean buildings were too broken down to be kept. Indeed, Aston had thought that this would be the case from the beginning, and from the moment he had first recommended the purchase of the buildings, he had made efforts to establish both the price and the availability of local building materials.[18] The proposal, with the prospect of additional expenditure, did not appeal to the Treasury in London.

Aston left in 1885, and was succeeded by E. C. Baber, from the China consular service, where he had been Chinese secretary. This was not apparently work which suited him, but he made an impression in Seoul, where he got on particularly well with the Chinese resident, Yuan Shikai. However, Baber fell ill, both physically – which some blamed on the poor condition of the buildings – and possibly mentally, and went home on sick leave. His temporary successor, E. H. Parker, was certainly somewhat odd, even if he was later to become professor of Chinese at the University of Manchester, and was hurridly moved. Only with the arrival of Walter Hiller, one of Parkes's protégés, in 1889, did Seoul settle down to a more peaceful regime.[19] It was against this background that the decision was finally taken to erect new buildings on the consular site.

Notes

1 For Captain Broughton's own account of his voyage, see William Robert Broughton, *A voyage of discovery to the North Pacific Ocean etc., etc.,* (London: Printed for T. Cadell and W. Davies, 1804), and his papers, which can be found in the Admiralty Records at the Public Record Office, in the National Maritime Museum archives at Greenwhich, and in the Hydrographer's Office at Taunton.

2 Andrew Hamilton, 'The Komundo affair', *Korea Journal*, vol. 22, no. 6 (June 1982), pp. 20–33; J E Hoare, 'Komundo-Port Hamilton', *Asian Affairs*, vol. 17, no. 3 (October 1986), pp. 298–308.

3 For a brief sketch of Aston, and some indication of how much Korean he had already acquired by 1883, see Peter Kornicki, 'William George Aston (1841–1911)', in Cortazzi and Daniels, eds., *Britain and Japan 1859–1991* pp. 64–75.

4 FO369/2042,/K10351, Report by H. Phillips upon his inspection of the British Consular Agent at Chemulp'o on Sunday 10 June 1928.

5 Details of Chemulp'o and other properties can be found in Works 10/342, Public Buildings Overseas, Korea. The detailed plans can be found in Works 40/162- 174.

6 Sir H. Parkes to Earl Granville, no. 35 confidential, 9 March 1883, enclosing Parkes to Aston, confidential and separate, 6 March 1883, in *Anglo-American Diplomatic Materials relating to Korea,* edited by Park Il-keun, (Seoul: Shin Mun Dang, 1982), pp. 185–89.

7 For Kim Ok-kyun and his friendship with Aston, see Harold F. Cook, *Korea's 1884 Incident: Its Background and Kim Ok-kyun's Elusive Dream,* (Seoul: Royal Asiatic Society Korea Branch, 1972, reprinted 1982), p. 74.

8 FO 17/1634, Jordan to Lansdowne, no. 25 consular, 15 December 1902, enclosing a report by Dr E. Baldock, 13 December 1902.

9 Aston to Parkes 24 April 1883, enclosed in Parkes to Earl Granville, no. 66, 28 April 1883, in Park, *Anglo-American Diplomatic Materials,* pp. 230–35.

10 'Tales of Chong-dong', KBS television, Seoul., 10 July 1994; letter from T. G. Harris, 11 July 1994.

11 Gregory Henderson, 'A history of the Chong Dong area and the American Embassy Compound', *Transactions of the Royal Asiatic Society Korea Branch* (TKBRAS), xxxv, (1959), 15–16; for an interesting sideline on the long occupation of the area, see Sheila Hoey Middleton, 'A collection of Choson Dynasty White Ware Sherds', *Oriental Art,* vol. Xl, no. 4, (Winter 1994–95), 21–28.

12 Stanley Lane-Poole, *Sir Harry Parkes in China,* (London: Methuen and Co., 1901), pp. 354–60; Parkes repeated his positive view of the house in Seoul in a desptach to the Foreign Office in London – see Works 10/389, copy of Parkes to Granville, Korean consular no. 1, 20 June 1884.

13 See the minuting in the Treasury files for 1882–84 in T/1/14809 and T/1/8146A/20447.

14 The best account of the Komundo incident, bringing in the political and diplomatic dimensions is Kim Yung Chung, 'Great Britain and Korea, 1883–87', unpublished PhD, University of Indiana, 1964, but see also her paper 'The Komundo incident 1885–87: an early phase in British-Korean relations', in *Korean-British relations: yesterday, today and tomorrow,* edited by Chong-wha Chung and J E Hoare, (Seoul: Korean British Society et al., 1984), pp. 9–38.

15 Works 10/389, Aston to Parkes, accounts no. 1, 30 May 1884; Parkes to Granville, Korean consular no. 1, 20 June 1884; *Ku Han'guk weigyo munso* (Diplomatic documents of old Korea), British series, I, (Seoul: Asia Research Centre, 1968), pp. 33–34, exchange of letters between Parkes and the Korean Foreign Office, 10 May 1884.

16 Works 10/389, Aston to Parkes, accounts no. 1, 30 May 1884. See also W. R. Carles, *Life in Corea,* (London and New York: Macmillan and Co., 1888), pp. 103–4.

17 Aston to Granville, no. 1, 3 January 1885, in FO 17/996; Foote to Freylinghuysen, no 128, 17 December 1884.Park, *Anglo-American Diplomatic Materials,* p. 998.

18 Aston to Parkes, 24 April 1883, enclosed in Parkes to Granville, no. 66, 28 April 1883, in Park, *Anglo-American Diplomatic Materials,* pp. 230–35.

19 Coates, *The China Consuls,* pp. 298–300.

Korea

The New Buildings

These new buildings were not to be erected without something of a struggle. By the late 1880s, the Foreign Office had become convinced that there was no alternative, and had asked the Office of Works in Shanghai to begin the process. The Office of Works, having been assured that it was intended to keep an officer of at least consul-general rank in Seoul, agreed to do so. The Treasury, however, was less accommodating, refusing to sanction any work:

> . . . so long as the consular establishment in Corea is only a provisional detachment from China and Japan, without any distinct organisation or recognition in the Parliamentary Estimates, My Lords [i.e. the Treasury] think it inexpedient to ask Parliament to provide for the erection of permanent Consular buildings in that country of the expensive nature indicated in your report.

The Treasury, however, did agree that some patching up of the existing buildings was necessary, and agreed to expenditure for this purpose.[1]

This was not a reply likely to find favour with the Foreign Office. It was not, after all, a new issue. It was somewhat disingenuous of the Treasury to argue that it was wrong to spend money on a temporary establishment, since the question of turning Seoul into a permanent post was already under discussion. In any case, the issue of whether or not the post in Seoul was to be treated as a separate establishment or as part of the Beijing or Tokyo establishments was irrelevant, since there was no doubt that some form of consular establishment would continue at Seoul. This was a different issue from that of accommodation; as far as the latter was concerned, the Treasury had been asked to give its opinion in a Foreign Office letter of 30 November 1886, and reminded in further letters of 27 April, 2 June, 21 September and 25 October of 1887, and 23 October 1888.

To the Foreign Office, it was a mistake and a '. . . waste of public money . . . to go on patching up buildings which had been medically condemned'.[2]

While these two departments of state exchanged letters, the Office of Works, clearly anticipating a decision in the Foreign Office's favour on this occasion at least, quietly proceeded with plans for new buildings in Seoul. On 18 January 1889, Mr Marshall at Shanghai forwarded preliminary drawings to London, together with some details of likely local costs. In particular, he noted that bricks, described as 'of fair quality', could be obtained in Seoul for about Mexican dollars $13 a ton. Timber was also available, but stone could only be bought in short lengths. Joinery would need to be done in Shanghai.[3]

Marshall's plans are still in the British Public Record Office at Kew near London. (There is nothing in the archives to indicate that anybody else had a hand in the drawings, although the consul-general at the time, Walter Hillier, was later accredited with drawing up plans for the Anglican Church Mission's hospital for women in Seoul, and with taking an active part in its construction.[4]) They show a standard set of China coast consular buildings, of a type which had been adapted from the British India style of official buildings. (Interestingly enough, however, Lady Evans, wife of the first British ambassador to Korea who was appointed in 1957, and who had been brought up in India, thought that '. . . except for the wide and deep verandas on the south side, our massive red brick Victorian house might have been that of any prosperous merchant on the outskirts of London or Birmingham'.[5]) Both buildings were two-storey, with wide verandas at both levels, though otherwise they indeed bore a strong resemblance to large suburban villas. The number one House, or the consul-general's house, stood at the top of the little hill on which the compound was situated. It was the bigger of the two. On the ground floor was a large L-shaped public room for receptions, an office/study for the consul-general, a drawing-room and dining-room overlooking the gardens. Kitchens and servants' quarters were in a detached building behind. Upstairs were four bedrooms, each with an attached bathroom. The number two, or assistant's, house, which sat half way between the number one house and the gate, was a smaller, squarer building. It lacked the large entrance hall of the number one house, and had only three bedrooms, but otherwise was very similar, and also had an external kitchen. Lower down the hill were the offices for the vice-consul and the writer, together with various other buildings which housed local staff and servants. These buildings have regularly been replaced since the 1890s, and the present set, erected in the early 1990s, bear no trace of the original Korean buildings or their various replacements.[6]

It is not clear how the buildings were heated. The plans show boilerhouses for the number one and the number two houses, and there are fireplaces in most of the rooms. In the plans of the offices, detached stoves seem to be indicated. Sir Arthur de la Mare, who was acting consul-general in the 1930s, claimed that the only form of heating for all the buildings was very inefficent pot-bellied 'Russian' stoves, which were removed in the summer. He may have been referring to the offices only, but some pictures of the two main buildings clearly show stove pipes sticking out of the windows. In 1898, the vice-consul at Chemulp'o, H. B. Joly, died of a chill caught in his apparently unheated bedroom, in a house dating from the same period, which perhaps tends to support de la Mare's memory.[7] The memory of unheated rooms lived on; Lady Evans writing in the 1970s, noted that the original heating had been totally inadequate, and that 'The cold in winter must have been paralysing'. Even in her day, with double doors and oil-fired central heating, American visitors often found the British residence a cool place in winter.[8]

Similar buildings erected by the British, and also dating from the late nineteenth century, can still be seen in good repair today in Shanghai and at Tamsui, Taiwan, and less well-preserved specimens are scattered about China. Despite the imaginative work by a Seoul university teacher, Professor Kim Chung-dong, there is nothing historically to link any of these properties to the garden city movement, which emerged in Britain at the end of the nineteenth century. Mr Marshall and his colleagues at Shanghai were working on essentially practical projects, rather than the visions of Ebenezer Howard. (Professor Kim is also mistaken in his belief that the Office of Works in Shanghai was somehow connected with the Shanghai International Settlement's Municipal Council.)[9]

The plans were sent to Aston, now retired on medical grounds and temporarily living in Switzerland, for comment. He had little to add, though he expressed the hope that as many of the old Korean-style buildings as possible might be preserved as servants' houses. He also suggested that there was a need for a new and substantial perimeter wall, since the existing one was '. . . of earth and is constantly falling to pieces in rainy weather'.[10]

Faced with the Foreign Office's insistence that the proposed new buildings should go ahead, and with the Office of Works' view that the exisiting ones could no longer be satisfactorily patched up, the Treasury gave in; if the money required, or a substantial part of it could be found from exisiting resources for the China or Japan establishments, then work could start. Treasury officials took some consolation from Aston's proposal that the exisiting buildings might be adapted for use as servants' quarters.[11]

That was in April 1889. By the time the decision reached Shanghai – building matters were still handled by letter, not by telegraph – it was too late to start work that year, but the Office of Works in Shanghai, with the approval of the minister in Beijing, who was technically the head of the mission in Seoul, began to collect the necessary building materials. A contract was siged in Seoul for the delivery of 300,000 red bricks, described as 'of excellent quality', by 31 December 1889. The contractor was a Chinese resident in Korea. Meanwhile, work was set in hand on the perimeter wall, which would be of local granite and erected by a local contractor.[12]

The work of accumulating supplies continued to take up much time in the winter of 1889–90. Despite the high hopes, the first contractor proved able to deliver only a small proportion of the promised bricks, and a new supplier had to be found. He, too, was Chinese, and he proved more reliable. By early April 1890, Marshall was in a position to begin ordering supplies from Britain. These included a 'superior front door [bell] pull', a

Chubb lock for the front door, and a 'Chubb rim lock . . . fro the wine cellar'. Beside this last request, an unknown official in London wrote 'Rubbish', though it is not clear whether this is a comment on the quality of the lock proposed or on the pretension of including a wine cellar in the main house.[13] Whichever was meant, the house did include a wine cellar.

The 1890–91 Office of Works' estimates had allowed £3000 for the buildings in Seoul, but by January 1890, it was clear that the real costs would be much higher. Based on Marshall's figures, the Office of Works reported to the Treasury that the final cost was likely to be double that figure. There was no comment from the Treasury.[14]

By mid-May 1890, work was ready to begin. Hillier moved out on 15 May, taking over one of the other buildings on the compound, and his house was pulled down. By the beginning of July, when Marshall sent back his first progress report, the foundations of the main house were almost finished, and the brickwork had begun. Marshall hoped to have the shell of the house finished within four months, if the weather held. On 19 July 1890, Mrs Hillier laid the foundation stone. The stone recorded that Marshall was the architect (he was in Seoul for the laying of the foundation stone), and that it had been laid in the 54th year of the reign of Queen Victoria, the 8th year of the Chinese Emperor 'Kuang Hsü' and the 499th year of the 'Corean era'. The original stone now stands in the entrance hall of the ambassador's residence, the number one house, while a replica has been placed in the original site.[15]

Photographs apparently taken by Walter Hillier during the construction period, show the main house at various stages of construction.[16] As with all building sites, bricks and tiles are piled everywhere. In one photograph, ponies stand around, with panniers of bricks on their backs – perhaps herein lies the origins of the Manchurian ponies. In one photograph, the labourers use a hoist while a group of Western men and women stand around watching. In all the photographs, tools and scaffolding are entirely local. Koreans, shown these pictures, invariably identify the workmen as Chinese.

Although it seems obvious from the speed at which the work progressed that the men worked hard, Marshall did not find it easy to manage his mixed crew, noting that '. . . Workmen here, a mixture of Coreans, Chinese and Japanese, are, as a rule, lazy and independent, and strike on the smallest provocation, while the headmen have but the smallest regard for truthfulness'. Matters were helped, however, when Hillier made available the services of Messrs Scott and Campbell, his consular assistants, who could both speak Chinese and some Korean, to help supervise the work.[17]

It was hoped that the consul-general's residence would be roofed by the autumn of 1890, but the necessary timbers failed to arrive in time and it was thus impossible to complete the work until after the winter. Despite such delays, and the difficulties with workmen, a year after the work had begun, Marshall was able to report that the main house and the servants' quarters were finished, except for internal work such as plastering, and that work was about to begin on the second house. It had all cost even more than the

January 1890 revised estimate, but the Treasury accepted an extra $10,000 without demur.[18]

By the autumn of 1891, the Hillier family was able to occupy the upper floor of the new house, and there only remained a small amount of finishing off to be done on the ground floor. Meanwhile, Marshall had turned his attention to the second house, though here work was delayed because summer 1891 was very wet, and was followed by a severe winter, with much snow. With the spring work proceeded apace and the acting vice-consul, W. P. Ker, noted in his diary on 1 May 1892 that he had 'Moved into new house', and that two members of the Anglican mission had dined with him there on the same day. Formally, however, it was not until Thursday 12 May 1892 that Hillier took delivery of the houses and the offices; in his diary, Ker noted that the safe was moved into the new offices on the twelfth, and that he had begun to work there the following day.[19]

Hillier reported all these developments in a despatch to the minister in Beijing on 31 May. He recorded his thanks to Marshall, and noted that the total cost of the project was £6213. The land had cost £225, and the buildings £5988. Hillier noted that the new buildings had aroused considerable local interest, and had caught the attention of King Kojong, who had carefully followed the progress of the works from the adjacent palace, and who had asked to see plans and photographs on completion. As a result, Hillier wrote:

> These latter have so taken his fancy that he has requested me to invoke Mr Marshall's assistance in constructing a similar building in the palace grounds, undertaking, if Mr Marshall will arrange a contract with Shanghai workmen for its erection, to lodge the money with a bank, to be drawn on from time to time.

The Foreign Office in London put this suggestion to the Office of Works. The latter informed Mr Marshall of this unexpected testimonial but decided that it was not possible to take him away from his other work in Shanghai, although he was allowed to offer plans and advice to the king, if the latter wished. There is no evidence that this offer was ever taken up, but it may well be that the origins of the Stone Palace (the Sokcho-jon) in the Toksu Palace are to be found in King Kojong's scrutiny of Mr Marshall's buildings.[20]

It was not only the king of Korea who was impressed by the new buildings. The United States minister, who was also aware of the king's interest, said that the new buildings could be seen '. . . as a guarantee of [British] interest in the country', while the a few years' later, the *Korean Repository*, commenting on Hillier's departure, described the main buildings as '. . . two of the best . . . in Seoul'.[21] Others were less sure. In 1892, Seoul was a low-rise city, which lay far below the legation and the site was not then, as it is now, surrounded by mature trees. It therefore presented a rather stark appearance to the world on first completion. A visiting British military officer, who saw the site just after the number one house was finished, described the house as being '. . . designed with the usual want of taste displayed in British official edifaces in the Far East', though he did concede that it was comfortable inside. Another, more famous traveller, Isabella Bird, who was generally a fearsome critic of British consular buildings – she called the vice-consulate at Chemulp'o a '. . . comfortless and unworthy building' – described a '. . . breezy hill, crowned by the staring red brick of the English legation and consular offices'[22] Such conflicting views have persisted since the buildings were first erected.

If there were conflicting views about the buildings, there was widespread agreement that the grounds were good. Mr and Mrs Aston had begun work in the compound to make gardens which would appeal to Europeans. Carles, arriving in Korea on his second visit in the summer of 1885 to take up a consular post, noted that one of the pleasures of escaping from Chemulp'o was to visit Seoul, where Mrs Aston had constructed a garden despite all the odds. He wrote that Mrs Aston,

> . . . By knocking down some division walls, and introducing more sunlight into the grounds, amd laying part of them down in turf, the compound had assumed the air of a very pretty garden, in which crab-trees, paulowanias, hawthorn, and lilac bushes flourished luxiuriantly.

So much so, indeed, that '. . . [a]s a visitor, it was impossible . . . to believe that so pretty a place could have drawbacks' Living there, however, would make him change his mind.[23]

Hillier, too, appears to have been a great gardener. He kept a greenhouse, and A. E. J. Cavendish was impressed by the gardens, whatever he may have thought about the house. The ground was well laid-out, and Hiller was having some success with his fruit trees, and was also producing good strawberries. The lawns, provided a site for special occasions. Queen Victoria's Diamond Jubilee was celebrated in fine style in 1897, with a formal party for foreign and Korean dignatories on the day itself, and, a few days later, a party hosted by the British children of the community for all other foreign children.[24]

And then there was tennis. One notable feature of the grounds was a tennis court, laid out as the new compound began to take on its final shape. W. P. Ker records frequent games of tennis, often at the British consulate-general, after his diary records on 27 April 1892 : 'Laid out tennis court'. This court was between the two houses, below the terrace of the number one house, and not where the present tennis courts are situated. Thereafter, there are regular references in newspapers and other sources to tennis parties there, though there appears to be no evidence for the charming story that King Kojong and Queen Min, viewing tennis being played next door to their place, wondered why these important foreigners did not get their servants to undertake such strenuous exercise.[25]

Notes

1 Works 10/389, Works to Foreign Office, draft no. 4, 4 July 1888; P. Currie (Foreign Office) to Works, 11 July 1888; Sir J. Walsham (Beijing) to F. J. Marshall, Works Shanghai, Public Accounts no. 10, 27 August 1888; and Treasury to Works, 23 January 1889.

2 Works 10/389, Foreign Office to the Treasury, 19 February 1889.

3 Works 10/389, Marshall to Office of Works, no. 1310, 18 January 1889.

4 *Morning Calm*, Vol. VI, no. 64, October 1895.

5 Maureen Tweedy, *A label round my neck*, (Lavenham, Suffolk: Terence Dalton Ltd., 1976), p. 131.

6 The drawings can be found in Works 40/ Maps and Plans, Buildings Overseas.

7 Letter from Sir Arthur de la Mare, KCMG, KCVO, 1 June 1984. For H. B. Joly at Chemulp'o, see Coates *China Consuls*, p. 300.

8 Tweedy, *Label round my neck*, pp. 151–52.

9 See Kim Chung-dong, '"Ku Kyong" for British Embassy was built by British Architect J. Marshall in Seoul', *Kyunchuka*, (January 1996), pp. 36–43. It may be churlish to say so, since Professor Kim draws heavily on my own *The British Embassy Compound Seoul, 1884–1984*, (Seoul: Korean-British Society, 1984), but it would be hard to find an article more full of mistakes. However, since he dismisses his main source as a work which appears 'somewhat perfunctory', I am that much less inclined to be apologetic!

10 Works 10/389, Foreign Office to Treasury, 22 April 1889, enclosing Aston to Foreign Office, 11 April 1889.

11 Works 10/389, Treasury to Works, no. 3307, 4 March 1889; no 7504, 30 April 1889.

12 Works 10/389, Marshall, Shanghai, to London, no. 1386, 10 October 1889.

13 Works 10/389, Marshall to London, no. 1441, 3 April 1890.

14 Works 10/389, 'Explanatory Statement by the Office of Works on the 1890–91 Estimates', 11 January 1890.

15 Works 10/389, Marshall to London, no 1469, 2 July 1890.

16 Some of these are reproduced in Hoare, *British Embassy Compound Seoul*. These were supplied by the Hillier family (see the introduction). Some of these, and others from the same period, are also reproduced in Park Yongsuk, *Soyangin-ei bon Koreya* (Western origins in Korea), (Seoul: Samsung Enron Chedan, 1997).

17 Works 10/389, Marshall to London, no. 1469, 2 July 1890.

18 Works 10/389, London to Marshall, no. 2069, 16 April 1891; Marshall to London, no. 1583, 18 May 1891.

19 Peabody Essex Museum, Salem Mass., Diary of W. P. Ker, 1892, entries for 1, 12 and 13 May 1892. I am most grateful to Frederic A. Sharf, who originally bought this diary and presented it to the Peabody Essex Museum, for providing me with a transcript of the diary and allowing me to quote from it.

20 FO17/1308, Walsham to Lord Salisbury, no. 30, 8 June 1892, forwarding Hillier to Walsham, public accounts no. 9, 31 May 1892. The exchanges about the royal interest are to be found in minuting about this despatch in Works 10/389. For a brief account of the Sokcho-jon, see Donald N. Clark and James H. Grayson, *Discovering Seoul*, (Seoul: Royal Asiatic Society, Korea Branch, 1986), p. 122.

21 A. Heard to the Secretary of State, no. 301, 12 September 1892, in S. J. Palmer, ed., *Korean-American Relations: Documents pertaining to the Far Eastern diplomacy of the United States* vol. II, (Berkeley and Los Angeles: University of California Press, 1963), 241–43; *Korean Repository*, October 1896.

22 A. E. J. Cavendish, *Korea and the Sacred White Mountain, being a brief account of a journey in Korea in 1891* (London: G. Philip and Son, 1894), pp. 16, 30–31; Isabella Bird, *Korea and her neighbours* (London: John Murray, 1897; reprinted Seoul: Yonsei University Press, 1970), pp. 30, 37.

23 Carles, *Life in Corea*, p. 103.

24 Cavendish, *Korea and the Sacred White Mountain*, p. 30; *Korean Repository*, June 1897; *The Indpendent*, 24 June 1897, 26 May 1898.

25 Ker diary, entries for 27 April and 9 May 1892; Cavendish, *Korea and the Sacred White Mountain*, p. 30–31; *The Independent*, 8 July 1897; *Korea Review*, April 1903.

Korea

$$\boxed{3}$$

From Consulate-general to Consulate-general, 1894–1942

K orea at the end of the nineteenth century was in a state of political turmoil and upheaval. The great powers, including Britain, competed for influence and control, and once again, the Korean proverb of the shrimp whose back is broken when the whales fight, seemed an appropriate description of the peninsula's plight.[1] For the British, the main concern was the Russians and their supposed designs on the peninsula. Much effort was devoted to preventing the Russians obtaining the upper hand at the Korean court. As was the case during the Komundo incident, Britain's real concern was to restraint the Russians elsewhere, especially on the edges of the Indian empire, but nevertheless, this still affected British policy towards Korea.[2]

At the more parochial level, the British consulate-general in Seoul was also involved in the upheavals of those years. During the 1894–95 Sino-Japanese War, the British posts at Seoul and Chemulp'o took on responsibility for looking after the interests of the Chinese community. At one time, the Chinese minister in Seoul took refuge in the British consulate-general. At Chemulp'o, so grateful were the Chinese community for British support that when the British vice-consul who had helped them, H. B. Joly, died in 1898, the Chinese Foreign Ministry sent £140 to his widow. It was all she got; since her husband had not been a substantive vice-consul she received no pension.[3]

One consequence of the Sino-Japanese War was that in 1897, the king of Korea, under Japanese pressure, announced that the ancient ties between Korea and China were now definitely at an end, and henceforward the kingdom of Korea would become the Korean empire, a wholly independent state. In these circumstances Britain reviewed its representation in Korea and decided that the existing arrangement whereby the minister in Beijing was also accredited to Seoul was no longer appropriate. So the consulate-general in Seoul ceased to be a subordinate post of Beijing and became a substantive post in its own right. The consulate-general, always technically a legation even if its head lived in Beijing, now became one in its own right, headed from 1898 at first by a chargé d'affaires, and then, from 1901, by a minister resident, the lowest independent rank in the British diplomatic service. Both roles fell to John Jordan, a relatively recent recruit to the British China consular service, who happened to be in the right place at the right time.[4]

The political upheavals and diplomatic changes had some surprising consequences for the British legation. The Korean king, having spent some time in the Russian legation after the murder of the queen by the Japanese, decided that there would be advantages in having escape routes available should he be threatened again. He therefore constructed a series of gates from the Kyong-un (now Toksu) Palace that would allow him easy access to the nearby legations, including the British legation. That gate survived until about 1985, when internal reconstruction of the Toksu Palace led to its disappearance. It would appear that nobody realized that the small old and cracked wooden door had any historical significance.[5] None of the gates was ever used. When the king suggested during the Russo-Japanese War of 1904–5 that he might take refuge in the British legation, Jordan firmly persuaded him not to do so.[6]

The restoration of the Kyong-un Palace after 1896, and its reoccupation as a royal residence, had some unfortunate consequences for its neighbour, the British legation. The habits of the guards and others who lived in the area left much to be desired, and in particular, had damaging consequences for the sanitary state of the legation. In 1902, the legation doctor wrote a report which the minister forwarded to London. It painted a dismal picture of the area in which the legation stood. The deep well dug in the 1880s could no longer be used, since it had become polluted by the garbage of the area. The palace walls, some twenty feet high, were soaked with filth up to four or five feet high, for all the sewerage and general refuse from the palace were thrown over the walls into open ditches at the foot of the walls. The stench was overpowering, and the legation was '. . . shut in by this huge cesspool'. These were among the reasons the legation advanced for opposing various plans to increase the palace area.[7]

The political tensions of the early twentieth century had another direct consequence for the legation. From the days of Korea's opening to the West, there had been regular visits to the peninsula by British naval vessels, and officers and men from these were frequent visitors to the consulate-general. It was no coincidence that the first head of the Anglican mission, and the first Anglican bishop of Korea, Charles John Corfe, had a long previous career as a naval chaplain; he, too, welcomed the visiting sailors to his small episcopal palace next door to the consulate-general.[8] At times of crisis, which grew more frequent in the last years of the nineteenth century, sailors or marines from the Royal Navy would be called upon to supplement the small guard which was a standard feature at many East Asian diplomatic and consular posts. During the Sino-Japanese War of 1894–5, for example, fifty British marines came up to Seoul from Chemulp'o, to join fifty Russian, forty American and nine German soldiers, sailors, or marines in protecting the foreign community.[9] In the British case, at least, such visits were always welcome, for apart from the added sense of security which the arrival of the marines conveyed, they were willing to help with community affairs and to organize shows and other events.

So frequent were the requests for military support that by 1898, it was felt in both Seoul and London that more permanent accommodation was needed in Seoul. Until then, troops appear to have been regularly billeted on land owned by the Korean Customs, but this was felt to be no longer satisfactory. The continued unsettled state of Korea indicated the need for a more permanent British military presence to match that at the Russian and American legations. After some delay, the Treasury agreed to the necessary works.[10]

There was no suitable piece of land available on the existing compound on which to erect a building to house the proposed troop of twenty men and two officers, until the Anglican mission, which owned land at the gate of the compound, offered to erect a building for the use of the marines and rent it to the legation, on condition that a high wall was built dividing the two compounds. When the offered land was examined more closely, it proved to be too small for its intended purpose. When Bishop Corfe was approached with a view to renting more of the church land, he proved unexpectedly difficult, although he had seemed in favour of the earlier proposal. Now he argued that he had no funds for the proposed building and gave every sign of wishing to abandon the whole project.[11]

Exchanges on the question dragged on until March 1900. Then Corfe was told by the London-based Society for the Propagation of the Gospel in Foreign Parts (SPG), the main source of funding for the mission, that he should sell the land to the legation. No doubt the Foreign Office in London had suggested to the SPG that it would be helpful if Corfe could be persuaded to change his mind; for the SPG, worried about the cost of the Korean mission, it may have been a useful way of raising some extra funds. Whatever the reason, the plan for a barracks could now go ahead. Additional land for the purpose came from some of the legation's stabling. The delay in persuading Corfe meant that the 1901 building season was missed, and it was not until 1902 that work began. It was completed the following year, at a cost of £1200. In the meantime, the exchange rate had worsened, and the contractor had lost heavily on the deal. As 'an act of grace' – the delays had not been the contractor's fault – the Treasury agreed to make good the difference.[12]

The permanent marines were as popular as had been their temporary colleagues. Again, they contributed to the social life of the small foreign community and they were useful in other ways too; they made valiant efforts to save the neighbouring palace in the great fire of 1904, though without success. In the event, however, the marines were a short-lived addition to the foreign community, and the barracks were only in use for a couple of years. Following the Russo-Japanese War, Japanese influence steadily increased in Korea. The defeat of the Russians, following the earlier defeat of the Chinese, and the general lack of interest of the other major Powers left the Japanese a free hand, and in 1905 they declared a protectorate over Korea. Korea's diplomatic relations would henceforward be handled by Japan, and the Japanese argued that it was no longer appropriate for diplomatic missions to be established in Seoul. The Seoul post ceased to be a legation. Jordan left to become minister in Beijing, and the post re-opened as a consulate-general, with Henry Cockburn, another China consul, as the first consul-general. For a few years more, the posts at Seoul and Chemulp'o were staffed from the China consular service, though they were now in a Japanese-controlled territory. After the annexation of Korea by Japan in 1910, both posts were absorbed into Britain's Japan consular service.[13] In these new circumstances, it was no longer felt necessary to keep a military presence in Seoul, and by 1906, the marines had gone. The barracks – the name continued in use until after the Korean War – were absorbed as offices and accommodation for servants.[14]

How long these arrangements lasted is not clear but at some point, the elaborate office arrangements of 1907 were abandoned. When Seoul was inspected in 1928, the inspector noted that the consul-general's office was in his house, while the vice-consul's office and the writers' offices were in the number two, or vice-consul's house. The inspector argued that a lot of time was wasted because of the need for the consul-general and the vice-consul to visit each other's offices – a comment dismissed as 'nonsense' in the margin of the Foreign Office copy of the report.[15] By the later 1930s, when Arthur de la Mare went to Seoul as acting consul-general, the main office was still situated on the ground floor of the number two house, while the buildings lower down the slope, towards the gate, were where a '. . . lodge and stabling housed the Writer and the two Korean gardeners, and of course the Police Box'.[16] There had clearly been some minor modifications to take account of the changes from Korean to Japanese staff as the colonial period progressed.

This is to run ahead. The last years of an independent Korea and the early period of Japanese rule saw minor problems over the roads near the consulate-general, eventually sorted out in May 1911 by an agreement between the British government and the Korean Imperial Household Agency, which provided for a new entrance. One of the important points for the British was not to allow an extension of the palace grounds, as far as this could be prevented, for fear of a further deterioration in sanitation. By the time of the second road agreement, the Japanese colonial government appears to have effected a change in the sanitary practices around the palace. Thereafter, there are no more complaints about the poor habits of the guards and other residents.[17]

The Japanese colonial period from 1910 saw the Seoul consulate-general become somewhat of a backwater. From about 1915 onwards, it became the only post in Korea, for Chemulp'o was abandoned as a career post, though it continued as a consular agency, under the talkative Mr Bennet.[18] Meanwhile, Seoul, though still a consulate-general, was often seen as less important than some of the other posts in the Japanese empire, for a number of reasons. While there was a modest amount to report on political developments in the years of the Japanese protectorate, after 1910, political work tended to decline. Only occasionally thereafter did the consul-general feel the need to report on political developments. The reporting of the independence rallies in March 1919, and the subsequent brutal suppression by the Japanese, was an exception, all the more marked because of its relative rarity.[19] Although Mr White, newly arrived as consul-general in 1928, claimed that he was busy with despatches on a wide range of subjects, including policy of the administration; Korean discontent; frontier troubles; movements of troops; communism; attitude towards education; attitude towards missionaries; morphine; and – oddly – Koreans; it is hard to believe that any of them were read with much interest, assuming that they were ever written. Reporting this list, and noting that Britain as a colonial power naturally had an interest in Japanese colonialism, the inspector-general of consular posts argued that Seoul should remain a consulate-general.[20]

The British community was small in 1910, numbering about 160 people, which figure included Australians, Canadians and other members of the empire. They were a mixed lot, occupying a variety of posts, but their variety could not make up for their lack of numbers. Unlike other East Asian ports, where they tended to dominate, the British in Korea were never the largest element in the foreign community. They always took second place to US citizens, and their numbers, increasing somewhat by the 1920s, thereafter hovered around 250–350, with a decline in the late 1930s. For most of the colonial period, this figure of course included Australians, Canadians and other empire and commonwealth citizens, as well as citizens of the Irish Free State – later Eire – after 1922, until the very end of the period. When the Japanese authorities compiled their last list of foreign residents in Korea just before the outbreak of the Pacific War in 1941, the 'British' had dropped to twenty – outnumbered by the 'Irish' at twenty-three, while there were nine Australians and ten Canadians. By that stage, the Americans numbered eighty-four, while there were eighty-two Turks, sixty-six French and 185 Russians.[21]

A high percentage of the British community, however defined, were missionaries, and these brought their own problems, although those of the British were rarely as difficult as those of other countries. Inspector Phillips noted in 1928 that there were then some 140 missionaries in a British community of 350. He also noted that since most of these did not speak Japanese, were scattered about a country the size of England, Scotland and Wales combined, and were in some cases engaged in education, there was plenty of potential for trouble. This reinforced the argument for the continuation of a senior officer in Korea.[22]

Trade, or rather its absence, was the other main preoccupation of the consul-general. British trade with Korea had been a disappointment from the first days of the 1883 treaty, and many visitors had commented on the lack of British shipping in Korea's ports and a similar lack of British companies. It was true that from the earliest days, and indeed, even before the treaty, British goods had found their way into Korea from China and Japan, and continued to do so until well into the colonial period, but clearly the lack of direct trade worried many British officials. There was some doubt about who was responsible for this failure. Some thought that it lay in the lack of enthusiasm shown by British merchants, others that it was the relatively unsophisticated nature of the Korean market which was at fault. Occasionally, a want of energy on the part of consular officials was seen as a factor. Whatever the reasons, British trade with Korea remained small.[23] The consul-general had to advise the business community on matters relating to Japanese law and sometimes had to intervene where there were disputes. It did not add up to a heavy burden.

Indeed, although the argument was accepted in London that Seoul should continue to be a consulate-general, in reality the post was effectively downgraded for long periods. When the consul-general went on leave, or fell sick, the post was sometimes left empty for several months at a time. For a period in 1937, it was agreed that it could be used to provide accommodation for refugees from the fighting in China, since there was no consul-general in residence. When temporary officers were appointed, they were often very junior, and sometimes had no experience at all. Arthur de la Mare, with nothing more than two years' Japanese language training, found himself acting consul-general in 1938 when the consul-general fell sick and returned to Britain (de la Mare claims in his memoirs that he died, which makes for a more dramatic story, but in fact he returned and took up his duties again). To make matters worse, de la Mare found on arrival in Seoul that he was to be acting everything else as well as consul-general, for the vice-consul promptly left on retirement. De la Mare had no consular training at that stage[24], but at least by his own account seems to have coped. His ability to speak Japanese gave him some advantage over his small number of consular colleagues, none of whom knew the language.[25] Even when the consul-general was present, he frequently found that he was the only officer, and had to do all the work including translation and typing. In commenting on this, and pleading for a vice-consul, Gerald Phipps in 1935 admitted that the work in Seoul was not as heavy as it had been in 1914, when he had last served there. Yet it had to be done, and it was not being done very efficiently.[26]

If the consul-general and his staff – when he had any – had little work to do, there were other attractions. Writing of the years 1914–19, one junior resident of the consulate-general noted that :

Seoul is a glittering prospect of mountains and palaces, with mushroom-roofed cottages on which red pepper laid out to dry on them presents a delightful Turkish-carpet effect seen from a hill-top, mingled with the blue smoke rising from thousands of kitchen fires as the evening meal is being prepared towards dusk. The whole picture – the molten sunshine and the filtered transparency of the air, the royal tombs, the winding river, the White Buddha, the imposing city gates, and the remnant of the old city wall crawling over Namsan (South Hill) – is rich with charm. We used to go for a walk of one or two hours nearly every day, except in the summer when we played tennis.[27]

Seoul (Keijo in Japanese) by the 1920s was becoming a modern city, with good roads and facilities, and it was at the centre of a growing rail system, which allowed relatively easy access to spectacular scenery in the Diamond mountains, and elsewhere. By 1928, there was electricity for lighting the compound, although light for the vice-consul's house was only available at night. The general cost of living was somewhat less than in Japan, even if the price of wine was higher. Heating was expensive and not very efficient; the long periods when the main residential buildings were not in use meant that they quickly deteriorated. De la Mare complained of huge gaps between window frames and walls in the number two house, through which the Siberian wind whistled. He also claimed that when Derwent Kermode and his wife arrived to take over from him in 1939 that the condition of the number one house, which by then had been left empty and unheated for four or five months over the winter, was such that Mrs Kermode's '. . . consumption of gin and cigarettes, already assuring her of a very creditable batting average, sent her soaring into the Guinness Book of Records'. It was not the first – or the last – unhappy experience for the Kermodes in Seoul. Inspector-general Phillips had noted in 1928 that Kermode seemed unhappy and was constantly ill.[28]

With the Anglican compound at the front, on which a cathedral was completed in 1926, and the Salvation Army headquarters at its rear, the area around the British consulate-general was seen as a small corner of Britain. Relations between the clergy of the English Church Mission and the staff of the consulate-general remained close as they had been in the past, and there were frequent comings and goings between the two small communities. As Arthur de la Mare somewhat unkindly put it, the cathedral clergy '. . . relied on the Consulate-General for their spiritual sustenance, of which they were always in great need'.[29] The Salvation Army did not share the same tastes, but relations with them were also cordial. Many photographs survive of members of the Seoul British community gathered together in the grounds of the English Church Mission for occasions such as St George's Day.

For the wider foreign community, the consulate-general was also a source of sustenance, and all agreed that the compound was an important centre for the social life of the foreign community. Empire Day (24 May) was an occasion for the whole foreign community, not just for the British, partly because the weather tended to be better than on 4 July. On Empire Day, adults took tea on the upper lawn, while the children played below. Other groups who regularly used the grounds for functions included the Seoul Women's Club, who gave an annual party, and the Seoul Society for the Prevention of Cruelty to Animals.[30] And while the offices might be undermanned, there were plenty of staff to look after the buildings and the grounds. As late as 1939, they included a superintending servant, a messenger, a gatekeeper, a coolie and a gardener.[31]

This gentle life came to an end in the late 1930s. From 1937 onwards, the fighting in China led to steady pressure on the foreign community in Korea. De la Mare noted severe restrictions on all travel outside the capital even for consular officers when he arrived in late 1938, and he was not able to visit Chemulp'o during his six months' residence.[32] Foreign businessmen found there were increasing limitations on their operations and on land holding.[33] Missionaries also faced Japanese suspicion, and their activities were subject to close scrutiny. The Salvation Army, with its military-style titles, had always worried some Japanese officials, and in December 1940 it was compelled to abandon these titles, break off links with its International Headquarters, and rename itself the 'Salvation Band'.

The English Church Mission, despite its long efforts to work with Japanese as well as Koreans, found that its activities were also increasingly viewed with suspicion. The bishop and some of his colleagues were accused of spying, while Fr A. E. Chadwell was detained in P'yongyang for possessing an illegal short-wave radio set. The mission's small rural hospitals found it difficult to obtain drugs and other supplies. By December 1940, the head of the mission, Bishop Cooper, had decided that the foreign clergy should also withdraw from Korea.[34]

When war came to Korea on 8 December 1941, the British community was therefore much reduced. As far as the consulate-general was concerned, there were two British consular officers and their wives, and one typist. Mr Bennett, the long-serving honorary consul in Chemulp'o soon joined them, and all were held there until they were moved to Japan for eventual repatriation in August 1942. Various books, sporting guns and radios were taken away, but on the whole, those detained were well treated. No attempt was made to stop the destruction of archives, and there were no cases of brutality. Indeed, the Clauson committee could find little to criticize in Japanese behaviour at Seoul except that '. . . wanton and unnecessary damage was done to the doors and windows of the buildings by nailing them up with immense nails'.[35]

Notes

1 For background, see G. A. Lenson, *Balance of intrigue: international rivalry in Korea and Manchuria 1884–99*, (Tallahassee, Florida: University Presses of Florida, 1982).

2 There is a considerable literature on this. See, *inter alia*, Synn Seoung Kwon, *The Russo-Japanese rivalry over Korea, 1876–1904*, (Seoul: Yuk Phub Sa, 1981); Ian Nish, *The origins of the Russo-Japanese war*, (London and New York: Longman Group, 1985.)

3 United Society for the Propogation of the Gospel (USPG) Archives, Oxford: Log of Bishop C. J. Corfe, Seoul 24 July 1894. I am grateful to Miss A. J. Roberts MBE, now of Leicester, for this reference. For the Chinese and Joly, see Coates, *China consuls*, p. 300.

4 Coates, *China consuls*, p. 302; J. E. Hoare, 'The centenary of Korean-British relations: the British diplomatic presence in Korea, 1883–1983', *Korea Observer*, vol. xiv, no. 2 (Summer 1983), 131–41.

5 A. and D. Clarke, *Seoul Past and Present: A Guide to Yi T'aejo's Capital*, (Seoul: Royal Asiatic Society Korea Branch, 1969), p. 105; letter from H M ambassador Seoul, T G Harris, 22 September 1992.

6 FO 17/1659, J. N. Jordan to Lord Lansdowne, no. 34, 8 February 1904.

7 FO 17/1634, Jordan to Lansdowne, no. 25 consular, 15 December 1902, enclosing a report by Dr E. Baldock, 13 December 1902.

8 See H. H. Montgomery, *Charles John Corfe: Naval Chaplain-Bishop*, (London: Society for the Propagation of the Gospel in Foreign Parts, 1927).

9 L. H. Underwood, *Fifteen years among the topknots* (Seoul: Kyung-in Co., for the Korea Branch Royal Asiatic Society, second edition, 1977), p. 108.

10 Works 10/98, Foreign Office to Works, confidential, 22 August 1898. The Treasury agreed in October; Treasury to Works, no. 15322, 15 October 1898.

11 Works 10/98, Works Shanghai to London, no. 2116, 20 October 1899; Foreign Office to Works, 7 March 1900.

12 Works 10/98, Memorandum 677/1902; Works to Treasury, no. F7793, 11 March 1903; Treasury to Works no. 4604, 14 March 1903.

13 Hoare, 'The centenary of Korean-British relations: the British diplomatic presence in Korea, 1883–1983', pp. 131–41.

14 Works 10/329, Plan 'for the conversion of the former marine barracks into offices . . .' 1906; 40/332, Seoul: Plan of Offices, Shanghai, 1907.

15 FO 369/2042/K10351/10351/223, H. Phillips to the Secretary of State, visits no. 12, 15 July 1928.

16 Letter from Sir Arthur de la Mare, 1 June 1984.

17 FO 17/1634, Jordan to Lansdowne, no. 12 consular, 1 July 1902; FO tel. no. 12 to Seoul, 27 November 1902; Seoul tel. no. 24 to FO, 29 December 1902. Copy of letter from T. G. Harris, HMA Seoul, to R. T. Sime, overseas estate department, FCO, 10 November 1994, enclosing a copy of an agreement between 'His Excellency Viscount Min Pyeng Suk, Steward of the household of His Highness Prince Yi, and His Britannic Majesty's Office of Works at Shanghai . . .', 14 April 1911.

18 FO 369/2042/K10352/10352/227, H. Phillips to Secretary of State, visits no. 13, 15 July 1928, Inspection report on Chemulp'o British Consular Agency. For earlier details of Mr Bennett's activities in Japan, see Angus Hamilton, *Korea*, (New York: Charles Scribner's Sons, 1904), pp. 144–49.

19 For an account which makes extensive use of British reporting of the March First movement, including reporting from Seoul, see Ku Dae-yeol, *Korea under Colonialism: the March First Movement and Anglo-Japanese Relations*, (Seoul: Seoul Computer Press for the Royal Asiatic Society, 1985).

20 FO 369/2042/K10351/10351/223, Report by Inspector-General Phillips upon his Inspection of His Majesty's Consulate-General at Seoul, 15 July 1928.

21 Figures for 1907–1909, 1912, 1924–25, 1927, 1929, 1937–38, and 1941–42 can be found in Yongsin Academy, Korean Studies Research Institute, compilers, *Chosun chaeryu ku-mi-in chosa rok*, ('Directory of Europeans and Americans in Korea'), (Seoul: Yongsin Academy Korean Studies Research Institute, 1981). Other sources will throw up occasional figures e.g. FO 262/1065, H. C. Bonar to MacDonald, no. 47, enclosing Bonar to Grey, no. 44, 20 July 1910, which includes a detailed breakdown of the British community by occupation, sex and place of residence; FO 369/2042/K10351/10351/223, Report by Inspector-General Phillips, 15 July 1928.

22 FO 369/2042/K10351/10351/223, Report by Inspector-General Phillips, 15 July 1928.

23 A. R. Michell, 'British commercial interests in Korea 1883–1941', in Korean National History Compilation Committee, editors, *Han-yong sugyo 100-nyon sa*, (Seoul: National History Compilation Committee, 1984), pp. 188–202. The lack of commercial activity at Seoul in the mid-1920s was blamed partly on A. H. Lay, who had just retired as consul-general, a post he held from 1914 to 1927. It was felt that he had been too long in Korea and lost interest in commercial work, and it was hoped that his much younger and more energetic successor, Oswald White, would do better. There is no evidence that he did. See minute by E. T. Crowe, 3 September 1928 on FO 369/2042/K10351/10351/223, Report by Inspector-General Phillips, 15 July 1928. For Lay, one of the few consular officers to learn Korean, see A. C. Hyde Lay, *Four generations in China, Japan and Korea*, (Edinburgh and London: Oliver & Boyd, 1952), pp. 22–28.

24 Not that this was unusual in the Japan consular service: See Hoare, 'Britain's Japan Consular Service', p. 102.

25 Letter 1 June 1984. See also the account in his autobiography: de la Mare, *Perverse and foolish*, pp. 68–70, which differs slightly from the account which he sent me in 1984.

26 FO 369/2413/K7412/26/23, Clive to Sir Samuel Hoare, no. 294, 5 June 1935, enclosing a memorandum 'Consular staff required at the Seoul Consulate-General', by G. H. Phipps.

27 Lay, *Four generations*, p. 25.

28 Arthur de la Mare, letter of 1 June 1984. For the more general picture of conditions in Seoul, as well as the comments on Kermode, see FO 369/2042/K10351/10351/223, Report by Inspector-General Phillips, 15 July 1928. Mr Phillips had also found him somewhat unprepossessing as acting consul in Tokyo in December 1927: see FO 369/2040/K2143/2143/223, Report on inspection of HBM Consulate At Tokyo, 10 December 1927.

29 Arthur de la Mare, letter of 1 June 1984.

30 Information from Dr Horace G. Underwood, Seoul 1983–84; conversation with Mrs Winifred Bland, 1 November 1983. See also FO 369/2042/K10351/10351/223, Report by Inspector-General Phillips, 15 July 1928, and Lay, *Four generations*, p. 27, who describes his mother as the 'presiding genius' of the Empire Day festivities.

31 FO 366/1778/XS3K/23/19, D. W. Kermode, Seoul, to FO Personnel Department, 18 June 1946.

32 Arthur de la Mare, letter of 1 June 1984.

33 FO371/21042/F1246, Clive to Eden, no. 43/5/57/37, of 16 January 1937, forwarding Phipps (Seoul) to Tokyo, no. 6, of 16 January 1937.

34 See various papers in FO 371/27951 of 1941, and A. Hamish Ion, *The Cross and the Rising Sun* volume 2 : *The British Protestant Missionary Movement in Japan, Korea and Taiwan, 1865–1945* (Waterloo, Ontario: Wilfred Laurier University Press, 1993), pp. 246–250.

35 FO 371/313736/F217/33/61, 'British officials in Japanese territory and Manchuria', minute by T. E. Broadley, 20 December 1941; FO 371/31839/F7575/867/23, L. H. Foulds to Lord Clauson, 27 November 1942, enclosing a memorandum 'Treatment of His Majesty's Diplomatic and Consular Establishments and their staffs by the Japanese Authorities'.

Korea

Seoul
Since 1945

The Beginnings

With the departure of the staff in 1942, the Seoul consulate-general passed to the care of the Swiss consul-general. There was little attempt at proper maintenance, and the conditions of the buildings steadily deteriorated. No attempt appears to have been made to look after them, as in Tokyo, and there was no foreign community to lodge in them, as in Beijing.

The British played no part in the occupation of Korea in 1945, and it was not until the very end of that year that the British military liaison mission in Tokyo was able to spare an officer to visit Seoul to examine the state of the buildings and to sound out the US occupation authorities about reopening the consulate-general. He reported that the Americans were keen to have additional allied representation in Seoul, and would like to see the British return. They were also willing to help over accommodation and other practical matters.[1]

Following this report, it was decided to appoint a liaison officer to the American occupation forces in Korea. As well as working with the US occupation government, the officer should also set in hand work to rehabilitate the consulate-general, pending the appointment of a foreign service officer to the post. The officer selected for this task was a Royal Naval Volunteer Reserve officer, Lt D. P. Lury. He was said to have had previous experience of Korea, and to speak the language, though his name does not appear in any of the Japanese lists of foreigners published during the 1920s or 1930s. His main task was to prepare the compound for the expected appointment of a consular officer early in 1946. His instructions noted that '. . . the necessity for substantial internal repairs, a thorough cleaning, overhaul of the plumbing and heating system is already apparent'. He was not, however, to set any of this in hand without reference to Tokyo and the Foreign Office, except that he was allowed to employ '. . . a total of three competent Koreans at not more than ten times the equivalent pre-war salaries'. In addition to this work preparing the way for a foreign service officer, Lury was to engage in naval intelligence – not an easy task in Seoul! He was not to carry out consular functions, which remained the responsibility of the Swiss.[2]

Although Lury's instructions were issued at the end of December 1945, it was not until February 1946 that he was able to take up his post as 'Liaison Officer to the Military Government Section of the United States Command'. Between his arrival on 15 February and the despatch of a Foreign Office representative on 16 April 1946, Lt Lury had little time to undo the ravages of years of neglect, although he somehow procured the help of the Royal Navy to provide a working party to start repairing the number one house. No doubt it would have been hard for anybody who was chosen to formally take-over Seoul for the Foreign Office and to move into the neglected buildings that occupied the site. It was particularly unfortunate, therefore, that the man who boarded the personal aeroplane of the head of the Tokyo liaison mission, together with Bishop Cooper of the English Church Mission, was that same Derwent Kermode whose past unhappy experiences in the post have already been chronicled.[3]

It is not clear from the surviving papers exactly how Kermode came to be selected. No doubt he was of the right seniority and experience, and there were many demands on Foreign Office staff at the end of the war. He now arrived in Seoul with the personal rank of consul-general, which put him on a par with the senior US diplomatic officer in the capital. But the number one house was dilapidated, and the naval party had been only able to patch things up, not to carry out the major repairs which were clearly required. This patching might last two years, but no longer. The garden, also totally neglected since 1942, was a jungle, and the one man now available to look after it, could scarcely keep on top of the work. By November 1946, Kermode seems to have worked himself into a state of misery. He felt that the other buildings on the compound could not be put right by another naval party, since they seemed to have deteriorated more than the number one house. Even if such a working party could put right the number two house, Mr Kermode felt that they would neither be capable of converting the offices – the old barracks – into Korean-style rooms, nor the servants' quarters from Chinese-style rooms to Korean. Such work, Mr Kermode concluded, could only be done by Korean builders, and he concluded with something like a note of triumph, even if it was possible to pay the exorbitant wages which Koreans now demanded, nothing could be done in 1946 because winter had already set in.

Mr Kermode also complained that water shortages made baths difficult, while a lack of glasses meant that he had to use old jam jars to serve drinks. He wrote that he did not mind doing this with American officers up to the rank of colonel, but he felt that generals might take offence. At a work level, he had neither cyphers – because he had no safe to keep them in – nor any other secure means of communication, and all telegraphic material except the most anodyne, had to be sent to Tokyo for transmission. It is perhaps not surprising that one of Mr Kermode's colleagues in London, who was on the receiving end of these diatribes, noted after a conversation with Arthur de la Mare, then in the Foreign Office's Japan department, that '. . . Mr Kermode . . . likes to have a grievance to nurse'.[4]

Nobody denied that there were problems. As Bishop Cooper noted, Mrs Kermode arrived in December 1946 to find '. . . a burst radiator, a tank in the roof leaking, and the kitchen range flooded by a broken pipe.' It was, wrote the Bishop, a '. . . good introduction to a Corea (sic) where most things [had] deteriorated after six years of neglect and misuse'.[5] But in the aftermath of war, there were few domestic staff available, and Seoul was as short of funds as any diplomatic service post. Mr Kermode did not seem to understand, and the complaints flowed in. After the Conservative MP, Fitzroy Maclean, paid a visit to Seoul, Mr Kermode's problems were raised in the House of Commons.

Various attempts were made to ease the burden by appointing a vice-consul to the post. Mr Kermode turned down each candidate offered, arguing that such an officer would have to live with him in the number one house and, he felt, US officers with whom he as consul-general would have to deal might well look down on junior officers. Even the suggestion from the US authorities in September 1946 that it would be a good idea if Mr Kermode was given the formal title of consul-general does not seem to have pleased him. His first reaction was that he had none of the required documents and seals to act as consul-general. The only seal which he had read 'British Consulate-General, Corea (sic)', and he felt that this would be claiming an authority to which he would not be entitled. When it looked as though London would accept the US proposal, Kermode wrote that while he could see no objection to such a move, he could not be expected to do any extra work.[6]

Whatever his objections, Kermode had the title of consul-general, and thereafter, life in Seoul seems to have got steadily better until his departure in 1948. Certainly the stream of complaints began to dry up, and in 1948, rewarded with a CMG (Commander of the Order of St Michael and St George), he passed from the Korean scene. Later, from 1950–53, he was appointed Ambassador in Indonesia, and then from 1953–55, to Czechoslovakia, and he added a KCMG (Knight Commander of the Order of St Michael and St George), to his earlier medal. After retirement, he was ordained as an Anglican clergyman in 1957, and at the time of his death in January 1960, he was the rector of Cocking with Bepton in West Sussex.[7]

Seoul again becomes a legation

By the time of Kermode's departure, Seoul was functioning as an independent consulate-general – following the end of the war, there had been no attempt to put it back under Tokyo's control. Kermode's successor as consul-general was Captain Vyvyan Holt, a former army officer turned diplomat, with much Middle Eastern experience but no knowledge of East Asia. With him as consul was Sydney Faithful, a career Foreign Service officer. From October 1948, they were joined by George Blake and Norman Owen, both members of the Secret Intelligence Service (SIS), or MI6, operating under consular cover. Blake had originally been destined for Urumchi in western China, but in summer 1948 was told that he would be going to Seoul. Apart from the fact that he would be the SIS head of station and thus running his own organization, it was not a posting he welcomed.[8]

Blake was briefed by an apparently more contented Kermode in London before flying out to Seoul in the autumn of 1948. The establishment of the SIS station meant that for the first time since 1884, there was no longer enough room on the compound to accommodate all staff. Blake's office, like those of the consul and consul-general were on the compound, but they did not live there. It was true that on arrival in Seoul, Blake was temporarily accommodated in the number two house. He noted that the ground floor was used as the chancery, or main offices, while Faithful, had an apartment on the first floor. Soon, however, Blake found accommodation for himself and his assistant, Norman Owen, in a Japanese-style house in the commercial district. Having two rooms spare, they rented them to the French vice-consul.[9]

Having found accommodation, Blake set about his main work. He had been charged with establishing an intelligence network in the then Soviet Far Eastern Provinces, since Seoul was the nearest British diplomatic post to the area. This he found an impossible task, and he turned instead to cultivating Korean contacts, who might assist him in his second role, which was to monitor developments in Korea should the Communists in the North occupy the whole peninsula. To do all this, he used the cover of a vice-consular post, developing links with the various missionary groups and issuing visas to Koreans. Like others, he found the Anglican missionaries at the gates of the compound both knowledgeable about Korea and not adverse to sharing the occasional drink.[10]

Normal diplomatic life also provided contacts for Blake. He found his boss, Captain Vyvyan Holt, who become minister with the establishment of diplomatic relations between Britain and the Republic of Korea in 1949, a man of great charm, but also something of an eccentric and an ascetic, preferring boiled vegetables, fruit and curds to what he disdainfully dismissed as 'hot meals'. He cleaned his own windows and repaired his own oil-fired central heating – one advance on the past – and was generally careful of staff welfare. Once, down with mumps and still as in pre-war days working from the office in the number one house, he arranged an elaborate system whereby papers could be left in the middle of his lawn, and were only collected when the bearer had retreated a safe distance from the infected head of post. Equally eccentric, perhaps, was the King's Birthday Party in June 1950, which, despite the pouring rain, Holt insisted on holding on the lawns, where he greeted his guests in gumboots and umbrella, rather than risk having people being sick over his furniture.[11]

The coming of the war

It was not long, however, before there were graver matters to worry both Holt and Blake. According to Blake's account, neither he nor Holt had instructions to leave in the event of a conflict; indeed, in Blake's case, he was specifically instructed to stay, to establish a network of informants behind North Korean lines. Whether or not they expected a conflict is not clear. The general view was that war was possible on the peninsula, and that neither North nor South wished to see the existing division perpetuated, but in the summer of 1950, it was not expected that either side would take action soon. In late May, Holt had asked the secretary to the UN Commission in Korea about reports of troop build-ups north of the 38th parallel, but had been told that these were South Korean stories designed to persuade the US to give more military equipment. Although early June 1950 had seen some unusual troop movements in the North, Blake thought that this was nothing special and that there was no need for concern. His US contacts reassured him that this was the case. They also added that if there was a conflict in Korea, the US would do nothing. Korea lay outside the United States perceived defence perimeter.[12]

For the British legation, Sunday 25 June 1950 began as most other Sundays. Blake had been at the French vice-consul's party the night before, but joined Holt at the regular English-language service held in the crypt of the Anglican Cathedral. During the service, an American officer arrived and spoke to several members of the US embassy and to US military officers, who all left. After the service, according to Blake's account, Holt and Blake learnt from the wife of an American colonel that North Korean forces had attacked the South, and there was heavy fighting along the parallel. Sydney Faithful, the consul, however, says that Holt was told in strict confidence by John Muccio, the US ambassador, that North Korean attack had begun, and that Holt then called at Faithful's house on his way back from church to pass on this news.[13] As the day progressed, South Korean troops began to appear on the streets in camouflage and it became clear that the fighting was more extensive than on any previous occasions, while the presence of North Korean aircraft over Seoul also indicated that this was different from a mere clash on the parallel.[14]

In the confusion that followed for the next few days, at first neither the US embassy nor the British legation expected that their countries would be directly involved in the conflict. In the British case, this led Holt to believe that there was no question but that he should stay at his post, a position he stuck to even when it began to seem likely that the US embassy would move out. However, he agreed that the British community should be encouraged to leave, and warned that there could be no guarantee of their safety if they did not. Blake, therefore, in his role as vice-consul, drove around the city informing the British community. The majority agreed to leave and were evacuated by the Americans. There remained the Anglican Bishop Cooper, his vicar-general Fr Hunt, the Anglican nun, Sister Mary Clare, and Commissioner Lord of the Salvation Army, who all decided to stay with their congregations. On 26 June, Holt sent a short telegram to the Foreign Office reporting in the barest detail what he knew and seeking instructions – like all Seoul's telegrams this had to be encyphered and then sent via commercial cable channels since the legation did not have its own wireless facilities. He knew that it would take at least two days for a reply to come, and in the meantime, told his staff that he intended to stay in Seoul.

Blake, whose main task as an SIS officer was to provide information following a North Korean take-over, clearly was also going to stay. In the end, Holt instructed Sydney Faithful to leave, taking with him a long reporting telegram of developments since the first news of the North Korean attack. Faithful resisted, but in the end gave in to a direct order. He was flown to Itazuke in Japan on 27 June, and arrived in Tokyo on 28 June 1950.[15]

The remaining staff waited in the legation compound. The US embassy left, following the retreating government of President Syngman Rhee first to Taejon, then to Taegu and finally to Pusan, but not before inviting the British to help themselves to the abandoned foodstuffs in their compound. The rain of 25 June gave way to sunshine, and light winds blew sheets of paper with the US embassy crest around the increasingly deserted streets of the capital. In the British legation compound, Holt, Blake and Blake's assistant, Norman Owen, were joined by Cooper, Hunt and Lord. Blake and Owen occupied the number two house, while the others stayed with Holt in the residence. By now fighting had extended to the city, and while they were not directly affected, one clash left a dead soldier at the legation gates. Since the body began to decay in the heat, they buried it in the garden. They also destroyed their codes and secret documents, and poured away the contents of the wine cellar. These essential tasks completed, the small group settled down to wait, talking and taking tea on the lawns, while the legation flag gently moved in the wind. While living thus, they learnt via the BBC World Service that Britain had condemned the North Korean attack on the South, and that Britain supported UN involvement in Korea. Any idea that as neutrals they would be safe from North Korean attention could no longer be sustained.[16]

By mid-week, the North Korean forces had taken Seoul, but the British found that they were not disturbed at first, although they were asked to take down the flag on the grounds that it might attract aircraft. Holt agreed. On Sunday 2 July, Bishop Cooper conducted a service in the number one house dining-room, and the rest of the day passed as normal until the late afternoon. Then, three jeeps arrived with North Korean officers, and all on the compound were taken to Seoul police headquarters. Holt and Blake were later taken back to collect the passports of all those detained, their last contact with the compound. That night, they began the journey which was to take them first to P'yongyang, then to the Yalu. For Father Hunt and Sister Mary Clare, it led to death, for George Blake, to a British prison as a Soviet spy and exile in Russia.[17]

The official history of Britain's part in the Korean War says that as Holt and his colleagues were taken away on 2 July 1950, the sack of the legation began.[18] It is not clear, however, what did happen to the compound after 2 July. Returning to Seoul in September 1950, following General MacArthur's successful landing at Inch'on, Harold Noble noted that while there was little sign of combat destruction in the centre of the city, many of the main buildings had been set alight as the North Korean forces retreated. He recorded that at least one US embassy compound had been spared, possibly for use as North Korean offices in a united Korea, but made no mention of the British legation.[19] Yet the Anglican Cathedral next door to the legation compound survived, albeit used as a store for furniture and other items collected from all over the city, including all the telephones from the US embassy, and destined to be taken north along with the collection of the National Museum from the Toksu Palace next door,[20] and it seems highly likely that the British legation compound was used for the same purpose. Perhaps the discovery of the processional cross in the legation building in 1954 indicates that this was the case.

After the recapture of the city by UN forces in September 1950, the furniture was distributed to the small group of diplomats and other foreign civilians in Seoul on the basis of need rather than ownership.[21] Even when Seoul changed hands again in January 1951, and retreating UN forces fired the city, the British legation appears to have escaped. Walter Graham, minister from 1952, claimed that the number one house was damaged in 1950 when the retreating ROK forces blew up the radio station next door; another account says that the radio station was bombed and flying debris damaged the house. The house was also hit by bullets either then or during the later occupation in early 1951, and many of the bricks had to be replaced.[22]

The wartime legation

After the departure of the head of mission into captivity, the British legation temporarily ceased to exist. However, on 13 July 1950, Henry Sawbridge, the British consul-general in Yokohama, was appointed chargé d'affaires in Korea, and flew to Taegu where the remnants of the Seoul diplomatic corps and the UN Commission were established. Sawbridge was not happy with his appointment to Korea. According to Harold Noble of the US embassy, who had found a house for the British legation in Taegu, Sawbridge disliked Korea and the Koreans, and was also unhappy with the primitive conditions in which he was now forced to live. He became steadily more unhappy, and eventually returned to Japan on 15 August, just before the legation moved further south to Pusan.[23] Meanwhile, Sydney Faithful had returned to Korea on 23 July 1950, with a communications clerk, and effectively re-established a permanent British diplomatic presence in Korea. In late September 1950, Alec Adams became chargé d'affaires. Noble found him a much more congenial companion than Sawbridge.[24] It was, presumably, Faithful who was representing the 'British legation' when General MacArthur formally 'returned Seoul' to President Syngman Rhee in a ceremony at the Capitol Building at the end of September 1950, for Harold Noble specifically notes the presence of the 'British legation' alongside the Chinese (representing Taipei) and US embassies.[25]

Apart from this brief return to Seoul, the legation operated from Pusan during the war period. From September 1952, there was a new minister, Walter Graham, formerly of the China consular service. According to an account by a former legation interpreter some forty years later, Graham had two advantages in his dealing with the ROK government in that period. One

was that the legation adjoined President Syngman Rhee's house, the other
that his wife became close to the Austrian-born Mrs Syngman Rhee. It seems
likely that any advantages so gained were more than offset by Rhee's belief
that the British had prevented the US from using atomic weapons in Korea,
and had thus prevented the reunification of the peninsula![26] Whatever his
contacts, however, Graham and the British legation were inevitably on the
side-line as far as the Korean War was concerned.

It is not clear what happened to the Seoul compound during the Korean
War from the time of the second Communist offensive against the city in
January 1951 to the end of the conflict. Together with the nearby Anglican
cathedral, it may well have been used as a refuge during the fighting in early
1951; forty years later, two Koreans who worked for the legation claimed
that in 1953, the house and grounds were still full of rubbish left by Chinese
forces, and the last foreign priest at the Anglican cathedral, Fr Clifford Smart,
also remembered stories of the Chinese occupying the legation compound
and the cathedral. Others have said that after the UN forces reoccupied the
city in March 1951, it was used at various times by both the British and
Australians as an army mess.[27] Oddly enough, of the thousands of
photographs relating to the Korean War held by the Imperial War Museum
in London, from British, US, Australian and Canadian official sources, as
well as from private collections, not one shows the British legation during
the war.

Whatever earlier use they may have been put to, when Colonel F. M. Hill,
an officer with the Royal Engineers, visited Seoul in February 1953, and
reported on their state to the Foreign Office, the buildings seem to have
been unused. Hill was both appalled and impressed by what he found:

> I passed through Seoul for the first time in six months about ten days ago and
> took the opportunity to go and have a look at the Legation buildings. When I
> tell you that they are of the same era (with red brick instead of grey) as the
> SME [? School of Mechanical Engineering] you will realise that although the
> decoration and woodwork may suffer from the weather, the main shells of
> the buildings are practically indestructible! Frankly I don't think I have ever
> seen before two such dreadful buildings and I think that it is a thousand pities
> that they were not bombed to bits so as to give an excuse for the building of
> more modern and comfortable replacements.[28]

Whatever Colonel Hill's views, the Foreign Office decided that repairs
should begin, in anticipation of a return to Seoul by the ROK government
and the diplomatic corps. The Ministry of Works estimated that repairs
would cost some £12,000, made up of £5000 for theresidence, £4000 for the
number two house, and £3000 for the writers' quarters and the offices. It
was estimated that the work would take some three months. They were
reluctant to begin, however, because of the continued uncertainty of both
the political and military situation in Korea. In June 1953, therefore, the
Ministry of Works asked the Foreign Office for a certificate that fighting
would not resume in Korea.[29] With armistice negotiations at a very difficult
stage, it was perhaps understandable that the Foreign Office was unable to

provide such a certificate. The signing of the armistice on 27 July 1953, and signs that the ROK government was beginning to return to Seoul, eventually overcame the Ministry of Works' reluctance, and work began on rehabilitating the compound in October 1953.[30]

Back to Seoul

There were no major difficulties. Even the old barracks, long since the writers' quarters, which at one time was thought to be damaged beyond repair, proved saveable. Towards the end of 1953, Walter Graham and his colleagues moved up from Pusan, and the British legation formally reopened in Seoul on 27 January 1954. The general lack of accommodation in the war-damaged city and the increase in staff numbers led to a rather cramped existence. Graham and two other diplomats, together with the military attaché, moved into the residence, while two other members of staff shared the flat above the offices in the number two house. (Blake's pre-war SIS station that had so singularly failed to deliver, was not revived.)[31]

As the likelihood of a renewal of the conflict receded, life for the inhabitants of the British legation returned to normal. More accommodation became available, and the overcrowding ended. The gardens, neglected for some three years, were overgrown but had not otherwise suffered. Gardeners could not be had but two paddyfield workers were found who were willing to cut the grass and keep the weeds at bay. The first function held in the re-opened legation was an informal reception attended by the ROK foreign minister on 12 February 1954, and summer 1954 once again saw the Queen's Birthday Party celebrated at the legation, the first time since Holt's rain-drenched party in 1950.[32]

During 1956–57, an old issue resurfaced. The Anglican mission made an attempt to get back the land it had sold to the legation over fifty years before for the erection of the barracks. The mission's argument was that the land was not being used as originally intended, and that therefore the original agreement was null and void. The Foreign Office view was that when first obtained, the land had been used as intended. Circumstances had changed, and so had the use to which the original building had been put, but that should not affect the validity of the transaction. There was some mutual recrimination, but the Foreign Office view eventually prevailed.[33]

By the late 1950s, it was clear that the old barracks no longer provided adequate office space. Work was set in hand to build a new office block, or chancery building, and the number two house was divided into two flats for staff accommodation. The new chancery building also contained two flats for staff. Other buildings were also erected to provide additional office and living space. Two sections of these 1957 buildings survived providing offices for the administration section and a small bungalow for the ambassador's personal assistant, until the major rebuilding of the 1990s.[34]

During 1957, Seoul became an embassy, with the then minister, H. J. Evans, (later Sir Hubert), becoming the first ambassador. There were other developments too that year. The British Commonwealth forces, organized during the Korean War, were finally withdrawn, and there were colourful ceremonies to mark the occasion. At one of these held on 13 June 1957 at the headquarters of the United Nations Command, to mark both the departure from Korea of the 1st Battalion The Royal Sussex Regiment and the Queen's Official Birthday, President Syngman Rhee himself attended. Later that month, there was a ceremony to unveil a monument at the small village of Solma-ri, site of the stand of the 1st Battalion The Gloucestershire Regiment and C Troop, 170 Light (Mortar) Battery Royal Artillery in April 1951.[35] At the same time, with the founding of the Korean-British Society in 1956, which provided a forum for many of those who had studied British politics and the British political system, the British legation/embassy became known as a focus for the opposition to Rhee, a reputation which was to last at least until the 1970s.[36]

During the 1960s and 1970s, the staff of the British embassy grew steadily. As South Korea's economy began to expand in the late 1960s, so the emphasis became more and more on commercial work; when Ian Mackenzie arrived as ambassador in February 1967, he announced that in his opinion what mattered most was promoting British trade; it was an attitude which would come to dominate both staffing of the post and thinking about Korea.[37] The increase in staff obviously affected the use of the compound. Changes to the residence were relatively minor. A porch was added to the front door in 1965 and a new terrace was added to the veranda in 1974, in order to provide better facilities in wet weather. This involved moving the original foundation stone, by then much weathered and overgrown by trees. It was relocated inside the house, and, after a brief period when the Royal Arms took its place, was eventually replaced by a copy. In turn, this too has become much weathered.[38] These two additions blended well with the original building. Less successful, at least from the outside, was a new dining-room added in 1980. While it met a long-felt need, and works well as an extension of the drawing-room, outside it has little to recommend it.

The 1957 office building was quickly outgrown, and in 1974–75, a new one was erected, the work being done in sections so that the old buildings remained in use while the new ones emerged. In 1974, a swimming-pool was added to the compound, and in 1980, the long disused tennis-courts behind the residence were restored and became very popular. By the 1980s, the majority of staff lived off the compound, in a variety of houses and flats scattered throughout the growing city of Seoul. For many years, senior staff lived in two delightful houses owned by Korean Standard Oil. As more modern housing became available, they gradually slipped down the ranks, until they were given up, with some regret in the 1980s.

By the late 1980s, there was once more a need for new office buildings. Those erected in the 1970s had a number of drawbacks. The roof was flat, which proved a constant problem in Korea's wet summers.[39] They had not been big enough from the beginning. Although they had included a flat, designed for a senior officer in the commercial section, the need for offices meant that the flat was never used as such, and from the very beginning, it had been pressed into service as offices. There was no room for expansion.

When the British Council decided to open an office in Seoul in the early 1970s, it had to be located off the compound. After a number of other locations were tried, the Council eventually acquired offices in the Anglican cathedral building just outside the gates of the embassy.

In 1989, therefore, plans for a new office block were put out to tender. Junglim Construction Company won the design contract, and Hyojung Development Company that for construction. The construction work began in June 1990, and took two years. At one point, the Seoul city authorities seemed inclined to raise questions about the height of the construction, and there was some short-lived press interest, but eventually the building was allowed to proceed as planned. During the works, the commercial section, the embassy's biggest single unit, moved out to the nearby Chosun hotel, while the remaining sections worked from the old number two house. The new building was completed in the autumn of 1992, and formally opened by the Prince and Princess of Wales on 2 November 1992 during their visit to South Korea. In a link with the origins of the compound, the main hall of the new offices, which provides a venue for political, business, cultural and social occasions was named 'Aston Hall', and includes a plaque recording how Mr Aston came to acquire the site long ago.[40] The new building is certainly handsome, with a fine granite facade, though not all problems associated with the old one have been solved; the flat roofs of the former building have been repeated in the new one, and have proved equally ineffective in heavy rain.[41]

Today, the British embassy compound, once one among a number of Western enclaves in the centre of Seoul, occupies a special position both physically and historically in the heart of the city. Most of the other remnants of the nineteenth century have long since gone from a city which prides itself on its increasingly glittering high-rise buildings and elevated highways. Yet the British compound, with its distinctive buildings and its relatively spacious gardens in a city which lacks open spaces, remains essentially as it was over a hundred years ago. The gardens, together with the Toksu palace and the grounds of the nearby US embassy compounds, provide an ecologically important 'green lung' for the city. One former British ambassador logged over forty different types of butterfly in his gardens in the 1970s, and the number is probably as high today.[42]

For the British, and perhaps to a lesser extent for the wider foreign community, the compound still has an important role for all sorts of functions. These range from grand, such as the annual Queen's Birthday Party – alas, no longer an occasion for all the thousands of foreigners who live in the city – and receptions for visiting dignitaries, such as that by the Prince and Princess of Wales in 1992, or the then Prime Minister, Mrs Thatcher, in 1986, and the Queen and Prince Philip in 1999, to smaller and more homely occasions. All form part of an historical pattern, stretching back to Sir Harry Parkes's dinners in 1883.

The compound and its buildings have aroused mixed feelings in the past, and still do. A distinguished British visitor, Sir Geoffrey Howe, then the secretary of state for Foreign and Commonwealth affairs, and now Lord

Howe, who appeared anonymously in the first version of this history,[43] said that the residence reminded him of a Victorian mental hospital. He meant solid and respectable, no doubt, but it was rather a harsh judgement. These may not be the most beautiful buildings in the world, yet in a city which has relatively few grand buildings, they can hold their own. They also provide a link to the past, and, as that long-dead US envoy said, they still serve as a token of Britain's interest and involvement with Korea over the last hundred years.

Notes

1 FO 366/1778/XS3K/23/19, D. McDermott, Tokyo, to FO, no. 76 confidential, 29 December 1945.

2 FO 366/1778/XS3K/23/19, D. McDermott, Tokyo, to FO, no. 76 confid., 29 December 1945, enclosure: 'Memorandum for Lt. Lury, British Representative in Seoul, 30 December 1945'.

3 Tokyo Liaison Mission Periodic Reports, February, April and May 1946, in *Japan and dependencies*, vol. 17, pp. 138, 182, 223; FO 366/1778/XS3K/23/19, Tokyo tels. to Foreign Office, nos. 166, 18 February and 516, 15 May 1946.

4 FO 366/1778/XS3K/23/19, minute by M. S. Henderson, 6 September 1946. This file is full of complaining letters from Mr Kermode, though one feels that perhaps de la Mare was not the most impartial judge!

5 Bishop's letter, 15 December 1946, *Morning Calm*, February 1947.

6 FO 366/1778/XS3K/23/19, Various letters, telegrams and minutes relate to this. See also: *FRUS*, 1946, vol. VIII, p. 685, note 5, and 735, note 48.

7 *Who was Who*, 1951–60.

8 George Blake, *No other choice: an autobiography*, (London: Jonathan Cape, 1990), p. 110.

9 Blake, *No other choice*, pp. 111–12.

10 Blake, *No other choice*, pp. 112–13.

11 Blake, *No other choice*, pp. 117–120.

12 Anthony Farrar-Hockley, *The British Part in the Korean War*, Vol. 1, (London: Her Majesty's Stationary Office, 1990), 30; Blake, *No other choice*, pp. 121–22.

13 Blake, *No other choice*, p. 121; Letter from Sydney Faithful, 13 October 1970, quoted in Harold Joyce Noble, *Embassy at war*, edited with an introduction by Frank Baldwin, (Seattle and London: University of Seattle Press, 1975), pp. 260–61.

14 Noble, *Embassy at war*, pp. 10–14.

15 Noble, *Embassy at war*, pp. 260–61.

16 Blake, *No other choice*, pp. 123–26.

17 Blake, *No other choice*, pp. 123–26. For Blake's recruitment as a Soviet agent, see pp. 143 et seq.

18 Farrar-Hockley, *The British Part in the Korean War*, Vol. 1, 58.

19 Noble, *Embassy at war*, pp. 202–203.

20 J. E. Hoare, 'The Anglican Cathedral Seoul 1926–1996', *TKBRAS*, vol. 61, (1986), 8. For the US embassy telephones, see Noble, *Embassy at war*, p. 206.

21 Hoare, 'Anglican Cathedral', p. 8; letter from T. G. Harris, 11 July 1994.

22 Letters from Walter Graham, 4 February 1984; T. G. Harris, 22 September 1994, and conversation with Alec Adams, 23 August 1985.

23 Noble, *Embassy at war*, pp. 146–47, 161.

24 Letter from the Foreign and Commonwealth Office, 27 July 1970 and letter from Sydney Faithful, 13 October 1970, in Noble, *Embassy at war*, p. 284, note 7. For Noble's view of Adams, see *Embassy at war*, p. 147.

25 Noble, *Embassy at war*, p. 203.

26 Letter from T. G. Harris, HM ambassador Seoul, 22 September 1994. For Walter Graham, see *Foreign Office List*. If his wife did have a close relationship with Mrs Rhee, it is odd that neither Graham himself, whom I knew in his later years and who commented on my earlier book *The British Embassy Compound Seoul*, nor Mrs Rhee, whom my wife and I met in Seoul in 1984 and who spent much of the time discussing Britain's 'betrayal' in the Korean war, ever mentioned it. There is a graphic description of the Rhees' house in Pusan in Robert T. Oliver, *Syngman Rhee: The man behind the myth*, (London: Robert Hale Ltd., 1955), pp. 312–13, but no mention of a British presence.

27 Letters from Walter Graham, 4 February 1984; T. G. Harris, 11 July and 22 September 1994, and conversation with Alec Adams, 23 August 1985.

28 FO 366/3024/XC01/81/253, Col. F.M. Hill, CRE 1, Commonwealth Division Korea to Brigadier C.D. Steel, Conference and Supply Department, FO, 14 February 1953.

29 FO 366/3024/XC01/81/153, R. H. G. Edmunds to Ministry of Works, confidential, 7 April 1953; XC01/18/353, Minute by Edmunds, 16 April 1953; and XCO1/81/853; R. B. Marshall, Works, to Edmunds, 8 June 1953.

30 FO 366/3024/XC01/81/2153, Minutes by J. Gaunt 31 October and 3 November 1953.

31 Letter from Walter Graham, 4 February 1984; *Korea Republic*, 27 January 1954.

32 *Korea Republic*, 13 February and 1 June 1954; conversation with Lt. Col. Bramwell Sylvester, Salvation Army, 22 October 1984.

33 Private information. Part of the Anglican mission's problem was a chronic shortage of funds, made worse since 1945 by land reform in South Korea. Before the Pacific War, Bishop Cooper had invested such surplus funds as the mission had in land, which had been lost during land reform. It could not afford to buy more land in Seoul, hence, perhaps, the attempt to regain that sold to the legation.

34 Letter from Colonel A. E. E. Mercer, former defence attaché, 9 November 1984.

35 Copies of programmes kindly lent by Lady Evans. See also the account which she gives in Maureen Tweedy, *A label round my neck*, pp. 138–39.

36 J. E. Hoare, 'The Korean-British Society: Some Past Events', *Bulletin of the Korean-British Society*, no. 2, (May 1982), 7–10.

37 F. F. Rainsford, *Memoirs of an accidental airman*, (London: Thomas Harmsworth Publishing, 1986), pp. 208–209.

38 Conversation with Sir Jeffrey and Lady Petersen, 10 October 1984.

39 As I found on more than one occasion between 1981 and 1985, when I returned to an office on the second floor swimming in water.

40 *British Industrial News*, (in Korean), 12 (1992), the then magazine of the British Embassy commercial section, has details of the royal visit, including the formal opening of the new offices; letters from Mrs Y S Park, British Embassy Seoul, 19 March and 4 April 1998.

41 As I found during a spell of temporary duty in Seoul in October 1997!

42 Conversation with Sir Jeffrey Petersen, 10 October 1984.

43 Hoare, *British Embassy Compound Seoul*, pp. 53–54.

Epilogue

S o the tale ends. But of course it does not. As this account has shown, there is nothing unchangeable about embassies. As well as the constant shifting human population, providing endless variety, there are also the changes of place. Cities change their centres and embassies move accordingly. In Beijing, the down-at-heel suburbs on the fringe of the city to which the Chinese moved the embassies in the 1950s are now a vibrant part of a very different city. The British embassies in Tokyo and Seoul still remain near the traditional heart of their respective cities, but in the latter case, this may not be for much longer; it is not only that the centre of Seoul seems to be moving south of the Han river, but also that plans to shift the capital away from the dangers of the Demilitarized Zone between the two Koreas are regularly put forward. So far, the difficulties and cost of such a move have held back the planners, but it may not always be so.

In any case, other considerations are also at work. For the present, the British embassy in Seoul seems likely to enjoy a period of relative stability. The new buildings opened in 1992, taken together with a partial move of the information section into premises adjacent to the embassy proper, will probably meet Britain's needs in the Republic of Korea (ROK) for the next ten years or so. The ROK's economic downturn following the 1997 Asian economic crisis will no doubt rein in more ambitious plans for some time. The first effect of the crisis has been the closure of a small, locally engaged-staffed post opened at Pusan in the early 1990s,[1] and there has been some redeployment of embassy staff while the economy is recovering.

Neither the Tokyo nor the Beijing embassies are likely to remain static, however. In the former case, the wish, which as we have seen stretches back to at least Sir Claude MacDonald in 1896, to make more use of the compound regularly resurfaces. While it is unlikely that anyone would now seek to remove all the post-earthquake houses, or to raze the chancery building, there are likely to be more imaginative developments to parallel the information and commercial offices. In Beijing, there seems to be a realization at last that there is a limit to the modifications and alterations that can be imposed on what are, basically, a pair of not very well designed houses. So, perhaps, the British government will finally do what it planned to do in 1960 and seek a new plot for a purpose-built embassy. In the meantime, as I write, growing consular and visa needs seem likely to mean that another section of the embassy will have to be out-housed, at least temporarily. One bright spot is that pressure on housing for foreigners has led to a further relaxation of controls, and at least one recent member of staff has been able to move out into a courtyard house.

Does it all matter? Is there still a need for diplomats and embassies, or can it all now be done by computers, the facsimile machine and visiting firemen? It is an old argument. Indeed, there have been revolutionary regimes which have begun with an expressed wish to abandon all the trappings of a traditional foreign policy. The new leader of Russia tried this in 1917 but quickly found that the reason why there had been a Russian diplomatic service was not because of some form of aristocratic out relief but rather that states did need to work together, even when they disagreed, and that to do so, they needed mechanisms that each side understood and accepted. 'Issuing a few proclamations and shutting up shop', in Trotsky's famous description of his approach to the post of foreign minister',[2] soon proved an untenable position.

The idea that modern methods of communication and transport will make traditional diplomacy a thing of the past is also not new, and predates the fax and the internet.[3] In practice, while there has been some modifications of work as a result of technological development, nobody has yet devised a better method for conducting relations between states than using people to talk to each other. And so that the leaders of one country can easily talk to each other when needed, no better method has yet evolved than having some of the talkers on one side resident in the country of the other. So diplomats still appear to have a role, and a continuing one.

It is clearly also important that those who conduct diplomacy project a positive image, however this is achieved. In the past, uniforms and mounted escorts did it. Sir Harry Parke's reluctance to see the departure of the legation guard – a reluctance shared by his successors until the 1890s – was less to do with safety than with effect. Indeed, in 1871 one visiting American contrasted the lack of diplomatic uniform and mounted escort of the United States' minister, with the splendour of his British counterpart, and argued that that this placed the American at a disadvantage, since '. . . Orientals cannot understand that a country which lets its officials go about like any cobbler . . . can amount to very much or be very powerful'.[4] About 100 years later, the same point was made, in very different circumstances, by a young Chinese diplomat at Beijing airport, in the days when the small diplomatic corps turned out for every visiting dignitary. By chance, this young man, probably in his twenties and impeccable in his 'Mao' suit, found himself standing next to a British diplomat of about the same age. In those days, it was possible still to visit Afghanistan as a tourist, and the British diplomat was wearing, and was immensely proud of, a shaggy Afghan coat, made of skins cured in the traditional way. The Chinese enquired of his companion what he did. On being told that he was a second secretary in the British embassy, the Chinese commented: 'If I was a second secretary in the British embassy, I would not wear a coat like that.'[5]

Clearly to one Chinese diplomat, despite being brought up in 'New China' and experiencing the Cultural Revolution, appearances did matter. It may be that diplomacy is largely a matter of bluff, of convincing the other side of your side's self-confidence and certainty. If so, it matters whether the ambassador sweeps out in a grand fashion from a majestic compound in the heart of a city, or slips away from an office that is far from the action. Styles change, and, Tokyo apart, diplomatic uniform has gone from the 'Embassies in the East', but there are those who still value an invitation to the British embassy and who are intrigued by the history they find there, and are impressed by the sheer style of it. Long may it continue!

Notes

1 Reported, somewhat ironically, under a headline '[British Foreign Secretary] Cook to recruit 200 envoys in fight for global markets', in *The Guardian*, 28 November 1998.

2 Frequently quoted; see, for example, Keith Hamilton and Richard Langhorne, *The practice of diplomacy: Its evolution, theory and administration* (London and New York: Routledge, 1995), p. 149.

3 For one example, see Geoffrey McDermott, *The new diplomacy and its apparatus* (London: Plume Press/Ward Lock, 1973).

4 Charles Appleton Longfellow, *Twenty Months in Japan, 1871–1873* (Cambridge, Mass: Friends of the Longfellow House, 1998), quoted in a forthcoming review by Sir Hugh Cortazzi: letter from Sir Hugh Cortazzi, 21 November 1998.

5 Story told by Ms Susan Pares, herself a second secretary in the British embassy at the time.

Appendix

Substantive Heads of the British Missions in China, Japan, and Korea, 1853–1998*

CHINA (from 1853)

1853 Sir John Bowring, pleniptentiary and chief superintendent of trade.

1857 James Bruce, Earl of Elgin and Kincardine, special mission.

1859 F. (later Sir Frederick) W. Bruce, envoy extraordinary and minister plenipotentiary.

1860 James Bruce, Earl of Elgin and Kincardine, special mission.

1861 F. (later Sir Frederick) W. Bruce, envoy extraordinary and minister plenipotentiary.

1865 Rutherford (later Sir R.) Alcock, min. plen. and envoy ext., and chief superintendent of British trade.

1871 Thomas (later Sir Thomas) F. Wade, min. plen. and envoy ext., and chief superintendent of British trade.

1883 Sir Harry Smith Parkes, min. plen. and env. ext. (Died at his post, 22 March 1885).

1885 Sir Robert Hart, min. plen. and env. ext. (Did not take up his post.)

1885 Sir John Walsham, min. plen. and env. ext.

1892 N. (later Sir Nicholas) R. O'Conor, min. plen. and env.ext.

1896 Sir Claude MacDonald, min. plen. and env. ext.

1900 Sir Ernest Mason Satow, min. plen. and env. ext.

1906 Sir John Jordan, min. plen. and env. ext.

1920 Beilby (later Sir Beilby) Francis Alston, min. plen. and env. ext.

1922 Sir J. W. R. Macleay, min. plen. and env. ext.

1926 Sir Miles (Wedderburn) Lampson (later Lord Killearn), min. plen. and env. ext.

---

*Information is mainly taken from the *Diplomatic Service List* and its predecessor, the *Foreign Office List*, supplemented from other sources.

1934 Sir Alexander M. G. Cadogan, min. plen. and env. ext.

1935 Sir Alexander M. G. Cadogan, amb. ext. and plen.

1936 Sir Hughe Montgomery Knatchbull-Hugessen, amb. ext. and plen.

1938 Sir Archibald John Kerr Clark (later Lord Inverchapel), amb. ext. and plen.

1942 Sir Horace James Seymour, amb. ext. and plen.

1946 Sir Ralph Clarmont Skrine Stevenson, amb. ext. and plen.

1949 John (later Sir John) Colville Hutchison, chargé d'affaires *ad interim*.

1951 Lionel (latr Sir Lionel) Henry Lamb, chargé d'affaires *ad interim*.

1953 Humphrey Trevelyan (later Lord Trevelyan), chargé d'affaires *ad interim*.

1954 Humphrey Trevelyan (later Lord Trevelyan), chargé d'affaires *en titre*.

1955 Con (later Sir Con) Douglas Walter O'Neill, chargé d'affaires *en titre*.

1957 Archibald Duncan (later Sir Duncan) Wilson, chargé d'affaires *en titre*.

1959 Michael (later Sir Michael) Norman Stewart, chargé d'affaires *en titre*.

1962 Terence (later Sir Terence) Wilcocks Garvey, chargé d'affaires *en titre*.

1965 Donald (later Sir Donald) C. Hopson, chargé d'affaires *en titre*.

1968 Percy (later Sir Percy) Cradock, chargé d'affaires *ad interim*.

1969 John Boyd Denson, chargé d'affaires *ad interim*.

1971 John Boyd Denson, chargé d'affaires e*n titre*.

1972 John (later Sir John) Mansfield Addis, amb. ext and plen.

1974 Edward (later Sir Edward) Youde, amb. ext and plen.

1978 Percy (later Sir Percy) Cradock, amb. ext and plen.

1984 Sir Richard Mark Evans, amb. ext and plen.

1988 Alan (later Sir Alan) Ewen Donald, amb. ext and plen.

1991 Sir Robin J. T. McLaren, amb. ext and plen.

1994 Sir Leonard V. Appleyard, amb. ext and plen.

1997 Sir Anthony C. Galsworthy, amb. ext and plen.

JAPAN (from 1859)

1859 Rutherford (later Sir R.) Alcock, consul-general, then minister plenipotentiary and envoy extraordinary.

1865 Sir Harry Smith Parkes, min. plen. and env. ext. (Accreditd to 'His Majesty the Tycoon'.)

1868 Sir Harry Smith Parkes (Accredited to 'His Majesty the Mikado'.)

1883 Hon. F. R. (later Right Hon. Sir Francis) Plunkett, min. plen. and env. ext.

1889 Hugh Fraser, min. plen. and env. ext. (Died at his post, 4 June 1894.)

1894 Hon. P. Le Poer Trench, min. plen. and env. ext.

1895 Sir Ernest Mason Satow, min. plen. and env. ext.

1900 Sir Claude MacDonald, min. plen. and env. ext.

1905 Sir Claude MacDonald, ambassador extraordinary and plenipotentiary.

1912 Rt Hon. Sir W. Conyngham Greene, amb. ext. and plen.

1920 Rt Hon. Sir Charles N. E. Eliot, amb. ext. and plen.

1926 Rt Hon. Sir John Tilley, amb. ext. and plen.

1931   Sir Francis O. Lindley, amb. ext. and plen.
1934   Sir Robert H. Clive, amb. ext. and plen.
1937   Sir Robert L. Craigie, amb. ext. and plen.

(Diplomatic relations suspended 1941–1952 – Sir R Craigie and staff repatriated August 1942.)

1946   Alvary (later Sir A.) D. F. Gascoigne, political adviser.
1951   Sir Maberley Esler Dening, political representative.
1952   Sir Maberley Esler Dening, amb. ext. and plen.
1957   Sir William David Lascelles, amb. ext. and plen.
1959   Sir Oscar Charles Morland, amb. ext. and plen.
1963   Sir Francis Brian Anthony Rundall, amb. ext. and plen.
1967   Sir John Arthur Pilcher, amb. ext. and plen.
1972   Sir Fred Warner, amb. ext. and plen.
1975   Michael (later Sir M.) Wilford, amb. ext. and plen.
1980   Sir Hugh H. Cortazzi, amb. ext. and plen.
1984   Sir (Charles) Sydney (Rycroft) Giffard, amb. ext. and plen.
1986   Sir John (Stainton) Whitehead, amb. ext. and plen.
1992   Sir John (Dixon Iklé) Boyd, amb. ext. and plen.
1996   David (later Sir D.) Wright, amb. ext. and plen.
1999   Stephen Gomersall, amb. ext. and plen.

Korea (from 1884)

(Residing at Beijing)
1884   Sir Harry S. Parkes, min. plen. and env. ext.
1885   Sir John Walsham, min. plen. and env. ext.
1892   Nicholas (later Sir N.) O'Conor, min. plen. and env. ext.
1897   Sir Claude MacDonald, min. plen. and env. ext.

(Residing in Seoul)
1898   John (later Sir John) N. Jordan, chargé d'affaires.
1901   John N. Jordan, min. plenipotentiary

Consuls-general (in the Japan consular service)
1906   Henry Cockburn, consul-general.
1909   H. A. C. Bonar, consul-general.
1912   A. M. Chalmers, consul-general.
1914   A. H. Lay, consul-general.
1927   O. White, consul-general.
1931   W. M Royds, consul-general.
1934   G. H. Phipps, consul-general.

(Post closed 1941–1945)
South Korea (from 1946)
1946   D. (Later Sir Derwent) W. Kermode, liaison officer (April-October 1946)
1946   D. W. Kermode, consul-general (October 1946)

Republic of Korea (from 1949)

1949 Captain Vyvyan Holt, minister plen. and envoy ext.

1950 Henry R. Sawbridge, chargé d'affaires.

1950 Alec C. S. Adams, chargé d'affaires.

1952 Walter G. C. Graham, minister plen. and envoy ext.

1957 H. (Later Sir Hubert) J. Evans, minister plen. and envoy ext. (18 February.)

1957 H. J. Evans, amb. ext and plen. (13 June.)

1961 Sir Walter Godfrey, amb. ext and plen.

1967 Ian C. Mackenzie, amb. ext and plen.

1969 Nigel (later Sir Nigel) C. C. Trench, amb. ext and plen.

1971 Jeffrey (later Sir Jeffrey) C. Petersen, amb. ext and plen.

1975 W. S. Bates, amb. ext and plen.

1980 J. (later Sir John) A. L. Morgan, amb. ext and plen.

1983 (J). N. (later Sir Nicholas) (T). Spreckley, amb. ext and plen.

1986 L. J. Middleton, amb. ext and plen.

1990 D. (later Sir David) J. Wright, amb. ext and plen.

1994 T. G. Harris, amb. ext and plen.

1997 Stephan (later Sir S.) D. R Brown, amb. ext and plen.

Bibliography

Unpublished Material

British Archives Public Record Office Kew
FO17/ Foreign Office records, China.
FO46/ Foreign Office records, Japan.
FO262/ Embassy and Consular records, Japan.
FO366/ Records of the Chief Clerk's Department.
FO369/ Records of the Consular Department of the Foreign Office.
FO371/ Foreign Office records, Political, 1906–66.
FCO 21/ Foreign and Commonwealth Office records, Political, 1967-.

T1/ Treasury Board records.

Works 10/ Office of Works (later Department of Public Buildings and Works, later Department of the Environment) records 1871–1971.
Works 40/ Office of Works, Plans and drawings.

Other archive material
BBC archives, Caversham, transcript of a talk, 'From our own correspondent' , 16 September 1991.
Jordan Papers (semi-official letters of Sir John Jordan), FO/350, Public Record Office, Kew.
Satow Papers (papers, diaries and letters of Sir E. M. Satow), Public Record Office Kew, (PRO/30/33).
United Society for the Propagation of the Gospel Archives, Oxford.
Yokohama Archives of History: 'Ernest Satow Exhibition File', Vol. 1.

Papers in private possession
'Some years in Korea' , ms. notes made by H. W. Davidson, c. April 1948. Copy supplied by Miss A. J. Roberts, MBE.
Letters, manuscript and photographs of W. P. Ker and Lucy Murray Ker, now in the possession of Ms Kate Ker, Surrey.
Diary of W. P. Ker, 1892, Peabody Essex Museum, Salem Mass.

Letter of Roger Keyes (Later Admiral of the Fleet and first Baron Keyes) from Beijing to Miss
    B. Jackson, 6 September 1900, now in the possession of Mr Frederic Sharf, Chestnut Hill,
    Mass.
'Memories of my stay in Peking 1936–38', Margaret McCallum, unpublished ms. 1990.

Letters and Oral Communications

A. Adams, formerly British legation, Seoul: 23 August 1985.
Sir John Boyd, formerly British mission in Beijing, HM ambassador Tokyo: 15 July 1996,
    25 April 1998.
Mrs Winifred Bland, 2 November 1983.
Sir Hugh Cortazzi, formerly HM ambassador Tokyo: letters 11 June, 16 July 1996,
    21 November 1998.
Margaret Cousins, formerly library and records department, FCO: letter, 16 April 1991.
Dr Nicholas Cox, Public Record Office: letter 2 January 1991.
Sir Percy Cradock, formerly HM ambassador Beijing: letter 10 March 1993.
Rodney Cummins, formerly British embassy Tokyo: letter 12 April 1996.
Dr Delia Davin, 23 January 1999.
Sir Arthur de la Mare, formerly British embassy Tokyo, consulate-general Seoul: letters 1 June
    and 18 October 1984.
Lady Evans, formerly British embassy, Seoul: 15 May 1996
P. L. Finch, formerly British embassy, Tokyo: letter of 19 August 1996.
Sir Sydney Giffard, formerly HM ambassador Tokyo: letter of 4 October 1996.
W. G. C. Graham, formerly British embassy Beijing, HM minister, Seoul: letters 4 February
    1984, 18 February 1994.
T. G. Harris, formerly British embassy Tokyo, HM ambassador Seoul: letters 11 July, 9
    August, 5 September, 22 September 1994, 29 July 1996, 28 February 1997.
Douglas Hurd, (now Lord Hurd), formerly British mission in Beijing, Secretary of State for
    Foreign and Commonwealth Affairs: conversation, Beijing, 5 April 1991.
Kate Ker, letter 22 October 1998.
Iain Lindsay, British embassy Tokyo: letter 26 April 1996, enclosing an undated
    memorandum by C. E. A. Ripley.
Mrs Margaret McCallum, letters: 9 October 1991, 19 February, 22 July 1992.
Sir Robin and Lady McLaren, formerly British embassy Beijing: various dates, 1991–97.
Colonel A. E. E. Mercer, formerly British embassy Seoul: letter 9 November 1984.
Sir John Morgan, formerly British mission in Beijing, HM ambassador Seoul: 5 May 1993.
Ms. Susan Pares, formerly British embassy, Beijing, various conversations.
Mrs Y. S. Park, British embassy Seoul: letters and faxes of 26 February, 19 March, and 4 April,
    23 July 1998.
Sir Jeffrey and Lady Petersen, formerly British embassy Seoul: conversations 10 October
    1984.
C. E. A. Ripley, formerly British embassy Tokyo: letter 21 May 1996.
Professor Michael Scohenhals, University of Stockholm: letter, 20 April 1994.
Frederic A. Sharf, Chestnut Hill, Massachusetts: letters and faxes, 1 March, 12 May, 13 May,
    14 May, 29 June, 16 September, 19 September 1996
Lt. Colonel Bramwell Sylvester, Salvation Army, conversation, 22 October 1984.
Ms Pippa Tristram, letter 25 June 1991.
Dr H. G. Underwood, conversations in Seoul, 1983–84.
Mr K. C. Walker, formerly British mission Beijing: letter 2 July 1994.
Alan Waters, formerly British embassy Beijing: 30 June 1995.
Sir Michael Wilford, formerly British mission Beijing, HM ambassador, Tokyo: undated letter,
    1996; conversations 1997.
Lord Wilson of Tillyorn, formerly British mission Beijing, governor of Hong Kong: letter 12
    June 1995.
Peter Wilson, formerly British embassy Beijing, conversation 1 February 1999.

Lady Wright, British embassy Tokyo: letters 5 and 7 May 1996; 14 August 1997; 25 January 1999.

R F Wye, research and analysis department, FCO: letter of 18 April 1991.

Published Archive Material

Archive Research Ltd., editors, *Japan and Dependencies: Political and Economic Reports 1906–1960* (Farnham Common Slough: Archive Research Ltd., 1994).

Asia Research Centre, Korea University, *Ku Han'guk weigyo munso* (Diplomatic documents of old Korea), British series, I, (Seoul: Asia Research Centre, 1968).

W. G. Beasley, translator and editor, *Select Documents on Japanese Foreign Policy 1853–1868* (London, New York and Toronto: Oxford University Press, 1955 reprinted 1967).

Foreign relations of the United States (FRUS): (Washington, DC: Government Printer, in progress).

Kessing's *Contemporary Archives* (London: in progress).

Lo Hui-min, *The correspondence of G. E. Morrison* vol. 1, (Cambridge: Cambridge University Press, 1976).

W. N. Medlicott and Douglas Dakin, editors, assisted by Gillian Bennet, *Documents on British Foreign Policy, 1919–1939* Second Series, Vol. XXI, Far Eastern Affairs, November 1936-July 1938. (London: HMSO: 1984).

S. J. Palmer, ed., *Korean-American Relations: Documents pertaining to the Far Eastern diplomacy of the United States* vol. II, (Berkeley and Los Angeles: University of California Press, 1963).

Park Il-keun, ed., *Anglo-American Diplomatic Materials relating to Korea* (Seoul: Shin Mun Dang, 1982).

Parliamentary Papers House of Commons:
    1867–1868, Vol. XLVIII, c. 135, *Reports from Major Crossman and Correspondence respecting the Legation and Consular Buildings in China and Japan.*

1902, Treaty Series No, 17 (1902), (Cd. 1390), *Final Protocol between the Foreign Powers and China for the resumption of Friendly Relations signed at Peking, September 7, 1901.*

1943, China No. 1 (CMD 6417), *Treaty for the relinquishment of Extra-Territorial Rights in China.*

Sir E. M. Satow, *The diaries and letters of Sir Ernest Mason Satow (1843–1929), A Scholar-Diplomat in East Asia* selected, edited and annotated by Ian C. Ruxton (Lewiston, N. Y; Queenston, Ontario; Lampeter: The Edwin Mellon Press, 1998).

E. L. Woodward and R. Butler, editors, *Documents on British Foreign Policy* Third Series, Vol. IX, (London: HMSO, 1955).

Yongsin Academy, Korean Studies Research Institute, compilers, *Chosun chaeryu ku-mi-in chosa rok*, ('Directory of Europeans and Americans in Korea'), (Seoul: Yongsin Academy Korean Studies Research Institute, 1981).

Newspapers and Journals

(Place of publication is London, unless otherwise stated.)
Beijing Review, Beijing
British Industrial News, Seoul.
The Builder, 17 November 1933.
China Daily, Beijing.
Daily Telegraph.
Eastern World, Yokohama.
Far East, Yokohama.
Far Eastern Economic Review, Hong Kong.
Financial Times.
Illustrated London News.

The Independent.
The Independent, Seoul.
International Herald Tribune, Paris.
Japan Advertiser, Yokohama.
Japan Weekly Chronicle, Kobe.
Japan Weekly Mail, Yokohama.
Kobe Chronicle, Kobe.
Korea Herald, Seoul.
Korea News Review, Seoul.
Korea Repository, Seoul.
Korea Republic, Seoul.
Korea Review, Seoul.
Korea Times, Seoul.
Morning Calm.
New York Times, New York.
Observer.
Peiping Chronicle, Beijing.
Summary of World Broadcasts, (BBC Monitoring Service, Caversham).
Sunday Telegraph.
Sunday Times.
The Times.
Washington Post, Washington D.C.
Washington Times, Washington D. C.

Other Works

Rutherford Alcock, *The Capital of the Tycoon* (London: Longman, Green, Longman, Roberts and Green, 2 vols., 1863).

Bernard Allen, *The Rt. Hon. Sir Ernest Satow, GCMG: A Memoir* (London: Kegan Paul, Trench and Trubner, 1933).

Roland Allen, *The Siege of the Peking Legations: The Diary of the Rev. Roland Allen, Chaplain to Bishop Scott, five years' acting Chaplain to HBM Legation* (London: Smith Elder and Co., 1901).

L. C. Arlington and W. Lewisohn, *In Search of Old Peking* (Beiping: Henry Vetch, 1935; reprinted Hong Kong: Oxford University Press, 1987).

Frank Ashton-Gwatkin, 'The meeting of John Paris and Japan', *tsuru*, vol. 3, no. 1, (September 1973).

Louise Atherton, *'Never Complain, Never Explain': Records of the Foreign Office and the State Paper Office 1500-c. 1960* (London: PRO Publications, 1994).

K. Baedecker, *Russia, with Teheran, Port Arthur and Peking: Handbook for Travellers* (Leipzig: Karl Baedecker, 1914; reprinted Newton Abbott: David and Charles, 1971; London: George Allen and Unwin, 1971).

Bao Ruo-wang (Jean Pasqualini) and Rudolph Chelminski, *Prisoner of Mao* (London: Andre Deutsch, 1975).

W G Beasley, *Great Britain and the Opening of Japan* (London: Luzac and Company, 1951; reprinted Folkestone: Japan Library, 1995).

——, *Japan Encounters the Barbarian: Japanese Travellers in America and Europe* (New Haven, Conn., and London: Yale University Press, 1995).

Anthony Best, 'Sir Robert Craigie as Ambassador to Japan 1937–1941,' in Nish, ed., *Britain and Japan: Biographical Portraits* , pp. 238–251.

——, *Britain, Japan and Pearl Harbor: Avoiding War in East Asia, 1936–41* (London and New York: Routledge, 1995).

Clive Bigham, *A year in China, 1899–1900, with some account of Admiral Sir E. Seymour's Expedition* (London: Macmillan, 1901).

Isabella L. Bird, *Unbeaten Tracks in Japan: An Account of Travels in the interior Including Visits to the Aborigines of Yezo and the Shrine of Nikko* (London: John Murray, second edition, 1911).

——, *Korea and Her Neighbours* (London: 2 vols., John Murray, 1897; reprinted in one vol., Seoul: Yonsei University Press, 1971; London, Boston, Sydney and Henley: KPI Ltd., 1985).

J. R. Black, *Young Japan: A narrative of the settlement and the city, from the signing of the treaties in 1859 to the close of the year 1879* 2 vols. (Yokohama: Kelly and Walsh; London: Trubner and Co., 1880–81).

Carmen Blacker, 'Laurence Oliphant and Japan, 1858–88', in Nish, *Biographical Portraits*, II, 35–47.

George Blake, *No Other Choice: An Autobiography* (London: Jonathan Cape, 1990).

J. O. P. Bland, *Something Light* (London: W. Heinemann Ltd., 1924).

Robert Boardman, *Britain and the People's Republic of China 1949–1974* (London and Basingstoke: The Macmillan Press Ltd., 1976).

Raymond Bourgerie and Pierre Lesouef, *Paliko (1860): Le sac du Palais d'Été et la prise de Pékin* (Paris: Economica, 1995).

Nigel Brailey, 'Sir Ernest Satow and *A Diplomat in Japan*', *Japan Society Proceedings*, no. 131 (Summer 1998), pp. 56–69.

Lady Brassey, *A Voyage in the Sunbeam: Our Home on the Ocean for Eleven Months* (London: Longman, Green and Co., 1878, reprinted London: Century Publishing House, 1984).

Juliet Bredon, *Peking* (Shanghai: Kelly and Walsh, 1931; reprinted Hong Kong: Oxford University Press, 1982).

Ann Bridge, *Peking Picnic* (London: Chatto and Windus, 1932).

——, *The Ginger Griffin* (London: Chatto and Windus, 1934).

——, *Facts and Fictions* (London: Chatto and Windus, 1968).

British Embassy Tokyo, *The Work of the Embassy* (Tokyo: British Embassy, 1995).

Timothy Brook, *Quelling the people: The military suppression of the Beijing democracy movement*, (New York, Oxford: Oxford University Press, 1992).

William Robert Broughton, *A voyage of discovery to the North Pacific Ocean etc., etc.*, (London: Printed for T. Cadell and W. Davies, 1804).

Roger Buckley, 'Britain and the Emperor: The Foreign Office and Constitutional Reform in Japan, 1945–1946', *Modern Asian Studies*, vol. 12, no. 4, (1978), 553–570.

——, *Occupation Diplomacy: Britain, the United States and Japan 1945–1952* (Cambridge: Cambridge University Press, 1982).

——, 'In proper perspective: Sir Esler Dening (1897–1977) and Anglo-Japanese relations 1951–1957', in Cortazzi and Daniels, editors, *Britain and Japan*, 271–276.

W. R. Carles, *Life in Corea*, (London and New York: Macmillan and Co. , 1888).

A. E. J. Cavendish, *Korea and the Sacred White Mountain, being a brief account of a journey in Korea in 1891*, (London: G Philip and Son, 1894),

Che Muqi, *Beijing Turmoil: More than Meets the Eye* (Beijing: Foreign Languages Press, 1990).

A. and D. Clark, *Seoul Past and Present: A Guide to Yi T'aejo's Capital*, (Seoul: Royal Asiatic Society Korea Branch, 1969).

Donald N. Clark and James H. Grayson, *Discovering Seoul*, (Seoul: Royal Asiatic Society, Korea Branch, 1986).

P. D Coates, 'Documents in Chinese from the Chinese Secretary's Office, British Legation Peking 1861–1939', *Modern Asian Studies*, vol. 17, no. 3 (1983), 239–255.

——, *The China Consuls: British Consular Officers 1843–1943*, (Hong Kong: Oxford University Press, 1988).

Paul A. Cohen, *History in Three Keys: The Boxers as Event, Experience, and Myth*, (New York: Columbia University Press, 1997).

Robert Coltman, Jnr., *Beleaguered Peking: The Boxer's [sic] War against the Foreigner*, (Philadelphia: F. A. Davis Company, 1901).

Sarah Pike Conger, *Letters from China: With Particular Reference to the Empress Dowager and the Women of China*, (London: Hodder and Stoughton, 1909).'

Harold F. Cook, *Korea's 1884 Incident: Its Background and Kim Ok-kyun's Elusive Dream*, (Seoul: Royal Asiatic Society Korea Branch, 1972, reprinted 1982).

Sir Hugh Cortazzi, 'The First British Legation in Japan (1859–1874)', *The Japan Society of London Bulletin*, No. 102, (October 1984), 25–50.

——, *Dr Willis in Japan: British Medical Pioneer, 1862–1877* (London and Dover, NH: Athlone Press, 1985).

——, *Victorians in Japan: In and Around the Treaty Ports* (London and Atlantic Heights, NJ: Athlone Press, 1987).

—— and Gordon Daniels, editors, *Britain and Japan 1859–1991: Themes and Personalities* (London and New York, 1991).

——, 'Sir Rutherford Alcock , the First British Minister to Japan 1859–1864: A Reassessment', *Transactions of the Asiatic Society of Japan*, Fourth Series, Vol. 9 (1994), pp. 1–42.

——, *Japan and back, and places elsewhere* (Folkestone, Kent: Global Oriental, 1998).

——, 'Sir John Pilcher, GCMG (1912–1990)', in *Britain and Japan: Biographical Portraits*, III, edited by J. E. Hoare (Richmond: Japan Library, forthcoming).

——, 'Sir Vere Redman, 1901–1975', in Nish, *Britain and Japan: Biographical Portraits*, II, 283–300.

Percy Cradock, *Experiences of China* (London: John Murray, 1994).

Sir Robert Craigie, *Behind the Japanese Mask* (London: Hutchinson and Co. Ltd, 1945).

Gordon Daniels, *Sir Harry Parkes: British Representative in Japan 1865–83* (Richmond: Japan Library, 1996).

Sir Arthur de la Mare, *Perverse and Foolish: A Jersey farmer's son in the British Diplomatic Service* (Jersey, Channel Islands: La Haule Books, 1994).

F. V. Dickins and S. Lane-Poole, *Life of Sir Harry Parkes* 2 vols., (London: Methuen and Co., 1894).

Dictionary of National Biography (Oxford: Oxford University Press, 1900 –).

Diplomatic Service List, (London: HMSO, 1967 onwards).

Sir Alfred East, *A British Artist in Meiji Japan* edited , with an introduction, by Sir Hugh Cortazzi, (Brighton: In Print, 1991).

Osman Edwards, *Residential Rhymes* (Tokyo: Hasegawa, n. d. [1899]).

Peter Elphick, *Far Eastern File: The Intelligence War in the Far East 1930–1945* London: Hodder and Stoughton, 1997).

Maurice Fabre, *Pekin: Ses Palais, ses Temples et ses Environs* (Tianjin: Librairie Française, 1937).

Anthony Farrar-Hockley, *The British Part in the Korean War* 2 vols. (London: Her Majesty's Stationary Office, 1990; 1995).

Zhong-ping Feng, *The British Government's China Policy, 1945–1950* (Keele, Staffs.: Ryburn Publishing/Keele University Press, 1994).

Dallas Finn, 'Josiah Conder (1852–1920) and Meiji Architecture', in Cortazzi and Daniels, eds., *Britain and Japan*, pp. 86–93.

——, *Meiji Revisited: The Sites of Victorian Japan* (New York and Tokyo: Weatherhill, 1995).

Wesley R. Fishel, *The end of extraterritoriality in China* (Berkeley, California: University of California Press, 1952; reprinted Taipei: Rainbow-Bridge Book Co., 1974).

Peter Fleming, *The Siege at Peking* (Hong Kong: Oxford University Press, 1986).

Foreign Office List, (London: Harrison and Sons, 1858–1965).

Grace Fox, *Britain and Japan, 1858–1883* (Oxford: Oxford University Press, 1969).

Mrs Hugh Fraser, *A Diplomatist's Wife in Japan: Letters from Home to Home* (London: Hutchinson and Company, 2 vols., 1899).

——, *A Diplomatist's Wife in Japan: Letters from Home to Home* (London: Hutchinson and Company, one volume edition, n. d.).

——, *A Diplomatist's Wife in Many Lands* (London: Hutchinson and Company, 2 vols., fourth edition, 1911).

A. B. Freeman-Mitford, *The Attaché at Peking* (London and New York: Macmillan and Co., 1900).

Berkeley Gage, *It's been a marvellous party! The Personal and Diplomatic Reminiscences of Berkeley Gage* (London: privately printed, 1989).

George S. Gale, *No Flies in China* (London: George Allen and Unwin, 1955).

Paul Gore-Booth, *With Great Truth and Respect* (London: Constable, 1974).

W. G. C. Graham, *China through one pair of eyes, or reminiscences of a consular officer 1929–1950* (London: The China Society, 1984).

Joseph C Grew, *Ten Years in Japan*, (London: Hammond, Hammond and Co. Ltd, 1944).

Anthony Grey, *Hostage in Peking* (London: Widenfeld and Nicholson, 1988).

Guide to 'Peking' (Beiping: The Leader, 1931).

Stephen Gwyn, editor, *The Letters and Friendships of Sir Cecil Spring Rice: A record* 2 vols., (London : Constable and Co. Ltd, 1929).

Kengi Hamada, *Prince Ito* (London: George Allen and Unwin Ltd, 1936).

Andrew Hamilton, 'The Komundo affair', *Korea Journal*, vol. 22, no. 6 (June 1982), 20–33.

Angus Hamilton, *Korea*, (New York: Charles Scribner's Sons, 1904).

Lord Frederic Hamilton, *Vanished Pomps* (London: Hodder and Stoughton; New York: George H. Doran Company, 1920).

Keith Hamilton and Richard Langhorne, *The practice of diplomacy: Its evolution, theory and administration* (London and New York: Routledge, 1995).

Denise Hardy, *En Chine avec Lady Hopson* (Paris: André Bonne, 1969).

Sir Robert Hart, *'These from the land of Sinim': Essays on the China Question* (London: Chapman and Hall, 1901).

Gregory Henderson, 'A history of the Chong Dong area and the American Embassy Compound', *Transactions of the Royal Asiatic Society Korea Branch*, xxxv, (1959), 15–16.

Philip Henderson, *The Life of Laurence Oliphant: Traveller, Diplomat and Mystic* (London: Robert Hale Ltd, 1956).

W. Meyrick Hewlett, *The siege of the Peking Legations, June to August 1900* (Harrow on the Hill: The Harrovian, 1900).

——, *Forty Years in China* (London: Macmillan and Co., second printing, 1944).

J. E. Hoare, 'The Korean-British Society: Some Past Events', *Bulletin of the Korean-British Society*, no. 2, (May 1982), 7–10.

——, 'The centenary of Korean-British diplomatic relations: the British diplomatic presence in Korea, 1883–1983', *Korea Observer*, vol. XIV, no. 2 (Summer, 1983), 131–41

——, 'The centenary of Korean-British diplomatic relations: aspects of British interest and involvement in Korea, 1600–1983' *Transactions of the Royal Asiatic Society Korea Branch*, vol. 58, (1983), 1–34.

——, *The British Embassy Compound, Seoul 1884–1984* (Seoul: Korean-British Society, 1984).

——, 'The Anglican Cathedral Seoul 1926–1986', *Transactions of the Royal Asiatic Society Korea Branch*, vol. 61, (1986), 1–11.

——, 'Komundo-Port Hamilton', *Asian Affairs*, vol. 17, no. 3 (October 1986), 298–308.

——, 'Building Politics: The British Embassy Peking, 1949–1992', *The Pacific Review*, vol. 7, no. 1 (1994), 67–78.

——, *Japan's Treaty Ports and Foreign Settlements: The Uninvited Guests 1858–1899* (Folkestone, Kent: Japan Library, 1994).

——, 'The Tokyo embassy 1871–1945', *Japan Society Proceedings*, no. 129, (Summer 1997), 24–41.

——, 'Britain's Japan Consular Service', in Nish, ed., *Britain and Japan: Biographical Portraits* vol. II, 94–106.

——, ed., *Britain and Japan: Biographical Portraits*, III, (Richmond: Japan Library, forthcoming).

C. Pemberton Hodgson, *A Residence at Nagasaki and Hakodate in 1859–1860* (London: Richard Bentley, 1861).

Mary Hooker, *Behind the scenes in Peking* (Hong Kong, Oxford and New York: Oxford University Press, 1987).

R. A. Humphries, *Latin America and the Second World War*, (London: Athlone for the Institute of Latin American Studies, University of London, 2 vols., 1982).

Douglas Hurd, *The Arrow War: An Anglo-Chinese Confusion*, (London: Collins, 1967).

A. Hamish Ion, *The Cross and the Rising Sun* volume 2: *The British Protestant Missionary Movement in Japan, Korea and Taiwan, 1865–1945* (Waterloo, Ontario: Wilfred Laurier University Press, 1993).

Ito Hirobumi den (Biography of Ito Hirobumi), (Tokyo: Sumpoko Tsuishikokai, 1940).

Iwao, Seiichi, *List of Foreign Office Records in the Public Record Office in London relating to China and Japan*, (Tokyo: Toho Gakkai, 1959).

D. Jacobs-Larcom, *As China fell: the experiences of a British Consul's Wife 1946–1953* (Ilfracombe: Arthur H. Stockwell Ltd., 1976).

Reginald Johnston, *Twilight in the Forbidden City* (London: Victor Gollanz, 1934; reprinted Hong Kong: Oxford University Press, 1987).

Tess Johnston and Deke Erh, *Near to Heaven: Western Architecture in China's old Summer Resorts* (Hong Kong: Old China Hand Press, 1994).

Kadata, Shozo, 'The Embassy in London, its History and Personalities', *The Japan Society of London Bulletin*, No. 86, (November 1978), 8–11.

G. N. Kates, *The years that were fat: Peking 1933–1940* (New York: Harper Brothers, 1952; reprinted Hong Kong: Oxford University Press, 1988).

Kawaseki, Seiro, 'Edo ni atta gaikoku kokan' ('Foreign missions in Edo'), *Gaimusho choso geppo*, 1987/No. 1, 31–103.

See Kim Chung-dong, '"Ku Kyong" for British Embassy was built by British Architect J. Marshall in Seoul', *Kyunchuka*, (January 1996), 36–43.

Kim Yung Chung, 'Great Britain and Korea, 1883–87', unpublished PhD, University of Indiana, 1964.

——, 'The Komundo incident 1885–87: an early phase in British-Korean relations', in *Korean-British relations: yesterday, today and tomorrow*, edited by Chong-wha Chung and J E Hoare, (Seoul: Korean British Society et al., 1984), pp. 9–38.

Sir H. Knatchbull-Hugessen, *Diplomat in Peace and War* (London: John Murray, 1949).

Peter Kornicki, 'William George Aston (1841–1911)', in Cortazzi and Daniels, eds., *Britain and Japan 1859–1991* 64–75.

Ku Dae-yeol, *Korea under Colonialism: the March First Movement and Anglo-Japanese Relations* (Seoul: Seoul Computer Press for the Royal Asiatic Society, 1985).

S. Lane-Poole, *Sir Harry Parkes in China* (London: Methuen and Co., 1901).

A. C. Hyde Lay, *Four generations in China, Japan and Korea* (Edinburgh and London: Oliver & Boyd, 1952).

G. A. Lenson, *Balance of Intrigue: International Rivalry in Korea and Manchuria 1884–99* (Tallahassee, Florida: University Presses of Florida, 2 vols., 1982).

Li, Shian, 'The extraterritoriality negotiations of 1943 and the New Territories', *Modern Asian Studies*, vol. 30, part 3, (July 1996), 617–650.

Peter Lowe, 'The Dilemmas of an Ambassador: Sir Robert Craigie in Tokyo, 1937–1941', Gordon Daniels and Peter Lowe, editors, *Proceedings of the British Association for Japanese Studies*, Vol. II, (1977): *History and International Relations*, 34–56.

——, *Britain in the Far East: A Survey from 1819 to the Present* (London and New York: Longman, 1981).

——, ' Sir Alvary Gascoigne in Japan, 1946–1951'. in Nish, *Britain and Japan: Biographical Portraits* pp. 279–294.

——, *Containing the Cold War in East Asia: British policies towards Japan, China and Korea, 1948–1953* (Manchester and New York: Manchester University Press, 1997).

Evan Luard, *Britain and China* (London: Chatto and Windus, 1962).

Peter Lum (Lady Crowe), *Peking 1950–1953* (London: Robert Hale, 1958).

Patricia McCabe, *Gaijin Bochi: The Foreigners' Cemetery, Yokohama, Japan* (London: British Association for Cemeteries in South Asia, 1994).

Duncan McCallum, *China to Chelsea: A modern pilgrimage along ancient highways* (London: Ernest Benn Ltd, 1930).

Geoffrey McDermott, *The new diplomacy and its apparatus* (London: Plume Press/Ward Lock, 1973).

Roderick MacFarquhar and John K. Fairbank, editors, *The People's Republic Part 2: Revolution within the Chinese Revolution, 1966–1982* (Cambridge, England: Cambridge University Press, 1991), (Cambridge History of China, vol. 15).

Colin Mackerras, *Modern China: A Chronology from 1842 to the Present* (London: Thames and Hudson, 1982).

John McMaster, *Sabotaging the Shogun: Western Diplomats open Japan 1859–69* (New York: Vantage Press, 1992).

Stephan Markbreiter, 'In search of an identity: the British Legation at Peking, 1861', *Arts of Asia*, vol. 13, no. 3, (May-June 1983), 120–130.

W. A. P. Martin, *A cycle of Cathay, or China North and South, with personal reminiscences* (New York, Chicago and Toronto: Fleming H. Revell Company, third edition, 1900).

——, *The siege in Peking: China against the World, by an Eye Witness* (New York, Chicago and Toronto: Fleming H. Revell Company, 1900).

D. Massarella, *A World Elsewhere: Europe's encounter with Japan in the Sixteenth and Seventeenth Centuries* (New Haven, Conn., and London: Yale University Press, 1990).

A. R. Michell, 'British commercial interests in Korea 1883–1941', in Korean National History Compilation Committee, editors, *Han-yong sugyo 100-nyon sa* (Seoul: National History Compilation Committee, 1984), pp. 188–202.

Alexander Michie, *The Englishman in China during the Victorian era, as illustrated in the career of Sir Rutherford Alcock, KCB, DCL., many years consul and minister in China and Japan* (Edinburgh and London: 2 vols., William Blackwood and Sons, 1900).

Sheila Hoey Middleton, 'A collection of Choson Dynasty White Ware Sherds', *Oriental Art*, vol. XI, no. 4, (Winter 1994–95), 21–28.

H. H. Montgomery, *Charles John Corfe: Naval Chaplain-Bishop* (London: Society for the Propagation of the Gospel in Foreign Parts, 1927).

H. B. Morse, *The international relations of the Chinese Empire* 3 vols., (London: Longman, Green, 1910–18; reprinted Taipei, Taiwan: Ch'eng Wen Publishing Co., 1978).

Lionel Munby, *How much is that worth?* (Salisbury, Wilts.: Philmore for the British Association for Local History, 1996).

Priscilla Napier, *Barbarian Eye: Lord Napier in China, 1834: The Prelude to Hong Kong* (London and Washington DC: Brassey's, 1995).

William L. Neumann, *America encounters Japan: From Perry to MacArthur* (Baltimore, Md: The Johns Hopkins Press, 1963).

Ian Nish, *The Anglo-Japanese Alliance: The Diplomacy of Two Island Empires, 1894–1907* (London: The Athlone Press, 1966).

——, *The Origins of the Russo-Japanese war* (London and New York: Longman Group, 1985).

——, editor, *Britain and Japan: Biographical Portraits* (Folkestone, Kent: Japan Library, 1994).

——, editor, *Britain and Japan: Biographical Portraits* vol. II, (Richmond, Surrey: Japan Library, 1997).

H. J. Noble, *Embassy at War* (Seattle and London: University of Washington Press, 1975).

L. L. Norris, *Handbooks of English Church Expansion: China* (London and Oxford: A. R. Mowbray and Co., 1908).

N. Oliphant, *A diary of the siege of the legations in Peking in the summer of 1900* (London: Longmans Green and Co., 1901).

Robert T. Oliver, *Syngman Rhee: The man behind the myth* (London: Robert Hale Ltd., 1955).

William J. Oudendyk, *Ways and by-ways in diplomacy* (London: Peter Davies, 1939).

Park Yongsuk, *Soyangin-ei bon Koreya* (Western origins in Korea), (Seoul: Samsung Enron Chedan, 1997).

Susan Pares, *Beijing: The Old Legation Quarter* (Beijing: Beijing International Society, 1992).

Cyril Pearl, *Morrison of Peking* (Harmondsworth: Penguin Books, 1971).

Niklaus Pevsner, *The Building of England: London except the cities of London and Westminster*, (Harmondsworth, Middlesex: Penguin Books, 1951).

Alain Peyrefitte, *The Collision of Two Civilisations: The British Expedition to China 1792–94* (London: Harvill, 1993).

F. S. G. Piggott, *Broken Thread* (Aldershot, Hants: Gale and Polden, 1950).

Brian Porter, *Britain and the Rise of Communist China: A Study of British Attitudes 1945–54* (London: Oxford University Press, 1967).

Sir John Pratt, *Britain and China* (London: Collins, n. d.).

Klaus H. Pringsheim, *Neighbours across the Pacific: Canadian-Japanese Relations 1870–1982* (Oakville, Ontario: Mosaic Press, 1983).

Asian-Gioro Pu Yi, *From Emperor to Citizen: the autobiography of Aisin-Gioro Pu Yi* (Beijing: Foreign Languages Press, 2 vols., 1964)

Qingji zhongying shiling nianbiao ('Yearlist of British and Chinese diplomatic and consular representation during the Qing period') (Beijing: Qinguo Jing, 1993).

F. F. Rainsford, *Memoirs of an accidental airman* (London: Thomas Harmsworth Publishing, 1986).

Jessie Ransome, *Story of the siege hospital in Peking, and diary of events from May to August, 1900* (London: Society for Promoting Christian Knowledge, 1901),.

Lord Redesdale, *Memories* (London: Hutchinson and Co., 1915).

Paul Reinsch, *An American Diplomat in China* (London: George Allen and Unwin, 1922).

D. F. Rennie, *Peking and the Pekingese during the first year of the British Embassy in Peking* (London: John Murray, 2 vols., 1865).

Rijkisuniversiteit Leiden, *Herrinnergen aan Japan, 1850–1870 – Yomigaeru Bakumatsu – Foto's en Fotoalbum in Nederland Bezit* ('s-Gravenhage: Staatsuitgeverij, 1987).

Sir Frederick St. John, *Reminiscence of a retired diplomat* (London: Chapman and Hall, 1905).

G. B. Sansom, *The Western World and Japan* (London: The Cresset Press, 1950).

Katherine Sansom, *Sir George Sansom and Japan: A Memoir* (Tallahassee, Florida: The Diplomatic Press, 1972).

Ernest Mason Satow, *A Diplomat in Japan* (London: Seeley, Service and Co., 1921; reprinted Rutland, Vt., and Tokyo: Charles Tuttle, 1983).

Edward Seidensticker, *Low City, High City: Tokyo from Edo to the Earthquake: How the Shogun's Ancient Capital became a Great Modern city, 1867–1923* (London: Allen Lane, 1983).

——, *Tokyo Rising: The City since the Great Earthquake* (New York: Alfred A Knopf, 1990).

Wenguang Shao, *China, Britain and Businessmen: Political and Commercial Relations, 1949–57* (Basingstoke and London: Macmillan Academic and Professional Ltd., 1991).

Fred Sharf, *Takejiro Hasegawa: Meiji Japan's Pre-eminent Publisher of Wood-Block-Illustrated Crepe-Paper Books* (Salem, Mass: Peabody Essex Museum Collections, 1994).

Bertram Lennox Simpson *Indiscreet letters from Peking: Being notes of an Eye Witness, which set forth in some detail, from Day to Day, the Real Story of the Siege and Sack of a Distressed Capital in 1900 – The Year of Great Tribulation* edited by 'B. L. Putnam Weale' (pseud.) (London: Hurst and Blackett; New York: Dodd, Mead and Company, 1907 – reprinted New York: Arno Press, 1970).

Beryl Smedley, *Partners in diplomacy* (Ferring, West Sussex: The Harley Press, 1990).

Dennis Smith, 'Sir Charles Eliot (1862–1931) and Japan', in Cortazzi and Daniels, *Britain and Japan*, pp. 187–197.

George Smith, *Ten Weeks in Japan* (London: Longman, Green, Longman and Roberts, 1861).

Anna M Stoddart, *The Life of Isabella Bird (Mrs Bishop)* (London: John Murray, 1908).

'A student interpreter', *'Where Chineses [sic] drive': English Student-Life at Peking*, (London: W. H. Allen and Co., 1885).

Synn Seoung Kwon, *The Russo-Japanese Rivalry over Korea, 1876–1904* (Seoul: Yuk Phub Sa, 1981.

T. Tamba, *Meiji tenno to Meiji jidai* ('The Meiji emperor and the Meiji period'), (Tokyo: Asahi Shimbun, 1966).

Richard Tames, *Encounters with Japan* (Stroud: Alan Sutton; New York: St Martin's Press: 1991).

James Tuck-Hong Tang, *Britain's Encounter with Revolutionary China, 1949–54* (Basingstoke and London: Macmillan Press Ltd., 1992; New York: St. Martin's Press, 1992).

——, 'Hong Kong's transition to Chinese rule: The fate of the Joint Declaration', in Judith. M. Brown and Rosemary Foot, editors, *Hong Kong's Transitions, 1842–1997* (Basingstoke and London: Macmillan Press Ltd., 1997), pp. 149–66.

W. H. Evans Thomas, *Vanished China: Far Eastern Banking Memoirs* (London: Thorsons Publishers Ltd., 1952).

H. P. Thompson, *Into all lands: The history of the Society for the Propagation of the Gospel in Foreign Parts* (London: Society for the Propagation of Christian Knowledge, 1950).

Sir John Tilley, *London to Tokyo* (London, New York and Melbourne: Hutchinson and Co. Ltd., n. d. [1942]).

Ronald P. Toby, *State and Diplomacy in Early Modern Japan: Asia in the Development of the Tokugawa Bakufu* (Princeton, NJ: Princeton University Press, 1984; reprinted Stanford, CA: Stanford University Press, 1991).

Lady Susan Townley, *My Chinese Notebook* (London: Methuen and Co., 1904).

H. Trevelyan, *Worlds Apart: China 1953–55; Soviet Union, 1962–65* (London and Basingstoke: Macmillan London Ltd., London, 1971).

H. Trevor-Roper, *A hidden life: the enigma of Sir Edmund Backhouse* (London and Basingstoke: Macmillan and Co., 1976).

Marcel Trouche, *Le Quartier Diplomatique de Pékin: Etude Historique et Juridique* (Paris: Librarie Technique et Économique, n.d.).

Maureen Tweedy, *A label round my neck* (Lavenham, Suffolk: Terence Dalton Ltd., 1976).

L. H. Underwood, *Fifteen years among the topknots* (Seoul: Kyung-in Co., for the Korea Branch Royal Asiatic Society, second edition, 1977).

J. van Ginneken, *The rise and fall of Lin Piao* (Harmondsworth: Penguin Books, 1976).

Daniele Varè, *Laughing Diplomat* (London, John Murray, 1938).

George Watt, *China 'spy'* (London: Johnson, 1972).

Michael Wenner, *So it was* (Edinburgh, Cambridge and London: The Pentland Press Ltd., 1993).

Clara Whitney, *Clara's Diary: An American Girl in Meiji Japan* (Tokyo, New York and San Francisco: Kodansha International, 1981).

Ray Whitney, 'When the Red Guards stormed our Embassy', *Sunday Telegraph*, 23 November 1980.

Who's Who (London: A. & C. Black, 1897–).

Harold S. Williams, *Shades of the Past: Indiscreet Tales of Japan* (Tokyo and Rutland, Vt: Charles E Tuttle Company, 1959).

Alan Winnington, *Breakfast with Mao: Memoirs of a Foreign Correspondent* (London: Lawrence and Wishart, 1986).

Nicholas Wollaston, *China in the morning: impressions of a journey through China and Indo-China* (London: Jonathan Cape, 1960).

Francis Wood, *No Dogs and Not Many Chinese: Treaty Port Life in China, 1843–1943* (London: John Murray, 1998).

Yokohama kaiko shiryokan/Yokohama Archives of History, *F Beato Bakumatsu Nihon Shashinshu* ('F. Beato: a photographer in Bakumatsu Japan'), (Yokohama: Yokohama shiryo kaikan, 1988).

——, *Meiji no Nihon: Yokohama shashin no sekai* ('Meiji Japan: The World of Yokohama Photographs'), (Tokyo: Yurindo, 1990).

L. K. Young, *British Policy in China 1895–1902* (Oxford: Oxford University Press, 1970).

Zhai Qiang, *The Dragon, the Lion and the Eagle: Chinese-British-American relations, 1949–1958* (Kent, Ohio: Kent State University Press, 1994).

Index